Conservation Tourism

Conservation Tourism

Ralf Buckley

International Centre for Ecotourism Research
Griffith University, Gold Coast, Australia

www.cabi.org

CABI is a trading name of CAB International

CABI Head Office	CABI North American Office
Nosworthy Way	875 Massachusetts Avenue
Wallingford	7th Floor
Oxfordshire, OX10 8DE	Cambridge, MA 02139
UK	USA
Tel: +44 (0)1491 832111	Tel: +1 617 395 4056
Fax: +44 (0)1491 833508	Fax: +1 617 354 6875
E-mail: cabi@cabi.org	E-mail: cabi-nao@cabi.org
Website: www.cabi.org	

A catalogue record for this book is available from the British Library,
London, UK.

Library of Congress Cataloging-in-Publication Data

Buckley, Ralf.
    Conservation tourism / Ralf Buckley.
        p. ; cm.
    Includes bibliographical references and index.
    ISBN 978-1-84593-665-5 (alk. paper)
 1. Ecotourism--Research--Case studies. 2. Ecotourism--Marketing--Case studies.
    I. Title.

    G156.5.E26B83 2011
    333.95'416--dc22

                                    2010018852

ISBN-13: 978 1 84593 665 5

Commissioning editors: Claire Parfitt and Sarah Hulbert
Production editor: Fiona Chippendale

Typeset by Columns Design Ltd, Reading, UK.
Printed and bound in the UK by the MPG Books Group.

Contents

_____

Tables

About the Author

———————————

Ralf Buckley is Director of the International Centre for Ecotourism Research, established in 1993 at Griffith University, Australia. He has ~750 publications including ~200 journal articles and a dozen books, eight of them on ecotourism and related topics. He has several decades' experience worldwide as a guide, participant and researcher in various forms of nature, eco- and adventure tourism and recreation. His research focuses on the various interactions between the tourism industry and the natural environment.

Contributors

Agustina Barros, J. Guy Castley, Clare Morrison, International Centre for Ecotourism Research, Griffith University, Australia

Julianna Priskin, Bruno Sarrasin, Département urbaines et touristiques, École des sciences de la gestion, Université du Québec à Montréal, Casier postal 8888, succursale Centre-ville Montréal (Québec), Canada

Zhong Linsheng, Qi Junhui, Institute of Geographical Sciences and Natural Resources Research, Academy of Sciences, 52 Sanlihe Road, Beijing, China 100864

Dedication

_____

With special recognition for Les Carlisle, pioneer in the
practicalities of conservation tourism and still
going strong!

Les Carlisle

Acknowledgements

The bulk of this book is the responsibility of the principal author, but critical segments have kindly been contributed by colleagues worldwide who share an interest in conservation tourism. Guy Castley, Senior Research Fellow at the International Centre for Ecotourism Research (ICER) at Griffith University, Australia is the principal author of Chapter 12, Southern and East Africa, based on 25 years living and travelling widely in southern Africa. Julianna Priskin and Bruno Sarrasin of the University of Quebec, Montreal contributed Chapter 10, France and Francophone Nations. Clare Morrison, Research Fellow at ICER, is the principal author of Chapter 7, Oceania, based on an extended period on the academic staff of the University of the South Pacific in Fiji. Agustina Barros of ICER contributed the section on her home country Argentina in Chapter 11, South and Central America. Linsheng Zhong and Junhui Qi of the Chinese Academy of Sciences contributed the Chinese case studies in Chapter 6, Asia. Many corrections and contributions to my draft were kindly contributed by Guy Castley, Katie Mossman and Cassie Wardle. Wendy Smith prepared the many successive versions of the manuscript and managed the ever-changing reference list.

This book also owes its format, content and reliability to a worldwide network of friends and colleagues who have contributed either to fieldwork, to data audit or directly to the compilation of individual sections and chapters. Previous publications, unpublished reports and personal expertise were contributed to the Americas chapter by our colleague Amanda Stronza at Texas A & M University. My own contribution to Guy Castley's Africa chapter, including sections on Namibia, Botswana, Uganda, and Sabi Sands and Madikwe in South Africa, were possible only through the generosity of colleagues in the conservation tourism sector. Similarly, fieldwork for Chapter 9, Arctic and Antarctic, was made possible with generous assistance from Explorer Shipping, Abercrombie & Kent, Aurora Expeditions, Southern Sea Ventures, Blackfeather Expeditions and Sunchaser Tours.

The four chapters on global leaders in conservation tourism owe their detailed information and insights to extended periods of cooperative research, over many years, with the four companies concerned. To Les Carlisle of Conservation Corporation Africa, now &Beyond, must go the primary credit for sharing his personal knowledge and enthusiasm for the practicalities in using tourism successfully to fund effective conservation. Les has infected a generation of guides, and an entire global corporation with his practical and effective enthusiasm for wildlife tourism and conservation. He kindly gave up time to join me in visiting most of the individual lodges and reserves described in the chapter on &Beyond. I must also thank Steve and Nicky Fitzgerald of &Beyond for giving Les and myself free rein, and funding, to carry out this work. Equally knowledgeable and hospitable were their counterparts at Wilderness Safaris. Malcolm McCullough, Chris Roche, Dave van Smeerdijk, Conrad 'Nad' Brain, Rob Moffett and Matt Ives made it possible for me to gain first-hand experience of the company's achievements in Botswana and Namibia; and individual lodge managers, environmental managers and guides have kept in touch and exhorted me to return. The opportunity to learn first-hand about the operation of Natural Habitat Adventures was kindly provided by its founder Ben Bressler, and I should also thank Caitlin Lepper for organizing my visit to Madagascar. Finally, my thanks to Peter Winn of Earth Science Expeditions and Travis Winn of Last Descents for making it possible for me to paddle down some of the great rivers of Tibet and Yunnan and to learn about their efforts to conserve the river corridors.

This book is offered to record and applaud the efforts of everyone involved in these enterprises, and in the hope that they may continue to prove successful.

Preface

_____

Conservation of biological diversity and functioning ecosystems is critical for human well-being; yet it is increasingly threatened through continuing population growth, consumption and contamination of natural resources and ecosystems, and now also by climate change.

The global protected area network has made enormous contributions to conservation, but it is not enough on its own and it also is under continual threat. Additional social and economic mechanisms are urgently needed to support the public reserve system and extend conservation efforts outside reserves. Conservation tourism is one component, small as yet but potentially significant.

Tourism is a multi-trillion dollar global industry with major economic, social and environmental impacts. In common with most industry sectors, most of its environmental impacts are harmful or negative. Indeed, since a large component of the industry takes tourists specifically to areas of high conservation value (Buckley _et al._, 2003a), these impacts are of particular ecological significance (Buckley, 2004a).

Unlike most other sectors, however, commercial tourism can on occasion make net positive contributions to conservation. These can operate either directly, or indirectly through local communities and national or international politics. Some of these ventures are marketed as ecotourism and are listed in global compendia of ecotourism case studies (Buckley, 2003a; Zeppel, 2006). This volume builds on previous research by assembling and analysing examples where commercial tourism has indeed contributed to conservation.

This is a field where reliable information is hard to come by. Many tourism operations claim environmental credentials, but most of these evaporate under closer scrutiny, even where they have received environmental certification or awards. This volume therefore focuses largely on cases where respected international researchers have made extended on-site investigations.

Recognizing that ecosystems, societies, economies and laws differ considerably between countries and continents, most of these cases are presented in geographical order, in an attempt to examine regional signatures in conservation tourism efforts. In addition, to illustrate what can be achieved by companies seriously involved in conservation tourism, four individual enterprises with particularly well-established credentials are first profiled in more depth.

1 Introduction

Gemsbok, Namibia

Definitions and Scope

Conservation tourism is, simply, tourism which operates as a conservation tool. More precisely, it may be defined as commercial tourism which makes an ecologically significant net positive contribution to the effective conservation of biological diversity. This is a narrower and more closely defined term than ecotourism. A contribution to conservation is one of the key defining criteria for ecotourism (Buckley, 1994, 2003b, 2009a; Weaver, 2001; Weaver and Lawton, 2007). Not all authors and analysts, however, treat the conservation criterion as critical (Buckley, 2003a; Donohoe and Needham, 2006; Wearing and Neil, 2009).

Academic research in ecotourism encompasses over 1000 articles during the past three decades, but very little of this examines its actual contributions to conservation (Weaver and Lawton, 2007; Buckley, 2009a). In commercial ecotourism marketing materials the proportion is even smaller. The bulk of such material, as well as the academic ecotourism literature, focuses on natural attractions, measures to reduce environmental impacts, the involvement of local communities and the role of interpretation (Weaver and Lawton, 2007).

A number of individual cases are presented in compendia such as those of Buckley (2003a) and Zeppel (2006) and in edited volumes such as those of Buckley et al. (2003a), Buckley (2004b), Gössling and Hultman (2006), Spenceley (2008a), Stronza and Durham (2008) and Saarinen et al. (2009a). None of those volumes, however, set out specifically to compile, consider or calculate the net contributions of tourism to conservation. The aim of the current volume is to commence this process and to catalyse future research along similar lines.

Significance

The growth in commercial conservation tourism enterprises is relatively new. While there are individual enterprises that have been following this approach for several decades, they have historically been too few, too small and too scattered to be recognized in their own

right as a definable subsector of either tourism or conservation. This volume seems to be the first attempt to survey and analyse the conservation tourism subsector specifically. Indeed, it appears to be the first publication, in either the academic or grey literature, which formally adopts the term conservation tourism. The practical approach is not new; and the idea that tourism can potentially contribute to conservation, and sometimes actually does so, is widespread, though contested, in the literature of ecotourism (Weaver and Lawton, 2007; Buckley, 2009a, b). What is new is that the number and scale of commercial tourism enterprises which may potentially qualify as conservation tourism have only recently grown to the point where comparative analysis is worthwhile.

Currently, conservation tourism is still, in statistical terms, a very small component of either tourism or conservation. While individual conservation tourism enterprises are now widespread worldwide, and some are quite substantial in scale, they are still very small in aggregate relative to the multi-trillion dollar scale of the global tourism industry. Similarly, while individual conservation tourism enterprises seem to have played a significant role in the conservation of particular areas and species, these examples are still few, and as yet make up only a very minor component of global conservation efforts as a whole (Buckley, 2008b). If current trends continue, however, conservation tourism approaches may well become more frequent in future.

The reasons that this is significant may be summarized as follows. Biodiversity is important not only in its own right, but as a key foundation and fundamental underpinning of human economic activity and indeed survival (Mooney and Mace, 2009; Sachs et al., 2009; Sukhdev, 2009; Marton-Lefevre, 2010): the 'biological basis of human civilisations' (Spangenberg et al., 2009). Biodiversity is under threat globally, with the global economic cost of biodiversity losses estimated at US$1.35–3.1 trillion annually (Marton-Lefevre, 2010). Global conservation efforts to date have had inadequate funding and political support, and consequently limited success (McCauley, 2006; Rodrigues, 2006). Indeed, it has been argued that 'the inability to halt loss of biodiversity is probably one of the most dramatic policy failures ever' (Spangenberg *et al.*, 2009). Hillman and Barkmann (2009), for example, noted that of the $53 billion needed annually for a globally representative set of protected areas, only $15 billion is actually available, half from national governments and half from multilateral funds: as compared, for example, with $5000 billion in 'economic stimulus' funds in 2009 and 2010, none of which is allocated to conservation.

Threats due to wilderness encroachment, resource consumption and pollution continue to grow with increasing human population size, with climate change now adding a further threat (Willis and Bhagwat, 2009). Threats from climate change are difficult to quantify precisely, largely because of inadequate scientific data on plant and animal biology (Mooney and Mace, 2009) and on human social responses (Barron, 2009; Moss *et al.*, 2010). Conservation can itself make a major contribution to mitigating climate change, more efficiently and cost-effectively than almost any other mechanism (Ricketts *et al.*, 2010). In fact, forest loss and clearance currently contribute around one-fifth of global greenhouse gas emissions (Marton-Lefevre, 2010). A wide range of different conservation measures and mechanisms are in place or under trial worldwide, ranging from the legal declaration and operational funding of national or international-level protected areas, to political and religious appeals (Bhagwat, 2009) and government, community or private economic incentives (Kiss, 2004; McCauley, 2006; Kareiva *et al.*, 2008; Gallo *et al.*, 2009; Sukhdev, 2009). While historically, public parks protecting relatively pristine areas of native vegetation and wildlife have proved by far the most effective type of conservation measure and are largely responsible for conservation successes to date, further expansion of the global public protected area network appears to be facing increasing resistance, principally because of the pressures of growing human populations and associated demands for natural resources (Buckley, 2009c).

Mechanisms which can successfully convert land use at least partially to conservation without changing land tenure or ownership are therefore becoming increasingly important (Buckley,

2008a). As plant and animal species and ecosystems are increasingly affected by climate change, mechanisms to provide landscape-scale connectivity rather than isolated islands of conservation are increasingly critical; and since connectivity corridors must often cross privately owned agricultural land, off-reserve conservation mechanisms are hence equally critical (Buckley, 2008a; Bierbaum and Zoellick, 2009; Willis and Bhagwat, 2009). In some countries and regions, such incentives may be provided by direct government payments or tax concessions for conservation or for associated environmental services such as watershed protection or carbon sequestration, but only if these incentives are deliberately designed, monitored and managed to conserve biodiversity (Buckley, 2008a; Venter *et al.*, 2009).

In a different but overlapping set of areas, income from commercial private-sector tourism enterprises can provide another and sometimes more targeted incentive. This success depends, however, both on natural attractions for tourism and on the broad-scale operational patterns of the global tourism industry. Conservation tourism aims explicitly to take advantage of this approach, and this is why it is significant.

Context

The tourism and conservation sectors exist independently of each other; neither exists to serve the other; and to a large degree they operate with little interaction or overlap. Where they do overlap significantly, however, the interactions between them become critical to both. Both tourism and conservation can mean different things to different people. Tourism includes individual leisure and holiday travel, and this in turn includes holiday visitation to national parks and other conservation areas. Many visitors to protected areas, however, especially for parks near to urban centres in developed nations, are local residents making day visits only. These are counted in park visitation statistics but not in tourism statistics. Conservation includes all measures and efforts to conserve biodiversity and ecosystem services on all types of land and water tenure, including all private and public holdings and landscape-scale connectivity approaches as well as national parks and other public protected areas.

In numerical terms, whether counted in tourists, visits or expenditure, the bulk of the tourism sector is urban. There is a large and financially significant outdoor subsector, estimated to comprise about one-fifth of the industry worldwide. This corresponds to an annual turnover of the order of one trillion dollars (US) globally, including mechanized equipment and fixed-site resorts, but not associated residential development. Most of the outdoor tourism sector, however, is adventure- rather than nature-based. It includes a number of large-scale mechanized activities with high environmental impacts (Buckley, 2004c). Most of these activities occur on land and water outside protected areas, but they have conservation impacts none the less, and some do also take place inside particular protected areas.

Contemplative nature-based tourism forms one component of the outdoor tourism subsector, smaller in economic terms than mechanized adventure activities but probably larger in the number of individual people involved, especially in older age groups. This component includes the majority of visitors to public protected areas. Ecotourism is a small segment of nature-based tourism, including both commercial and non-profit operations and defined by additional management, education and conservation criteria (Buckley, 2009b).

The core of global conservation efforts consists of the formal public protected areas in the national reserve systems of individual countries, as recognized by IUCN. Since these formal reserves cover only a tenth or so of global land area, however, conservation also depends on remnant ecosystems in other land tenures, which are undergoing continuing attrition (Lees and Peres, 2008). As a result, and given the increasing political difficulties in expanding formal protected area systems in countries with growing populations, conservation efforts have begun to include various landscape-scale connectivity approaches (Brooks et al., 2006; Crooks and Sanjayan, 2006). These include both community and private landholdings (Murphy and Noon, 2007) and public forests and rangelands nominally allocated for multiple use (Gardner et al., 2007). The relative scale and significance of different land tenure types for both tourism and conservation differ greatly between continents and between developed and developing nations. In addition, there are remote wilderness areas either within or outside national jurisdictions, but with little or no infrastructure or permanent human presence, which can be highly significant for conservation irrespective of formal tenure.

Under the broad definitions outlined above, the major interactions between tourism and conservation may be summarized as follows. Outdoor tourism operates largely outside protected areas; partly inside protected areas; and to a small degree in remote wilderness areas. In multiple-use areas, even though adventure tourism produces significant environmental impacts, it may sometimes help to focus land managers' attention on recreation and conservation rather than primary production (Buckley, 2006). In protected areas, many forms of adventure tourism produce major negative impacts on conservation and major practical difficulties for management agencies; but are tolerated either because of historical precedent or current political pressures, or in order to maintain a political constituency. In remote wilderness areas, outdoor tourism takes the form of expeditions, which may help to attract public attention to conservation values and issues, but may also create impacts especially if large-scale rescues are required.

Contemplative nature-based tourism operates largely, though not entirely, in protected areas, private as well as public. The impacts and management of visitors to public protected areas, the fees they may be charged and the political support they may engender have been studied extensively (Watson and Borrie, 2003; Buckley, 2004a, 2009b; Lockwood et al., 2006). They need not be re-examined here, except to reiterate that these are still the principal current links, both positive and negative, between tourism and conservation. We should also note that there are commercial wildlife-watching tours in other land tenures and in remote wilderness areas, and these are often significant for conservation.

The focus here is on mechanisms by which tourism can make a net positive contribution to conservation, through positive contributions large enough to outweigh negative impacts. The mechanisms may be political, social or economic, or commonly some combination of these. Tourism is often invoked as one political justification for the establishment of protected areas, for example, in both developed and developing nations. Park fees offset management costs in developed nations, and may generate net foreign exchange earnings for governments in their developing counterparts. Continuing political support is needed to maintain conservation management in the face of other pressures, whether for oil drilling in Australia's Great Barrier Reef or the Arctic National Wildlife Reserve, or for clearance and subsistence agriculture in parts of Asia and Africa.

This volume presents some examples of such models and mechanisms, and attempts to illustrate the social, environmental, economic and political dimensions in different countries. It also contains contributions by colleagues worldwide who have expertise in particular countries, cultures and languages. It focuses on examples where the principal and contributing authors have some direct on-site experience; but, even so, one cannot always be confident of understanding political processes, especially in countries with different languages and cultural traditions – or, indeed, even in one's own local neighbourhood. That is, we present our perceptions of particular models involving tourism and conservation, but with the proviso that others with greater local experience might well see additional aspects of each case.

Models and Mechanisms

A number of different mechanisms by which tourism could potentially contribute to conservation have indeed been identified (Buckley, 2009a), and are summarized in Table 1.1.

The approaches used to harness tourism as a tool in conservation differ considerably between continents and countries and between tour operators and organizations. There are no standard models, but a menu of approaches which may be tailored to different circumstances. Approaches which have proved successful in one set of circumstances do not necessarily

work as well in another, even for the same organization.

Possible mechanisms for tourism to contribute to conservation include: mandatory fees and voluntary contributions in cash or in kind to public protected area agencies; conversion of other public lands to conservation use through direct political lobbying by tour operators or clients; support for non-government conservation organizations to conduct such lobbying; and the conversion of private or community landholdings from primary production to conservation use through direct financial means.

Many public protected areas charge entry, camping and activity fees both for individual visitors and for commercial tour clients. In most developed countries, per capita fees are generally less than per capita costs of visitor infrastructure, so there is no net contribution to conservation. In some developing nations, park fees from international visitors do constitute a net financial contribution, but governments often appropriate these funds centrally, with no direct link to conservation. A few tour operators do also make direct voluntary in-kind contributions to conservation management in particular public protected areas. Examples include: staff salaries for park rangers and anti-poaching patrols; vehicles and radios; bounties for animal snares; and ecological monitoring (Buckley, 2003a).

Tour operators have sometimes supported non-government conservation groups. Approaches include: sponsoring transport and accommodation, as at Khutzeymateen in Canada (Buckley, 2010, p. 153); providing land and infrastructure, as at Walindi in Papua New Guinea (Buckley, 2006, pp. 172–174); running tours for conservation organizations, with cash contributions from the price paid by participants; direct cash donations from the tour operator; and donations from tour clients. These activities are not necessarily motivated by concerns over conservation, nor are they necessarily effective or significant in scale (Buckley, 2009b, pp. 175–192); but in some cases they may be so.

Tour operators could lobby directly on behalf of conservation, but this seems to be rare in practice. Attempts to promote tourism as a conservation alternative to whaling in

Table 1.1. Mechanisms for ecotourism to generate positive environmental effects.

Mechanism	Potential environmental significance	Breadth of adoption in ecotourism sector	Achievement in practice, global scale	Attributable to ecotourism	
				Devel[a]	Select[a]
Political					
parks policies	***	*	**	–	**
CTO[b] lobby	**	*	*	*	**
Clients lobby	*	*	*	*	*
Support NGOs[b]					
CTO cash	**	*	*	**	**
CTO in kind	*	**	*	**	**
Clients local	**	*	*	–	**
Clients global	*	**	**	–	*
NGO as CTO	**	*	*	**	**
Contribute to parks agencies					
Compulsory fees	**	**	*	–	*
Cash donations	*	*	*	*	*
Staff salaries	**	*	*	*	**
Equipment	**	*	*	*	**
Operations	**	*	*	*	*
Community conservation					
Lease land	***	*	**	**	**
Employ locals	**	**	*	**	**
Client purchases	*	**	*	**	**
Community-owned ops	*	**	*	**	**
Revenue-sharing	**	*	*	*	*
Private reserves	***	*	**	*	**

Key: ***, major; **, medium; * , minor; –, nil or not applicable.
[a] Devel = role of ecotourism in developing this mechanism; Select = degree to which ecotourism enterprises have selected this mechanism.
[b] CTO = commercial tourism operator; NGO = non-governmental organization.

Iceland (Parsons and Rawles, 2003) or to logging or hydroelectric dams in Australia, Chile, China, Indonesia or Papua New Guinea (Buckley, 2009b) rarely seem to have been successful. There seems to be little evidence that a nature tourism experience converts commercial clients to conservation lobbyists (Beaumont, 1998; Lee and Moscardo, 2005); and, even if it did, there would be no net conservation benefit unless their lobbying outweighed impacts.

A number of major international environmental NGOs are indeed involved in tourism projects, sometimes with commercial tourism partners. The World Wide Fund for Nature is reportedly involved in tourism projects in South Africa, Namibia, Belize and Greece; Conservation International in the Philippines, Indonesia, Brazil and Panama; and the Nature Conservancy in China and Mexico (Buckley, 2003a, 2009b). In Australia, the Mareeba Wetlands Foundation runs tourism and conservation operations in a private reserve in the tropical north (Nevard, 2004). There are other examples in Chile, Ghana, the Seychelles, the United Arab Emirates and Zambia (Buckley,

2009b). I have not visited or audited any of these in person, except for the Al Maha oryx reserve in the UAE.

Private Reserves and Community Conservancies

The most effective approach for tourism to contribute to conservation seems to be the most direct. Tourism generates revenue, which can be used to fund private or community conservation reserves. Examples have been described for case studies in South Africa (Lindsey et al., 2005), Brazil (de Oliveira, 2005), Greece (Svoronou and Holden, 2005), Australia (Tisdell et al., 2005) and worldwide (Buckley, 2003a). The importance of involving local residents in such efforts has been re-emphasized by recent research in Nepal (Allendorf, 2007), Tanzania (Holmern et al., 2007) and a number of southern African nations (Spenceley, 2008a). Some successful models of this approach are outlined below.

If a reserve is funded entirely through tourism, then the service and hospitality components must generate a sufficient surplus to cover conservation management costs. In practice this is rarely possible unless the property has an icon attraction for which there is a strong demand. In most instances this is scenery and/or wildlife. In addition, since the need to cover conservation costs means that prices must be relatively high, clients will then expect a high level of service quality, and this in turn will increase prices still further. The most successful model for private conservation reserves funded by tourism hence seems to be through upmarket luxury game lodges with skilled staff who can provide a particularly memorable wildlife watching experience, often with animals which are at least partially habituated and which may be managed to maintain particular population densities.

Private conservation reserves and community conservancies funded by tourism are becoming increasingly commonplace worldwide (Buckley, 2003a, 2008a, 2009b; Krüger, 2005; Shultis and Way, 2006; Murphy and Noon, 2007; UNEP, 2007; Spenceley, 2008a). The best-known and earliest examples are in southern Africa, particularly in Botswana,

Namibia and South Africa itself (Spenceley, 2008a). Companies such as &Beyond (2010) (formerly Conservation Corporation Africa) and Wilderness Safaris (2010) have developed successful business models which rely on wildlife tourism to fund quite large-scale conservation efforts, including habitat restoration, anti-poaching efforts and wildlife relocation programmes. Wilderness Safaris (2010), for example, has apparently brought around 20,000 km^2 of land in Botswana and Namibia, principally community land, at least partially into conservation use. &Beyond (2010) has successfully established a considerable number of private conservation reserves funded through tourism, largely in South Africa, and has pioneered restoration, restocking and wildlife relocation techniques.

Tourism funds the private reserves of the Sabi Sands area, which has effectively added 650 km^2 to Kruger National Park in South Africa (Buckley, 2003a; Spenceley, 2008a) and the Madikwe private reserve adjacent to the Botswana border (Buckley, 2008a; Relly, 2008) (see Chapters 2 and 12). There are many individual operators in each. In Madikwe, the individual landowners have removed internal fences and operate the entire area as a single co-managed reserve. In Sabi Sands, they have removed fences not only between private reserves but also between these and the public national park. &Beyond also established the Phinda private reserve, which extends the iSimangaliso World Heritage Area in South Africa; and operates the Kwandwe reserve, which provides critical habitat for the endangered blue crane. In addition, its conservation staff pioneered capture, translocation and 'soft release' techniques for active population management of a number of endangered wildlife species, a key step in using tourism as a conservation tool (Chapter 2).

Similar approaches have been followed by Wilderness Safaris (2010) (see Chapter 3). Its Ongava private reserve, adjacent to Etosha Pan National Park in northern Namibia, effectively extends the area of the public park and is separated from it by a 'semipermeable' fence, which allows some animal species through while retaining others. A series of adjacent community conservancy areas leased by Wilderness Safaris and funded by tourism is gradually building a conservation corridor between the Etosha Pan ecosystems of north-eastern Namibia and the arid ecosystems of the Skeleton Coast in the north-west, habitat for desert-adapted elephant. This corridor runs adjacent to the border with Angola, and, once politics allow, cross-border connectivity will also be feasible. In late 2006 the tourism ministers of Angola, Botswana, Namibia, Zambia and Zimbabwe signed an MOU to set up a five-nation Kavango–Zambezi Transfrontier Conservation Area (Suich, 2008). It is intriguing that the countries concerned were represented by tourism rather than environment portfolios in such negotiations. Internal corporate goals for both &Beyond and Wilderness Safaris include even more ambitious multi-country conservation corridors.

South of the Skeleton Coast, Wilderness Safaris leases a community conservancy which supports what is apparently the largest remaining population of desert-adapted rhinoceros outside the public protected area system. It also supports research on rhino populations, ecology and conservation, both directly and through an NGO (Save the Rhino Trust, 2010). In Botswana, it funded the reintroduction of rhino, previously poached to local extinction, into the publicly owned Moremi reserve in the Okavango Delta, and leases large areas which it runs for conservation funded by tourism.

A large number of smaller companies have adopted similar models, though with fewer sites and smaller areas. Similar tourism-based models, often run by the same companies, also help to fund conservation in public conservation reserves and conservancies in East Africa and elsewhere. &Beyond (2010), for example, operates a series of private reserves in East Africa, leased from the national governments and converted from subsistence agriculture and hunting to wildlife conservation (Buckley, 2006). These effectively extend the protected area of the Serengeti ecosystem. The same company has established a marine reserve at Mnemba Island off the coast of Zanzibar (Buckley, 2006), similar to the private marine reserve at Chumbe Island (Buckley, 2003a). Through a joint venture known as Taj Safaris, &Beyond has recently built four tourist lodges to support tiger conservation in India

(Chapter 6). It has also provided technical expertise to relocate gaur, the endangered Indian wild ox, as part of a continent-wide conservation programme.

Critiques of the approach adopted by companies such as these have been provided recently by Spenceley (2008a) and Relly (2008) for Madikwe and Sabi Sands in South Africa; Spenceley (2008a) and Barnes (2008) for conservancies in Namibia; Massyn (2008) for the Okavango area in Botswana; and Nelson (2008) for Tanzania, including the Klein's Camp concession operated by &Beyond. The focus of those authors was on community benefits rather than conservation, and they concluded that a number of local communities in these areas have indeed benefited considerably from upmarket private game lodges, through a variety of mechanisms.

There are also private reserves funded by tourism, though generally at a smaller scale, in various countries in the Americas, Asia, Europe and Australasia (Buckley 2003a, 2009b; Conservation Finance Alliance, 2003; Lindsey et al., 2005; Svoronou and Holden, 2005; Tisdell et al., 2005). Tourism is not always the sole source of income for these reserves. Some receive support from bilateral or multilateral aid. Some were established and operated by philanthropic individuals or conservation organizations such as Conservation International (2010), The Nature Conservancy (2010), the World Wide Fund for Nature (2010) or the Australian Wildlife Conservancy (2010). There are examples of private reserves with NGO involvement and ecotourism operations in, for example: Australia, Belize, Brazil, Chile, China, Ghana, Greece, Indonesia, Mexico, Namibia, Nepal, Panama, the Philippines, the Seychelles, South Africa, the United Arab Emirates and Zambia (Buckley, 2008b). There are also public reserves which have been established with the assistance of particular tour operators, such as the Khutzeymateen grizzly bear sanctuary in Canada (Buckley, 2008b). Both Conservation International (2010) and the World Wide Fund for Nature (2010) now advertise a global suite of tours through their own websites, as one way to generate political and financial support. They use particular commercial tour operators with good environmental credentials, such as Natural Habitat Adventures (2010) (see Chapter 4), to provide those tours.

Social and Geopolitical Challenges

There are many other countries where similar tourism-funded conservation models have operated in the past and/or could operate in the future, but where political circumstances prevent them operating effectively at present. Tourism-funded conservation models cannot function well in countries where war or terrorism threatens the safety of tour clients; where basic infrastructure such as roads and airports are too run-down; or where land tenure is too unstable for a private tourism operator to invest. If and when such countries adopt or return to relatively stable democratic systems of government, they will probably be able to call on significant international aid funding to help rebuild infrastructure, perhaps including parks infrastructure. Such aid programmes are typically short-lived, however, and a longer-term source of income is needed once aid funding comes to an end. The opportunity for tourism to take over conservation funding in nations such as these is thus particularly significant, since companies already operating in the region have established clienteles who would visit new destinations.

Conservation seems likely to face increasing challenges worldwide in future (Pressey *et al.*, 2007). The global human population continues to grow, and the greatest growth is in large newly industrialized nations such as China and India, where protected area systems are relatively weak. In addition, both developed and newly industrialized nations in both the East and the West continue to exploit natural resources in areas of high conservation value in developing nations, where conservation frameworks are even weaker and conservation impacts correspondingly more severe. These effects will also be compounded over forthcoming decades with those of anthropogenic climate change. This will increase pressures on existing national reserve systems and simultaneously reduce public funding for conservation by creating other urgent social needs which will compete for public funds.

To conserve biological diversity and ecosystem services under such circumstances, existing public protected areas and landscape-scale connectivity approaches will both be critical. If the impacts of tourism in parks can be reduced through better monitoring and management of visitors, that will help to increase the resilience of protected area ecosystems to other stresses such as those from climate change. And, if the revenue-generating potential of tourism can be harnessed through social and political processes as a tool to help in off-reserve conservation, that will help to alleviate the continuing loss in remnant ecosystems outside the national reserve systems. Various mechanisms have been proposed, including an attempt to link connectivity conservation approaches across national boundaries into a single globally branded 'world wild web' able to attract major funding from carbon mitigation measures (Buckley, 2008a). One such mechanism is the so-called REDD component, Reducing Emissions from Deforestation and Degradation, in international climate-change agreements. Meanwhile, models developed by tourism operators such as &Beyond, Wilderness Safaris and their counterparts elsewhere surely deserve expansion, replication and encouragement. At the same time, if these approaches expand, then efforts to monitor and evaluate their positive and negative social, environmental and economic impacts will also require attention.

At a global scale, tourism has become a significant source of funding for connectivity conservation, though currently much more prevalent in particular regions and restricted to a relatively small set of tourism operators. The tourism industry more broadly does not necessarily contribute to conservation, and indeed generates a wide range of ecological impacts; but if an adequate conservation framework is in place, tourism can generate significant funding to support it. Indeed, for a small number of leading ecotour operators whose owners are driven by conservation concerns, they may also help to establish such conservation frameworks, by providing examples of what can be achieved.

Of the various mechanisms by which tourism can contribute to conservation, those which currently have the greatest reach and consequence are also the most difficult to quantify reliably (Buckley, 2009a). This is because they involve broad-scale and indirect social and political processes which extend beyond the commercial tourism industry. Local expenditure by independent visitors, for example, can play a role in modifying the tenure, use or management of public lands such as parks, forests and rangelands. Income from tourism, in conjunction with other income streams such as payments for ecosystem services, conservation incentives or carbon offsets, can also play a role in persuading private landowners to manage their lands more for conservation and less for intensive primary production (Buckley, 2008a, b). More direct and readily quantifiable mechanisms, such as the use of tourism to establish and operate private conservation reserves, are as yet relatively few in number and small in scale. They may indeed become significant, e.g. in creating conservation corridors (Buckley, 2008a, b), but only if they are integrated into broader conservation planning.

Whether the mechanisms are direct or indirect, local or broad-scale, the opportunity and ability of the tourism sector to contribute to conservation depend heavily on the legal, social, political, economic and institutional frameworks of the particular countries concerned (Buckley, 2008a, 2009c; Honey, 2008). The contexts within which commercial tourism enterprises operate and the types of products they offer also depend strongly on human as well as physical geography (Buckley, 2007a, 2010). Adjacent nations with similar ecosystems may provide widely different opportunities for conservation tourism if they differ in wealth, population density, form of government, history of war and conflict or the structure of land tenure and taxation systems. Even countries with rather similar social, political and legal systems, such as Australia and the USA, may differ in key aspects such as the perceived role of the public forestry agencies in regard to recreation and conservation. Opportunities for tourism and conservation also change over time within individual nations. At the most extreme, there are countries which once had effective and well-funded systems of parks and protected areas which supported thriving tourism industries, but where both parks and tourism were subsequently destroyed by military dictatorships or insurgencies, or through terrorism or state-sanctioned militias. Depending on the degree and duration of damage, it can take a very long time for tourism and conservation to recover after such episodes. Uganda, Zimbabwe, Nepal and Chile provide historical examples. Less dramatically, changes in government or in the policies, laws and budget allocations of individual governments can have substantial effects on tourism and conservation, either positive or negative, even in politically stable, peaceful, well-off and democratically governed nations.

Methodological Approach

The principal focus of the current volume is on the conservation contributions of commercial tourism enterprises, rather than the role of private recreation in promoting or hindering conservation on public lands. Large-scale political histories of individual countries, however, set the contexts within which individual private enterprises operate, and therefore cannot be ignored. In addition, in countries which have effective public conservation systems, the role of tourism and private conservation reserves may be rather different from those where public protected area agencies are unable to operate effectively or, in some cases, do not exist at all. For all these reasons, this volume is organized along geographical lines, considering general models and particular examples of conservation tourism on a continent by continent basis.

This volume does not attempt to provide a comprehensive compendium of case studies or an aggregate estimate of net outcome at a global scale. Such exercises would indeed be valuable and are in fact under way, but will take a large team several years to complete. Instead, this contribution concentrates on leaders in commercial conservation tourism, and aims to provide some insight into their motivations, mechanisms and achievements. Chapters reviewing the overall structure or regional signature of conservation tourism models in different continents are therefore supplemented by chapters which present the detailed operations of individual conservation tourism enterprises. The latter are derived from on-site audits and interviews by the principal author over the past decade, coupled with published materials where available, and interviews with staff, clients and other stakeholders of the enterprises concerned. Despite their limitations, especially those involving language and cultural barriers, such on-site approaches remain the most reliable means to analyse the operations and net outcomes of conservation tourism endeavours (Buckley, 2003a, 2006).

From a methodological perspective, the task attempted in this volume is fraught with difficulties. Essentially, for each case study included here, there are three methodological steps. The first is simply to identify it, to know that it exists at all. Some examples are easy to find. They are long-established, are well-known, have well-publicized awards and have been described on many occasions in electronically searchable publications in English. Others, however, may be described only in other languages, only in localized parks-agency or tour-operator marketing materials, or not at all. They are not necessarily any less important for conservation than better-known examples; indeed, they may well be much more important. But, if nobody has written about them, they may be hard to find.

The second step is to assemble reliable information about individual cases identified. This is also difficult, for similar reasons. There are rather few publications in the refereed academic literature which set out specifically to describe the conservation parameters of tourism ventures. Even for the best-known examples, much of the material available originates ultimately from the owners and operators, or from other agencies with a stake in their success, such as NGO partners, aid agencies or other donors, retail tour packagers who want to sell trips to clients, or government agencies who want to promote their portfolios through so-called success stories. Even where particular cases have been described in the refereed academic literature, most such descriptions focus on other aspects such as community dynamics, economics and equity, or social

justice and legal rights. These are all significant issues, and relevant to conservation outcomes, but they do not necessarily provide the data needed here.

The third step is to evaluate the contributions of tourism to conservation. This requires reliable information on both tourism activity and conservation outcomes, as above, but also on internal processes and mechanisms and external factors and disturbances, which may influence either tourism, conservation or the links between them. In addition, including and describing any given case study in a volume such as this in itself contributes to advertising it. Moreover, if an academic publication uses data from an unrefereed report, popular publication or website, that process in itself brings unchecked data into the research literature. Ultimately, these difficulties with identification, reliability and evaluation are unavoidable. No one researcher can check every case study worldwide in person. This volume aims to find a balance between extensive but relatively uncritical compendia, such as those of Zeppel (2006), and critical but localized studies, such as those of Stronza (2007). It aims to provide at least a first, incomplete global perspective on conservation tourism, as a basis and catalyst for more detailed and extensive studies in future. It aims to include enough examples to assess patterns at continental and worldwide scales, but to be sufficiently selective for it to avoid any unintentional propagation of inaccurate claims.

It is a sobering reminder that the 170 or so case studies in ecotourism compiled by Buckley (2003a) were drawn from an initial list of around 500. The other two-thirds were culled out either because no detailed information could be found or because comments from colleagues who had actually visited them revealed that advertised information was inaccurate. Because of these concerns, most of the examples presented in this volume are long established and previously described. This has both advantages and disadvantages. The disadvantage is that the material presented is selective rather than comprehensive. The advantages are, first, that available information refers to actual outcomes over an extended

period, not merely to optimistic prognosti-
cations; and, second, that different sources of
data can be cross-checked between multiple
authors and agencies and weighted according
to the type of publication.

This volume therefore presents examples
and analyses of conservation tourism from
around the world, using a range of different
mechanisms at a variety of scales, with a focus
on models, approaches and cases which seem
to have been successful. It starts by presenting
four particular companies in detail, and continues
with a geographically structured overview which
is less detailed but broader in scope.

Cases Presented

The format, comprehensiveness and level of
detail differ between chapters, contributors,
countries, companies and cases presented,
depending on data available. In general this
volume focuses principally on instances where
the author or contributors have direct

experience or access to reliable publications or
colleagues. Some chapters present individual
examples of conservation tourism in a case
study format, whereas others describe general
patterns with reference to named examples but
without presenting these examples in detail.
The list of cases given in Table 1.2 indicates
which sites have been audited or visited in
person by the principal author or relevant
contributors. In most cases the majority of
information has been verified on site. The main
exception is for much of Latin America and
Oceania, where only some of the case studies
have been audited by the authors. For the
former, a variety of recent documentary sources
are cited. For the latter, the principal contributing
author relies on up-to-date on-site reports from
colleagues in the countries concerned.

Acknowledgements

Previous versions of parts of this chapter have
been presented in Buckley (2008a, b, 2009b).

Table 1.2. Cases presented.

Chapter and country	Company, agency or area[a]	Case study or named example[a]	Audited by principal author	Audited by section or chapter author[b]
&BEYOND				
South Africa	&Beyond	Phinda	Yes	–
South Africa	&Beyond	Kwandwe	Yes	–
South Africa	&Beyond	Exeter	Yes	–
South Africa	&Beyond	Kirkmans	Yes	–
South Africa	&Beyond	Dulini	Visit	–
South Africa	&Beyond	Leadwood	Visit	–
South Africa	&Beyond	Ngala	Yes	–
South Africa	&Beyond	Madikwe	Yes	–
Botswana	&Beyond	Nxabega	Yes	–
Botswana	&Beyond	Sandibe	Yes	–
Tanzania	&Beyond	Mnemba	Yes	–
Tanzania	&Beyond	Grumeti	Yes	–
Tanzania	&Beyond	Kleins	Yes	–
Tanzania	&Beyond	Ngorongoro	Yes	–
Kenya	&Beyond	Kichwa Tembo	Yes	–
WILDERNESS SAFARIS				
Botswana	Wilderness Safaris	Mombo	Yes	–
Botswana	Wilderness Safaris	Savuti	Yes	–
Botswana	Wilderness Safaris	Duma Tau	Visit	–

Table 1.2. Continued.

Chapter and country	Company, agency or area[a]	Case study or named example[a]	Audited by principal author	Audited by section or chapter author[b]
Botswana	Wilderness Safaris	Kings Pool	Visit	–
Botswana	Wilderness Safaris	Vumbura	Yes	–
Namibia	Wilderness Safaris	Ongava	Yes	–
Namibia	Wilderness Safaris	Skeleton Coast	Yes	–
Namibia	Wilderness Safaris	Serra Cafema	Yes	–
Namibia	Wilderness Safaris	Desert Rhino	Yes	–
Namibia	Wilderness Safaris	Damaraland	Yes	–
Seychelles	Wilderness Safaris	North Island	Yes	–
NATURAL HABITAT ADVENTURES				
Canada	Natural Habitat Adventures	Ultimate Polar Bear	Yes	–
Madagascar	Natural Habitat Adventures	Wild Madagascar	Yes	–
LAST DESCENTS				
China	Last Descents	Mekong	Yes	–
China	Last Descents	Salween	Yes	–
China	Last Descents	Yangtze Great Bend	Yes	–
ASIA				
India	Taj Safaris	Baghvan	Yes	–
India	Taj Safaris	Mahua Kothi	Yes	–
India	Ultimate Descents	Kameng River	Yes	–
Nepal	Annapurna	Conservation Area Project	Yes	–
Mongolia	Various	Grassland tourism	No[c]	–
Russia	Kamchatka	Kurilskoye grizzly bears	Yes	–
Borneo	Various	Orang-utan	No	–
China	Various	Xianggelila	No	Yes
China	Various	Juzhaigou	No	Yes
China	Various	Tianmushan	No	Yes
OCEANIA				
Cook Islands	Rarotonga	Takitumu	No	No
Fiji	Vanua Bouma	Bouma Reserve	No	Yes
Fiji	Waisali community	Waisali Reserve	No	Yes
Fiji	Rivers Fiji	Upper Navua	Yes	Yes
Fiji	National Trust	Sigatoka	No	Yes
Fiji	Beqa Adventure Divers	Beqa Shark Corridor	No	Yes
Solomon Islands	Tetepare Descendants Association	Tetepare	No	Yes

Continued

Table 1.2. Continued.

Chapter and country	Company, agency or area[a]	Case study or named example[a]	Audited by principal author	Audited by section or chapter author[b]
Solomon Islands	Local residents and stakeholders	Kolombangara Reserve	No	Yes
Solomon Islands	Peava Lodge	Gatokae	No	Yes
Solomon Islands	Consortium of NGOs	Bauro Reserve	No	Yes
New Caledonia	Province Sud	Blue River Reserve	No	No
French Polynesia	National government	Tiahura MPA	No	No
AUSTRALIA				
Australia	World Heritage	3 sites	Yes	–
Australia	Western Australia	2 sites	1 of 2	–
Australia	Northern Territory	5 sites	3 of 5	–
Australia	South Australia	4 sites	3 of 4	–
Australia	Victoria	3 sites	1 of 3	–
Australia	Tasmania	5 sites	Yes	–
Australia	New South Wales	5 sites	3 of 5	–
Australia	Queensland	9 sites	7 of 9	–
Australia	Private Reserves	7 sites	4 of 7	–
ARCTIC AND ANTARCTIC				
Russia	89° North	Barneo	No	–
Canada	Baffin Island	Pond Inlet	Yes	–
USA	Alaska	Various	Yes	–
Canada	Sunchaser	Khutzeymateen	Yes	–
Norway	Aurora Expeditions	Svalbard	Yes	–
Antarctica	Abercrombie and Kent	Peninsula and Islands	Yes	–
FRANCE AND FRANCOPHONE				
France	National government	Cévennes National Park	No	Yes
France	111 communes	Vosges du Nord Park	No	Yes
SOUTH AND CENTRAL AMERICA				
Mexico	Conservation International	Ixcan	No	–
Mexico	National government	Monarch butterflies	No	–
Mexico	Singayta	Singayta	No	–
Belize	Women's Conservation Group	Community Baboon Sanctuary	No	–
Belize	Belize Audubon Society	Cockscomb Basin	No	–
Belize	Chaa Creek Lodge	Chaa Creek	No	–

Table 1.2. Continued.

Chapter and country	Company, agency or area[a]	Case study or named example[a]	Audited by principal author	Audited by section or chapter author[b]
Belize	Toledo Ecotourism	Toledo guest houses	No	–
Guatemala	Ecomaya	Ecomaya	No	–
Guatemala	RARE	Tikal NP	No	–
Guatemala	Various	San Pedro	No	–
Costa Rica	Monteverde	Cloud Forest	No	–
Costa Rica	Rara Avis	Lodge	No	–
Costa Rica	Costa Rica Expeditions	Various	No	–
Costa Rica	Horizontes Tours	Various	No	–
Panama	ODESEN	Wekso	No	–
Panama	Kuna Blas	Nusagandi	No	–
Ecuador	Capirona	Napo	No	–
Ecuador	RICANCIE	Oriente	No	–
Ecuador	Huaorani	Ecolodge	No	–
Ecuador	Cofan	Zabalo	No	–
Ecuador	Various	Galapagos	Yes	–
Ecuador	Neotropic Turis	Cuyabeno Lodge	Yes	–
Ecuador	Napo	Wildlife Centre	No	–
Ecuador	Napo	La Selva	Yes	–
Ecuador	Mindo	El Monte Lodge	Yes	–
Bolivia	Various	Mapajo	No	–
Bolivia	San Jose de Uchupiamonas	Chalalan ecolodge	No	–
Peru	National Park	Huascaran	No	–
Peru	Rainforest Expeditions	Posada Amazonas	No	–
Peru	Heath River	Wildlife Centre	No	–
Brazil	Conservation International	Fazenda Rio Negro	No	–
Brazil	Estancia Caiman	Pousada Caiman	No	–
Brazil	Cristalino Jungle Lodge	Cristalino reserve	No	–
Brazil	Conservation International	Una Ecopark	No	–
Argentina	Yacutinga Lodge	Yacutinga Refuge	No	Yes
Argentina	Reserva del Yaguaroundi	Wildlife refuge	No	Yes
Argentina	Aurora del Palmar	Wildlife refuge	No	No
Argentina	Fundación ProYungas	Rutas del Alto Bermejo	No	Yes
Argentina	National government	Monte Leon National Park	No	No
Argentina	Conservation Land Trust	El Socorro	No	No

Continued

Table 1.2. Continued.

Chapter and country	Company, agency or area[a]	Case study or named example[a]	Audited by principal author	Audited by section or chapter author[b]
SOUTHERN AND EAST AFRICA				
South Africa	SANParks	Kruger NP	Yes	Yes
South Africa	SANParks	Addo Elephant Park	Yes	Yes
South Africa	Tswalu	Desert Reserve	No	No
South Africa	Thanda	Game Reserve	No	No
South Africa	Kuzuko	Game Reserve	No	Yes
South Africa	‡Khomani San	!Xaus Lodge	No	Yes
South Africa	Hunter Hotels	Gorah Elephant Camp	No	Yes
South Africa	Madikwe	Game Reserve	Yes	Yes
South Africa	Mantis Group	Shamwari	No	Yes
Kenya	Fauna and Flora International	Ol Pejeta Conservancy	No	No
Various	African Parks Foundation	Various	No	Some
Botswana	Khama	Rhino Sanctuary	No	No
Botswana	Mokolodi	Nature Reserve	No	No
Mozambique	Manda Wilderness Trust	Nkwichi Lodge	No	No
Uganda	National Park	Mgahinga	Yes	No
Rwanda	Mantis Group	Gorilla Nest Lodge	No	No

Notes: [a] The names and information in this table are abbreviated. Full details are given in the main text.
[b] Data for contributing authors are shown only for cases written by contributors. [c] Cases not audited by either the principal author or section or chapter contributors are drawn from published literature and/or information provided by colleagues with direct relevant experience as acknowledged in the chapters concerned.

2 &Beyond

Leopard, Phinda

Introduction

The conservation tourism enterprise currently known as &Beyond has a long history under the name of Conservation Corporation Africa, variously abbreviated as ConsCorp and later as CC Africa. Some of the individual private reserves and game lodges involved were already pursuing a conservation tourism model before they became part of the &Beyond portfolio. &Beyond currently operates 28 fixed-site lodges and tented camps and three mobile safari operations in six countries in sub-Saharan Africa, and a further four lodges in India. The Indian lodges operate in association with public national parks, and are considered separately in Chapter 6. Most of the African lodges operate either on concessions or leases, community landholdings or private reserves, depending on the land title systems of the countries concerned.

The philosophy of &Beyond has been expressed (Carlisle, 2007) as 'care of the land, care of the wildlife, care of the people'. The metaphor of the three-legged cooking pot has been used to illustrate the argument that each of these three components is equally critical to the overall success of the enterprise. Similar metaphors have also been adopted by a number of other African conservation tourism operators. In practice, active management of land and vegetation, wildlife populations and interactions, and good relations with staff and neighbouring communities are indeed equally critical core components of business operations for companies such as &Beyond. These components are as vital for commercial success as smoothly operating lodges, transfers and global marketing systems. The land, wildlife and local people provide the assets on which the business is based, and the lodges and tourism operations provide the mechanism by which these assets are used to generate revenue, including the revenue to maintain the assets in good condition.

The very close integration between these components is indeed recognized in the internal structure of &Beyond, and a central role is accorded to conservation management and community interactions, as well as the commercial tourism and hospitality components. This does not mean, however, that the hospitality or marketing components can be neglected. &Beyond has a well-deserved reputation for outstanding and individualistic design and fit-out for each of its lodges, world-class catering and seamless logistics. A number of its lodges have been granted membership of prestigious luxury syndicates such as Relais et Châteaux or Small Luxury Hotels of the World. These aspects, coupled with the opportunity to watch wildlife at very close range from open safari vehicles, by night as well as by day, maintain an international clientele prepared to pay the prices needed to keep such an operation running. Indeed, the same clients return again and again, year after year. High levels of repeat business and word-of-mouth recommendations are both measures of &Beyond's reputation within the worldwide wildlife tourism sector.

Relationships between &Beyond and the local communities at its various lodges appear to be uniformly cordial, and incorporate four key components in addition to any commercial arrangements involving leases and licences on community landholdings. Like the majority of remote-area tourism operations in sub-Saharan Africa, &Beyond houses the employees of its various lodges in on-site staff quarters. These are quite separate from any nearby villages, and indeed form sections of the lodge sites themselves, though typically separated by a tall hedge or fence from the front-of-house areas accessible to guests. They share some infrastructure, such as power supply, with the front-of-house areas; but they usually have separate facilities such as kitchens and ablutions areas. The standard of these staff facilities, and especially the level of hygiene in the kitchens and the operation of plumbing and drainage in the showers and toilet areas, is a very good indication of the respect which tourism operators pay their staff and the pride which staff take in the operations. While there is always a significant gap between the facilities provided for staff and those provided for guests, the former can still meet basic standards of comfort and cleanliness. This applies to a game-watching lodge on private or community land in sub-Saharan Africa, just as it does to an urban hotel or a ski resort in Western nations. In practice, with one or two minor exceptions, the lodges operated by &Beyond have generally achieved a high standard, relative to the rest of the industry in this area, for all their staff quarters (Buckley, 2003a, 2006).

The incidence of HIV/AIDS is high throughout sub-Saharan Africa, and no successful business can afford to ignore it or to leave countermeasures purely to government agencies or international initiatives. Companies such as &Beyond have in fact taken a very proactive role in addressing HIV/AIDS within their own staff and local communities. They have carried out education campaigns, offered free and confidential blood testing, made condoms readily available through staff stores at each lodge, and created a social climate where the issue can be discussed and addressed rather than hidden and ignored. In addition, through their on-site staff stores they have made available a commercial nutritional supplement known as e-Pap, at a subsidized price and in large quantities. Employees at the lodges are encouraged to purchase as much of the supplement as they want and take it back to their own families and villages. Irrespective of the mechanisms of HIV transmission, the onset of AIDS symptoms apparently depends heavily on general health and nutritional status. To combat the continuing spread of HIV/AIDS in sub-Saharan Africa, therefore, nutritional supplements such as e-Pap are an important complement to educational programmes, improved health care and the availability of condoms.

Of course, it is in the interests of tourism operators such as &Beyond that their staff remain healthy, because staff training involves significant investment, particularly at managerial levels. In addition, for members of local communities to reach managerial levels of expertise generally requires many years of experience. It is therefore in the company's interests that staff who have gained such experience and expertise should remain healthy so that they can continue to contribute to ongoing operations, to corporate memory and to training new staff. This utilitarian aspect, however (Mahal, 2004), does not diminish the humanitarian contribution made by these programmes, which do indeed demonstrate the third tenet of the &Beyond philosophy, 'care of the people'.

In addition to these particular programmes related to HIV/AIDS, &Beyond runs a much broader programme of community support, both at a corporate level and at individual lodges. The corporate-scale programmes are run through the Africa Fund, an independently managed organization set up to channel client donations to community welfare projects. At the level of individual lodges there is a wide variety of initiatives, with local schools and health clinics as the principal focus.

The other two components of the three-legged philosophy, namely 'care of the land' and 'care of the wildlife', are also closely integrated into routine daily operations at each of &Beyond's reserves and lodges. The detailed management measures and opportunities available depend on the different circumstances at each lodge and reserve, including the ecosystem type, reserve area, land tenure and land uses in neighbouring areas. Perhaps most importantly, some of the reserves are fenced and hence represent closed systems, where wildlife can be bought or sold on and off the property. Others are unfenced open systems, where individual animals can enter or leave the &Beyond reserve at any time. Some of these areas are co-managed with adjacent properties, as part of larger multi-owner private reserves with a boundary fence around the external periphery of the area as a whole, but no internal fences. Others are adjacent to public protected areas, and may be unfenced along the boundary with the park but fenced around external boundaries adjoining agricultural or communal land.

In unfenced areas operated under lease from community landholders, the terms of the agreement typically make the tourism operator responsible for land management measures, such as weed control, and for upkeep of infrastructure such as roads and tracks, but do not provide any rights for direct intervention in wildlife management. In large isolated multi-owner private reserves such as Madikwe in South Africa (see Chapter 12), an agreement between the individual lodge owners provides for a joint land and wildlife management agency with considerable powers over the individual operators. This joint management agency can decide to buy or sell wildlife on and off the reserve area as a whole, and can also impose sanctions on individual operators that breach agreed operating codes, e.g. by driving vehicles off-track. In the case of Madikwe, this agency is the North-West Parks and Tourism Board (2010). In areas which have open boundaries shared with public protected areas, individual wildlife can typically cross unimpeded between public and private land, and the private operators have the ability to manage wildlife habitat on their properties, but generally not to manage wildlife directly, except in some cases through hunting. Finally, on entirely private reserves, operators have considerable freedom to modify habitat, clear or plant vegetation, drive on- or off-track as they decide, and buy, sell and translocate wildlife.

The capture, translocation and release of large game animals have been developed to a high degree in sub-Saharan Africa, with a range of well-tested techniques currently in routine use (Ebedes et al., 2002). Public protected area agencies, as well as private reserve managers, routinely take part in such programmes. The conservation management staff of &Beyond played a significant role in pioneering some of these techniques, most notably helicopter capture and soft release strategies for translocated animals. Under this approach, animals introduced into a reserve are first kept in a small pen where veterinary treatment is available if needed; then released into a large fenced area where they can adapt to the landscape but do not interact with resident territorial wildlife; and finally released to roam freely throughout the reserve. These approaches have greatly improved the success of translocation programmes.

In the remainder of this chapter, the considerations outlined above are examined in more detail for a series of individual lodges and reserves operated by &Beyond. A number of these have been described previously by Buckley (2003a, 2006). Information presented in the following sections is derived from on-site audits by the author at 17 of the 20 individual &Beyond properties, some with multiple lodges, as described by Buckley (2003a, 2006). These audits were carried out over the past decade, and updated as required. The individual reserves and lodges are listed in Table 2.1.

The descriptions given in Buckley (2003a, 2006) involved a somewhat different focus from the current volume. The 2003 study aimed to test each case study against the four

principal defining criteria for ecotourism (Buckley, 1994). The 2006 volume examined four lodges operated by &Beyond in the Northern Circuit of Tanzania, as an example of wildlife adventure tourism. The current volume, in contrast, focuses specifically on what &Beyond has contributed to the conservation of biological diversity. Such contributions include a range of mechanisms, including private reserves, leases of community landholdings, management agreements with public protected areas and contributions to local communities which encourage conservation through more indirect means.

Maputaland: Phinda

Phinda Private Game Reserve in South Africa is in many ways the flagship of the &Beyond portfolio, incorporating and exemplifying many aspects of the company's conservation tourism philosophies. It is 230 km^2 in area, and lies immediately adjacent to the World Heritage-listed iSimangaliso (formerly Greater St Lucia) Wetland Park, in the Maputaland region of Kwazulu-Natal. Phinda was previously a privately owned cattle property, which &Beyond bought in 1991 with funds from a bank loan and other investors. The entire perimeter had to be fenced with a wildlife-proof fence, very much stronger and more expensive than a standard stock fence. This was needed not only to protected the company's investment in new wildlife, but to prevent any potential losses to neighbours which might have occurred if wildlife had escaped. The vegetation was rehabilitated, notably through control and eradication of the introduced triffid weed, Chromolaena odorata. The reserve was restocked with wildlife purchased from elsewhere, including the Big Five and other charismatic species such as cheetah. Since that date, &Beyond has built six new lodges, all to high environmental standards: Forest, Vlei, Mountain, Rock, Zuka and the Homestead.

The boundaries and ownership of the Phinda private reserve have changed at least twice since it was first established. The original property purchased in 1991 has been quoted as either 150 km^2 or 170 km^2 in area (Buckley,

Table 2.1. &Beyond camps and lodges.

Country	Region	Reserve	Type	Lodge or camp
South Africa	iSimangaliso	Phinda	Private Game Reserve	Phinda (× 6)
South Africa	Eastern Cape	Kwandwe	Private Game Reserve	Kwandwe (× 4)
South Africa	Sabi Sands	Sabi Sand	Game Reserve	Exeter
South Africa	Sabi Sands	Sabi Sand	Game Reserve	Kirkman's
South Africa	Sabi Sands	Sabi Sand	Game Reserve	Dulini
South Africa	Sabi Sands	Sabi Sand	Game Reserve	Leadwood
South Africa	Timbavati	Ngala	Private Game Reserve	Ngala (× 2)
South Africa	Northwest	Madikwe	Game Reserve	Madikwe
Namibia	Namib	NamibRand	Nature Reserve	Sossusvlei[a]
Botswana	Okavango	Moremi	Wildlife Reserve	Nxabega
Botswana	Okavango	Moremi	Wildlife Reserve	Sandibe
Botswana	Okavango	Moremi	Wildlife Reserve	Xaranna[a]
Botswana	Okavango	Moremi	Wildlife Reserve	Xudum[a]
Zimbabwe	Victoria Falls	Matetsi	Private Game Reserve	Matetsi[a]
Tanzania	Zanzibar	Mnemba	P and P	Mnemba
Tanzania	Serengeti	Serengeti	National Park	Grumeti
Tanzania	Serengeti	Kleins	WMA	Kleins
Tanzania	Ngorongoro	Ngorongoro	Conservation Area (P and P)	Ngorongoro
Tanzania	Lake Manyara	Lake Manyara	National Park	Lake Manyara
Kenya	Mara	Masai Mara	National Reserve	Kichwa Tembo

[a]Not audited or included in this chapter.
P and P = public conservation area, lodge on adjacent private land or leasehold. WMA, Wildlife Management Area, leasehold concession

2003a; Druce *et al.*, 2008). In 2004, boundary fences between Phinda and two neighbouring properties, Zuka and Mziki Pumalanga, were removed (Druce *et al.*, 2008), increasing the total area by 34 km². The additional area was soon utilized by resident wildlife from Phinda, including elephant (Druce *et al.*, 2008). In 2008, an area of 95 km² was transferred to the neighbouring communities of Makhasa and Mnqobokazi, with a 72-year leaseback to &Beyond and an indefinite conservation covenant. The total area of the conservancy is currently quoted as 230 km² (&Beyond, 2010), presumably including both the contiguous titles and the leaseback area.

The Phinda reserve contains a variety of different ecosystem types. Rarest of these in conservation terms (Gaugris and van Rooyen, 2008) is the patch of dry sand forest where Forest Lodge was built. The sand forest provides habitat for a number of rare plants, for smaller antelope such as suni and red duiker, and for rare birds such as Neergard's sunbird and the lemon-breasted canary (Barnes, 2000).

Phinda has acted as a model and proving ground for translocation and reintroduction of large wildlife, notably elephant, rhino, lion and cheetah. Between 1992 and 1994, 58 elephant were introduced, and by 2003 there were over 100 (Druce *et al.*, 2006). The population has since been reduced by outward translocations. Lion had been extinct in Maputaland since 1938, and 15 were reintroduced successfully between 1992 and 2003, using a newly developed 'soft release' strategy which has since been duplicated widely and adapted for other species. Fifteen cheetah were also reintroduced and have thrived, with many since relocated to other reserves. In 2004, 16 black rhino were introduced as part of a joint programme with the World Wide Fund for Nature and Ezemvelo KwaZulu Natal (Sherriffs, 2007). Programmes have been introduced to reduce hunting of leopard on neighbouring properties (Balme *et al.*, 2009).

Part of Phinda's conservation success derives from its good relations with its three local communities. It is a major employer, producing ten times the total income and 30 times the salary income of the previous farming properties. It has provided funds for schools, a computer training centre and health care facilities. It runs a ranger training school and a construction trade training course. In 2008 it apparently paid approximately US$2.5 million to two local communities as part of the land hand-back mentioned above (&Beyond, 2010).

Eastern Cape: Kwandwe

Kwandwe is a 220 km^2 privately owned conservation reserve about 100 km inland from the south coast of the Eastern Cape province of South Africa. The Eastern Cape ecosystems are rather different from those commonly associated with African wildlife safari tourism. The principal landscape is of low rolling hills with a low but relatively dense shrub vegetation cover which supports a wide variety of succulents and other plant species. The Great Fish River also flows through the Kwandwe reserve, providing a separate landscape of steep cliffs and riverine sandbars. Kwandwe supports small populations of lion, leopard, cheetah and black-footed cat; elephant, buffalo and both black and white rhino; some of the rarer herbivores such as Cape grysbok and black wildebeest; and a wide range of bird species, including crowned eagle and Knysna woodpecker.

Kwandwe is of particular significance for conservation of the endangered blue crane. Indeed, the name Kwandwe means 'Place of the Blue Crane' in the Xhosa language (&Beyond, 2010). This species is also of special political significance as South Africa's national bird. The blue cranes are seasonal visitors to Kwandwe, with nesting sites in a particular area of short grassland.

Black rhino were reintroduced in 2001, purchased from Ezemvelo KwaZulu Natural Wildlife Service at a cost of R2.24 million (US$300,000) each. There are now 11 individuals at Kwandwe (&Beyond, 2010).

Cheetah were also reintroduced in 2001, with an initial population of nine individuals.

The owners of the Kwandwe property also operate a community development fund, the Angus Gillis Foundation, which is funding optical services and community development infrastructure in neighbouring schools and villages, and which has assisted &Beyond in offering conservation lessons at Kwandwe to children from the nearby Fort Brown Primary School. One game drive vehicle from Kwandwe, with ranger and tracker, is allocated to these lessons one day each week (&Beyond, 2010).

Sabi Sands and Timbavati: Kirkman's, Exeter, Dulini, Leadwood, Ngala

The Sabi Sands area consists of a total of 29 individual properties, totalling 650 km^2 in aggregate area, formerly managed for commercial cattle production, adjacent to the 19,000 km^2 Kruger National Park in south-eastern South Africa. Most of the Sabi Sands area is now operated as private reserves, with a total of 18 named reserves, some including more than one land tenure block. Most of these also operate one or more game lodges, with 35 lodges in total. Several of these lodges were described previously by Buckley (2003a) including Chitwa Chitwa, Sabi Sabi and Londolozi. This section considers the four properties currently operated by &Beyond.

There are several features of the Sabi Sands area which combine to make it particularly successful as a conservation tourism proposition. The rainfall is sufficient to support a dense savannah woodland, which in turn supports a dense population of the larger herbivores and hence the larger carnivores. The wildlife have been habituated to tourists in safari vehicles for several generations: that is, the individuals currently present in the area learnt from their parents to ignore the vehicles. Tourists can hence be driven by experienced guides, in open-topped safari vehicles, extremely close to large and potentially dangerous wildlife such as lion and leopard, even at night and even when they are hunting, mating or suckling young. The biological productivity of the area, and hence the density of large wildlife, is high; and the area is traversed by a large number of roads and tracks, so it is relatively straightforward for the skilled game trackers at each of the lodges to locate individual animals each morning. Indeed, they recognize many of the individuals and know their territories and behavioural characteristics quite well.

Individual vehicles and trackers cooperate both within and between lodges to hasten the tracking process and also to manage access to individual sightings, so as to avoid crowding other tourists or disturbing the animals. The various lodges operate in syndicates which grant each other traversing rights across each others' properties, under various conditions. Many of the fences which used to separate the properties when they were used by cattle grazing have long since been dismantled, and the fence separating the entire Sabi Sands area from Kruger National Park was also taken down some time ago, so that wildlife can roam freely between the two. Because Kruger National Park itself is a major tourist destination, there is a well-maintained local airport near the main Kruger Park gateway. Individual lodges can shuttle visitors to their own airstrips using light planes, or ground transfers which double as wildlife-watching safaris.

In tourism terms, the private reserves and lodges of the Sabi Sands area are a highly successful cluster of very similar enterprises, which have built up a global reputation and clientele over a number of decades and are marketed heavily by travel agents worldwide. In addition, several of these enterprises have established their own loyalty programmes to maintain a solid year-round base clientele from within South Africa itself. With year-round road access for consumables and other supplies, their operating costs are lower than competing lodges in more remote areas. As long as South Africa itself remains politically stable and safe for visitors, the principal commercial issue for the Sabi Sands enterprises is probably the value of the local currency, the South African rand, relative to international benchmarks such as the US dollar and the euro. Since these enterprises are on private landholdings, they do not need to renegotiate leases with local communities, as occurs in some other regions; and, since they are relatively small in area and employ numerous staff from the local Shangaan-speaking communities, they are able

to avoid the pressures of poaching, harvesting and incursions of domestic livestock which occur in some other areas.

From a conservation perspective, the private reserves of the Sabi Sands area effectively extend the size of Kruger National Park by 650 km^2. This is a substantial area of wildlife habitat, and while it comprises only 3.4% of the area of Kruger National Park itself, this proportion is small because Kruger National Park is large, not because the Sabi Sands are insignificant. Dropping the fence between the Sabi Sands area and Kruger National Park allowed some of the habituated individuals in the private reserves to move out into the much larger public protected area, where they were no longer accessible to clients of the private reserves. Equally, however, it allowed wildlife from the much larger reservoir area in the public park to move into the private reserves, bringing new genetic diversity to previously isolated populations. Even if the private enterprises may have gained greater net benefits than the public park in this exchange, the bottom line is that the Sabi Sands lodges and reserves have increased the Kruger conservation estate by about one-thirtieth; and presumably the protected populations of the plant and animal species occurring in the Kruger ecosystems have increased by similar proportions. There are some differences, because some of the individual reserves are managed more intensively than Kruger National Park, in order to boost populations of particular icon species which are highest in tourism value though not necessarily in conservation value. Even so, it appears that the Sabi Sands tourism enterprises do indeed make an unequivocal contribution to conservation of biological diversity.

Over the past decade, the situation at Sabi Sands has experienced an interesting twist. Noting the significant revenues earned by the private lodges of the Sabi Sands area, the public parks agency decided to copy their model itself. SANParks identified seven individual areas within Kruger National Park which were relatively remote and generally inaccessible to self-drive visitors, and invited tenders from commercial tour operators to build and run exclusive lodges in those areas, directly analogous to the private lodges of the Sabi Sands area. This venture is examined in more detail in Chapter 12. In summary, the new lodges inside Kruger National Park did not generate as high an income as those in the adjacent Sabi Sands area, because the latter have developed international reputations over a number of decades and are in high demand. Their facilities, infrastructure and operations are well polished; their wildlife are already habituated; and they have an established clientele of repeat customers. The new lodges within Kruger National Park had none of these things.

&Beyond currently operates four properties within the Sabi Sands area: Kirkman's Camp, Exeter, Leadwood and Dulini. They are all relatively small in area, but they share traversing rights with a number of their neighbours, and they are all operated as integral parts of the broader Sabi Sands Reserve. The Kirkman's property was previously owned by one of the early pioneers of the area, and has recently been remodelled to reflect that heritage, with historic firearms and even furniture on display. Dulini Lodge currently supports an ongoing external research programme on pangolin population ecology.

Each of these lodges offers conservation lessons to nearby schools, where children and their teachers visit the lodge for a day, go on game drives and learn about wildlife and conservation. Kirkman's has also contributed kitchens and permaculture gardens to nearby schools, while Exeter has carried out tree-planting programmes and funded local students to go to university, through the &Beyond Community Leaders Education Fund. These contributions, in addition to local employment, continue to maintain community support for wildlife conservation in the Sabi Sands area.

In the Timbavati area near Kruger National Park, &Beyond operates the 150 km^2 Ngala private game reserve. The Timbavati area is separate from the Sabi Sands area from a land management perspective, but it forms part of the same cluster from a tourism marketing perspective. The Ngala property was donated to the South Africa National Parks Trust, via the World Wide Fund for Nature, by landowner Hans Hoheisen. The SANParks Trust leases exclusive tourism operating and traversing rights to &Beyond in return for a lease fee, a traversing fee and a proportion of profit. Over the past 10 years, the SANParks Trust has earned about US$2.7 million from this arrangement. Ngala Game Lodge is a member of the Small Luxury Hotels of the World. It also has a particularly comprehensive minimal-impact environmental management system (Buckley, 2003a). Community contributions include construction of classrooms at the Mdluli High School in Hluvukani, and a craft market at Bohlabela near the Orpen Gate of Kruger National Park (&Beyond, 2010). Ngala also offers conservation lessons to nearby schools.

Madikwe

Madikwe is a group of former farms established in 1991 as a syndicated private game reserve, 760 km^2 in total area. It lies at the north-western border of South Africa, adjacent to Botswana, and is bisected by the Mafikeng–Gaborone Road. Its western boundary is formed by the Marico River. Derelict farm buildings, old fences and weeds were removed; other buildings were renovated for parks staff; a 157 km electrified perimeter fence was installed to enclose a 600 km^2 area of the reserve; and 8000 individual animals, from 28 wildlife species, were translocated and released in the reserve through a programme known as Operation Phoenix. In addition to the Big Five, these species include cheetah and wild dog. Both black and white rhino now occur in Madikwe, which is also known for the less common brown hyena. Over 350 bird species are recorded.

A number of game lodges have been built in the reserve using private capital, and these lodges pay concession fees to the North West Parks and Tourism Board. Fees are also received from trophy hunters and other tour operators in the reserve. These funds are used to: repay the development and restoration costs for the reserve; maintain its conservation infrastructure; provide regional development funding for local communities; and establish a conservation trust fund to develop similar areas elsewhere in the north-west province.

Community development has also been funded by bilateral aid from the UK. &Beyond operates a lodge on one of the Madikwe properties.

Okavango Delta, Botswana: Sandibe, Nxabega, Xaranna, Xudum

The Okavango area is a large inland flood plain fed by the Okavango River, which originates in the highlands of Angola (Mbaiwa, 2004). The waters flood outwards to form a maze of interconnected channels, reed swamps and grassy plains, interspersed with slightly higher-elevation sand islands which support low open woodland (Ross, 1987). The extent of the flooded area varies both seasonally and from year to year, and the entire ecosystem is at risk from proposed large-scale water diversion projects in Angola and Namibia, which would reduce the net inflow to the Delta area (Mbaiwa, 2004). The area is world-famous both as a habitat for endangered wildlife and because of the cultural traditions of the Okavango Delta San or Bushman peoples (Ross, 1987).

The area includes a large national park, Moremi, and large areas owned under community title and subject to community-based natural resource management. Private tourism lodges on these community lands are operated under lease agreements, which typically grant the lessee an exclusive right to access and traverse the area concerned and to construct and operate lodges and facilities, for a fixed and often relatively short period of years. The agreements may stipulate a fixed annual rental, a proportion of profit or turnover, a fee per customer bed-night or other financial arrangements.

Typically, these agreements make the lessee responsible for upkeep and maintenance of infrastructure, such as roads and tracks, bridges and jetties, as well as the operational infrastructure, such as power and water supplies and sewage treatment systems at the lodges themselves. The agreements may also specify that members of specific local villages should have preferential access to employment opportunities, either in the lodge itself or for contract labour such as road maintenance and bridge repairs.

Most of the lodges in the Okavango Delta offer wildlife watching by *mokoro*, dugout canoes poled along the shallow channels among the reed swamps, and *mokoro* guides are commonly local residents who are already adept at manoeuvring and navigating the *mokoro* canoes. Some of the lodges also operate launches or dinghies powered by electric or outboard motors. In addition, most of the lodges offer more conventional game drives in open-topped 4WD safari vehicles.

The ecosystems, wildlife, human settlements and management of the Okavango Delta area have been described in an illustrated volume by Ross (1987). From a wildlife-watching perspective, the area is particularly well known for two relatively unusual antelope species, the red lechwe and the much more shy and elusive sitatunga. It is one of the particular characteristics of the Okavango Delta area that large expanses of nearly level ground are flooded at times by sheets of water only a few centimetres or tens of centimetres in depth. Herds of red lechwe generally frequent open grassland areas close to water or flooded to a shallow depth, which does not hinder their movement. Sitatunga are more solitary animals, seen only singly or in pairs. They are much more shy than the lechwe and are likely to run as soon as they become aware of humans in the vicinity. While relatively small, they have a particular springing or bounding gait which enables them to run at speed even in areas with relatively deep water. While sitatunga sightings are by no means guaranteed, they are one of the key attractions for more experienced wildlife tourists. Many areas of the Okavango also boast a high density of other game, including Big Five and less common species such as aardwolf.

The Okavango area is also extremely rich in bird life. Most particularly, it provides opportunities to see the rare and beautiful Pels fishing owl, and other charismatic species such as the giant eagle owl and the tiny pearl-spotted owl. There are also excellent opportunities to watch a wide range of water-loving bird species, including a variety of different kingfisher species.

All of these, and particularly the rarer and more specialized species, depend heavily on the seasonal flooding of the Delta ecosystems:

first, because this maintains their habitat and food supplies, and second, because it limits encroachment from cattle farming. By providing a wildlife-based income which is significant both for local resident communities and also at a national scale, tourism helps to maintain both the public protected area and the community lands in a relatively well-conserved state. In addition, it contributes to the international pool of conservation advocates who are prepared to campaign against large-scale water diversion schemes, which represent a particular threat to the area.

No single lodge or tourist operation can lay claim to the overall conservation benefits, but each of them contributes; and some are more active than others in relation to conservation management, community support and international advocacy. &Beyond is a leader along all these lines. Its lodges have adopted a range of minimal-impact environmental management practices and enjoy good relations with local communities (Buckley, 2003a). &Beyond operates four lodges in the Okavango Delta region of northern Botswana. These are Sandibe, Nxabega, Xaranna and Xudum. I have visited only Sandibe and Nxabega. Xaranna and Xudum are recent additions to the &Beyond portfolio.

Nxabega Tented Camp is set in riverine forest in an 80 km^2 private wildlife concession south-east of Moremi Wildlife Reserve in the southern section of the Delta. It can accommodate up to 18 guests and employs over 200 local staff. The tented cabins are set on raised wooden platforms and can be removed completely in future if required. Operations and environmental management were described by Buckley (2003a). The Camp contributes to research on wetland birds, including the endangered wattled crane.

Sandibe Lodge lies in an 80 km^2 private concession near Moremi. It is built on a low sand island, but has close access to reed-lined permanent channels accessible in a small electric-powered launch. Operational aspects were described by Buckley (2003a). Staff live in an on-site village. Locals also operate a herb and vegetable garden, established with assistance from &Beyond's Africa Fund, which sells its produce to the Lodge.

Zanzibar: Mnemba

Mnemba Island is a small sand cay on a reef just off the north-eastern tip of Zanzibar in Tanzania. It supports typical vegetation for small subtropical reef islets: open woodland dominated by beach casuarinas; salt-tolerant trees such as the cannonball mangrove; and pan-tropical sandy-beach shrub species. The island's position moves slightly on the reef top from season to season as wind and wave patterns change. It is reached by boat from the nearest beach on Zanzibar. The reef around the island is a marine park, protected from fishing, and many guests come to dive. The Lodge has placed artificial Fish Aggregation Devices outside the reserve to provide additional opportunities for local fishermen. There are a number of other dive operators based on Zanzibar itself, and Mnemba Reef is a popular destination since it is one of the few protected as a marine park. The reef was declared a reserve after lobbying from &Beyond. The dives are relatively shallow, but there are rather few dive resorts in this part of the world, so even highly experienced and well-travelled divers are likely to see species which are new to them. Staff and guests of &Beyond's Mnemba Island Lodge are the only residents. There are ten individual villas, with maximum total occupancy of 20 guests. The island's beaches provide one of few remaining safe nesting sites for the highly endangered green turtle, and also support a significant population of the rare crab plover. There is a very successful breeding population of the small suni antelope in the forested sections, with individuals translocated to other reserves at intervals.

Greater Serengeti: Grumeti, Kleins, Lake Manyara, Ngorongoro, Kichwa Tembo

The Greater Serengeti ecosystem of northern Tanzania and southern Kenya is one of the world's premier wildlife conservation and tourism destinations. It is centred on Serengeti National Park itself in northern Tanzania, and the adjacent Maasai Mara National Park in southern Kenya. Both of these are large areas of semi-arid savannah grassland, which are world-famous both for Big Five wildlife-watching opportunities and for the annual migration of large herds of wildebeest and other herbivores such as zebra.

The areas around these large national parks contain mosaics of villages and Wildlife Management Areas, some of them used for hunting tourism and some for photographic wildlife tourism. There is a certain degree of conflict at times between these different uses, especially when governments grant hunting licences over areas where photographic wildlife tourism enterprises are already operating, with existing government licences and agreements with local villages. Local village economies rely principally on cattle grazing, with the cattle protected from predators by herdsmen during the day and by being driven into enclosures at night. These areas, known as bomas, are surrounded by dense hedges of thorny bushes, and typically include dwellings as well as livestock. Areas subject to cattle grazing suffer a degree of degradation to soils, vegetation, wildlife populations and aesthetic appeal for tourism, so wildlife tourism operations generally aim to maintain exclusive-access conservation areas, and visual separation between lodges and villages.

In this overall ecological, social and political context, wildlife tourism operations can indeed make significant contribution to conservation at a regional scale, effectively by extending the area of the public national parks. Unlike South Africa, where many of the best-known areas for conservation tourism are on private range-land, &Beyond's lodges in Kenya and Tanzania are on areas held under concession arrange-ments with a fixed life. To continue their contributions to conservation, therefore, re-quires that concessions must be renewed at intervals. Typically this requires not merely profitable operation and good relations with local communities, but also a favourable political context at a national level. This requires a stable national government which recognizes existing land tenure and manage-ment systems, and which values the ongoing development of its wildlife tourism industry – in

preference, for example, to a quick one-off cash return from a wealthy shooting party.

Grumeti

Grumeti Serengeti Tented Camp is a permanent camp on the banks of an oxbow lagoon, attached to the Grumeti River in the north-western part of the Serengeti National Park. The Camp has ten large guest tents with en suite bathrooms and verandas. The central lodge area incorporates a dining room and lounge built around a tree-studded lawn which slopes to the river. The Camp is close to an area of plains which are used routinely during the annual wildlife migrations, and also offers spectacular wildlife viewing when the migrating herds cross the Grumeti River itself. Hippo are frequently seen – and heard – browsing close to the tents at night and early morning. The river is flanked by tall gallery forest which supports a resident population of black-and-white colobus monkeys. The main contributions to conservation seem to be: first, control of invasive plant species such as water lettuce; and, second, contributions to and extension of the Park's anti-poaching patrols by the &Beyond rangers.

Kleins

Kleins Camp lies in a 100 km^2 Wildlife Management Area which is directly adjacent to the north-eastern corner of the Serengeti National Park in northern Tanzania. It is a very well-appointed lodge with ten individual stone villas, built inconspicuously on the side of a hill slope which looks out over the concession area. The concession area includes some large open plains and dry hill slopes with good opportunities to watch cheetah and a strip of riverine forest frequented by leopard. Guests at Kleins Camp can also take advantage of the great expanse of the Serengeti Plains, with quick access into the National Park and the opportunity to watch the migrating herds at the appropriate season. Guests can also take a guided walk to the crest of the Kuka Hills behind the Camp, with views out over the Serengeti. There is a village not far from the lodge, though not directly in view, and there are close links between the lodge and the village. The lodge provides employment, buys fresh produce and loans equipment as required. The village provides a residential area for lodge staff and a local supply of fresh food. The villagers continue to graze cattle in some areas. The overall outcome appears to be an effective addition to the Serengeti National Parks system.

Ngorongoro Crater

Ngorongoro Crater is one of the world's best-known wildlife-watching destinations, and also one of the more contentious. The crater and its immediate surrounds lie within the Ngorongoro Conservation Area. Conflicts arise first, because of the extremely heavy use of the crater floor by tourist vehicles, which crowd both each other and resident wildlife populations; and, second, because of a certain degree of contention between the NCA management agency and tour operators on the one hand, and resident Maasai cattle herders who occupy the surrounding areas and also graze their cattle on the inner walls of the crater. The crater is closed to tourist access at night, and a large proportion of visitors stay in the nearby town of Arusha and visit the park only during the middle of the day. There is no accommodation within the crater itself, but there are a small number of tourist lodges around the rim. Guests at these lodges are first into the crater in the morning, and last out in the evening, and generally get much better, less crowded and more relaxed opportunities to watch wildlife, including the less common and more reclusive species.

&Beyond operates one of these lodges, which it took over from Abercrombie and Kent a number of years ago. There are three separate lodges on the &Beyond concession (Buckley, 2006). North and South Camp, with 12 suites each, have the more opulent lounge areas, but the smaller six-suite Tree Camp has picture-postcard views to the crater floor and beautifully designed timber cottages with their own fireplaces and four-posters, private butlers and baths perched in oval annexes with their own views across Ngorongoro. These lodges

represent only a rather small proportion of the total tourist volume at Ngorongoro Crater, and are probably not critical to its continued role as a conservation reserve. The company has taken an active role, however, in ongoing management negotiations for the crater and surrounding area, with particular reference to maintaining the conservation value of the park while still maintaining the rights and livelihood of neighbouring cattle-herding communities.

Lake Manyara

Lake Manyara National Park is a narrow strip of forest bounded by Lake Manyara itself on one side and a rift scarp on the other. It is separated from Ngorongoro Crater National Park by an expanse of largely denuded subsistence farmland. It is a public national park open during the day to self-drive visitors and a wide range of commercial tour operators. Since there is only one entrance to the park and one road, however, most vehicles do not drive very far down the edge of the lake. In addition, Lake Manyara National Park has historically been famous for its lions which, unlike those of the open savannah country, have developed the habit of climbing trees. While this behavioural difference is not of any particular significance from a conservation perspective, it has become the icon attraction for the majority of tourists, who judge the success of their visit by this feature alone.

The lodge operated by &Beyond in Lake Manyara National Park, in contrast, is near the far end of the access road, beyond the area generally accessed by day visitors. While lion may certainly be seen, either climbing trees or behaving more conventionally, they are not the primary attraction for the majority of the lodge's guests. Rather, it is the opportunity to experience the diversity of the forest ecosystem at dawn and dusk, when a particular wealth of bird life can be seen and heard, along with monkeys and the smaller forest-dwelling herbivores. The individual suites at the lodge are built at the level of the forest canopy, like enormous tree houses. While screened and protected from insects and any larger night wildlife, they are completely open to the sounds of the forest at night. This provides a very different and complementary experience to the lodges of the open plains.

From a conservation perspective, the &Beyond lodge in Lake Manyara National Park provides two major benefits for the parks service. The first is funding, in the form of lease payments. The second is patrols and protection against poaching in this more remote section of the park.

Kichwa Tembo

One of the best-known sights in wildlife documentaries on East Africa is the river crossings, during the annual migrations, when the herds of wildebeest and zebra are at particular risk from crocodile attacks. One such crossing site on the Mara River is accessible from the &Beyond Lodge at Kichwa Tembo on the western side of Kenya's Maasai Mara National Park. The Lodge is built on community land, with several villages in the vicinity, as well as a staff residential area on site.

Local government arrangements include a district council, and there has apparently been a certain degree of historical dispute between that council and individual villages over allocation of the various fees paid by the tour operator. Payments include: lease arrangements for the lodge itself; daily access fees for traversing rights; and payments for dances performed for guests at the lodge. The Kichwa Tembo Lodge is larger than many of those operated by &Beyond, and provides substantial local employment. It also provides opportunities for local artisans to market their wares directly to lodge guests at certain times of the week. Relations between &Beyond and the local villages are thus very good.

From a conservation perspective, the Kichwa Tembo tourism operation effectively creates an area of wildlife habitat which would otherwise be used only for cattle grazing. It also provides logistic support for an externally operated anti-poaching and animal rescue team (&Beyond, 2010). It carries out invasive plant control, and reduces clearance for fuel wood by local residents by providing them with fuel bricks made from waste paper and coal dust.

Philosophy and Future Plans

The scale of &Beyond's operations has grown greatly over recent years, in both economic and geographical terms, and this is perhaps the reason behind the change of name from Conservation Corporation Africa. The company has amply demonstrated the success of its model within southern and eastern Africa, and continues to consolidate and expand both within the African continent and also within Asia and elsewhere, with appropriate adaptations to local circumstances. The company's initiatives in Asia are described in Chapter 6.

Within Africa, &Beyond's principal focus is sub-Saharan, and its overall vision is to create a giant subcontinental-scale complex of conservation areas linking Ethiopia in the north-east, Angola in the west and South Africa in the south. This would include areas of Kenya, Tanzania, Uganda, Rwanda and Burundi, Malawi, Zambia, Zimbabwe, Namibia, Angola, Botswana, Mozambique, Lesotho and South Africa. It would also include Madagascar, though there is of course no land link to mainland Africa. To create such a conservation complex is an enormous but not impossible undertaking. Most of the countries concerned already have public protected areas at least in name, though actual on-the-ground protection is not always effective. Some of these countries are war-torn and severely poverty-stricken, and all of them face a range of intractable social and political pressures, ranging from disease and malnutrition to international debt and ethnic conflict. Essentially, the model proposed by &Beyond contains three complementary components.

In the wealthier countries such as South Africa, assuming that land tenure and government systems remain stable, the principal approach is to extend the public protected area system by creating private reserves funded by tourism. As outlined in this chapter, a number of such ventures have already proved their success. There are, however, several barriers to extending this model indefinitely. It takes time to rehabilitate vegetation, restock wildlife and habituate individual animals to ignore tourist vehicles, so as to provide a wildlife-watching experience for which tourists are prepared to pay the high prices necessary to fund a private reserve. In addition, these prices are maintained partly by exclusivity. If a large number of new private reserves and lodges were to commence operations simultaneously, this might simply spread the total available revenue more thinly, unless global demand for African wildlife-watching experiences increases at a comparable rate. In addition, if social concerns over climate change, coupled with government measures to mitigate greenhouse gas emissions, jointly reduce the attractiveness of long-haul international travel, this could also reduce the supply of clients for Africa's private reserves and game lodges. All of these factors, however, remain uncertain, and currently the private-reserve model funded by upmarket wildlife lodges, as adopted by &Beyond, does indeed seem to work well in sub-Saharan Africa.

The second component of a subcontinental-scale conservation complex is the widespread adoption of wildlife tourism and conservation as a key component of community-based natural resource management (CBNRM), in countries such as Namibia and Botswana, which have large areas of lands held under various forms of community title (see Chapter 12). Issues associated with international tourism markets are similar for these areas to those for the private reserves as outlined above, but there are additional legal, economic and social complexities. The legal complexities relate to the precise bundle of rights conferred by national governments on local residents under various types of community title, and the precise rights and responsibilities provided for tour operators under lease and permit arrangements both with local communities and with national government agencies. These can differ quite significantly between countries and between individual land areas.

The economic complexities relate to issues such as: the difficulties in raising investment capital without freehold land title; the ability of fledgling wildlife tourism enterprises to jointly service debt, cover operating costs for conservation management as well as tourism infrastructure, and simultaneously yield a sufficient return to local communities for them to continue to support the tourism and conservation operations. Larger companies with a substantial asset base and current cash flow are better placed to make new investments where outgoings are likely to exceed income for a number of years initially. The social complexities can vary greatly from place to place, but typically include: concerns over local employment and other opportunities; the types and allocation of benefits received by local communities; conflicts between individuals involved in tourism and those involved in agriculture or other activities; and arguments between and within different communities in relation to ownership and access rights for particular areas of land (Spenceley, 2008a; Saarinen et al., 2009a, see also Chapter 12).

The third key component of the subcontinental-scale conservation complex is the restoration of infrastructure and technical capability in countries recovering from extended civil conflicts, such as Angola, Zimbabwe and Mozambique. In general, once a degree of stability and democratic order is established, both multilateral and bilateral aid agencies are prepared to fund a wide variety of restoration works, which may include transport and tourism infrastructure and in some cases the re-establishment of protected areas. Such funding, however, is generally on a limited-term project basis. The period concerned is typically not long enough to build up local institutional and technical capacity from scratch, if it has been eroded severely over an extended number of years or indeed decades. Therefore, a mechanism is needed to provide a transition from entirely external international donor funding to an entirely domestic economy which can support a fully functioning public protected area system.

A number of organizations, including &Beyond, have proposed that one mechanism for such a transition would be to establish private protected area management corporations. National governments in the nations concerned could grant or lease operating rights to public protected areas to such corporations, which could also receive funding directly from international aid agencies. These corporations, which would draw their staff from existing parks agencies and similar organizations worldwide, would provide conservation management expertise and operational capability. They could then lease tourism operating rights to conservation tourism companies such as &Beyond, with a gradual transfer of income streams from international aid to tourism revenue. This type of approach has already been commenced by the organization African Parks, as described in Chapter 12.

There are two further critical issues. The first is that neither &Beyond nor any other single conservation tourism corporation can achieve conservation connectivity throughout sub-Saharan Africa solely through its own efforts. It will need to work together, as indeed it already does, with other conservation tourism operators, community landholders, public parks agencies, and potentially also with private conservation organizations, NGOs and international donors. The second is that both the particular areas under conservation management and the organizations involved will almost certainly change over time. The overall structure therefore needs to be resilient and to contain some redundancy so that it can survive political or financial setbacks. For example, even those countries which are currently stable politically may in future potentially be subject to terrorism, armed conflict, dictatorships or other political destabilization which damages the conservation capabilities of both public and private reserve areas, at least for a while. Similarly, where conservation depends on income from tourism, then either large-scale financial shocks, increased travel costs or individual corporate failures may create set-backs in part or even the whole of the conservation complex.

The ambitions of conservation tourism corporations such as &Beyond, therefore, will not be easy to achieve. They are, however, well within the realm of possibility and well worth pursuing. In the meantime, &Beyond has already achieved a great deal for conservation. It has protected significant areas of wildlife habitat in the form of private and community reserves funded by tourism. Within some of these areas, it has successfully protected significant populations of endangered species, such as the great blue crane at Kwandwe. It has developed, demonstrated and shared techniques for successful capture, translocation and release of individual animals of many different species. This is a critical component of current conservation management practices, so as to be able to restock rehabilitated areas and in some cases so as to actively maintain genetic diversity in isolated subpopulations. And, finally, it has provided a model which many other tour operators have successfully followed and emulated, so that its efforts have been amplified well beyond the scale of the company itself. The three-legged-pot philosophy of caring simultaneously for the land, the people and the wildlife has successfully made &Beyond into one of the few organizations which can legitimately claim a triple bottom line where social, financial and environmental components are all positive.

3 Wilderness Safaris

Safari vehicle, Serra Cafema

Introduction

The strategic business philosophy of Wilderness Safaris (2010) is enunciated in the corporate website and other marketing materials. These emphasize that, in terms of its *raison d'être*, Wilderness Safaris sees itself as a conservation organization as well as an ecotourism company. To survive and operate as such, however, it must also function successfully as a tourism operator in a globally competitive industry.

Since 2003, Wilderness Safaris has generally pursued a policy of expansion. There are several reasons for this. The first is simply to achieve financial growth as a corporation, so as to increase funds available. The second is to extend its successes in conservation tourism to a broader area. The third is to expand the range of lodges and reserves so as to offer more variety to repeat customers. The fourth, however, is that, unlike many similar operators, Wilderness Safaris has relied entirely on travel agents for its sales. This means that it must have enough bed-nights available to sell for it to be worthwhile for the agents to invest in the sales effort, including agent-branded marketing materials and staff information and training.

Since small exclusive lodges and camps are a key aspect of high-priced products, the only way to increase the number of bed-nights available is to operate more lodges. There are at least four main ways to achieve this, and Wilderness Safaris has pursued them all. The first is to add one or two extra rooms to existing lodges, each time they are refurbished. The second is to build several separate lodges on each property or lease – either at the same level of luxury, such as at Vumbura, or at different levels, such as at Ongava. The third is to buy or lease new areas, for example when previous leases expire. And the fourth is a franchise-style model where independently owned and operated lodges are marketed under the Wilderness Safaris brand.

From a business perspective, the agents-only sales strategy used by Wilderness Safaris is unusual in this sector, and it is worth examining why the company follows this approach. Essentially, it occurs because of commercial pressures from particular travel agents. These agents insist, in order for them to continue selling Wilderness Safaris' products, that

Wilderness Safaris refrain from selling the same products directly to clients. Effectively, this means that the company cannot add an additional sales stream or make a gradual transition to direct Internet-based sales. It can only offer direct sales if it has the confidence, the client database and the marketing mechanisms in place to make a complete instantaneous transition. That is, it would have to be prepared for agents to boycott its products – or, at least, it would have to be able to convince travel agents that it was prepared to survive such a boycott. Given that Wilderness Safaris operates a number of highly prestigious and heavily coveted properties which well-informed and well-heeled clients ask for by name, it actually seems unlikely that agents would stop selling its products. It would not enhance their reputation with clients. Indeed, it would encourage clients to move from agents to direct bookings, not only for Wilderness Safaris but more generally. It would also provide a major market advantage for any agents who broke ranks. In addition, large-scale collusion by agents would be illegal in many countries. So the agents-only sales strategy may not survive. But, in reality, a direct-sales-only strategy is also unlikely. Therefore, the company does indeed need to maintain agent sales if possible. It will be interesting to watch how this dilemma is resolved in future.

The philosophies and operations of Wilderness Safaris are in many ways parallel to those of &Beyond, though in some respects it has taken different strategies. In this volume I have presented &Beyond first, since it commenced operations earlier and has in many ways led the development of this model; but the two companies are now of a similar scale and follow very similar approaches. Wilderness Safaris espouses the same three-legged-pot philosophy as &Beyond and indeed many other conservation tourism operators (Walpole, 2006), aiming to include benefits for local communities as a key component in the practicalities of conservation in the developing world. For historical reasons and due to the particular interests and prior experience of its founders, its principal areas of operation are in Botswana and Namibia, and, because of the land tenure systems in those countries, it relies more heavily on CBNRM approaches and less on the private freehold reserves which are more commonplace in South Africa. One of its flagship properties, however, is North Island in the Seychelles, which is indeed a private reserve. As outlined later in this chapter, Wilderness Safaris and four other equity partners have invested heavily in rehabilitation works on North Island, including the successful reintroduction of three critically endangered species.

One of the founders of Wilderness Safaris resigned his role in the company a few years ago so as to pursue the same goals independently. It is commonplace that the skills and approaches needed to manage the routine operations of a large and complex tourism corporation with numerous individual properties in a range of different countries, are rather different from the skills and approaches needed to identify new conservation tourism opportunities and establish new enterprises. This applies across many areas of business and other endeavours, and does not reflect any deficiency in either approach. It should, therefore, perhaps be considered normal and indeed advantageous that conservation tourism entrepreneurs move on to new ventures, handing over their established enterprises to be run by conservation tourism managers.

One of the consequences of a geographical focus in northern Botswana and Namibia is that Wilderness Safaris has successfully brought a very significant area of community-managed lands into conservation. The company currently estimates that this area is close to 20,000 km^2 in total, about the same size as the whole of Kruger National Park in South Africa – though of course in rather different ecosystems. Wilderness Safaris also operates lodges, camps and reserves in several other countries, especially Zambia and Zimbabwe (Table 3.1). The remainder of this chapter, however, describes only those which I have visited myself in Namibia, Botswana and the Seychelles, as indicated in Table 3.1. In addition, the lodge operated by Wilderness Safaris at Rocktail Bay in Maputaland, South Africa, was described by Buckley (2006, pp. 183–186). Rocktail Bay Lodge contributes to conservation by protecting coastal vegetation and associated rare bird species, and through its role in the Maputaland Sea Turtle Project, which guards leatherback

and loggerhead turtles laying eggs on the beaches. The lodge pays a concession fee which funds turtle scouts who guard the nests and patrol the beaches, and lodge staff also take part in these patrols directly.

Namibia

Introduction

Namibia has a total area of 824,000 km^2 and a population of about two million people. As of 2007, 16.5% of the country was in national parks and game reserves, 14.4% in community conservancies and 7.4% in freehold conservancies, tourism concessions and community forests (NACSO, 2008). As of 2007, there were over 50 registered Community Conservancies in Namibia with a further 25 in preparation for registration. These conservancies support over 220,000 residents and earned around N$39 million (~US$5 million) in 2007 (NACSO, 2008). Community-based natural resource management (CBNRM) has received substantial support from international donors, with a focus on tourism. Many conservancies, however, focus largely on farming. Wilderness Safaris operates extensively in Namibia, with 360 beds in 18 individual camps and lodges at six different concession areas and community conservancies (Table 3.1). This represents 1.5% of the total tourist bed capacity of Namibia. In writing this chapter I visited five of these camps and lodges for at least 2 days each to check environmental and conservation operating practices, and three others briefly to check lodge construction and environmental management practices only. Those examined in detail were: Ongava, Skeleton Coast, Serra Cafema, Desert Rhino and Damaraland. They are described in turn below.

Because of the history and land tenure arrangements in Namibia, relationships with local communities are particularly critical for conservation (NACSO, 2008). Each of the Wilderness Safaris lodges operates under different circumstances, but all have adopted similar approaches to ensure that local communities receive and perceive benefits. There are direct financial payments: either through community equity in the lodge enterprise, as at

Table 3.1. Wilderness Safaris camps and lodges.

Country and region	Reserve and type[a]	Lodges and Camps
Botswana, Okavango	Moremi, Game Reserve	Mombo[b], Little Mombo, Xigera
Botswana, Okavango	Jao, Concession	Jao, Jacana, Tubu, Kwetsani
Botswana, Okavango	Linyanti, Concession	Savuti[b], Duma Tau[c], Kings Pool[c]
Botswana, Okavango	Selinda, Concession	Seba, Selinda, Zarafa
Botswana, Okavango	Vumbura, Community Conservancy	Vumbura[b], Little Vumbura[c]
Botswana, Okavango	Duba Plans, Community Conservancy	Duba Plains
Botswana, Kalahari	Central Kalahari, Game Reserve	Kalahari Plains
Namibia, Etosha	Ongava, Private Game Reserve	Ongava[b], Little Ongava[b], Ongava Tented Camp[c], Andersson's Camp[c]
Namibia, North West	Skeleton Coast, Concession	Skeleton Coast[b]
Namibia, Kunene	Marienfluss, Community Conservancy	Serra Cafema[b]
Namibia, Kunene	Palmwag, Concession	Desert Rhino[b]
Namibia, Damaraland	Torra, Community Conservancy	Damaraland[b]
Namibia, Damaraland	Doro !Nawas, Community Conservancy	Doro !Nawas
Namibia, Kulala	Sossusvlei, National Park	Kulala, Little Kulala, Kulala Wilderness
Namibia	Mudumu National Park, Lianshulu Concession, Balyerwa Conservancy	Lianshulu
Malawi	Lake Malawi, National Park	Mumbo Chintheche
Malawi	Liwonde, National Park	Mvuu
Seychelles	North Island, Private	North Island[b]
South Africa, Mpumalanga	Kruger, National Park	Pafuri
South Africa, KwaZulu Natal	iSimangaliso Wetland Park	Rocktail Bay[b] (2)
Zambia, Kafue	Kafue, National Park	Busanga, Kapinga
Zambia, Luangwa	South Luangwa, National Park	Kalamu
Zambia	Mosi-oa-Tunya, National Park	Toka Leya
Zimbabwe	Hwange, National Park	Makalolo (2)
	Mana Pools, National Park	Ruckomechi

[a] In National Parks, Game Reserves and Community Conservancies, the lodges operate on (generally unnamed) leases or concessions within those tenures. For Private Game Reserves and named Concessions, Wilderness Safaris owns or leases the entire reserve.
[b] Audited by author.
[c] Visited briefly.

Damaraland; or fixed lease fees, as at Serra Cafema; or revenue-sharing agreements, as at Skeleton Coast and Desert Rhino Camp (Wilderness Safaris, 2010). There is direct employment at the lodges, with 42% of staff drawn from community conservancies and 99% from within Namibia. Desert Rhino Camp employs 97 staff, Serra Cafema 42, Damaraland 40 and Skeleton Coast 23 (Wilderness Safaris, 2010). At some lodges, particular services such as laundry and road maintenance are outsourced to local communities. At others, notably Serra Cafema and Skeleton Coast, guests routinely visit local communities to buy curios and artefacts made locally for the tourist trade. At most sites, the company and its guests have contributed in kind to community services such as water bores, school buildings and computer equipment. Most lodges and their staff also contribute to the programme Children in the Wilderness, which brings disadvantaged children to the Wilderness Safaris camps for fully sponsored 6-day educational programmes. CITW is also co-sponsored by 18 other Namibian businesses (Wilderness Safaris, 2010).

Ongava

The Ongava Reserve, 300 km^2 in area, is adjacent to the 20,000 km^2 Etosha National Park on its southern side. It is separated from the park by a fence which is designed to allow some wildlife species through, but not others. In particular, since 2005 Ongava has been stocked with both black and white rhino, through a partnership with the World Wide Fund for Nature and the Namibian Ministry of the Environment and Tourism. As well as providing a tourist attraction, the rhino are better protected against poachers in the smaller reserve where their daily whereabouts are generally known. There is also a small rhino research station within the Ongava Reserve. In addition to rhino, the Ongava Reserve generally contains the same range of wildlife as Etosha National Park itself, and effectively adds to the size of the public protected area. As well as lion and leopard, there are brown hyena, caracal and aardwolf; and in addition to the large herbivores there are smaller antelope such as klipspringer, steenbok and the endangered black-faced impala.

Ongava Reserve was established in 1991, and consists of four individual land titles which are owned jointly by a landholding company with numerous individual shareholders and four directors. There are four lodges and camps in the Reserve: Little Ongava, Ongava, Andersson's Camp and Ongava Tented Camp. The lodges and reserve are run by Wilderness Safaris through a management company called Ongava P/L, which pays Wilderness Safaris a management fee and a marketing fee calculated as percentages of revenue. There are around 120 staff in total, including hospitality and technical staff at the lodges, wildlife guides, land and wildlife managers and an anti-poaching unit. This is about the same number as the number employed at Etosha National Park headquarters at Okaukuejo.

Ongava Lodge, the main lodge, is built on one rib of a rocky hill which forms part of the foothills of the Ondundozonanandana Range. It overlooks an artificial waterhole which attracts wildlife at dawn and dusk. Little Ongava, on the top of the hill, consists of three large and luxurious suites with their own pools and dining areas. Andersson's Camp is built largely of recycled materials and designed for minimal impact. The tented camp is at the base of a hill with views over a small pan frequented by wildlife.

Serra Cafema

Serra Cafema Lodge is one of two tourism lodges in the 3000 km^2 Marienfluss Conservancy on the southern bank of the Kunene River, the border between Namibia and Angola. The local Himba people, some 12,000 in total number, apparently live in both countries and cross between them. There is a modern Himba settlement not far from the lodge, and a hut built in traditional style which is used as a demonstration village and craft outlet. It is staffed during the day by Himba people in traditional dress and hairstyles, including various braid styles caked with red mud, which indicate family circumstances. Concession and lease fees, employment at the lodges, village visit fees and sales of artefacts provide the Conservancy members with income, which leads them to maintain the area largely under conservation, though they do also run domestic livestock in some sections.

Quad bikes are used for guests to visit an area of dry grassland with small mobile barchan sand dunes, and a granite hill with views and an opportunity to hike and scramble to the summit. One can also walk downriver from the lodge itself to a narrow rock gorge and cascades. Serra Cafema does not have the density of big game characteristic of the Etosha area, but it has very different scenery and bird life and the cultural interests associated with the Himba. Most of the staff at the lodge itself are local Himba people. Staff live on site in a staff village immediately adjacent to the lodge, and visitors are allowed during the daytime. The lodge has a generally high standard of environmental management and well-maintained working areas.

Damaraland Camp

Damaraland Camp in the Torra Conservancy is one of Namibia's best-known examples of a community conservancy supported by tourism. The Torra Conservancy has over 700 registered members and manages an area of over 3500 km^2. There is apparently a dispute with the neighbouring #Khoadi//Hoas Conservancy over one boundary. The Torra Conservancy holds a Permit to Operate a tourism business, which it leases to Wilderness Safaris. Under the terms of this agreement, which commenced in 1996, equity in the tourism business remained 100% with Wilderness Safaris for the first 10 years, with the Torra Conservancy receiving an annual rental plus 10% of turnover, as well as salaries for individual staff employed directly. Historically (in 2002) cash payments have totalled about two and a half times salaries. From the tenth to the fifteenth year of the agreement, equity in the assets was also transferred to the Conservancy, 20% per annum so as to complete the transfer in the final year, i.e. 2011.

The agreement was endorsed by the Namibia Ministry of Environment and Tourism, which grants the Permit to Operate a tourism business; and the former Namibian Wildlife Trust, now the Integrated Rural Development and Nature Conservancy, IRDNC. The camp first started operations in 1994, with start-up funds provided by a grant from the World Wide Fund for Nature. The commercial lease agreement with Wilderness Safaris commenced in 1996. The lease is subject to the Traditional Authorities Act 2000 and the Communal Land Reform Act 2002. Currently, all 1200 members of the Torra Conservancy (NACSO, 2008) benefit from this agreement, and 60 members of the Torra Conservancy are employed directly by Wilderness Safaris at its various Namibian lodges (Wilderness Safaris, 2010).

Torra Conservancy was one of four Namibian community conservancies which commenced operations in 1998, the first year of registration, along with #Khoadi//Hoas, Nyae-Nyae and Salambola (Skyer, 2004). The early operations of Nyae-Nyae and #Khoadi//Hoas are described by Buckley (2003a). Torra Conservancy is controlled by a six-member community committee with eight staff. In addition to its permit to operate a tourism business, it also owns a game harvest quota, which allows limited hunting and game sales, and employs six game guards. Of over 50 Community Conservancies in Namibia (NACSO, 2008), Torra is one of only three that is fully self-supporting financially.

The Torra Conservancy and the Wilderness Safaris lease agreement are believed to have made a significant contribution to increases in elephant and gemsbok (oryx) populations in north-western Namibia by reducing hunting and poaching. Between 1982 and 2006, the elephant population rose from 250 to 700 and the oryx population from 400 to 15,000. The population ecology of the elephants in the Kunene area was described by Leggett (2006). In particular, 24 black rhino were captured and relocated from Kunene, and nine of these were taken to the Torra Conservancy. The total cost of this operation was over a million Namibian dollars, about US$130,000. Only about 4% of this was paid by the Namibia Ministry of Environment and Tourism, and the remainder by the Save the Rhino Trust and Wilderness Safaris.

During 2008 the former tented camp was replaced with a newly built lodge, with Wilderness Safaris providing materials and the Conservancy providing the labour. The new lodge is designed throughout to minimize water and energy requirements, through both architecture and fittings. Buildings are shaped to take advantage of natural ventilation (Buckley, 2009b, p. 148). The main central area has solid walls but an open construction, illustrated by Buckley (2009b). The guest rooms are large tents on wooden decks, with bathrooms constructed of sandbags and cement. Hot water is provided by passive solar heaters, and room lighting by 12 V photoelectric systems. Sewage treatment is by a single gravity-fed septic system well removed from living areas.

Skeleton Coast

The Skeleton Coast is the northernmost section of the Namibian coastline, heavily dotted with historical shipwrecks. For the modern nature tourist the terrestrial landscape is arid, forbidding, dramatic and beautiful, with low rocky hills, dry or near-dry desert washes and small barchan dunes, including 'roaring dunes' famous for the booming sound made by their slip faces. From a wildlife perspective the area is known particularly for its desert-adapted elephant herds and its coastal seal colonies, though its antelopes and bird life are also impressive.

Skeleton Coast Camp is built near the dry bed of the Khumib River in a 16,400 km^2 private concession held on a 10-year lease from Skeleton Coast National Park. During 2009 the lodge suffered a severe fire, but was rebuilt. There is also a camp built originally to house research staff and now under redevelopment, as less upmarket accommodation aimed at 'overlander' tours. There is a separate staff village not visible from the main lodge. Major external research projects based at the Camp have focused on lichen communities, characteristic of the Skeleton Coast ecosystems; and on desert-adapted giraffe and elephant. The Skeleton Coast Camp has also contributed to a school in the local community of Purros.

Desert Rhino Camp

Desert Rhino Camp lies in the 4000 km^2 private Palmwag Concession in the Damaraland region of central Namibia. It is particularly well known for the opportunity it provides for tourists to track and watch desert-adapted black rhino on foot, accompanied by skilled guides and trackers (Bakkes, 2010). This is made possible through a partnership with an NGO, the Save the Rhino Trust. SRT is an international effort started by Blythe Loutit, which now has an international fund-raising arm in the UK, SRT International (Save the Rhino Trust, 2010). It also raises funds in the USA, especially for research, through a US-based NGO (Round River, 2010). Save the Rhino Trust Namibia receives funds from Wilderness Safaris to pay three trackers who follow the rhino day by day – both to guard against poaching and to help guide tourists to them quickly. There are apparently 25 rhino in the area but most guests see one, two or three individuals with well-known habits and accessible territories. There are over 900 black rhino in Namibia as a whole, but this is apparently

the largest group of desert-adapted rhino outside the public national park system.

There is a guest camp, with six double tents and a central dining area, and a separate staff village. Both are scheduled for reconstruction. Currently, for example, washing water is carried to each guest tent in large hot and cold vacuum flasks, but there is a good local supply from a bore, and reticulated supplies are planned.

Botswana: Mombo, Linyanti, Vumbura

Introduction

An independent nation since 1966, Botswana is a comparatively wealthy country, at least in an African context, since it produces around 30% of the world's gem-quality diamonds. Mining is the principal source of national income, but tourism contributes around 12% of GDP. Much of the country's population, however, still relies largely on subsistence cattle farming, and cattle are considered a major measure of individual wealth. The country has a total area of 582,000 km^2 and a total population a little below two million. International tourism is largely focused in the northern part of the country, especially the Okavango Delta Region. Much of the south lies within the largely waterless Kalahari Desert.

Mombo

Mombo Camp and Little Mombo lie within the Mombo Concession on Chief's Island, at the western end of the 4870 km^2 Moremi Game Reserve in the central part of the Okavango Region. This is in the drier section of the Okavango, with open savannah and raised islands rather than the flooded reed-lined channels found elsewhere in the Okavango Delta. Both black and white rhino have been reintroduced to this area, and staff at Mombo Camp contribute to routine tracking, monitoring and anti-poaching patrols. This is of critical importance since previous attempts at reintroducing rhino to Botswana have failed because of poaching (Hitchins, 1992). The Botswana Rhino Reintroduction Programme is managed by the Botswana Department of Wildlife but financed largely by Wilderness Safaris. According to Pitlagano (2007) a total of 11 male and 21 female white rhino were released at Mombo between 2001 and 2003, in four separate batches. Five of these died, two from poaching, one from capture stress, one from a territorial fight and one in a bush fire. Of the surviving 27, 21 have established themselves in Moremi Game Reserve. The first calf from these translocated individuals was born successfully in 2004. Some of those in the fourth batch have now moved up to 250 km away.

Since these lodges lie within the Okavango Delta and any effluents may contaminate the freshwater ecosystems, environmental management practices are particularly critical. Mombo Camp includes ten rooms, Little Mombo an additional three, and there is a staff village with around 25 rooms. Sewage from both staff and guest rooms is pumped to a central four-stage treatment system, including chlorination, with sludge from the final stage recirculated for redigestion and final effluent distributed through an irrigation system. Generators are housed in a clean and well-insulated generator room with lagged exhausts and industrial-quality mufflers, and fuel tanks are bunded. Kitchens are equipped with grease traps and separation bins. Organic catering residues are buried in a covered pit, though monkeys do dig under the cover on occasion.

Linyanti

Wilderness Safaris operates several camps and lodges in the Linyanti Concession, part of the 1250 km^2 Linyanti Game Reserve, which abuts the western boundary of Chobe National Park. The area is leased from the Botswana Land Board as a hunting concession but operated for wildlife-watching tourism. The Concession includes a section of the Linyanti River, and also the sporadically flowing Savuti Channel, which was dry from 1980 to 2007 but filled in 2008. Savuti and Duma Tau Camps are both close to Savuti Channel, and Kings

Pool Camp lies on the Linyanti River. Savuti is an extremely well-run and organized camp. It operates a centralized septic system which takes grey water as well as sewage, from staff as well as guest rooms. The system incorporates three digestion chambers, chlorination and final irrigation on to a well-vegetated area of deep sand. Kitchen waste separation is excellent, and solid wastes are disposed of in fenced and covered burn and compost pits. Vehicle wash-down areas are also bunded so as to minimize any possible contamination of waterways.

Vumbura

Vumbura Plains Camp, which includes two individual camps with central services, lies in the Kwedi area at the far northern edge of the Okavango Delta. Kwedi is part of Moremi Wildlife Reserve, but the camps are in a concession leased from five neighbouring villages through the Okavango Community Trust, OCT. The Trust leases the land from the Botswana Land Board. There are around 5000 residents in the five villages, which are north of the Wilderness Safaris camps. OCT leases two areas to Wilderness Safaris, the Vumbura Plains and the Duba Plains Concessions totalling 890 km^2 in area. The camps employ 120 staff from these local communities, and also outsource tasks such as road maintenance. Almost all (95%) of the employees at Vumbura and Duba Plains are from these five villages. All game drive vehicles are also required to carry an OCT escort as well as the Wilderness Safaris guide.

Vumbura operates a single centralized sewage treatment system with three chambers and chlorination, including venturi aeration in the aerobic digestion chamber. Final effluent is led to a small wetland area planted with papyrus. As with most such systems, elephant damage is a recurrent maintenance issue. The organic-wastes disposal pit is particularly well designed, with planked walls and a heavy mesh cover which overlaps well beyond the walls. Instead of dumping wet organic waste directly into this pit, it is placed on a mesh drying rack supported on a wooden frame inside the pit, and raked off once it has dried out. Little

Vumbura, on an island reached by boat from Vumbura Plains South, uses similar systems.

The Vumbura Plains Concession also contains Capirota Camp, the Wilderness Safaris Botswana guide training camp. Potential guides, who must have a driving licence and a Botswana guide licence, can be accepted into Capirota for a 4-week intensive training course, which is fully sponsored by Wilderness Safaris. The course involves a very detailed knowledge of local natural history, as well as tracking and safety skills, and accepts only very highly motivated applicants. It has an 80% pass rate, and those who pass are then given a paid internship at one of the Wilderness Safaris camps, though with no guarantee of permanent employment. Between 2005 and 2008 the Capirota Camp trained about 70 guides in total.

Seychelles

Introduction: endangered birds

The Seychelles are an archipelago of over 40 granite islands about 4½°S of the equator and about 1800 km from the eastern coast of Africa. Since 1976, the Seychelles have been an independent republic, following a period as a French colony from 1756 to 1814 and a British colony subsequently. The principal population centre is on the large granite island of Mahé, some 155 km² in area. There are a number of smaller granite islands not far from Mahé. Coral atolls such as Aldabra up to 1150 km further south are also part of the Seychelles.

As a long-isolated archipelago, the Seychelles support a number of endemic plant and animal species, notably a number of birds. There are no native terrestrial mammals, so the birds had no ground-based predators until the introduction of cats and rats. These introduced species caused devastation through nest predation among many of the bird species, leading to the extinction of several.

Several of the smaller granite islands are privately owned, and several have been restored and rehabilitated from low-key livestock and copra production in the past to private reserves supporting endangered endemic species and funded at least partly by tourism. One of these is North Island, operated by Wilderness Safaris. The contributions of tourism to conservation in these islands may be considered in three principal categories. The first is simply provision of access. Even for completely independent organizations to carry out conservation works, they need permission from the landowner. The second is through in-kind support. The single key prerequisite to successful conservation on these islands, particularly of these endangered bird species, is to eradicate rats and cats from the entire island concerned. This is neither easy nor cheap, but has been accomplished successfully for some of the islands with funding from the landowner or tour operator. The third is financial and in-kind support for ongoing conservation efforts.

The smaller granite islands are particularly critical for conservation of various endemic and endangered bird species. Most critically endangered are the Seychelles white-eye, the Seychelles magpie-robin, the Seychelles warbler and the Seychelles black paradise flycatcher (Table 3.2). The number of individual birds remaining for each of these endangered species is rather small, having dropped as low as a dozen birds at one time in the case of the Seychelles magpie-robin. Even now, there are only a couple of hundred magpie-robins in total, and these are distributed between five islands as a result of translocation and re-establishment programmes. Cousin Island provides critical habitat for the Seychelles warbler and the Seychelles fody. It was bought in 1968 by the (UK) Royal Society for Nature Conservation, declared as a Special Reserve in 1975, and managed initially by BirdLife International and subsequently by BirdLife Seychelles, which was later renamed Nature Seychelles. Aride Island was purchased by the Royal Society for Nature Conservation in 1973, and 29 Seychelles warblers were moved there from Cousin Island, breeding successfully to a current population of >2000 birds. Concepcion Island supported 245 of the 400 Seychelles white-eyes in existence as of 2007, with the remainder on Fregate and Mahé. Fregate Island was invaded by Norway rats in 1995 (Thorsen et al., 2000), with disastrous consequences for conservation. In 2007, 20

Table 3.2. Scientific names of rare bird and reptile species mentioned in text.

Common name	Scientific name
Seychelles black paradise flycatcher	*Terpsiphone corvina*
Seychelles blue pigeon	*Alectroenas pulcherrima*
Seychelles kestrel	*Falco araea*
Seychelles magpie-robin	*Copsychus sechellarum*
Seychelles sunbird	*Nectarinia dussumieri*
Seychelles warbler	*Acrocephalus sechellensis*
Seychelles white-eye	*Zosterops modestus*
Seychelles 'black' terrapin	*Pelusios subniger parietalis*
Aldabra tortoise	*Dipsochelys dussumieri*

white-eyes were relocated to Cousine Island and 25 to North Island, as described below.

Cousine Island is a dry granite island 0.26 km^2 in area. It is privately owned and has been rehabilitated gradually since 1992 (Samways *et al.*, 2010). It has never been invaded by rats or mice, and feral cats have been eradicated. It previously supported a population of Seychelles warbler but these were killed by rock blasting in the 1970s (Samways *et al.*, 2010). Breeding populations of seabirds, previously subject to severe poaching, have now recovered; rehabilitation of vegetation is well under way; and Seychelles warbler, Seychelles magpie-robin and Seychelles white-eye have all been introduced or reintroduced, with 39 magpie-robins and 350–400 warblers as of 2009 (Samways *et al.*, 2010). Seychelles warbler also occurs on Denis Island, which operates a small resort with helicopter access. Seychelles black paradise flycatchers occur on La Digue Island, but that island is run for agriculture and copra production and the flycatcher population is now <200 pairs.

North Island

North Island was operated as a copra plantation from 1826 until 1970, and when it was purchased by Wilderness Safaris and four other equity partners in 1997 it had been abandoned for many years and was severely infested with weeds as well as feral animals. By mid-2008, vegetation rehabilitation works commenced over about 40 ha (20%) of the island, with advice from two NGOs, the Island Conservation

Society and the Plant Conservation Action Group. Around 100,000 native plants had been planted out from a plant nursery established on the island. By the end of 2009, the company aims to have commenced rehabilitation over twice this total area, 80 ha or 40% of the island. Not all areas require rehabilitation.

In order to reintroduce endangered bird species to North Island, it was first essential to eradicate all feral animals, particularly rats. This is a difficult and expensive task, and strict measures are required to maintain quarantine and prevent rats accidentally being reintroduced. On North Island it took two large-scale campaigns to eradicate rats successfully, with the help of experts from New Zealand. The second campaign was completed in 2005. Since then, strict measures have been used to guard against accidental reintroductions. All supply boats are baited against rats before being loaded. There is no jetty on the island, and the supply boats are anchored in shallow water off the beach and all goods carried ashore by hand. Traps are set in the surrounding section of beach and nearby buildings, and the goods are loaded directly into a rat-proof trailer which is towed into a rat-proof room for unpacking. To date these measures have proved successful.

The most critical conservation role played to date by North Island has been the establishment of a small breeding group of the endangered Seychelles white-eye. In July 2007, following the successful eradication of rats on North Island, ten male and nine female birds were moved there to start a new subpopulation. The translocation was managed by a local NGO, the Island Conservation Society, with support from FFEM, the Fondation Français pour l'Environnement Mondial. The birds were moved by helicopter, sponsored by ZIL Air, and kept initially in large aviaries where they were fed with sugar water and termites on honey sticks, as a soft release technique. All the birds translocated to North Island survived, and once released the males established territories and began territorial songs and the females began nest building. A total of 12 chicks hatched and survived successfully on North Island in 2008. North Island thus supports about 8% of the world's total population of Seychelles white-eye.

The other endangered Seychelles bird species mentioned above may also be introduced to North Island in future. Three further bird species listed by IUCN as vulnerable also occur on North Island: the Seychelles sunbird, at least nine individuals of the Seychelles blue pigeon and one pair of the Seychelles kestrel. Rehabilitation of vegetation and eradication of rats have also enabled two native seabird species, the wedge-billed shearwater and white-billed tropic-bird, to recommence nesting on North Island, though to date only in very small numbers.

North Island has also reintroduced two endangered reptile species, the Aldabra tortoise and the Seychelles terrapin. There was one old male tortoise already on the island when Wilderness Safaris took it over, and three adult females were introduced in 2003. Their first eggs were eaten by rats, but, following the successful rat eradication in 2005, 11 hatchlings from two nests survived in 2005. Seven more tortoises were introduced in 2007.

There are two recognized Seychelles subspecies of African freshwater terrapins (Table 3.2). One of these, known locally as 'black terrapin', has been reintroduced to North Island. The terrapin lives in North Island's central wetland area, a perched groundwater body fed by underground drainage from higher granite areas which surround it on three sides. The lodge draws about 100,000 litres of freshwater per day from bores, and monitors the wetland to ensure that it is not affected. Extending the area of vegetation under rehabilitation will increase water requirements (for irrigation), but the lodge

intends to use grey water (sullage) to irrigate rehabilitation areas, reducing freshwater consumption. Currently, sewage and sullage are treated jointly, and after aerobic digestion and chlorination are discharged on to the land surface on the seaward face of one of the granite hills, so as not to affect the drinking water supply. Organic solid wastes are buried, and inorganic solid wastes are separated and taken off the island for disposal on Mahé. All these steps are intended to maintain the purity of the freshwater source, critical for tourism as well as conservation.

All of these small populations of endangered bird and reptile species need active ongoing conservation management, which costs money. For the bird species, management includes captive breeding programmes, soft release through field aviaries and routine monitoring of individual birds, including blood samples for genetic fingerprinting. All of these involve live trapping and release. Conservation also requires ongoing quarantine measures and monitoring to prevent the reintroduction of cats or rats, which can be carried inadvertently in the barges which bring supplies to the tourism operations. Now that populations of the bird species concerned have recovered somewhat, it is difficult for international NGOs to continue to raise funding for these programmes when there are so many other critically endangered species elsewhere in the world. Since there are now local NGOs and local and profitable tourism operations on privately owned islands, the expectation is that these islands should operate as private conservation reserves with locally generated operational funding. In practice, this does seem to be the case for some of the islands, but not for others.

On North Island, the upmarket tourist lodge operated by Wilderness Safaris has indeed successfully funded ongoing rehabilitation of native vegetation, eradication of rats and cats and reintroduction and conservation of Seychelles white-eyes and other species, in conjunction with local and international conservation and research organizations. Expertise in eradicating rats and cats on island ecosystems, for example, was provided from New Zealand. Blood sample analysis is carried out in the Netherlands. Bird conservation ecologists from various parts of the world have developed the techniques to trap, translocate and release the bird species concerned without injury or mortality. Restoration ecologists have designed techniques to restore the island habitats to a condition suitable for successful breeding by the bird species concerned.

In addition, the particular characteristics of these island ecosystems mean that a number of active conservation measures are possible, which might not be feasible elsewhere. Perhaps most importantly, because there are no native ground-dwelling terrestrial mammals (there are two bat species), it is possible to eradicate rats and cats through intensive blanket poisoning across an entire island simultaneously, using baits laced with the mammalian poison sodium monofluoracetate, commonly known as '1080'. This would not be possible if the islands were larger or if they supported native mammal species which would also be affected. The birds themselves are relatively easy to catch and release safely and repeatedly. This means, first, that they can be removed from harm's way during rat baiting exercises, and, second, that populations can be increased through captive breeding programmes, and birds can then be translocated and released successfully on other feral-free islands, to provide some insurance against the possible reintroduction of rats or cats on any one island. Capturing birds prior to poison baiting is essential, since previous attempts to bait selectively for rats only on Fregate Island led to the death of several endangered Seychelles magpie-robins (Thorsen et al., 2000).

To a certain degree, the endangered-bird conservation programmes on these smaller islands of the Seychelles provide a model for a three-step conservation programme where: initial measures are funded by international aid and carried out by international NGOs; on-ground operations are then handed over to local NGOs with newly built capacity; and ongoing funding streams and in-kind support are provided by successful nature tourism enterprises which operate the conservation areas as private reserves. This is essentially the same model as that proposed by several operators, including Wilderness Safaris, for future conservation in war-torn African nations such as Zimbabwe and Angola, once their political structures become sufficiently stable. The Seychelles thus provides something of a test case for this approach.

Conclusions

Especially through its partnerships with community conservancies in Namibia and Botswana and the North Island private reserve in the Seychelles, it does indeed seem that Wilderness Safaris has made net positive contributions to conservation and community development. The company has pursued a policy of expansion in recent years and, economic circumstances permitting, this seems likely to continue, though only within southern Africa. The company's plan to contribute to a conservation corridor across northern Namibia is of particular note.

4 Natural Habitat Adventures

Ruffed Lemur, Madagascar

Introduction

Natural Habitat Adventures (2010) is a global nature and wildlife tour operator which constructs, markets, runs and guides a worldwide portfolio of specialist retail tour packages to iconic wildlife tourism destinations. It does not own its own private reserves, and it is a commercial tourism company, not an NGO. Natural Habitat Adventures and other companies like it none the less form an important piece in the jigsaw of conservation tourism, because they provide one of the major mechanisms to bring a continuing stream of international tourists to the places which need the money and political attention which tourists can provide.

Founded by Ben Bressler in 1985, Natural Habitat Adventures is run out of Boulder, Colorado. It assembles packages in its destination areas by selecting appropriate local accommodation, transport and tour guides, and also sends its own trip leaders from the USA or elsewhere to handle logistics and provide additional interpretation. It currently offers a global portfolio of over 100 mid- to upmarket tours to iconic wildlife-watching destinations worldwide. The details of itineraries and local providers are continually adjusted on the basis of new opportunities and feedback from both clients and guides. This is a successful model which is followed by a number of international nature and adventure tour operators.

There are many individual companies in this particular market niche, and over the past two decades they have shown a considerable degree of convergent evolution. While, historically, different companies specialized in different destinations and different icon wildlife species, now there are many different companies which all offer similar portfolios, often by subcontracting the same on-ground local operators and sometimes even the same individual guides. The reasons for this seems to be strictly commercial. It takes less investment of company time and resources to sell another tour to a previous client than to attract a new client; and, for large-scale retail tour operators, the local on-ground components are simply costs, and the profit derives from the markup applied in retail sales of the package as a whole. No tour company wants its clients to book their next holiday with a competitor and so risk losing future business. To counteract this possibility, each company tries to offer all the icon destinations and experiences that would be available through their competitors. Thus, for example, a wide range of different companies all offer: game lodges and wildlife safaris in sub-Saharan Africa; tiger-watching in India; expedition cruises to Antarctica; polar bear packages in Hudson Bay, Canada; jungle lodges or riverboat cruises in the Amazon; and, at least until recently, bird- and lemur-watching tours in Madagascar.

Whether or not these retail tour operators contribute to conservation depends on the details of their packages and operations. If they rely preferentially or exclusively on local accommodation, transport and activities which operate or support private conservation reserves or other conservation mechanisms as outlined in Chapter 1, then they do indeed contribute to conservation benefits by providing part of the funding for those local enterprises. If they pay no attention to such considerations in assembling their packages, however, then they may be more likely to boost high-impact tourism with negative effects on conservation. As with environmental aspects of any tourism operation, there is no way to be sure without going to look. This chapter features Natural Habitat Adventures because it seems to be a well-established and highly regarded company, and because I have had the opportunity to examine two of its icon products in person: the 1-week 'Ultimate Polar Bear Adventure' in Hudson Bay, Canada; and the 2-week 'Wild Madagascar' tour of wildlife in Madagascar. These particular products are described in more detail below.

Polar Bears

The location and operations of the polar-bear-watching industry on the west coast of Canada's Hudson Bay were described by Buckley (2006). The bears congregate on the bare coastal plains near Churchill in October and November to await freeze-up of the sea ice. This is the most southerly and accessible part of the bears' range and the prime site for tourists to see them. Unlike more northerly populations of polar bears, which remain on the polar ice year-round, the Hudson Bay bears must come ashore when the sea ice melts in spring, and remain ashore until it re-forms for winter (Lunn and Stirling, 1985; Derocher and Stirling, 1990a, b, 1995). On the ice the bears eat seals, but while ashore they have very little food. They are therefore very keen to get back on the winter ice as soon as it forms. Because of the shape of the coast and fresh water from Churchill River, the sea ice forms first at Churchill. Every year, therefore, the bears congregate there to wait for access to the Arctic. The port of Churchill, at the mouth of the river, was thus built exactly where the polar bears congregate every year. Historically, management of interactions between people and bears around Churchill was poor, with hungry bears foraging in an open tip and then being confined in a so-called bear jail or in some cases shot. There is still some conflict and criticism (Pilkington, 2002; Buckley, 2003a, pp. 176–181; Dyck and Baydack, 2004). Overall, however, the treatment of polar bears seems to have improved considerably. Polar bear tourism is now of sufficient economic significance to the town for its residents to have cleaned up their garbage instead of shooting the bears. Bears do still forage in the town dump, however, and there is still at least one landowner who uses the need to feed his sledge dogs as an artifice to attract hungry bears and hence paying tourists.

At the time when I took part in it myself, Natural Habitat Adventures' flagship polar bear tour was billed as the 'Ultimate Polar Bear Adventure', and included: two days and one evening in tundra buggies in the main bear-viewing area east of Churchill town on the southern side of the river; a day by helicopter, viewing bears from the air along the ice edge south of Cape Churchill; and two nights in a lodge on the northern side of the Churchill River, in an area adapted for ground-level viewing of polar bear cubs and their mothers. The lodge, known as White Whale Lodge, has subsequently burnt down, and the flagship tour, currently marketed as the 'Classic Polar Bear Expedition' (Natural Habitat Adventures, 2010), instead spends more time in the vehicles

formerly known as 'tundra buggies' and currently described as 'polar rovers'. The former lodge was an old single-storey building north of the river, in an area used by female bears with cubs. The building's open areas were protected with metal bars, so that tourists could watch bears in the open at very short range when the bears came up to the building. There was also an open viewing deck on the roof and an enclosed and heated viewing room. Tundra buggies, or polar rovers, are specialized vehicles with enormously oversized tyres and a coach body raised beyond the reach of the bears, and provide the main mechanism for tourists to watch bears at close range. They are illustrated on the NHA website. The bears largely ignore the buggies, or investigate them casually. The helicopter tours provide good viewings, but with higher impact. In particular, they cause the less habituated individual bears to panic and run in circles. This represents an additional energy expenditure which may decrease the bears' probability of survival, since they are very severely limited by lack of food and fat at this time of year.

Particularly at Hudson Bay, at the southern limit of their range, polar bears are threatened by climate change and the consequent melting of the Arctic ice, and polar bear tourism has helped to popularize their plight. While Natural Habitat Adventures does not seem to have been involved directly in polar bear conservation efforts, it does appear that, as one of the principal contributors to the bear-watching tourism industry in Hudson Bay, it has had sufficient local economic impact to influence human behaviour in Hudson Bay to the bears' net advantage. It is selective about the local on-ground tour products it purchases, and with its clients making up 25% of the polar bear tourists travelling to Hudson Bay, it has sufficient market power to influence how those local products operate.

Madagascar

Natural Habitat Adventures offers tours to Madagascar to watch a wide variety of rare, endangered and charismatic wildlife including lemurs, birds, frogs and chameleons. The tour includes both the wetter north-eastern and drier south-western ecosystems, and visits both public national parks and smaller private and community reserves. It includes day hikes along forest trails, spotlighting at night and boat rides to otherwise inaccessible areas. Wildlife species commonly seen include: rare lemurs such as the greater bamboo lemur, the tiny grey-brown mouse lemur and Hubbard's sportive lemur; giant chameleons such as the green and brown Parson's chameleon, *Calumma parsonii*; rare frogs such as the bright vermilion tomato frog and the tiny *Mantidactylis*; endemic members of bird families such as couas, vangas, mesites and ground rollers, and rare bird species such as Archbold's newtonia, Benson's rock thrush and Appert's greenbul. Guests also see a wide range of vegetation types and plant species, including endemics such as the spiny octopus tree. Scientific names for the bird and lemur species mentioned are listed in Table 4.1.

Madagascar is one of the world's mega-diverse countries. It has a complex history, including a colonial period, and a heterogeneous modern social structure which seems to be somewhat unstable politically. In particular, there are several different social groups with different political histories, who still do not always interact on an equal footing. In addition, historically there was a complex system of taboos known as fady, which prohibited hunting or eating some particular animal and plant species, but this system is apparently breaking down (Jones *et al.*, 2008).

The government in power during the early 2000s adopted a deliberate national-scale policy to expand the public national park system and associated international wildlife tourism, as an economic development and poverty alleviation strategy. At the World Parks Congress in South Africa in 2003, for example, the then president of Madagascar stated that by 2008 he would triple the country's protected areas, from 3% to 10% of total area (Marie *et al.*, 2009). Some substantial additions were indeed made, and as of late 2008 these parks supported a substantial nature and wildlife tourism sector with a broad international clientele, in addition to the long-standing beach resort sector with stronger ex-colonial con-nections. One effect of this wildlife-watching industry was to encourage the growth of small community-owned conservation areas outside the public parks system. Some of these, though small in area, are highly significant ecologically as they provide the only remaining habitat area for particular threatened plant and animal species, and habitat fragmentation and hunting are the major threats to many native animal species in Madagascar (Craul *et al.*, 2009). Without the local income from tourism, there is a much greater risk that the small areas of remnant native vegetation will be cut for firewood and timber and used to graze goats and cattle.

In early 2009, the then government of Madagascar was overthrown in a military coup. This appears to have been relatively bloodless but none the less led to significant political destabilization, including security risks to foreign researchers, conservation groups and NGOs and tourists, and a considerable reduction in foreign investment. Since then, international tourism has declined sharply. Natural Habitat Adventures, however, still offers its Wild Madagascar tour several times each year during the prime bird- and lemur-watching periods. Its current marketing for this tour notes specifically that the tours are helping to protect conservation areas.

The Wild Madagascar tour commences in the country's capital city of Antananarivo, in the central highland area. The group travels, partly by air and partly by road, to a series of specific sites in two main areas, the wetter north-east and the dry south-west. This provides opportunities to experience a range of ecosystems and their associated rare, endemic and localized birds, lemurs, reptiles and amphibians. The tour first visits an area owned by Vakona Lodge, in a corridor of vegetation between Analamazoatra Reserve and Matadia National Park, in the region of Madagascar known as Perinet. The group visits the national park during the day and the area around the lodge at night. It also visits a small outdoor zoo area near the lodge, in the form of an island surrounded by an artificial moat. Lemur species on the island include the black-and-white ruffed lemur, the brown lemur, the grey bamboo lemur and the diadem sifaka. Visitors access the island in canoes, and, though the moat is quite shallow and narrow, it is apparently sufficient to keep the lemurs on the island. Supposedly, the island is run as a

Table 4.1. Scientific names of bird and lemur species mentioned in text.

Common name	Scientific name
Lemurs	
Aye-aye lemur	*Daubentonia madagascariensis*
Black-and-white ruffed lemur	*Varecia variegata*
Blue-eyed black lemur	*Eulemur flavifrons*
Brown lemur	*Eulemur fulvus*
Crowned lemur	*Eulemur coronatus*
Diadem sifaka	*Propithecus diadema*
Eastern lesser bamboo lemur	*Hapalemur griseus*
Greater bamboo lemur	*Hapalemur simus*
Grey-brown mouse lemur	*Microcebus griseorufus*
Hubbard's sportive lemur	*Lepilemur hubbardi*
Red-bellied lemur	*Eulemur rubriventer*
Red-fronted lemur	*Eulemur rufifrons*
Ring-tailed lemur	*Lemur catta*
Verreaux' sifaka	*Propithecus verreauxi*
Birds	
Appert's greenbul	*Phyllastrephus apperti*
Archbold's newtonia	*Newtonia archboldi*
Benson's rock thrush	*Monticola bensoni*
Black parrot	*Coracopsis nigra*
Blue coua	*Coua caerulea*
Blue pigeon	*Alectroenas madagascariensis*
Crested coua	*Coua cristata*
Cuckoo roller	*Leptosomus discolor*
Green-capped coua	*Coua olivaceiceps*
Hook-billed vanga	*Vanga curvirostris*
Long-tailed ground roller	*Uratelornis chimaera*
Pitta-like ground roller	*Alelomis pittoides*
Running coua	*Coua cursor*
Scaly ground roller	*Brachypteracias squamiger*
Sickle-billed vanga	*Falculea palliata*
Subdesert mesite	*Monias benschi*

refuge, orphanage and veterinary facility for the lemurs, but effectively it seems to be a small outdoor zoo funded by tourist entry fees. Given the difficult political situation in Madagascar currently, however, and the many threats to free-living lemurs outside protected areas, even this may provide some conservation benefits. Birds seen in this area include characteristic Madagascar species such as the black parrot, the blue pigeon, the blue coua and the cuckoo roller, as well as endangered endemics such as the scaly ground roller and the pitta-like ground roller.

On the east coast, the group visits the Parc d'Ivoloina in the region known as Toamasina. The Parc, which is sponsored by the St Louis Zoo in Missouri, USA, through the Save the Lemur Foundation, includes a zoo which is used for research, education and captive breeding. The environmental education programme receives 14,000 visitors a year, mostly local school groups. It does charge entrance fees, but about half of the Parc's annual budget of US$300,000 is met by member organizations and other sponsors. The breeding programme includes a number of rare lemur species including the crowned lemur, the blue-eyed black lemur, the red-bellied lemur and most notably the greater bamboo lemur, with an estimated wild population now of fewer than 100 individuals. There are two adult females and one adult male greater bamboo lemur in Parc d'Ivoloina, and they have successfully produced four offspring to date. Other species held in the zoo section include the eastern lesser bamboo lemur and the black-and-white ruffed lemur.

In the Maroantsetra region of north-eastern Madagascar, the group visits Masaola Nature Reserve, a World Heritage Area, and the island of Nosy Mangabe. There is a lodge in the reserve itself, the Masaola Forest Lodge, but the Natural Habitat Adventures groups stay in the very comfortable seafront Relais de Masaola. The group makes day visits to the two reserves, by boat, and takes guided hikes through the forest. At Masaola Nature Reserve, the species seen in the wild include the red-ruffed lemur and the white-fronted brown lemur, as well as the highly cryptic leaf-tailed geckos and the tiny *Mantidactylis* frogs. Additional species seen at Nosy Mangabe included some extremely small and cryptic pygmy chameleons. Night spotlighting from the Relais de Masaola, led by a local guide, allowed the NHA guests to see the rare tomato frog and aye-aye lemur. These encounters, however, were clearly staged by the individual involved, and, because of ethical concerns over the provenance of the actual animals, this component will apparently be excluded from future NHA tours. For similar reasons, the NHA group did not visit a caged fossa, Madagascar's endemic arboreal dog-like predator famous from the movie *Madagascar*, which was apparently on display – for a price – near Vakona Lodge.

In the Tulear region on the south-western coast of Madagascar, the NHA group visits the community-owned Reniala Reserve, an area of dry forest characterized by the baobab *Adansonia*, the pirogue tree *Givotia* and the octopus tree *Didiera*. A number of rare and endemic species can be seen in Reniala Reserve, despite its small area. These include the green-capped coua, the running coua, the crested coua, the hook-billed vanga, the sickle-billed vanga, Archbold's newtonia and

the particularly rare subdesert mesite and long-tailed ground roller. The NHA group stays at a seafront lodge, Le Paradisier, which is surrounded by an area of dry forest within the privately owned lodge grounds. This area supports a population of the tiny nocturnal and arboreal grey-brown mouse lemur, which can be seen by spotlighting at night.

The group returns from Tulear to the capital city of Antananarivo by road, so as to visit two national parks en route. At Isalo National Park, a hike up a river valley on to a plateau provides excellent views of forest and surrounding areas, as well as ring-tailed lemur and Benson's rock thrush. At a small park near the sapphire mining settlement of Ilakaka, local rangers guide the NHA group to see birds such as Appert's greenbul and cuckoo rollers, the giant grey chameleon and the small, rare and cryptic Hubbard's sportive lemur. Because of the nearby township, there is significant pressure on surrounding vegetation. Lemur-watching, however, provides employment for a number of local guides, who wait during the day at a small visitor centre. These guides know where individual lemurs can commonly be found, generally half-hidden in tree hollows. They are therefore able to lead visitors along small walking tracks to points where they can get a good view, even though the Hubbard's sportive lemur is small and cryptically coloured.

The precise dynamics of local social situations such as these can be difficult to elucidate even for people who are closely familiar with the circumstances, so for clients of a commercial tourism enterprise who make only a brief visit any analysis is necessarily speculative. One can, however, observe the activity, new buildings and squatter shacks around the mining town, all of which indicate local population growth. One can observe the degradation of the woody vegetation in areas adjacent to the reserve, on the side of the mining town. One can see that the visitors' centre and associated car park, though low-key, is used and not abandoned; and that a number of local guides do indeed wait there. One can hear the NHA leader making arrangements by telephone with particular local guides. Available evidence, therefore, suggests that the income available to local guides through commercial tourism operations does indeed play a significant role in conserving this particular patch of remnant vegetation, and its resident lemurs against a real and immediate threat of clearance.

Evaluation

In the case of Madagascar, at least before the coup in March 2009, the contribution to conservation was very clear. There are a number of highly endangered bird, lemur and chameleon species which survive only in small remnant populations in small reserves. Some of these reserves are public protected areas, some are communally owned and some are private, but in each case tourism is a key to their survival. In the publicly owned reserves, tour operators such as Natural Habitat Adventures pay local guides to lead tour groups through the reserve, finding and pointing out the rare and hard-to-spot species of wildlife which the tourists have come to see. Since the guides watch the individual animals concerned every day, they know where they are likely to be, what they are likely to be doing at any given time and what to look for, at a level of detail that individual tourists or international guides cannot hope to emulate. The local guides earn enough money from this for it to be worth their while to prevent other local residents from hunting the animals concerned or cutting trees for firewood. Of course, technically such activities are prohibited anyway inside a public protected area, but without funding for enforcement such prohibitions are ineffective except where policed by locals. Not all inbound operators, however, have as strong links to local guides as those shown by Natural Habitat Adventures (Jensen, 2009).

Essentially the same economic incentive also operates in private and communally owned reserve areas, but with two significant differences. The first is that the owners do indeed have the right to cut or clear the areas concerned if they want, and they will leave them undisturbed only: (i) if they have no need or incentive to cut or clear them; or (ii) if they gain greater net benefits by protecting them. The second difference is that private or communal owners can charge and keep whatever entry or activity fees they choose,

subject only to what the market will bear. Public protected areas may also charge entry fees, sometimes with differentials between domestic and international tourists. At least in theory, however, both the size of the fees and the allocation of the funds collected are determined centrally by the parks agency concerned. In countries with a long-established public parks system and an effective public sector, the roles and operations of private and public reserves respectively are typically quite different. In Madagascar, however, the Natural Habitat Adventures tour visits a number of public, private and community-owned reserves, and in an operational sense they all seem rather similar, at least to the individual tourist.

For all three categories of reserves in Madagascar, the key features for tourism to contribute to conservation seem to be as follows. First, the areas do have defined boundaries and people or organizations who either own them or are responsible for managing them. As long as someone has an incentive to protect them, therefore, there is a legal and social foundation for their actions. Second, while there are people who might hunt, cut timber or firewood or graze livestock in each of these areas, the incentives for them to do so are relatively minor. At least prior to the 2009 coup, local residents around each of the areas visited by Natural Habitat Adventures did have other sources of food and fuel wood and other places to graze livestock. Only two of them are immediately adjacent to settlements of any significant size. One is near the rather lawless sapphire mining settlement at Ilakaka, and the area between the town and the reserve is almost completely cleared; but there are still shrubs growing close to the town, and other sources of firewood in other directions. The other, Isalo National Park, is also close to a town, but separated from it by a stretch of farmland; and, in addition, the park is particularly popular because of the banded lemurs, so tour groups and their guides are almost always present. The third factor is that each of these reserves provides opportunities for a small group of local people to earn a living from tourism in one way or another, so these individuals have a direct personal incentive to protect these reserves and their wildlife in order to maintain their own livelihoods. This is possible since the Madagascan currency is relatively weak, average incomes and living costs in these rural areas are relatively low and the principal legal alternative is subsistence agriculture and hunting. Indeed, when tourism arrivals and hence income fell suddenly after the 2009 coup, local hunting for bushmeat apparently increased considerably, with severe consequences for several species of lemur.

Poaching for the black-market international wildlife trade, however, does provide an illegal alternative cash income to wildlife tourism, and we met at least one individual who was apparently suspected of such activities by local authorities and guides. Since the individual concerned is also involved in wildlife tourism, the incident is described below as an example, or indeed warning, of how well-intentioned tourists may inadvertently be led astray by unscrupulous locals. It also demonstrates well how Natural Habitat Adventures responded appropriately to a potentially difficult situation.

The particular local resident concerned claimed to be able to guide tourists, including NHA groups, to sightings of two rare Madagascan endemic species, namely the tomato frog and the aye-aye lemur. The former is a large frog, *Dyscophus antongili*, named for its vermilion colour. The latter is famous for its elongated bony middle finger, which allows it to extract edible grubs from narrow tree cavities. It has been hunted historically because of local superstitions. Both these species are now rare and difficult to see in the wild, so it naturally generates a degree of suspicion when someone offers to provide sightings within walking distance of a lodge on the outskirts of a coastal town, in return for a rather substantial fee. Accordingly, during the trip in which I took part, the NHA guide asked me to investigate whether or not these sightings were likely to be genuine. The local 'guide' led us along the main dirt road near the hotel, and almost immediately 'found' a tomato frog on the short grass verge. By waiting quietly until the rest of the group had moved on, I was able to determine that the frog was unnaturally cold and immobile and had clearly been refrigerated to prevent it hopping away. In addition, I had brought a powerful spotlight, and by turning this on suddenly I was able to locate two people hiding in the ditch, presumably so as to recapture the frog.

Meanwhile, the tour group had been led down a side road to a single tree in the middle of a large, flat, bare expanse of sand, a hectare or two in area. In this tree there was, most improbably, a single aye-aye. As the tour group rushed around the tree taking photographs, I walked around the outside of the entire group, searching for lemur footprints in the soft dry sand. There were none. As the group left the tree, I swung my spotlight around and saw two people squatting in the grass in the dark at the edge of the bare area. I lagged behind the group, walking in the dark, and when I was about 100 m from the tree I shone my spotlight back towards it. Two men were standing beside the tree and, as my light illuminated them, they both jumped behind it, one behind the other. As it was a rather thin tree, it did not hide them very successfully. It seems fairly clear that the aye-aye had been placed in the tree shortly before the tour group arrived, and was then recaptured when they left.

Overall, therefore, it seems fairly clear that this particular local 'guide' actually keeps captive individuals of the species concerned, and has accomplices release them just ahead of a group of tourists and then catch them again once they have taken photographs. In addition to keeping endangered wildlife captive for temporary release as a tourist attraction, we were given to understand by other locals that this particular individual is probably also involved in illegal wildlife trade. That is, these animals are caught illegally and sold illegally overseas. Releasing them for tour groups and then recapturing them is a secondary source of income, albeit quite a substantial one. Interestingly, even though most of the participants in this particular trip were quite experienced wildlife tourists, only one or two made any comment about the rather unlikely encounters with two endangered species so close together and so near to town, especially without seeing any other wildlife at all. Most of them seemed concerned only with the quality of their photographs. The NHA guide, however, was indeed concerned and Natural Habitat Adventures deserves credit for investigating such instances.

While the majority of sites visited by the Natural Habitat Adventures tour involved guided hiking through reserves to look for lemurs, birds and other wildlife, the tour does include two locations with captive wildlife, as described above. One of these is a zoo established specifically to assist in conservation of particularly endangered lemur species. The animals are caged, there are organized captive breeding programmes and the zoo is supported by funding and technical assistance from international counterparts. It also maintains an educational programme for Madagascan schools. Tourists are welcome, and there are tourist facilities such as formed trails and a small restaurant, but it does not seem to be run principally as a tourist attraction. This is straightforward.

The other is less straightforward. It is advertised as a lemur rehabilitation centre. Effectively, it is a small patch of forest surrounded by a shallow water-filled moat to form an artificial island. There are small populations of several lemur species ranging freely on the island, and staff to feed them. We did not see any veterinary facilities, but we did not explore the entire island, and they could have been elsewhere. Tourists reach the island by crossing the moat on canoes, and this seems to be an organized system. The facility is close to a moderately sized and well-frequented forest lodge which could provide it with a steady stream of tourists. It is presented as if it were a separate organization from the lodge, but we had no way to check the reality. From a conservation perspective, the key question is where the lemurs came from. If they were rescued from forest subject to logging or agricultural clearance, then this facility is effectively acting as a small zoo which keeps the individual lemurs alive. If they were captured from within reserve areas, in contrast, then the net contribution to conservation would be negative. Realistically, there was no way for us to tell. The Natural Habitat Adventures staff also mentioned that there is another facility nearby where a fossa, *Cryptoprocta ferox*, is kept in a cage specifically for paying tourists to observe, but that NHA does not take its tour groups there, because this is not a practice they wish to support.

Any single natural history tour company such as NHA makes up only a small proportion of the total market for any one lodge or local attraction, private reserve or wildlife guide. Natural Habitat Adventures, or other similar retail tour packaging operators, can influence these in-country operators to some degree through: their selection of specific destinations within Madagascar; their selection of specific operators at each destination, if there is a choice; and, to some degree, direct discussion with the owners or operators of individual enterprises. As in any country, there are some individuals and some local enterprises which take advantage of international nature tourism without any net contribution to conservation. At the broader scale, however, international tourism is one of the main factors providing political support for conservation in Madagascar; and, at the scale of the individual company, NHA does indeed seem to do its best to patronize local operations which make positive contributions to conservation and avoid those which do not.

The tour described above thus provides an example of the conservation benefits that can accrue from tourism operations of this type, and also some of the challenges they face in dealing with unscrupulous local entrepreneurs. The coup in Madagascar in early 2009, and its consequences for both tourism and conservation, also showed the critical importance of political stability and safety for this particular conservation tourism model to work. Short-term and localized arrangements which depend on a continuing supply of international tourists to provide revenue are highly susceptible to breakdown if this stream of visitors dries up.

Lacking direct experience of the entire portfolio, it is not possible to make a reliable assessment of Natural Habitat Adventures' overall contribution to conservation at a global scale. Judging from the polar bear and Madagascar products presented above, however, it does indeed seem that the company is sufficiently selective in its choice of local providers for it to make a positive contribution. At the very least, within this category of global nature and wildlife tour retailers, Natural Habitat Adventures seems to deserve its reputation as a world leader.

5 Last Descents

Jinsha Gorge, China

Chinese Context

Last Descents is a Chinese river-rafting tour company owned by two partners, one Chinese and the other a Chinese-speaking expatriate. It is a small commercial enterprise with a very large conservation goal, namely to protect the relatively few remaining free-flowing rivers in the gorges of western China against continuing exploitation for hydroelectric dams. To understand what Last Descents is attempting, why it is significant and what it has achieved, it must be considered in the modern Chinese context for tourism and conservation.

China is a rapidly changing country, socially and politically as well as economically (Grumbine, 2007). Within living memory of its older citizens, China has gone through two enormous political changes which have penetrated the deepest fabrics of family life: first, the change to military communism and extreme collectivization; and, subsequently, the change to a very fast-paced capitalist economy, but under powerful political constraints. China is a very large and populous country, with a very powerful and fast-growing economy, and in recent years it has become one of the world's principal economic and political players, with its influence still growing. At the same time that China is testing its power on the international stage, it still maintains a wide variety of cultural traditions which have been millennia in the making. One of the key outcomes is a pervading belief that there are Chinese ways of doing things which are different from Western ways. This applies to everything from commercial transactions and business ethics to large-scale political processes, and from perceptions of nature to perceptions of appropriate group behaviour. In addition, this economic growth has come at enormous and still-expanding social and environmental cost, owing particularly to a long-standing policy of 'industrialise now, clean up later' (Liu, 2010), which has been in force for at least 25 years (author, personal observation, 1985–2010).

Over the past two decades, the central government has devolved more and more power to provincial, prefectural and local governments, and granted more and more autonomy to semi-private quangos, some of them very large. These steps have boosted the pace of economic growth, but with concomitant increases in financial opportunism, and in some cases corruption, at lower levels.

At the same time, a certain degree of public expression is now possible in China, though still under very close central scrutiny, and perhaps only in tones and topics which reflect central government interests. There have been increasing public calls, for example, to reduce environmental pollution at prefectural levels, and to reduce localized corruption, both of which perhaps serve central interests. At the same time, however, it seems that critical comment on central government initiatives or policies is still difficult to make and likely to be punished (Ponseti and Lopez-Pujol, 2006).

Two such policies are particularly relevant here. The first is the continuing drive to bring China's 56 or more ethnic minorities into the dominant Han culture, retaining only those aspects of their own cultures which are marketable as attractions to Han domestic tourists. The second is the very large-scale push to exploit the natural resources of rural western China on behalf of urban eastern China, the 'Western Development Strategy' (Grumbine, 2007). Irrespective of the intentions, motivations and beliefs of the officials involved in this, the net outcome for western China is the very considerable social and environmental disruption commonly associated with large-scale population movement, resource exploitation and infrastructure construction, anywhere in the world. Indeed, as noted by Grumbine (2007), the scale of internal west–east migration within China is equivalent to the entire populations of Canada and Mexico crossing into the USA in search of work.

In socio-economic terms, there is a significant divide between the massive cities of the eastern and southern coastal fringe, and the more rural areas of the west and north. Most of China's minority peoples and ethno-linguistic cultural groups live in these more peripheral provinces. They are increasingly outnumbered, however, by citizens from the dominant Han Chinese ethnic majority, who have moved into these provinces either as government employees or in search of economic opportunities including those provided by taxation incentives. From a national economic development perspective, the eastern cities see the western provinces as 'underdeveloped'. The term 'underdeveloped' actually refers to mean per capita income, which in the rural western provinces is 40% lower than the national average, including the eastern megacities, and equal to one-third of the average income in urban areas (Grumbine, 2007). Such income patterns are common in all continents, and show only that the highest-paid jobs are mostly in cities. It is interpreted by western provincial governments, however, as political justification to exploit natural resources.

As in other countries, there have already been opportunistic frontier-style booms in uncontrolled logging and mining in much of western China, leading to enormous losses in biological diversity, disruption of rural lifestyles and widespread soil erosion and water pollution (Liu, 2010). These have taken place under many different central governments from the Guomindang onwards (Ponseti and Lopez-Pujol, 2006; McDonald, 2007). Some steps, albeit small as yet, have been taken centrally to curb such excesses (Liu, 2010). More recently, however, two new booms have started: hydroelectric power development and mass tourism.

From a conservation perspective, it is the western provinces which contain much of China's remaining biological diversity, from the rainforests of Xishuangbanna in the far south-west to the high montane ecosystems of the Tibetan plateau and the northern Himalayas (Grumbine, 2007). One of the most important landscapes, from both cultural and natural conservation perspectives, is the gorges of the great western rivers, which originate on the Tibetan Plateau and cut southward to the lower-lying areas of India and Yunnan. In particular, three of these great rivers form three giant parallel gorges at the extreme south-eastern corner of Tibet and the adjacent areas of Yunnan. These are the Nu River, also known as the Salween; the Lancang, also known as the Mekong; and the Jinsha, also known as the Yangtze. The gorges of these three rivers are particularly deep and inaccessible, so there are extended sections with little or no human settlement. The main gorge of the Salween, in particular, is more than three times as deep as the Grand Canyon of the Colorado River in the USA, if measured from the base of the gorge to the mountain peaks which form its upper edges. The upper sections of these rivers form part of the traditional territory of the Kham Tibetan ethnic group, and the Yunnan sections form part of the traditional territories of the Yi, Bai, Naxi and other ethnic minority peoples.

These great rivers of western China, which provide water not only within China but also for other nations downstream, are currently subject to intense campaigns of dam building for flood control, electricity generation and possibly large-scale water transfer schemes (Ponseti and Lopez-Pujol, 2006; McDonald, 2007; International Rivers, 2010). Some of the power output is for new local industries, but the majority is intended to supply increasing demand in eastern cities, where expectations of material living standards are growing rapidly in line with increasing economic wealth. Patterns in power demand and production are detailed by Ponseti and Lopez-Pujol (2006).

The economic, social and environmental consequences of China's cascaded mega-dam developments, especially on the Yangtze and the Mekong, have become issues of global concern (Grumbine, 2007; International Rivers, 2010). This concern was triggered when international opposition to the giant Three Gorges Dam on the Yangtze led the World Bank to withdraw funding, even though that dam and many other giant dams subsequently have still been constructed using domestic finance (Ponseti and Lopez-Pujol, 2006). Except perhaps by governments of downstream South-east Asian nations which are affected by the greatly reduced monsoon flows in the Mekong, the scale of recent and ongoing dam construction in the western Chinese river corridors is not generally appreciated. Dams currently under construction on the Yangtze upstream of the Three Gorges Dam, for example, have a total capacity several times greater than that dam (China Gezhouba Group Corporation, 2010).

The Nature Conservancy, an international environmental NGO, gained considerable credit from its role in the successful establishment of the Three Parallel Rivers National Park and a cluster of World Heritage sites in Yunnan Province. The boundaries of the Park, however, were apparently drawn by the Yunnan Provincial Construction Bureau so as to exclude the lower-elevation sections which would be flooded by proposed dams, and include only the higher-elevation slopes and ridges of the mountain ranges which separate the three rivers concerned. A book by O'Shea (2006) about a source-to-sea descent of the Mekong River did lead to limited publicity in the form of a television documentary, but with no apparent change in Chinese national or provincial government policies or the pace of dam construction by the government-backed private hydroelectric consortia. A local conservation campaign led by a group of residents of Naxi ethnicity, and assisted by domestic conservationists and mass media, did successfully avert the construction of one dam on the Yangtze. That dam would have flooded the entire First Bend of the Yangtze and all the Naxi villages concerned and displaced 100,000 Naxi residents. In addition, it was intended as the 'valve reservoir' for an eight-step dam cascade downstream, and one of these dams would have flooded a major tourist destination and source of national pride, Tiger Leaping Gorge.

Last Descents

The approach taken by Last Descents is different from all of these, and the company is included here as a case study because of its innovative ideas and its clear dedication to conservation. Essentially, the model used by Last Descents is simply to take extremely influential individual Chinese on raft expeditions down the sections of river where conservation action is particularly critical and urgent, so as to inspire those individuals to use their influence within the Chinese domestic political system. In most cases, these sections of the river corridors are only accessible along the rivers themselves; and Last Descents is the only rafting company which has the equipment, the expertise and the local contacts to run such expeditions both safely and legally.

Key to this approach is that Last Descents is incorporated within China. It is effectively a business partnership between an American raft guide, with particularly good credentials and contacts in the international white-water world, and a Chinese entrepreneur, with connections both in the growing world of Chinese outdoor

adventure sports and within the prefectural and provincial governments of western China. It thus has some similarities with Expediciones Chile, profiled by Buckley (2003a, 2006), which is a commercial white-water raft and kayak company working to help protect the Futaleufu River in Patagonia.

Last Descents, in its current form, evolved from two previous rafting companies operating in western China. The first of these was a US-based company called Earth Science Expeditions (ESE), established by two American geologists and white-water experts, Peter Winn and Mike Connelly. The primary goal of ESE was to carry out geoscience exploration of the western river corridors. Most of China was still closed to foreign tourists at the time when ESE was established, and the company arranged its permits through the Chinese Academy of Science, the peak national scientific body. Earth Science Expeditions carried out a number of first descents, which are mapped and described on its website (Earth Science Expeditions, 2010) and in some cases also by Buckley (2003a, 2006).

Earth Science Expeditions first established arrangements with the Chinese Academy of Sciences to conduct an expedition in the Yunnan section of the Mekong River in the mid-1980s, but these plans were interrupted by the Tiananmen Square massacre in 1989, which severed diplomatic relations between China and the USA. The expedition was reactivated in 1994, but provincial authorities diverted it from the main flow of the Mekong to a large tributary, the Yangbi River (Buckley, 2003a; ESE, 2010). In following years, ESE ran a series of raft trips down different sections of the Mekong, all in conjunction with the Chinese Academy of Sciences. It also began to investigate the other major river corridors in this region and started to lobby for conservation measures.

By the early 2000s, political circumstances in this region had changed significantly. Access had become considerably easier, and China had also begun to establish its own domestic outdoor tourism enterprises, with several small rafting companies keen to take advantage of ESE's skills and experience. A group of individuals with relevant interests, including provincial government officials as well as private entrepreneurs, had formed an organization known as the Sichuan Scientific Expeditionary Association, SSEA, which was keen to be involved in any new internationally led expeditions or tourist ventures in western China. The western gorge region had also begun to market itself as a tourist destination, with one town in a Tibetan region of Yunnan Province deliberately rebranding itself as Shangri-La, the name of a legendary Himalayan valley of peace, beauty and tranquillity. Finally, the Chinese government began to allow foreigners to enter Tibet, albeit under much more restricted conditions than for the rest of China.

Earth Science Expeditions adapted to these changing circumstances by forming a subsidiary company, Shangri-La River Expeditions (SLRE), in order to operate commercial rafting tours rather than geoscience expeditions. As noted in Chapter 6, Shangri-La was the name of an imaginary region which formed the setting for a 1933 novel, and has now been appropriated by Zhongdian County in north-western Yunnan. This area, an ethnic Tibetan township and county, has renamed itself first from its original Tibetan name of Gyalthang to Zhongdian, and more recently to Shangri-La or Xianggelila, specifically as a tourism market-ing device. Since this is the same general region that Shangri-La River Expeditions operates, this was a particularly appropriate name. Shangri-La River Expeditions also ran a number of first descents, most notably in previously inaccessible areas of Tibet.

During this period, in discussion with Chinese members of these expeditions, it became increasingly apparent that while SLRE was training Chinese raft guides and kayakers to work in the newly established Chinese white-water industry, the great rivers of western China which provide the foundation for that industry were rapidly disappearing under dams. When ESE first investigated the possibility of rafting on the upper Mekong in the mid-1980s, both the Lancang and Yangbi branches were free-flowing rivers largely unpolluted by any industrial effluent. By the time the Yangbi River expedition ran in 1994, there were very extensive logging and brick-making industries in the area, a pulp mill discharging untreated effluent into the Yangbi and a large hydroelectric

dam below the junction of the Yangbi and the Lancang. During the period when ESE and later SLRE were continuing exploration of the western river corridors, proliferation of dams emerged as the greatest threat to conservation in this region. A cascaded series of dams on the lower portions of the Lancang Jiang raised international concerns over interruption to water supply and alteration of river flow regimes in the downstream nations of the Mekong River basin. The Chinese government constructed the Three Gorges dam on the Yangtze, despite international concern and condemnation of the forced relocation of residents from the area concerned. The continuing growth in population and power demand in China's enormous eastern cities created a political and financial climate which favoured the large engineering consortia, which relied on a continuing supply of new construction contracts to maintain their existence and profits. These organizations are structured as corporations, but with strong shareholdings by provincial government agencies, which made it relatively straight-forward for them to obtain development approvals for new dams. The political parallels with the development of dams in the American West, and notably the conflicts between hydro-electric power and river conservation on the Colorado, were not lost on the founders of ESE and SLRE.

The need to provide some protection for the remaining river sections, largely in the upper reaches in southern Tibet and northern Yunnan, was thus becoming increasingly urgent and important, for tourism as well as for local communities and conservation. As new dams were continually built, and yet more sections of river were flooded, it became clear that many of these first descents were in fact also the last and only descent of that particular river section. As a small foreign-owned cor-poration, SLRE had rather little political influence, especially since its local partner was no longer the Chinese Academy of Science, but instead a private outdoor association based in Sichuan. To create a more effective force for conservation, the owners of ESE and SLRE concluded that they would need to catalyse the growth of a Chinese domestic river rafting tourism industry, so as to create a significant internal constituency for conservation on river corridors.

Accordingly, Peter Winn's son Travis, who had studied and travelled extensively in China and spoke Mandarin Chinese, established a new Chinese-based rafting company in conjunction with a Chinese partner who already had an outdoor business and whom they had previously trained as a river guide. They named this new company Last Descents, a deliberate counterpart to the adventurer's goal of first descents, in order to emphasize the increasing threats to river conservation. Travis is a world-class kayaker, with many first descents to his credit, and a former river guide on the Grand Canyon of the Colorado River. He speaks Chinese and has lived in China for extended periods. He took part in many of the expeditions run by ESE and SLRE, and has organized many more himself. His efforts have attracted the attention of a number of well-known Chinese academics, conservationists, politicians and entrepreneurs, as well as international media attention (Bowerman, 2008). Last Descents does exactly what its name implies, bringing passengers and participants safely down sections of China's great western rivers which are about to be flooded by new dams – in the hope that this may help to conserve other river sections where dams are planned but construction has not yet commenced.

As more and more of the western rivers are dammed, the sections remaining become increasingly scarce and hence increasingly valuable for tourism as well as for conservation and local community use. That is, the supply of raftable river sections is being reduced through continued dam construction. At the same time, recreational demand for these rivers is increasing. Within China's enormous urban populations, the domestic demand for outdoor recreation continues to grow. This also raises the value of remaining raftable rivers, both for commercial tourism and for social welfare through individual recreation.

As yet, however, there is apparently no organized political lobbying force representing the tourism industry in Chinese domestic politics (Airey and Chong, 2010). National, provincial and prefectural governments do have tourism agencies or portfolios, but, as in

other countries, their main interests are in marketing the regions for which they are responsible, as tourist destinations for people from outside those regions. They do not seem to have taken an active role in defending prime tourist attractions against the demands of other industry sectors. The same applies in other countries: tourism organizations are relatively ineffective lobbyists, and they focus their lobbying on demands for government-funded marketing campaigns. In addition, the outdoor tourism sector in particular is as yet little developed within China. There is no organized river rafting industry, for example, which could act as a political counter to the continuing demands of the hydroelectricity quangos. There are Chinese domestic rafting companies, but they are as yet very small and low-key, and certainly not in a position to oppose what they see as the state-sanctioned hydropower sector.

Under such circumstances, Last Descents might well seem to be facing an impossible uphill struggle in its efforts to contribute to conservation of these great western river corridors; but it has achieved some successes none the less. It has adopted a four-part strategy, with all components running in parallel. It runs new rivers, to demonstrate that western China has world-class resources for an international white-water rafting industry. It helped to train Chinese kayakers associated with the Beijing Olympics, and is continuing to train kayakers and raft guides. It has established a US-based NGO, the China Rivers Project (2010) as a coordinating point for conservation efforts. And, perhaps most importantly, it has run or assisted in a number of river trips with influential participants, some of whom have subsequently contributed to conservation lobbying.

Two of these efforts are of particular note. The first involves links with river trips by members of The Nature Conservancy (2010). One such trip, run in 2003 by some famous kayakers associated with TNC's senior staff, provided a significant component in the campaign by TNC for China to declare the Three Parallel Rivers National Park. This trip relied heavily on Last Descents' forerunners, ESE and SLRE, for technical information and assistance. Indeed, as noted by Buckley (2006), it appears that earlier expeditions by ESE and SLRE provided both information and a trigger for the TNC campaign. Last Descents and its predecessors have run a number of expeditions in the headwaters of the Lancang, Nu and Yangtze in Yunnan and Tibet (Buckley, 2003a, 2006; Last Descents River Expeditions, 2010; Shangri-La River Expeditions, 2010). This collaboration between Last Descents and TNC is continuing currently (T. Winn, personal communication, 26 April 2010).

In many sections of these gorges, the only access is along narrow rocky foot trails carved out of the cliffs or built up from many metres below by stacking rocks against the cliff face. Crossings are very few, on suspension bridges high above the river. In some sections, the only settlements are tiny terraced villages carved out where side streams enter the main canyon. Elsewhere, there are small agricultural plots on ridges high above the gorge, or tracks which lead into the gorges for hunters or timber cutters. There are significant patches of relatively undisturbed natural forest cover, with remnant populations of endangered native bird and mammal species. These areas are thus of high conservation value on a global scale. The same applies for some of the river corridors in India, Bhutan and Nepal on the southern side of the Himalayas, but the gorges of the three great Chinese rivers mentioned above are particularly deep and inaccessible.

The second Last Descents project of particular note was a 2009 trip on a section of the Yangtze River known as the Great Bend, downstream from Tiger Leaping Gorge. This upper part of the Yangtze is known in China as the Jinsha Jiang and has a total catchment of 500,000 km^2. Several mega-dams have already been built on this section, and more are under construction, moving gradually upstream (Ponseti and Lopez-Pujol, 2006; China Gezhouba Group Corporation, 2010). A number of US-based rafting companies, including Last Descents, have offered trips on the Great Bend on the Yangtze during the past decade. During 2008 and 2009, however, the raftable sections became shorter and shorter as more and more rapids were rendered inaccessible by new dam construction.

Which particular raft trip on a river section upstream of a new dam will prove to be the last

descent is rarely known for certain, for several reasons. First, there is no publicly available information on the exact dates at which each dam's diversion tunnels will be closed, starting to fill the dam reservoir above. (Sections of river may also be closed off years earlier, while dams are constructed.) Second, the rate at which each reservoir fills, flooding the river upstream, depends on rainfall and stream flow. Third, there are commercial and political uncertainties as to whether any particular individual raft trip will actually run. Each raft trip depends both on permits and on an adequate supply of commercial customers. As a result, any of the 2009 trips might indeed have been the very last descent of the Great Bend. One trip in particular, however, was widely expected to be the last to pass through the Inner Gorge of the Great Bend. It was run as a scientific, social and policy workshop, the Floating Forum on the Jinsha River, by the Centre for Nature and Society at Beijing University, in partnership with Last Descents. Participants included: members of Beijing University; members of the Chinese Academy of Science and the Chinese Academy of Social Sciences; a number of nationally and inter-nationally known Chinese entrepreneurs and financiers; and a small number of invited international contributors.

Run in April 2009, this trip took participants through the inner gorge, an astonishing rock chasm with near-vertical walls stretching up several hundred metres high from the river, as well as more open gorges between neighbouring mountain peaks. It passed the legendary Stone City of Baoshan, a fortified village over 700 years old, close to the point where Genghis Khan's armies swam across the Yangtze using inflated animal skins as flotation devices. Although the river is tranquil for much of the gorge section, there are several rock-walled rapids which require modern rafting equipment and skills to negotiate safely. As a result, it seems highly likely that nobody at all has ever seen these inner gorge sections except for the few participants in recent rafting expeditions, most of whom have been expatriates.

The Chinese members of the April 2009 Floating Forum formed the largest and best-connected group of Chinese citizens ever to see this gorge, which may soon be submerged under the rising waters of new dams not far downstream. The Great Bend of the Yangtze lies right in the middle of an area which is promoted and used heavily for domestic tourism, and which includes Lijiang Old Town and Tiger Leaping Gorge as well as the Stone City of Baoshan and the famed Lugu Lake. Even so, it seems that the insatiable demand for electricity from the opposite side of China may well ensure that Chinese tourists never have the opportunity to experience this particular natural wonder. As of 12 June 2009, the Ministry of the Environment had apparently suspended permitting on nearby projects. Liyuan Dam, immediately downstream of the inner gorge section, apparently does not have approvals in place, but as of April 2010 construction is still continuing none the less. If Liyuan Dam were to be completed as proposed, it would inundate the lower and central sections of the famed Tiger Leaping Gorge. This would include a large rock where several brave Chinese rafters drowned in an attempted first descent some decades ago, and which is now the principal tourist attraction.

The politics of the dam construction in China's great western rivers are opaque even to Chinese investigators. Last Descents does not attempt to take a direct political role. What it does is to show some of China's own citizens, who may potentially have such a role, just what is at stake and what there is to be lost. If this approach succeeds in saving even one section of the great river canyons of western China, that would be a globally significant conservation outcome.

Conservation Tourism vs Hydropower in China

Conservation depends on political decisions. Economics can influence political decisions, but it is not the only factor. Current conservation decisions are nearly always made in competition with development demands, and conservation only continues if economics and politics continue to favour it. Economics is not only about cash flow, but cash has the greatest political weight. A person who joins a private river rafting trip incurs most of the same real costs and gains most of the same real benefits as a person who uses a commercial tour operator or outfitter to undertake the same trip; but the latter counts for more politically because the cash transactions are larger. In analysing the economics of river recreation, there are many different possible economic valuations, and these numbers represent political tools rather than market transactions. Conservation can indeed be carried out simply by buying land, but that option is not realistically available for river corridors in western China.

The annual value of the outdoor nature and adventure tourism sector worldwide is estimated at around US$1 trillion (Buckley, 2010) and according to the UN World Tourism Organization there are about 900 million international tourist trips each year. In China, there are around 20 million international visitors each year, but around two billion domestic tourist trips. Chinese wealth is continuing to grow very rapidly indeed, and the future of tourism in China probably depends far more on domestic than on international markets. Currently, the expectations of most Chinese domestic tourists are quite different from those of international tourists, but this is likely to change, as it has in other countries.

Therefore, the key issue for the economics of river recreation as compared with hydropower development in western China is to make a rational projection for the potential scale of domestic river-based tourism in a wealthy China. To do this, we can use per-trip values derived from existing upmarket international tours on Chinese rivers, and calculate numbers of participants based on physical and social crowding limitations in an intensively developed industry such as that on the Grand Canyon of the Colorado. In addition, it is critical to note that tourists who actually raft down rivers make up only a tiny proportion of the total number of tourists who visit rivers simply to look at them, and also that the economic value of a river used for conservation and recreation includes that of ecosystem services as well as those of tourism and recreation. Finally, it is important to factor in the costs of social and environmental impacts associated with large hydropower schemes, which are not incurred in the case of conservation and recreation. For mega-dam cascades such as those under construction on

China's great western rivers, these impacts are enormous. The Three Gorges Dam alone has caused actual or incipient extinction of three endangered and endemic fish species and one freshwater dolphin species, as well as loss of fisheries downstream, disease and pollution in reservoirs and emission of the potent greenhouse gas methane from rotting vegetation (Ponseti and Lopez-Pujol, 2006). We should also consider the costs of transferring power from the western river corridors to the eastern seaboard cities.

There seem to have been few attempts to make direct economic comparisons between river tourism and hydropower development. There is one published comparison from Ireland, but at a very small scale for both sectors. There are, however, figures from Colorado, USA, which can be used to calculate the current value of tourism in the Grand Canyon, and compared with the current value of hydropower produced by the dams upstream and downstream of the Grand Canyon. The social and environmental impacts of dam construction in western China can be deduced from existing dams built on the Lancang Jiang or Mekong River over the past 15 years. These include dams such as Manwan, Dachaoshan, Xiaowan and Jinghong, which have a total installed capacity of 8.5 GW and a reservoir area of 54 km^2, displacing 45,000 people.

On the Yangtze itself, the projected power outputs of the various dams are publicly available, and so are approximate construction costs. Revenues depend on electricity prices paid at the dam generators. In most countries, electricity prices are not fixed, but are in fact very different for different consumers and at different times. Individual residents pay far higher retail prices than large-scale industries which purchase electric power in bulk for many years ahead. In addition, social and environmental costs per kWh consumed also depend on cross-country transmission losses.

The five largest dams proposed for the Jinsha section of the Yangtze are named Xiangjiaba, Xiluodu, Baihetan, Wudonghe and Hutiaoxia, also known as the Upper Tiger Leaping Gorge Dam. Xiluodu is already built, flooding 90 km^2 and displacing somewhere between 30,000 and 50,000 people. It has a dam wall 278 m high, and total installed generating capacity of 12.6 GW (China Gezhouba Group Corporation, 2010). Xiangjiaba is also recently completed, with a dam wall 161 m high. Baihetan and Wudonghe are under construction, with completion expected by 2020. Hutiaoxia is currently suspended for an indefinite period. These five dams would have a total installed capacity of about 44 GW. That means that, if every generator ran at full capacity year-round, the total power which they could potentially generate each year would be about 186,000 GWh, i.e. 186 billion kWh. Actual power production, however, would generally be well below that. Even when the dams are full, guaranteed power output is only one-third of total installed capacity (China Gezhouba Group Corporation, 2010). In reality, dams do not release full capacity all the time, especially not if there are several dams in series. So a more realistic figure might be about 30 billion kWh or less. In addition, output will fall in future as the reservoirs fill with sediment. One reason to build the upstream dams is to reduce sediment input to the downstream reservoirs, but, even so, sedimentation in some of China's dams has reduced power output by up to 80% in a few decades (Ponseti and Lopez-Pujol, 2006). At the official electricity price of RMB 0.25 per kWh, this would represent total potential annual revenue of about RMB 7.5 billion (US$1 billion). This compares with total construction costs of around RMB 180 billion (around US$26 billion).

Ignoring the social, environmental, infrastructure and operating costs, therefore, and assuming indefinite demand and US-parity retail power prices, these dams would produce a straight cash return on investment of only around 4%. These assumptions, however, are not in fact valid. The rivers are in the west of China and most of the power demand is in the east, so there would be enormous costs for power transmission infrastructure and significant transmission losses. Assuming that a separate power supply company builds the power lines, buys electricity from the dams and sells it to consumers, the company building the dams and generators would receive a far smaller return, perhaps only a third of this, i.e. RMB 2.5 billion (US$0.36 billion). These figures are very approximate estimates, since there are no publicly available data on wholesale power prices in China, or indeed in most other countries. From a public accounting perspective we should deduct social and environmental costs from this; but if nobody plans to pay compensation, the actual hydropower corporation may well ignore these.

Against this we must compare potential net benefits from river tourism, recreation and conservation. If the rafting industry developed to a similar scale to that of the Grand Canyon, it would generate around RMB 500 million per annum directly, and around RMB 1.2 billion p.a. (US$0.17 billion) in total for the local region. If a million visitors a year also came just to look at the river – as they do at Tiger Leaping Gorge – and if each spent, say, RMB 1500 locally, with a typical local economic multiplier around 2.0, that would add another RMB 3 billion (US$0.43 billion). So these numbers are not so very different from the hydropower numbers. If we also add the costs of travel, expenditure in surrounding areas, the value of time and consumer surplus, then the total social economic value of tourism might be several times higher.

In addition, the comparison should also consider the value of ecosystem services from a free-flowing river, as compared with, for example, the agricultural value of flood control or the agricultural costs of preventing flood sediment deposition. It should consider the expected life of the dams and the maintenance costs of generators. And it should disaggregate costs and benefits geographically, e.g. for the province cf. nationally. Any of these issues could become politically significant. But, at the broadest scale, the issue is simply that the economic scale of river tourism, in the 'underdeveloped' western provinces, could be as great as that from supplying power to the east.

As in other countries, however, building dams creates a dam-building industry, and in order to survive this industry needs to keep building more dams. Especially if many megadams are under construction at the same time, as in China, this industry develops a huge financial and political momentum which it is difficult to divert to other activities. The same applies for other industry sectors and for dam construction in other countries such as the

USA, Chile, Australia and New Zealand among others. In all of these countries, continued dam construction has come under heavy criticism both domestically and internationally and has now largely been halted. Indeed, in some countries, the principal political emphasis is now on dismantling some of the existing dams so as to restore free-flowing rivers. This has already happened quite extensively in some parts of the USA (Chatterjee, 1997; Doyle et al., 2003; Ponseti and Lopez-Pujol, 2006). It has also been under serious consideration for a number of years for a large hydroelectric dam in Tasmania, Australia, which submerged a world-renowned scenic lake in order to generate electricity for which there was no demand within Tasmania and which could not be transmitted across the Bass Strait to mainland Australia. Instead, the electricity generated from this dam was sold at a very heavily discounted rate to the aluminium smelting industry, which began shipping bauxite from thousands of kilometres away to take advantage of such low-priced electricity, rather than smelting near the mine site using full-price power.

In the case of western China, there is indeed a real and growing demand from the major cities of the eastern seaboard, several thousand kilometres away, and this demand is currently met mainly from coal-fired power stations. These have environmental and political consequences as China tries to meet its international obligations related to greenhouse gas emission reductions and climate change mitigation. These obligations, however, are rather weak, since they are expressed only as carbon emissions per unit GDP, which are likely to fall in any event as the Chinese economy modernizes and diversifies. Large dams also have severe social and environmental costs and risks of their own; and, per kWh at final consumption, these costs and risks are effectively multiplied by the high proportional transmission losses occurring when the final consumers are so far away from the initial source of power.

Most of the world, including neighbouring Himalayan nations and other wealthy developing countries, as well as Europe and the USA, has stopped building giant dams because of their net negative outcomes. Indeed, as noted above, they are dismantling a number of existing dams. China already has almost half the world's large dams (Ponseti and Lopez-Pujol, 2006) and is apparently the only nation worldwide which continues to construct mega-dams. The argument used in China is that proportionally less of the country's total hydropower potential is developed in China than in the USA. But, if the net outcomes of such development are negative, countries lose rather than gain from increasing that proportion. The other argument is that, if China is to limit its greenhouse gas emissions while continuing economic growth, it will need sources of power other than coal, which is currently the mainstay of its electricity generating industry. The first few hydroelectric schemes may indeed have generated some environmental gains if they did in reality replace coal-fired generation – which is far from clear. Now that few of the western rivers remain undeveloped, however, for those remaining the economic, social and environmental benefits of conservation and tourism far outweigh those of hydropower.

Meanwhile, however, as in other parts of the world, hydropower development to date has built a number of large organizations and construction groups whose continued existence and/or profitability depends on continuing development of new dams, roads and electricity transmission systems. These organizations have created their own financial and political momentum to continue exploiting publicly owned natural resources long past the threshold of net public well-being. This is, of course, a common feature of primary production sectors worldwide, notably in fisheries and forestry as well as dam construction. Examples from other countries indicate that central governments generally do not act until too late, despite multiple warnings from NGOs both domestic and international, because of political capture by the industries concerned. Overexploitation continues unless and until a competing industry sector, also commanding money and votes, makes a more powerful demand for the same resources. Occasionally, such conflicts arise directly between primary industries such as forestry and fisheries, e.g. where pulp-mill effluents pollute rivers and oceans. Occasionally, water requirements for urban use may also compete with demands by industry.

More commonly, however, the only industry with potential interests in conserving natural landscapes and ecosystems is the tourism sector. In western China, there are currently large-scale conflicts between continuing construction of hydropower dams and conservation of remnant forest along major river corridors. These are complicated by the high proportion of minority ethnic groups living along these rivers, which allows development proponents to paint concerns over conservation, or economic critiques of continuing hydropower development, as ethnic unrest. Such unrest is contrary to one of the national government's overriding policy objectives, cannot be criticized with impunity, and may indeed be subject to powerful military intervention.

Ethnic minorities have, in fact, played a significant role in a number of river conservation efforts, but they do so at some risk. The most notable is the role played by a Naxi farmer in a successful campaign to prevent construction of one hydropower dam on the Yangtze river, which would have flooded his village. The same dam, however, would also have created severe impacts on a very heavily visited scenic spot known as Tiger Leaping Gorge, which is nationally famous since several Chinese rafters drowned there while trying to beat a US team to be the first to raft the entire length of the Yangtze, source to sea. The relative importance of national pride, tourism and the Naxi people in this case is not known. It seems likely that they all played some role, in combination. Certainly, the charismatic Naxi leader became the spearhead and public face of the successful campaign to halt that particular dam. Many other dams, however, are still going ahead.

The goal of Last Descents' approach is to focus public and political attention on the relative value for the regional economy of western China of conservation and tourism cf. dams and hydropower. As China grows richer, the balance tips to tourism. Dams last decades, and by then China will be as wealthy as the USA. The Colorado Grand Canyon grew to be a global tourism icon, and mainstay of the regional economy, in just a few decades. The great gorges of the Nu, Lancang and Jinsha are larger, deeper and equally spectacular – but hardly anyone has yet seen them. There are two billion domestic tourist trips in China every year, and the number is growing. If Chinese national and provincial governments and the Chinese tourism industry want these tourists to travel and spend in China rather than overseas, they must keep places for them to visit. Based on a Colorado model, for example, the Great Bend section of the Yangtze could earn about the same through tourism as it could from hydropower – because power operations are intermittent, costs and losses in transmission to eastern cities are high and bulk purchase prices are well below retail. And tourism has far lower social and environmental costs than hydropower dams, and far lower risks. The Western USA learnt this lesson at the last moment, conserving only the Grand Canyon for tourism when equally beautiful sections upstream and downstream were already dammed. China need not make the same mistakes. Last Descents is a very tiny tourism company in a giant global economy, but its efforts are very highly focused and may yet bear fruit.

6 Asia

Chitwan, Nepal

Introduction

The Asian region is very large and diverse in its topography, ecosystems, cultures and economies. Approaches to conservation tourism are equally diverse. In the dry open forests of central India, opportunities to search for tiger and Asian rhinoceros, as well as a number of spectacular bird species, provide opportunities for conservation tourism approaches which are comparable to those of sub-Saharan Africa. In the dense rainforests of South-east Asia, in contrast, the rich and mixed biological diversity in a dense and multilayered forest ecosystem provides opportunities which are more directly comparable with those of tropical and sub-tropical Latin America. The great mountain ranges and river corridors of central Asia provide potential opportunities comparable to those of the Rocky Mountain states and provinces of North America. For the Arctic and subarctic areas of northern Asia, there are opportunities analogous to those of Alaska, the Canadian Arctic and northern Scandinavia. All of these opportunities are in fact being pursued to some degree, but to date the number of enterprises concerned and the economic and geographical scale of the outdoor tourism sector in general are much smaller in Asia than in comparable areas in North America and Europe. In addition, historically the outdoor tourism sector in Asia has relied largely on international tourists, as for sub-Saharan Africa and Latin America.

In recent years, however, this has changed enormously, with rapidly increasing wealth in a number of Asian nations, and associated growth and domestic demand for outdoor tourism activities, including nature and wildlife experiences. The sources of wealth, the social and cultural characteristics of the newly wealthy, and the types of tourist experiences they want, differ between individual countries in the Asian region, and so also do the history and current context of public protected areas and other land tenures relevant to conservation tourism. As just one example, countries with a former colonial period may well have a national parks system modelled on that of the colonial nation concerned, whereas other nations have their own land tenure systems which do not have direct international analogues. The

zapovedniks of Russia, for example, are not quite the same as the so-called Yellowstone model of national parks; and the forest parks of China are not quite the same as either the national forests of the USA or the USFS wilderness areas. Similarly, where these nations have concepts comparable to the Western notion of ecotourism, there are often differences both in principle and in practice. The concept of *shengtai luyou* in China provides one example (Buckley *et al.*, 2008a).

Despite these differences, the same basic social, economic and political links between tourism and conservation which operate in other continents can also apply throughout Asia. This chapter presents case studies of conservation tourism from only six Asian nations: India, Nepal, China, Mongolia, Russia and Malaysia. Earlier volumes by Buckley (2003a) and Zeppel (2006) listed a much more extensive set of examples, including a number from Thailand, Vietnam, Cambodia, Laos, Indonesia and the Philippines, as well as additional cases from Malaysia, Nepal and China. Information currently available for those cases, however, is insufficient for reliable evaluation of possible conservation benefits.

Taj Safaris' Tiger Lodges, India

Taj Safaris is a joint venture between the well-known African conservation tourism operation &Beyond (formerly Conservation Corporation Africa) and a large Indian hotel group, Taj Hotels. Essentially, Taj Safaris aims to apply the successful conservation tourism model used in eastern and southern Africa, to an area of central India known for its tiger-watching opportunities. There are significant political differences between India and Africa, as indeed there are between different countries within Africa; and operational aspects reflect these differences. Within these constraints, however, the aim of Taj Safaris has been to provide an experience recognizable by regular guests of &Beyond's African lodges; and also to attract the large and newly wealthy sector of the Indian domestic tourist market, which has an interest in wildlife tourism generally and tiger-watching in particular.

The joint venture company has constructed four lodges, each in a well-known tiger-watching protected area. The lodges are on private estates which provide a peaceful ambience and some local wildlife-watching opportunities, but the main opportunities to look for tiger and other larger animals are within nearby public national parks. Guests at the Taj Safaris lodges, therefore, do not have exclusive access to the wildlife-watching areas in the way that they are accustomed to in &Beyond's African lodges. They do, however, have open African-style safari vehicles and particularly skilled naturalist guides who know the geography of the parks and the behaviour of their wildlife, and can thus provide Taj Safaris' guests with much better wildlife viewing than would typically be experienced by independent visitors. The lodges themselves follow local Indian vernacular architectural styles, but with the same theme of low-key luxury as for &Beyond lodges in Africa; and the same exemplary standard of service, including skilled chefs who can provide either local delicacies or Western fare as the guests prefer.

The first two lodges were at Mahua Kothi and Baghvan, adjacent to Bandhavgarh and Pench National Parks respectively. Two further lodges have opened more recently, Banjaar Tola at Kanha National Park and Pashan Garh at Panna National Park. I have visited the first two only. When these lodges first opened there was no direct air access, and guests were transported by road from the nearest regional airport, using chauffeured four-wheel drive vehicles. This was an interesting journey but took several hours. Direct air access is now available, however, using the local charter operator, Chimes Aviation.

At both Mahua Kothi and Baghvan Lodges, the main objective of most guests is to get good sightings of tiger, and this is the aspect on which the guides focus initially. All tourists' vehicles, including those operated by Taj Safaris, must first stop at a control point at the park entrance gate for the day's permits. The section of the park which is open to the public has a network of dirt roads, and the permit system directs each vehicle to a particular area or road circuit initially, so that the vehicles do not all cluster in the same place. Inside the park, the behaviour of wildlife-watching vehicles

is very different from that in the private reserves of southern Africa. In the latter, the vehicles all drive slowly, remain in quiet but efficient radio contact and follow a strictly observed protocol to avoid crowding at individual sightings.

In the Indian parks, vehicles are not permitted to carry radios, so they communicate by stopping and talking to each other and by watching where other vehicles are going. Most of the vehicles are private cars driven by individual tourists with little or no wildlife-watching experience. In theory there is a speed limit, but this is rarely observed. There are no limits on the numbers of vehicles which may assemble at any given sighting, and it is commonplace for large crowds of vehicles to assemble very quickly. In addition, there is no protocol for new vehicles to approach a sighting, and in practice many vehicles arrive at high speed with considerable dust and noise and drive directly in front of vehicles which are already on site, blocking their view and disturbing the animals under observation. For guests who are used to the practices followed at &Beyond's African lodges, this free-for-all melee does detract significantly from the ambience of the tiger sightings.

Fortunately, however, these scrambles apply only for sightings of tiger in heavily visited areas of the more heavily visited parks. Pench and Panna National Parks are much less well known, and crowding is far less severe. Even in Bandhavgarh, the Taj Safaris naturalists use their greater knowledge of tiger behaviour patterns to locate tiger in areas without other vehicles, providing some close, undisturbed and unforgettable sightings. In addition, they know to the minute how long it takes to reach the Park gate at closing time, so they can offer their guests sightings in the late afternoon light when the other cars have already left and the tigers are relaxed. There is also a wide variety of other wildlife within these parks, including leopard, deer, the giant cattle known as gaur, the bluebuck known as *nilghai*, and a wide variety of bird life, including wild peacocks. The Taj Safaris naturalists are expert at finding all of these species and providing guests with good viewing opportunities.

There are also options to watch tigers from elephant-back. This operation is run directly by the park staff. Visitors book in at the park entry gate on the morning of the day concerned, and are given an approximate time at which to proceed to the elephant station. This is generally not until late morning at the earliest, in order to give the park staff time to locate a tiger. When their turn comes, the visitors are taken cross-country on elephant-back, crossing slopes or swamps as needed, typically to see a tiger resting in dense bush. The elephants can push into thick scrub, and the tigers allow them to approach quite closely. The elephants carry four passengers at a time, however, and only those on the side towards the tiger get good sightings and photographic opportunities. The mahouts do turn the elephants round before leaving the site, but only very briefly. They seem to be motivated principally by the urgency to get back to the base station in order to take another group, and the actual tiger sighting seems to be treated more as a formality than as a lifetime experience for the visitors.

The parks service in India has a long tradition of its own, deriving originally from British colonial days. Approaches to visitor management are perhaps derived from days when there were very few visitors. Currently, however, because of India's rapidly increasing wealth, there are large numbers of visitors with their own 4WD vehicles who do not have a history of low-impact wildlife watching and are, perhaps, not even aware of the impacts which their behaviour may have on wildlife and on other visitors. This does detract considerably from the wildlife-watching experience.

In these national parks, there are zones which are open to public access as described above, and zones which at present are completely closed to any visitors, principally because there is no road access. The parks agency is considering whether to extend the road system so as to expand the area accessible for wildlife watching. Taj Safaris has proposed that the parks service might consider an experimental pilot trial of an African-style system, an exclusive lease of part of this area to a single operator which could establish a more carefully controlled and much lower-impact wildlife-watching system using expert trackers and radio contact between safari vehicles to control access to individual sightings of tiger or leopard. It remains to be seen whether this suggestion will be adopted.

To assist in establishing its credentials in proposing such an approach, &Beyond has made some significant conservation contributions to the Ministry of Environment and Forests, which manages national parks and wildlife in India. In particular, they have made available their expertise in large-animal live capture, translocation and soft release so as to help the parks service move a number of gaur, the giant ancestral wild Indian cattle, from one area to another. As of April 2010 the holding pens have been built and the vehicles, darting and tracking equipment purchased, but the Indian Government has not yet issued the necessary permits (L. Carlisle, personal communication, 24 April 2010).

If the proposal goes ahead and &Beyond can successfully demonstrate the advantages of limiting indiscriminate access by private vehicles with unskilled drivers, the next step might be to impose tighter management measures in the public-access zone. One option would be to transfer all visitors from their own vehicles into small multi-seater vehicles driven by parks staff, a practice followed in a number of national parks worldwide. An alternative might be to require that every private vehicle pick up a park ranger at the gate, with their own parks service radio, and that these rangers would have the power to determine where each vehicle went and how it drove. This would be analogous to the system in the Galapagos Islands in Ecuador, where every tourist boat must take on board a national parks guide and follow their instructions. A third possibility might be that private vehicles would be required to proceed in small convoys of three or four vehicles each, led by a parks vehicle. In each case, the aim of the system would be to ensure that all vehicles drive slowly, that they proceed to tiger or leopard sightings in an orderly manner, taking turns according to some pre-defined protocol; and that each vehicle approaches and departs from individual sightings slowly and quietly, without disturbing the animals or interrupting the view of other groups.

Examples from elsewhere, e.g. at Madikwe in South Africa, show that it is perfectly possible for such low-impact practices to be followed by all the vehicles in a given reserve, even if they are not operated by the same owner, as long as there is a system in place to take action against any vehicles which infringe the protocol. In the Madikwe case, however, all the vehicles belong to tourist lodges which have a shared interest in the joint management system. It would be more difficult to achieve this with private vehicles, whose owners may only visit the park once; but it might be possible with a strong enough education and enforcement system.

While the opportunity to see tigers in the wild is certainly the principal tourist attraction to these parks and lodges, there are also cultural and historical attractions. At Bandhavgarh National Park, there is an ancient stone fort at the top of a nearby hill, accessible by a 4WD track and on foot. Though long since abandoned, this fort remains an astonishing feat of construction, with temples, statues, fortifications and enormous water tanks carved from solid rock. It is currently a very peaceful place, with a single resident priest, some troops of monkeys, one or two tourists, and eagles soaring along the rocky cliffs. It certainly provides a very different ambience from the flurries of vehicles rushing to and fro in the principal tiger-watching area.

The Taj Safaris venture is still new, and the net conservation outcome will not be known for some years. If the Taj Safaris joint venture approach is successful, however, it may be able to harness the growth in domestic Indian wildlife tourism to contribute to conservation of India's biological diversity, rather than the reverse.

Montane Forests of Arunachal Pradesh, India

The Province of Arunachal Pradesh occupies the far north-eastern corner of India. It is bordered to the north by Tibet, to the east by Myanmar and to the north-west by Bhutan. To the south-west lies Bangladesh and to the south-east lies the Indian province of Assam. Arunachal Pradesh and Assam are connected to the rest of India along a narrow corridor running between Bhutan and Bangladesh. Topographically, the northern section of the province forms part of the Himalayan Ranges, running up to the eastern end of the Tibetan

plateau. The province slopes down to plains in the southern section, and much of the northern half forms part of the great Brahmaputra River system, fed by a series of tributary rivers from the Himalayas. There are no major cities in the northern section, and the main gateway is the town of Guwahati, which has a population of about one million but is still small by Indian standards.

The mountainous northern sections of the province, particularly those close to the borders, still contain areas of uncleared forest along the major river corridors. The province is some 83,700 km^2 in area, 80% of it is still forested, and it is considered one of the world's top 20 high-biodiversity regions. It also has high ethnic and cultural diversity, with around 25 different local tribes and peoples. These areas do not have any formal protection at present and survive only because access is difficult and they are only sparsely settled. These forests are of considerable conservation significance, supporting some of the few remaining wild populations of Indian elephant and a high diversity of forest bird species such as hornbills. Indeed, some of the older local residents of the area wear decorative headdresses which feature hornbill beaks.

Arunachal Pradesh is not routinely open for international tourism. Currently, a series of permits are required to enter the province and then to enter a particular local government area or police zone. According to Shackley (1995), parts of the province were indeed opened and promoted for tourism in 1993 and 1994, but were closed again in 1995 at the request of the local inhabitants themselves, who felt that tourism was bringing negative rather than positive changes. Currently, international tourists can visit the province, but not routinely. Infrastructure is limited and tourism is thus largely of an expeditionary nature. It does indeed have the potential to contribute to conservation.

There are currently 16 local tour operators approved by the provincial government of Arunachal Pradesh (Arunachal Tourism, 2010). Fewer than half of these have operational websites, however, and only three or four actually offer local tours in the more remote areas, focusing principally on cultural and ethnic diversity. Two of these also offer 14-day white-water rafting tours on the Siang River, a tributary of the Brahmaputra near the eastern end of the province.

Another such tributary is the Kameng, which runs south from the Himalayas, through an area of largely inaccessible forest, past the town of Seppa. The Himalayan rafting company Ultimate Descents (2010), operated by David Allardice and well-reputed for its extensive portfolio of raft tours in Nepal, Bhutan and Myanmar (Buckley, 2006), ran the first commercial descent of this river in 2007 with an international team of guides and participants. This trip demonstrated the logistic possibilities of a river rafting industry as a way to generate local interest and finance for conservation, as has occurred elsewhere in the world. Additional Kameng River rafting tours have been run subsequently.

The 2007 group brought most of its equipment by road from Nepal, but there are skilled rafters and kayakers elsewhere in India and it would not be difficult to establish a locally based operation, especially since locally based rafts already run the Siang River. Access to the upper Kameng is by road to the village of Seppa. From there a narrow and eroded dirt road runs along the eastern side of the river, providing access to scattered smallholdings inside the forest. The local inhabitants keep pigs and chickens, draw their water from small side creeks and rely on fuel wood for cooking and heating. It is not clear whether there are any formal land tenure systems, but a number of these houses are recently constructed and it seems likely that this area of forest will come under increasing pressure from new settlement radiating out from the town of Seppa.

Currently, while these forests are inhabited at low density by indigenous peoples who may or may not have formal title to the land, they are as yet of low financial value in modern-day property markets. It would therefore still be feasible to establish these areas as community conservation reserves, with tourism to provide a cash income for the traditional inhabitants. In the absence of such an approach, there is a strong probability that these areas will gradually be occupied, legally or illegally, by settlers who will cut timber and clear forest for farmland. Even if a traditional communal land title prevents such encroachment, the local inhabit-ants are likely to look at ways in which they can obtain cash to buy some of the conveniences of urban civilization; and their easiest options, as in other countries, would be to sell logging rights or hunting concessions. While local residents are not necessarily thinking about either conservation or tourism at this juncture, therefore, and tour operators are not necessarily thinking about either conservation or communities, there might well be an opportunity to link all of these components while the economic, social and environmental contexts are still favourable.

Community Conservation, Annapurna, Nepal

In addition to its publicly owned national parks such as Sagarmatha, Chitwan, Bardia and others, Nepal possesses a number of community conservation areas such as Annapurna, Makalu-Barun, Mustang and Baghmara. Some of these have been quite successful in linking tourism and conservation, others somewhat less so. Perhaps the most heavily studied of these areas (Gurung, 2008; Spiteri and Nepal, 2008) is the Annapurna Conservation Area. The ACA lies on the southern side of Annapurna itself and covers an area of over 7500 km^2. Much of the ACA lies within the region traditionally occupied by the Gurung peoples, and the ACA itself extends from the uninhabited high-altitude mountain ranges to lower-altitude hill spurs and valleys dotted with villages.

From its outset, the Annapurna Conservation Area was established and has been run as an inhabited, multiple-use, community conservation area, not as a national park. The history of its establishment and the key role of particular far-sighted individuals have been detailed by Gurung (2008). The successful establishment and operation of the Annapurna Conservation Area was by no means straightforward, and involved a great deal of effort by its founders and many others. It seems that it was successful because it was able to integrate social and institutional structures, both new and existing, at all levels from individual villages to the national government.

There seem to have been four critical components. The first is that, instead of English-language terms such as parks or conservation, the proposal was phrased as *samranchan*, a local term which had positive connotations in the simple sense of good practices in land management. The second is that the founders were able to gain support from leaders among the village women as well as men, and women's groups then played a critical role in grass roots involvement, including responsible management of income and assets.

The third key component was that, with the approval of the national government, the founders were able to establish an independent trust which had the right to charge fees to tourists entering the conservation area and then to retain and use those fees within the area itself. This trust was originally called the King Mahendra Trust for Nature Conservation, later renamed as the Nepal Trust for Nature Conservation. These arrangements differed from those for the centrally managed national parks, first, in that the tourist entry fees were significantly higher, and, second, in that these fees were retained and spent locally, rather than paid into the central government treasury. The advantages and disadvantages of high or low visitor fees for conservation areas and of local or centralized control of funds have been debated extensively in different countries and circumstances, but in the Annapurna case it certainly does appear that this approach was a key factor in the success of the ACA.

The fourth and final key factor was the establishment of a management agency, the Annapurna Conservation Area Project, which set up the mechanisms to collect visitor fees, to establish priorities and budgets for community projects within individual villages, to maintain equity between different interests and stakeholder groups and to manage the expenditure of cash and also the in-kind contributions to community projects from individual villages. Such organizations have not always been successful, because of either corruption or inadequate management skills, but, in the case of ACAP, it does indeed seem to have played a key role in the operation of the Annapurna Conservation Area.

Within the ACA there are particular treks which are especially well known, such as those to the pass of Jomsom or to Annapurna Base Camp. Along these routes there are well-established commercial tourist facilities, small-scale but numerous. The key components are, first, the guest houses and tea-houses which provide accommodation and food for trekkers; and, second, the guides and porters. Trekkers can travel either independently or with international tour operators such as World Expeditions (2010), as described by Buckley (2006). There are fixed prices for food and accommodation, which reflect the greater time and labour required to operate the higher-altitude establishments which are more remote from road access. When trekking tourism first boomed in this region it produced significant environmental impacts, especially through cutting of montane forests for firewood and timber. Under ACAP's organization these impacts have been reversed, and commercial tourism does now make significant contributions to conservation.

Ecotourism in China's West and East

Zhong Linsheng, Qi Junhui and Ralf Buckley

Modern ecotourism in China originated in the 1980s, though it has far older cultural antecedents (Buckley *et al.*, 2008a; Airey and Chong, 2010). Today, it has become an important component of China's tourism sector, with a strong development momentum. Over the past 20 years or longer, the scale and range of outdoor tourism activities have continued to expand, including forest tourism, birdwatching and wildlife watching, and activities such as bicycle tourism, off-road desert adventures and river rafting (see also Chapter 5).

This has been matched by growth in the number and types of destinations such as forest parks, nature reserves, geological parks, wetland reserves and water parks. As of late 2007, China had established 2531 nature reserves, with a total area of over 1.52 million km^2, or ~15% of the country's land area (China, Ministry for Environmental Protection, 2008). In addition, by late 2008 it had established almost 2300 forest parks, with a total area of 163,000 km^2, i.e. a further 1.6% of the nation's total area. Most forest parks are tourist destinations. In 2008, for example, they received 274 million tourists, bringing RMB 18.7 billion (US$2.7 billion) in direct revenue and generating over RMB 140 billion (US$20 billion) in indirect economic activity. Finally, as of late 2007, China had also established 241 geological parks covering 72,000 km^2, with RMB 9.7 billion (US$1.4 billion) in infrastructure construction. Taken together, these three types of parks thus represent over 17% of China's total land area.

This growth in nature-based and outdoor activities and destination has been driven by national policy. Ecotourism is promoted in China, as elsewhere, as a way to achieve economic development and environmental protection simultaneously. In particular, as in other countries, ecotourism is seen in China as a way for local rural residents to generate income without intensive consumption of natural resources. As elsewhere, however, newly developing tourism economies are under threat in some regions because of conflicting large-scale development in other sectors, including transport infrastructure, hydroelectric dams and mining operations. Different government agencies, at all levels, have different goals and they are not always coordinated. Accordingly, the economic scale and social benefits of ecotourism are of prime political importance for it to contribute effectively to conservation. Here we present three case studies from different regions of China, which illustrate both what can be achieved and what obstacles may be faced. These are: Shangri-La County in Yunnan Province; Jiuzhaigou Nature Reserve in Sichuan Province; and Tianmushan Nature Reserve in Zhejiang Province. These are, of course, not the only examples in China. Chapter 5 describes the operations of a rafting tourism business concerned with conservation of river corridors. WWF China (2008) has also included ecotourism in its Giant Panda conservation programme in the Qinling Mountains in central China.

Shangri-La County lies in Yunnan Province at the southern margin of the Qinghai–Tibet plateau. It is about 11,600 km^2 in area and lies in the hinterland of the Three Parallel Rivers

National Park east of Hengduan Mountain. Formerly known as Zhongdian County, Shangri-La was renamed specifically for tourism marketing, since it is claimed that the area may have provided the inspiration for the fabled place 'Shangri-La' in a popular novel, *The Lost Horizon*, written in 1933 by British author James Hilton. The name has since been adopted in general use as a metaphor for a land of peace, tranquillity and extended youth. Within China, Shangri-La County received an additional marketing boost when it was selected nationally as one of six 'golden century-crossing tourism products'. Xianggelila County, as it is now officially known, has a population of nearly 1.3 million from over a dozen different ethnic groups. The majority are Tibetan, with Han, Naxi and Bai also well represented.

Historically, human populations were relatively sparse and mostly Buddhist, and the area remained largely forested with significant wildlife populations. Around 20 years ago, as in much of western China, there was a boom in logging and lumbering, with widespread and severe soil erosion and losses in forest biodiversity. At that time, 80% of the County's revenue was derived from forestry. The national government took over control of the forests in 1994, with a complete prohibition of logging and hunting from 1998. Surveys of local residents indicate that 97% would like to see an end to 'activities harmful to the environment' (Hong and Zhuo, 2001). Of course, this is a rather poorly defined consideration, and may also be ineffective if the other 3% control the major industries.

In addition to highly scenic mountainous landscapes and some remaining forested areas, the area includes some well-known natural attractions such as Lake Bitahai, the whitewater terraces of Napa Lake, Tiger Leaping Gorge on the Yangtze River and the First Bend of the Chang River at the town of Shigu. There is a wide range of cultural attractions, both modern and historical. There is now a well-developed tourism industry in Shangri-La, growing at around 12% annually. If tourism can successfully stave off large-scale hydroelectric development (McDonald, 2007), encourage reforestation and maintain protected areas, it will indeed make a contribution to conservation.

Western academic views of Shangri-La are recorded by Hillman (2003) and Kolas (2004). The former described the area in terms of 'minorities, myths and modernity', noting that the Zhongdian County government had lobbied for the change of name for many years before the Yunnan State government finally granted permission in December 2001. The latter argued essentially that minority cultures, principally Tibetan, had been 'sacralised', 'ethnicised' and 'exoticised' as a tourist attraction. The area is currently presented to Han domestic tourists as an exotic destination: a tranquil, beautiful and idyllic rural contrast to fast-paced and polluted eastern cities. And, indeed, at the coarsest level, it is. This marketing message, however, ignores factors such as: the influx of immigrants cashing in on commercial tourism opportunities; the environmental impacts of rapid growth in tourism; the social impacts of commodifying minority ethnic cultures for tourism; and the other development pressures affecting the natural environment.

One of the key environmental issues in western China, especially in the area around Shangri-La County, is the continuing pressures by electricity quangos to build cascades of giant hydropower dams along major rivers and smaller hydropower dams on their tributaries. The history and politics of these hydropower dams and their role in national development policies for western China have been examined by Goodman (2004), Yang and Naughton (2004), Magee (2006) and McDonald (2007). In particular, McDonald (2007) conducted a detailed study of hydropower development and its social consequences on the Nu or Salween River, including Chayu County, immediately west of Shangri-La. Chayu and neighbouring counties are part of Nu Prefecture, where only 10% of residents are of Han ethnicity.

McDonald (2007, p. 173) reported that Prefectural government policies are based on 'two pillars and one brand' where the pillars are mining and hydropower development and the brand is World Heritage, relying on the Three Parallel Rivers National Park. She noted that conflicts between tourism based on the World Heritage brand for river corridors and hydropower development, which is flooding those same corridors, do not seem to have been addressed, since different government agencies are involved. She found that, in Gongshan County at least, tourism is more important than dams. In this area as a whole, however, hydropower quangos and the Prefectural government are continuing dam construction despite lack of legal approvals, following the developers' dictum of 'xian zuo, hou shuo' which translates roughly as 'first do, then say' – i.e. just go ahead anyway. The largest proposed dam, for example, would create a reservoir 100 km long, displacing around 20,000 people (Mertha, 2008).

Jiuzhaigou Nature Reserve, the second case study considered here, is a 600 km^2 protected area in Nanping County, Sichuan Province, at around 33°N, 104°E. Its mountainous terrain ranges from 2264 m to 4764 m in elevation, and it is famous for its 108 lakes, linked by dozens of waterfalls. The Reserve was first established in 1978, the first reserve in China declared specifically for the protection of natural landscapes. It became a National Nature Reserve in 1988, a World Heritage area in 1992 and a Biosphere Reserve in 1997. It is named after a 60 km long valley with nine Tibetan villages.

As a national nature reserve, Jiuzhaigou is expected to treat nature conservation as its primary goal. Since the area was already inhabited before the reserve was declared, however, this has required negotiation, compensation and offset projects for the local residents, developed over an extended period. When the reserve was first established, its resident population was relatively small and engaged largely in small-scale subsistence agriculture. As it became popular for tourism, however, it attracted entrepreneurs who built home-stay hotels and other tourist facilities, with significant impacts. In May 2001, therefore, the reserve managers established new regulations requiring that all tourist accommodation must be moved out of the reserve, so as to comply with the policy directive 'sightseeing inside the nature reserve, lodging outside'. To compensate the immigrants who had previously moved into the reserve, the reserve management agency distributed about one million yuan (~US$150,000) per annum from the Jiuzhaigou gate takings.

The Reserve has created more than 600 jobs for local residents, ranging from fire control to forest rangers, ticket agents and tour operators. Tours include hiking, adventure, photographic and cliff sightseeing. The Reserve has also provided new infrastructure including two sewage treatment works, a household garbage collection programme, and an environmental monitoring programme. As a result, residents in the Reserve area have reconverted 64 km^2 of farmland for forest restoration, so that forest cover – albeit mostly secondary – has now returned to 63.5%.

Jiuzhaigou Nature Reserve is described by UNESCO (2010a) and featured in a number of English-language travel guides and travel magazine articles. The *Lonely Planet* guide (Anon., 2010a) says that is an overcrowded mass tourism destination with 20,000 beds in gateway hotels, but that it is so beautiful that you should go anyway. The Wikitravel guide (Anon, 2010b) says, in summary, that Jiuzhai (Nine Villages) Valley is 720 km^2 in area, 460 km north of Changdu, and consists largely of high-altitude limestone karsts. It is famous for over 100 lakes and waterfalls. It was inhabited only by people of Tibetan and Qiang ethnicities until 1972, when it was subject to a wave of intensive logging from 1972 to 1979. It was then declared as a reserve and promoted for tourism. Annual visitation rates grew from 5000 in 1984 to 2.5 million in 2007, with over 12,000 visitors per day in peak seasons. While local residents still live inside the park, it is no longer legal for them to provide accommodation for tourists, who must stay in the gateway town and take day trips into the park. The daily park entry fee is 220 yuan (US$32) plus 90 yuan (US$13) for the shuttle bus. One subsidiary valley, Zaru, has been 'dedicated to ecotourism', which apparently means that tourists can take a 3-day hike along a traditional pilgrimage route around a mountain known as Zha Yi Zha Ga.

Most recently, an article in *National Geographic* by Hoagland (2009) says that visitor numbers have now reached 18,000 per day, with 280 shuttle buses and 80 hotels. Hoagland notes that one area is advertised as '"primeval forest" … which translates as groves which were not levelled by loggers'. He also reports meeting people illegally collecting sacks of medicinal herbs in Zaru Valley, and that snow leopard skins are still openly on sale in a town nearby. The area is marketed as habitat for wild panda, but it is not clear if any of the 20 or so believed present are actually still there. Travel guides refer to a complex of boardwalks, and it appears that these were built to overcome continuing erosion along the tracks from the bus stops to the lake lookout points. According to Li *et al.* (2005), tree roots were suffering damage despite formed trails. According to Shen *et al.* (2008), the large number of tourists in Jiuzhaigou is overwhelming its capacity. In their view, the number of tourists should be reduced and conservation efforts increased. According to Shen *et al.* (2008), the 'scenic area' totals 90 km^2, about one-eighth of the total. Recent descriptions of Zaru Valley thus suggest that, rather than decreasing the number of tourists, the reserve managers are expanding the accessible area.

The third case considered here is Tianmushan Nature Reserve, a much smaller reserve in eastern China. Tianmushan, 'Eye on Heaven Mountain' near Linan in Zhejiang Province, is a famous peak 230 km SW of Shanghai in China's heavily populated eastern seaboard. Tianmushan Nature Reserve is a small but highly biodiverse reserve. It has a total area of 43 km^2, but a core area of only 12 km^2. It is recognized none the less as a Biosphere Reserve (UNESCO, 2010b). A recent analysis by Wang *et al.* (2008) concluded that the reserve is too small for effective conservation management, and that forests of the giant moso bamboo *Phyllostachys pubescens* and Chinese cedar *Cryptomeria* are being degraded.

Tianmushan has a long cultural history, blending Buddhism, Taoism and Confucianism. The Reserve ranges from 300 m to 1556 m elevation, and provides protection for a key area of temperate broadleaf forest (UNESCO, 2010b). It was established as a Forest Reserve in 1958, recognized as a provincial-level nature reserve in 1986 and declared as a UNESCO Biosphere Reserve in 1996. Despite its small area, Tianmushan Nature Reserve supports 2160 species of higher plants, including 35 species which are declared as protected at national level and 37 species which are named for the Tianmu location. Similarly, there are 2274 species of vertebrates, of which 34 are nationally protected and 48 are named for

Tianmu, and over 2000 insect species. The Reserve is thus of considerable importance for conservation, both within China and globally.

Because of its fertile soil and warm temperate to subtropical climate, however, local residents have used Tianmushan for growing fruit and vegetables, cutting firewood, digging up medicinal roots, hunting and grazing livestock. Nine villages are involved. This has led to conflict between local residents, who want access to resources, and the reserve managers, who are concerned to promote conservation and tourism and want to expand the boundaries of the area available. To resolve these conflicts, the reserve managers commenced negotiations with the villages concerned under the principle 'ownership not changed, farmers not moved, unified management, interests shared' (Chu and Xu, 2004). For those parts of the reserve which originally belonged to a farm collective or were leased to individual families, farmers retain the rights to use natural resources. In 1987 a community management committee was established through an initiative of the Linan City local government, in order to 'manage resources jointly', 'protect resources collaboratively' and 'utilize resources considerately' (Feng, 2005). Through this approach it was possible to expand the outer zone of the reserve quite considerably, improving both scenic resources and biodiversity conservation. As part of these arrangements, local residents have gained employment opportunities both in conservation management and in tourism.

Central Asian Grasslands, Mongolia

Mongolia contains 1.3 million km^2 of central Asia's higher altitude grasslands, which also extend to an additional 0.4 million km^2 in neighbouring Inner Mongolia (White et al., 2000; Zhong, 2001). These areas support wildlife such as argali sheep, ibex, bear and sable, and birds such as black stork, Altai snowcock, Baikal teal and barheaded goose. They are also the homelands of ethnic groups such as the Tuvan reindeer herders. Eleven of Mongolia's 38 parks and reserves contain grasslands (Batjargal, 2004), and there are six grassland reserves in Inner Mongolia. About 85% of Mongolia and 35% of Inner Mongolia are grassland. Mongolia's grasslands support almost three million residents, and Inner Mongolia has a total population of over five million. Mongolia receives about 300,000 tourists annually and Inner Mongolia about 800,000. Most of these are business travellers, but Mongolia receives about 40,000 visitors each year from Korea and Japan and 20,000 from North America and Europe. Most of these international tourists arrive in mid- to late summer (Yu and Goulden, 2006). Grasslands, especially as a cultural landscape, are the principal attraction, with various degrees of commodification (Buckley et al., 2008b). Despite various tourism laws and plans (Buckley et al., 2008b), grassland tourism has not always been well managed and has produced environmental impacts additional to those of pastoralism (Wei et al., 1999; Yang and Gan, 2001; Zhong et al., 2005). In the Lake Khovsgol area, however, it appears that international tourism has contributed to maintaining the grassland landscape and culture, including habitat for native plant and animal species.

Grizzly Bears, Kamchatka, Russia

The Kamchatka Peninsula in Far Eastern Russia is an area of considerable conservation significance, notably for brown or grizzly bear. Remaining bear populations, however, are under significant threat from poachers, who shoot and snare bears for the international illegal trade in wildlife body parts, especially gall bladders, which command a high price for certain traditional Asian medical preparations. There are a number of national parks where both the bears and the salmon they feed on are nominally protected. The salmon, however, are systematically poached by organized crime syndicates, which catch spawning female salmon in order to strip and sell salmon roe, considered a delicacy within Russia. It appears that salmon poaching is a lucrative business, and the poaching gangs are thus well funded and equipped, which makes it easy for them to kill bears as a sideline business. Suggestions have been made that senior park officials may historically have been complicit in the poaching business. The politics and practical outcomes of the poaching activities in the parks and attempts to counteract them have been described by Russell and Enns (2002).

Kamchatka is also a significant tourist destination, for both Russians and international visitors. Domestic tourists include self-drive local residents from Petropavlovsk and wealthy tourists on holiday from Moscow and other major Russian cities. Kamchatka's most famous tourist attraction is its volcanoes, but in recent years its bears have also become well known, with a number of companies offering bear-watching tours to Lake Kurilskoye in Yuzhno-Kamchatsky Reserve.

One such tour, operated by Explore Kamchatka, is described in Buckley (2006). From a conservation perspective, the key issue is whether or not this tourism operation makes any net contribution to conservation of the bears. From the brief visit described by Buckley (2006), it was not possible to provide a definitive answer to this question. Increasing the number of international visitors to the area may potentially improve the resources allocated to park management for anti-poaching meas-ures, but there is no guarantee of this. If the poachers are heavily armed and have their own ex-military helicopters, as stated by the park rangers, then they may well ignore both park staff and tourists.

Orang-utan, Borneo

In conservation tourism terms, Borneo is known principally as a place to see orang-utan and other South-East Asian rainforest primates. Borneo is also well known for its birdwatching opportunities and for some spectacular rain-forest plants such as the giant *Rafflesia* flower, but orang-utan is its icon species. Orang-utan can also be seen in some parts of Indonesia, but orang-utan tourism seems to have been developed much more intensively in Malaysia, apparently as a result of its greater political stability and safety.

An extended discussion thread on the *Lonely Planet*® Thorntree® blog site, started and moderated by Wagner (2003–2009), has compared the merits, management, logistics and conservation aspects of national parks and orang-utan tourism enterprises throughout Malaysia and Indonesia. According to this discussion, there are four main reserves in Malaysian Borneo, three of them in Sabah and one in Sarawak. There are at least eight in Kalimantan in Indonesian Borneo and one in Sumatra. Further information on the Malaysian parks is available from National Parks of Malaysia (2010) and the Orangutan Conser-vancy (2010). The Indonesian National Parks mentioned by Wagner (2003–2009) are: Kutai, Gunung Palung, Betung Kerihun, Bukit Baka Bukit Raya, Danau Sentarum, Tanjung Puting, Gunung Leseur, Gunung Niyut and Muara Kaman. Information on these parks is also available from the Indonesian Environmental Conservation Information Center (2010) and National Parks of Indonesia (2010).

In Malaysian Borneo the most popular area is reportedly Kinabatangan Wildlife Sanctuary, with tourism accommodation available at Sukau Rainforest Lodge (2010) or a range of less expensive guest houses. Apparently, how-ever, the main reason that orang-utan sightings are good at Kinabangatan is that there is 'only such a narrow strip of forest left sandwiched between the oil-palm plantations along the river that they just can't hide' (Wagner, 2003–2009, p. 2). Particularly recommended by Thorntree® bloggers is Danum Valley Con-servation Area, cited by Wagner (2003–2009) as 'probably the very best place in Malaysia to see wild orang-utans in pristine habitat'. The forest outside the conservation area itself is logged. The main tourist accommodation in Danum Valley is Borneo Rainforest Lodge (2010). The third reserve in Sabah is Tabin Wildlife Reserve, with tourist accommodation at Tabin Lodge (2010).

In Sarawak the only area with wild orang-utan is Batang Ai National Park (Wagner, 2003–2009). The park seems to be protected as the watershed for Batang Ai Reservoir, a large hydroelectric dam. There is an expensive hotel, the Batang Ai Hilton Longhouse Resort, on the shores of the reservoir 2 hours from the reserve. Upstream from the reservoir is Ulu Ai Longhouse, built in 1996 by Borneo Adventure (2010) as an Iban village guest house in the Nanga Sumpa community, adjacent to Batang Ai National Park and the Lanjak Entimau Wildlife Sanctuary (Basiuk, 2000, cited in Buckley 2003a). According to Borneo

Adventure (2002, cited in Buckley 2003a), the Ulu Ai project was providing economic benefits for the local Iban community and economic incentives to track orang-utan and report poachers.

Orang-utan forest habitat is under severe threat from logging and agricultural clearance, both legal and illegal, and orang-utan are also hunted both by traditional means and by modern poachers. Despite the relatively large scale of orang-utan tourism, it is by no means clear whether the tourism industry has made any significant contribution to conservation of rainforest. In particular, in addition to the uncertain opportunities to see wild orang-utan and other icon species such as proboscis monkeys in national parks, there are a number of establishments which provide opportunities to see captive orang-utan in so-called 'rehabilitation' centres, now largely renamed as viewing centres since it became apparent that rehabilitation was not in fact taking place. These establishments are aimed squarely at the mass tourism market. Some are adjacent to large public protected areas but others have only tiny patches of forest nearby. These centres keep individual orang-utan alive in the same way as zoos, but do not contribute to conservation of wild populations or habitat.

Conclusions

Asia embraces a very wide range of ecosystems, social and economic circumstances, and political systems. The contexts for conservation tourism are equally varied. Countries such as China and India, Russia and Indonesia contain both densely settled and sparsely inhabited areas, and both heavily visited national parks and remote and rarely visited wilderness areas. All these nations have spectacular scenery and rare plants and animals well worth conserving. In both China and India, there is an enormous range of ecosystems, from Himalayan peaks to lowland tropical forests and mangroves, from arid deserts to humid rainforests. Both these countries now have large wealthy middle classes, who support correspondingly large domestic tourism industries, including visits to national parks.

The countries of South-east Asia and the larger Pacific Island nations such as Papua New Guinea, Fiji, Samoa and the Solomon Islands support dense forest with high biodiversity and endemicity, under threat from logging. In many of these countries, traditional landownership is still predominant and greatly influences both conservation and tourism. In India and Nepal, there are tiger-watching lodges comparable to the lodges on the private game reserves of sub-Saharan Africa, and in Borneo there are orang-utan lodges comparable to the rainforest ecolodges of South and Central America, though neither have yet developed to the same degree. There are, however, many more new lodges and exploratory nature and adventure tourism ventures throughout Asia, not described in this chapter, which have started up recently and whose potential contributions to conservation are as yet unstudied.

7 Oceania

Clare Morrison and Ralf Buckley

Rendova, Solomon Islands

Introduction

Many islands are significant conservation areas for a number of endemic species, and many are also major tourist destinations. There is an entire subsector of the tourism industry based around island beach resorts, especially in the tropics and subtropics. The majority of such islands worldwide are in the Pacific and Indian oceans. The South Pacific, in particular, has enjoyed a reputation as a tourist destination ever since the Rodgers and Hammerstein Broadway musical of that name shortly after the Second World War. This chapter therefore focuses on the South Pacific, which also forms something of a bridge between mainland Asia (Chapter 6) and Australia (Chapter 8).

The South Pacific region has 22 small island countries and territories. These countries have approximately five million people, living on 550,000 km^2 of land spread over 29 million km^2 of the Pacific Ocean. The great majority of people live in relatively small and isolated coastal or rural village communities, and remain closely reliant on their local natural resources for subsistence and economic development. The countries in the region range in size from Papua New Guinea, which at 452,860 km^2 is almost twice the size of the United Kingdom, down to Nauru which is the world's third smallest country at 22.5 km^2. Even the smaller countries, however, control large marine Exclusive Economic Zones (EEZ). This chapter focuses principally on Fiji, the Solomon Islands and the Cook Islands. Examples from Samoa were presented by Buckley (2003a).

The tropical islands of the South Pacific have particularly high proportions of endemic species, as a result of an extended period of isolated evolution (Keast and Miller, 1996). Terrestrial biodiversity in the South Pacific is highly variable and generally decreases from west to east, reflecting both island size and the distance from Melanesian biodiversity dispersal centres (Flannery, 1996; Keast, 1996; Keast and Miller, 1996). Despite this global conservation significance, however, only 0.15% of total land area and less than 20% of known ecosystems are in designated protected areas, and few of these areas are well managed

(Chape et al., 2003). With rapidly growing populations and related pressures, the terrestrial biodiversity of the South Pacific islands is among the most threatened in the world. The region also has vast and complex marine ecosystems, including the world's most extensive coral reef systems. These are essential in maintaining the subsistence lifestyles of most Pacific Island peoples.

With only a few people as custodians, the region faces great difficulties in protecting its fragile environment from internal and external influences. This problem is exacerbated by poor public and political awareness of the conservation principles and practices. While environmentally sound development practices are widely expressed and touted, there is a distinct lack of funding, staffing and institutional frameworks allocated to plan and administer development and conservation programmes (Baines et al., 2002). Alternative Income Generating Activities (AIGAs), particularly tourism, are increasingly promoted and utilized by Pacific Island governments as a means of alleviating poverty and conserving valuable natural resources (Connor et al., 1996).

Tourism is one of the highest income generating activities in parts of the South Pacific, accounting for as much as 80% of GDP in some countries (Table 7.1). In other countries, however, the economic scale of tourism is still small in comparison with agriculture, fisheries, mining and other extractive industries. Historically, tourism in the South Pacific has been based around coastal areas, promoting beaches, diving, fishing, sailing and local cultures. Only recently have alternative tourism activities based in inland areas, such as white-water rafting, birdwatching and hiking, been promoted as tourism activities in the region. Even more recent has been the promotion of ecotourism. Ecotourism is still in its infancy in many South Pacific countries, and is based largely on guided tours of reserve areas (both marine and terrestrial) or local village stays.

Despite the great potential for sustainable tourism in the South Pacific region, many past projects have proved unsustainable in practice. Once external start-up funding was exhausted, many projects suffered financial mismanagement, poor marketing, lack of facilities

Table 7.1. Visitor numbers, GDP and tourism in the South Pacific.

Country	Visitors per year	GDP, US$ million	Tourism as % GDP	Tourism GDP, US$ million
Cook Islands	101,000	183	60	101
Fiji	580,000	3,590	18	646
French Polynesia	196,500	6,100	80	4,880
Kiribati	3,380	137	2	3
New Caledonia	103,500	3,300	2	66
Niue	4,748	10	~4	0.4
Papua New Guinea	104,100	8,092	<4	324
Samoa	122,163	537	–	–
Solomon Islands	13,748	473	2	9.5
Tonga	41,000	258	(12)[a]	31
Tuvalu	1,130	15	~7	1
Vanuatu	90,657	573	~10	57

All data are for 2008 except for Cook Islands (2009) and Tuvalu and Papua New Guinea (2007). –, data unavailable. GDP data are from IMF (2008).
[a]GDP for Tonga is for the whole commerce sector including tourism.

maintenance, disputes over distribution of profits and failure to include local landowning communities adequately (Baines *et al.*, 2002). This is particularly important in the South Pacific, where the traditional owners still exercise full control over and access to their land and reefs.

A number of individual projects, however, do indeed seem to have been successful to date. Twelve of these are summarized in Table 7.2 and described in detail below. Except for one, all of these projects are still operational as of March 2010.

Takitumu Conservation Area, Rarotonga, Cook Islands

The Takitumu Conservation Area (TCA) is a private rainforest reserve managed by three landowning clans, the Kainuku, Karika and Manavaroa families. It was established in 1997 by the Cook Islands Government, South Pacific Biodiversity Conservation Program (SPBCP) and the local community, in order to preserve the endangered Rarotonga flycatcher or kakerori, *Pomarea dimidiata*. It built on a pre-existing government programme, the Kakerori Recovery Project, initiated in 1987. The TCA was funded by the SPBCP initially, with follow-up funding from the Cook Island Environmental Protection Fund and the New

Zealand Overseas Development Agency (SPREP, 2003).

The TCA lies approximately 800 m from the main coastal road on Rarotonga and extends over 1.55 km^2 of forested ridges and valleys. It includes the headwaters of two major streams and basins of a third. Located on the wettest part of the island, the conservation area provides most of Rarotonga's drinking water. It also contains the only protected population of the Rarotonga flycatcher. In 1989 only 29 individuals remained in the wild. Since the establishment of the TCA and subsequent conservation actions, the numbers had recovered to 180 individuals by 1999 (Sherley, 1999; Read, 2002). Of the 17 Conservation Areas funded by the SPBCP, the TCA is one of only two projects that were considered a success based on conservation achievements and sustainability of the project (Hunnam, 2002). The main tourism activity is a nature walk and birdwatching venture, which started in 1998. Income is also derived from a souvenir shop and an 'adopt-a-nest' programme. The TCA's success has prompted active interest from other places in the Cook Islands. Residents of both Mangaia and Mitiaro Islands have visited the TCA to get ideas for protecting their own endemic species, and the Cook Islands Tourism Department frequently uses the TCA nature walk and birdwatching business as a case study in its ecotourism workshops.

Table 7.2. Conservation tourism projects, South Pacific.

Country	Name	Principal stakeholders	Start date	Funds from[a]	References, data sources
Cook Islands	**Takitumu, Rarotonga** Community nature reserve, endangered Rarotonga flycatcher.	Community	1996	SPBCP NZODA	Sherley, 1999; Read, 2002; Buckley, 2003a; CM, pers. obs.
Fiji	**Bouma** Community conservation area.	Community	1990	NTF, NZAID	SPREP, 2003; National Trust Fiji, 2010; CM, pers. obs.
Fiji	**Waisali** Remnant rainforest, endemic birds and frogs.	NGO and Community	1996	NTF, NZAID	National Trust Fiji, 2010; I. Rounds, personal communication; CM, pers. obs.
Fiji	**Upper Navua** Tourism-funded conservation area. Leased from landowners.	Private and Community	1998	USP, WWF, CI, BI	Bricker, 2001, 2003; Rivers Fiji, 2010; CM, pers. obs.
Fiji	**National Park, Sigatoka** Coastal dune vegetation, archaeological sites.	Government and NGO	1989	Fiji Government	National Trust Fiji, 2010; I. Rounds, personal communication; CM, pers. obs.
Fiji	**Beqa Shark Corridor, Fiji** Marine reserve set up by dive tour operator. Now managed by local communities.	Private and Community	2002	Private	Brunnschweiler and Earle, 2006; Brunnschweiler, 2010; CM, pers. obs.
Solomon Islands	**Tetepare** Integrated land and marine conservation area.	Community and NGO	2002	EU, TDA, CI, WWF, NZAID, SICCP, AMNH	Read and Moseby, 2006; Filardi and Pikacha, 2007; Farrington, 2009; Pikacha, 2009; Tetepare, 2010; CM, pers. obs.
Solomon Islands	**Kolombangara** Conservation area run by NGO.	NGO and Community	2008	AMNH, SICCP, KFP	Filardi and Pikacha, 2007; CM, pers. obs.
Solomon Islands	**Gatokae** Small lodge, runs tours with local village guides.	Private	2002	–	Wilderness Lodge, 2010
Solomon Islands	**Bauro** Highland rainforest. Programme collapsed in 2008.	NGO and Community	1997	CI	Russell and Stabile, 2003; Pikacha, 2007; Conservation International, 2010; CM, pers. obs.

Continued

Table 7.2. Continued.

Country	Name	Principal stakeholders	Start date	Funds from[a]	References, data sources
New Caledonia	**Blue River** Rainforest, endemic Kagu bird (~600–800 individuals)	Government	1980	PSNC, SPC, DRN, DDRP	Letocart and Salas, 1997; Ekstrom *et al.*, 2002; New Caledonia Southern Province, 2010; New Caledonia Tourism, 2010
French Polynesia	**Tiahura MPA** Government-run marine protected area with private hotels, dolphin centre and stingray feeding tours, and NGO sea turtle clinic.	Government and Private	2004	French Polynesia	Petit, 2008; CM, pers. obs.

[a]Abbreviations used: AMNH, American Museum of Natural History. BI, Birdlife International. CI, Conservation International. DDRP, Direction du Développement Rural et de la Pêche. DRN, Direction de Ressources Naturelles. EU, European Union. KFP, Kolombangara Forest Products Ltd. NTF, National Trust of Fiji. NZAID, New Zealand International Aid and Development Agency. NZODA, New Zealand Overseas Development Agency. PSNC, Province Sud de Nouvelle-Calédonie. SICCP, Solomon Islands Community Conservation Program. SPBCP, South Pacific Biodiversity Conservation Program. SPC, South Pacific Commission. SPREP, South Pacific Regional Environmental Program. TDA, Tetepare Descendants Association. USP, University of the South Pacific. WWF, World Wildlife Fund for Nature. CM, pers. obs., Clare Morrison, personal observation.

Bouma National Heritage Park, Taveuni, Fiji

Taveuni is the third largest island in Fiji and is known as the Garden Island. It supports large tracts of relatively undisturbed tropical rainforest and a number of endemic and endangered plant and animal species. One key reason for this is the absence of mongoose, an introduced predator throughout many of the Pacific Island nations. Taveuni is the second- largest mongoose-free island in the Pacific, after Kauai in Hawaii (Morley, 2004). Taveuni has 22 regional endemic bird species, including the orange dove *Chrysoenas victor* and the silktail *Lamprolia victoriae* (Watling, 2001). Endemic plant species include the iconic tagimaucia flower, *Medinilla waterhousei*. Like forests throughout the Pacific, Taveuni has been threatened by logging, and about half of Taveuni is covered by logging concessions (Ceballos-Lascurain, 1996). In 1988 three *mataqali*, the landowning clans within Fijian traditional society, became concerned over the likelihood of logging in eastern Taveuni. In 1990 these *mataqali*, from the Vanua Bouma lineage, established a reserve, Bouma Forest Park, in conjunction with the Native Lands Trust Board, Fijian Affairs Board and National Trust of Fiji, with funding from NZAID (SPREP, 2003). Later renamed Bouma National Heritage Park, the area has grown to 150 km^2 in area, almost a third of Taveuni. It also includes 0.27 km^2 of coastline and reefs.

Areas and activities added include the Tavoro Waterfalls and Tavoro Forest Park in 1991 (Buckley, 2003a), the Lavena Coastal Walk and Lodge (2010) in 1993, the Waitabu Marine Park in 1998 and most recently the Lekutu Forest Hike. Tourist activities available include hiking, swimming and birdwatching. The waterfalls are also used as a site for weddings. Local residents in villages around the park work as tour guides, park managers and lodge staff and the project seems to have been successful in using tourism to conserve a biologically important area against imminent threats from logging.

Waisali Forest Reserve, Vanua Levu, Fiji

Waisali Forest Reserve is a small community conservation area in Fiji's second largest island of Vanua Levu. The Reserve protects 1.3 km^2 of forest, including a dense patch of Fijian kauri, *Podocarpus vitiensis*, known locally as *dakua salusalu*. Despite its small size, Waisali Forest Reserve contains about 30 species of orchid, some of them endemic (Tuiwawa, 2004); several endemic frog and reptile species; and 21 bird species, including at least four endemic. The bird fauna represents 40% of Fiji's breeding land birds (Tuiwawa, 2004) and includes the orange dove, red shining parrot, collared lory and orange-breasted myzomela. The Reserve also contains mainland Fiji's only protected population of the endangered Fiji ground frog, *Platymantis vitanus*, and the largest known population of the endemic Fiji tree frog, *Platymantis vitiensis* (Morrison *et al.*, 2004). Waisali Forest Reserve is owned by the Waisali community and operated by the National Trust of Fiji. Most visitors are from beach resorts in the nearby town of Savusavu. The main activities are self-guided hiking and birdwatching and guided rainforest walks. Visitors are charged an entry fee of around US$15 per person, with revenue used to pay lease fees, ranger salaries and maintenance costs. Larger infrastructure costs have been funded by NZAID. Waisali villagers are employed as rangers and park maintenance crews.

Upper Navua Conservation Area, Fiji

The Upper Navua Conservation Area is a corridor along a 17 km stretch of the Navua River in the southern hinterland of Viti Levu, Fiji. It was established in 1998 in conjunction with local landowning clans or *mataqali* and the Native Land Trust Board, as an initiative by a white-water rafting company, Rivers Fiji (2010). The company and its operations have been described extensively in the academic literature by one of its founders (Bricker, 2001, 2003). It negotiated a management plan for the conservation area which protects it from logging or gravel extraction in return for lease payments, user fees and employment opportunities for local residents. In 2006, with assistance from NGOs and the University of the South Pacific, the Upper Navua Conservation Area became Fiji's first Ramsar site. Overall, Rivers Fiji does indeed seem to have been successful in conserving a section of river and surrounding forest from logging and local extractive industries, using tourism to supply funding. This success relied heavily on the commitment of the company's founders to extended negotiation with local landowners. Initially this was one of the commercial keys to establishing the tourism business, since it gave the company exclusive access and protected its resource. Ultimately, however, the founders have quite justly gained more fame for their achievements in conservation.

Sigatoka Sand Dunes, Fiji

Sigatoka Sand Dunes National Park, 6.5 km^2 in area, was established in 1989 to protect archaeological sites (Anderson et al., 2006). It is managed by the National Trust of Fiji and was the first national park in the country. It supports a number of endemic coastal plant species (Kirkpatrick and Hassall, 1981). It also supports 22 bird species, eight of them endemic to Fiji. These include the Fiji bush warbler, Fiji goshawk and orange-breasted myzomela. The National Trust of Fiji funds the reserve by charging entry fees of around US$5 per person. There are self-guided tracks and a visitors' centre. Tours of the park are promoted by local resorts.

Shark Corridor, Beqa, Fiji

The Shark Corridor is a community-owned shark reserve along 40 km of the southern coastline of Viti Levu, Fiji, funded by private dive tourism operations. It was initiated by Beqa Adventure Divers (2010) at a site called Shark Fin Reef, which was well-known to shark diving enthusiasts. The company reached an agreement with two villages, Waniyabia and Galoa, which owned traditional rights to the reef. The villages agreed not to fish on parts of the reef and granted the dive tour company

exclusive access rights, in return for a daily levy of $US10 collected from each diver. In 2004, this agreement was formalized by the Fiji Ministry of Fisheries to establish the Shark Reef Marine Reserve. In 2007, a third village joined the agreement. As well as giving up fishing rights within the marine reserve, the villages banned shark fishing throughout their entire *qoliqoli*, the areas where they maintain customary control over fishing (Brunnschweiler, 2010). This produced an extended shark protection area, the Shark Corridor.

A survey of the Shark Reef Marine Reserve (300 × 350 m) in 2004 recorded 267 fish species, including eight species of shark. A 2008 survey reported over 400 species, high by Pacific standards for such a small reef (Brunnschweiler and Earle, 2006; Brunnschweiler, 2010). The Shark Reserve and Corridor provide an example of conservation initiated by a private tourism operator, funded by tourism and successfully involving multiple local communities in an area where marine rights are finely subdivided. The tourism levies paid to the villages totalled US$58,000 from 2004 to 2008 inclusive, and are predicted to rise to around US$100,000 over the 5-year period from 2009 onwards (Brunnschweiler, 2010). In addition, the no-fishing area itself is relatively small, and fish production outside the no-take zone has increased. The principal obstacle has been illegal fishing by communities outside the three involved in the agreement, especially targeting the larger fish. To overcome this, in 2004 Beqa Adventure Divers sponsored the training of 12 Reef Wardens, who have police powers from the Fisheries Department to monitor and halt illegal activities.

Tetepare, Solomon Islands

Tetepare is a 120 km^2 forested island in the New Georgia group in the western province of the Solomon Islands. A total of 73 bird, 24 reptile, four frog and 13 mammal species are recorded from the island, including a number of rare and endemic species (Read and Moseby, 2006). The critically endangered leatherback and hawksbill turtles and the endangered green turtle nest on Tetepare's volcanic black sand beaches. Its seagrass meadows support dugong and crocodile, and its coral reefs support a particularly high diversity of fish species (Filardi and Pikacha, 2007; Farrington, 2009).

When Tetepare was threatened by logging in 2001, Tetepare islanders and their descendants, now living across the entire Western Province, established the Tetepare Descendants Association (2010) to convert the entire island to a community conservation area, including marine as well as terrestrial ecosystems. The 13 km long Tetepare Marine Protected Area was established in 2003. The reserve is supported by the European Union's Sustainable Forestry Conservation Project, the World Wide Fund for Nature and Australian Volunteers International. The Tetepare Descendants Association (2010) operates a five-room guest house, the Tetepare Ecolodge, built in 2002 with EU funding. The lodge offers forest hikes by day and night, bird- and turtle-watching trips, canoeing and boat trips and snorkelling in the lagoon. Rates are around US$45 per person per night including meals and there is a one-time reserve entry fee, known as a *kastom* fee, of around US$6 per person. Transfers and boat trips cost more because of the cost of fuel.

The Tetepare Descendants Association employs 12 rangers to run conservation programmes, and 30 casual staff at the lodge (Farrington, 2009; Pikacha, 2009). The lodge also purchases fruit and vegetables locally. Overall, the programme seems to have been successful in using tourism to conserve Tetepare's forest and turtles. A major factor, however, was that the Tetepare islanders and descendants were opposed to logging.

number of ecological research projects have used this trail (Burslem *et al.*, 1998) and there is a campsite known as Professors Camp at 1050 m elevation. The Kolombangara Reserve, 300 km^2 in area, was established in 2008 as a community-owned reserve, through an initiative of the American Museum of Natural History. It appears that both Conservation International and the World Wide Fund for Nature have also been involved to some degree, though neither has active Web links to this project as of March 2010. The Reserve is variously described as 'Coast to Cloud Forest' or 'Reef to Ridgeline'. Establishment was also supported by a local NGO and a local logging company with Forestry Stewardship Council certification. According to blogs on the *Lonely Planet®* Thorntree® website in late 2009, tourists hiking the trail are required to pay an entry fee of about US$25 per person and hire a local guide and porter at about US$30 per day each. The hike normally takes 2 days, camping overnight at Professors Camp, which is 2 km from the summit of Mt Rano. Additional lease payments to local communities have apparently been made by the partners mentioned above. There is now a new accommodation facility, Imbu Rano Lodge (2010) at the road head at 380 m elevation, immediately outside the reserve. It has capacity for up to 14 people, and seems to have been built largely to support research and educational groups. It is also open for tourists at around $US120 per night including meals. This is a very high rate relative to other comparable accommodation in the area.

Kolombangara, Solomon Islands

Kolombangara is a volcanic island near the north-western end of the Solomon Islands chain. It is relatively accessible for tourism, an hour by boat from the town of Gizo, which is accessible by air from the capital at Honiara. The island has been subject to logging at lower elevation, but montane cloud forests from 400 to 1700 m elevation are relatively intact. There are a number of logging roads and tracks, and also a well-established trail which runs 15 km from the coastal village of Iriri to Mt Rano, the highest point on the rim of the volcano. A

Gatokae, Solomon Islands

Gatokae, Gatukai or Nggatokae is a small island at the eastern end of the New Georgia group in the Western Province of the Solomon Islands, adjacent to the larger island of Vangunu. There is a small private lodge, the Wilderness Lodge (2010) in Peava village on the eastern side of the island, with two guest rooms which can accommodate up to six people each. The lodge offers fishing, snorkelling and rainforest hikes. It has partnerships with Conservation International, the American Museum of Natural History and various NGOs and university research groups as well as local communities, and provides some income for the villagers of Peava and Biche. According to its website, it was established in order to contribute to local conservation efforts around Marovo Lagoon.

Bauro Highlands, Makira, Solomon Islands

Makira Island, also known as San Cristobal, lies at the south-eastern end of the main chain of the Solomon Islands. Separated by a deep ocean channel from the other islands of the archipelago, Makira supports 12 locally endemic bird species and a number of endemic plants. As elsewhere in the Pacific, the Solomon Islands have been subject to extensive logging with little control. In 1995, a consortium of NGOs established a 630 km^2 community conservation area in the central highlands of Makira, in an area known as Bauro. The members of the consortium were Conservation International (2010), a development NGO known as the Solomon Islands Development Trust and a small former New Zealand NGO known as the Maruia Society. The consortium received a grant of US$347,000 from USAID via an organization known as the Biodiversity Conservation Network, which ceased operations in 1999 (World Wide Fund for Nature, 2010). It apparently used these funds to negotiate with villages inside the conservation area regarding the area's boundary and possible commercial enterprises. The main enterprise was a 2- to 3-day tourist trek along a forest trail (Russell and Stabile, 2003). Despite winning an award in 1998 and establishing a myspace® site in 2007, it appears that this trek never became a commercially viable enterprise. The conservation area was subsidized by Conservation International and collapsed when funding ended in 2008. Its future is now uncertain.

Blue River Provincial Park, New Caledonia

Also known as le Parc Provincial de la Rivière Bleue, this is a 90 km^2 rainforest reserve established in 1980 by the government of the Province Sud de Nouvelle-Calédonie. It supports a high diversity of rainforest plants, but is best known for the only protected population of the endemic, endangered and flightless kagu bird, *Rhynochetos jubatus*, national emblem of New Caledonia. This species is highly susceptible to attack by feral dogs and other introduced predators, so the reserve runs a feral animal control programme as well as a kagu breeding programme. In consequence, Blue River Provincial Park protects around 600–800 individual kagu birds, the largest population in the country and hence the world (Letocart and Salas, 1997). It also provides habitat for the crow honeyeater *Cymnomyza ambryana*, listed as critically endangered, and for the horned parakeet *Eunymphicus cornutus*, listed as vulnerable (Ekstrom *et al.*, 2002). The park is run by the provincial government, which collects revenue from entry fees (~US$10), nature tours and a visitor centre. Visitors take part in activities such as forest hikes, birdwatching and river kayaking. There is no publicly available information on the proportion of the park's operating budget covered by tourist revenue. The park also receives park operating funds directly from the provincial government. Kagu conservation programmes are funded by the provincial government, the national government and the South Pacific Commission.

Tiahura Marine Protected Area, French Polynesia

French Polynesia has one of the world's largest marine territories, and its tropical islands and lagoons attract thousands of tourists every year. The Tiahura Marine Protected Area (TMPA) is a 2.5 km^2 marine reserve on the north-west of Moorea Island. It is one of eight MPAs established in 2004 by the French Polynesian Government. One of the primary reasons for its establishment was to protect stingray populations which support the local tourism industry. Stingray feeding at Tiahura began in 1994 and currently involves at least ten tour operators and around 60,000 visitors annually. The TMPA is also host to the Moorea Dolphin Center, a private tourism business that allows visitors to interact with captive dolphins housed in the TMPA. The Dolphin Center funds 50% of the work conducted by a local non-profit marine conservation organization known as Te mana o te moana, which runs a clinic to treat and re-release sick and wounded turtles. It also runs education progammes on sea turtles. Since the Tiahura MPA was established, the abundance and biomass of marine life within the TMPA have increased significantly (de Loma *et al.*, 2008).

General Conclusions

Within the Pacific region, customary resource tenure systems prevail and must be considered in the management of resources and conservation (Reti, 2003). Any sustainable development projects, including tourism, must integrate these resource tenure systems and involve local communities at all levels if they are to be successful and sustainable in the long term. This is particularly important in developing or cultivating a sense of ownership by the communities. Most of the unsuccessful community-based projects in the Pacific pay inadequate attention to the social foundation needed for community-based management of development and conservation (Baines *et al.*, 2002). This foundation needs to be clearly understood and incorporated in order to develop and maintain truly sustainable tourism projects. The failure to clearly establish the long-term commitment from landowners and other stakeholders, their capacity to follow through with the project and their capacity building needs is also common to unsuccessful projects. In addition, there is a perceived preoccupation with biodiversity over the subsistence needs of the community (where local communities are totally excluded from an area

open to tourism activities) as well as the pressure to produce quick financial benefits.

Keeping the focus on conservation is important but, even in the best of circumstances, ecotourism is only a partial solution to defining the balance between conservation and development in the South Pacific (Baines *et al.*, 2002). A common mistake made is to define ecotourism potential based on biodiversity values without adequate consideration of the market prospects for each site or project. Conservation areas in the Pacific need a range of viable activities and enterprises, strongly supported at both the community and national levels. Communities need appropriate consultation, policies, markets for their products and links to like-minded organizations to fulfil their roles in sustainable projects.

The case study projects described in this chapter (with the exception of the Bauro Highlands Reserve) have been successful in the short to medium term primarily due to the commitment and communication between the different stakeholders involved, adequate involvement and consultation of the local communities, local capacity building in the areas of project management and finances, good marketing strategies, transparent distribution of profits and the support of national and international governments and conservation organizations.

Acknowledgements

We thank the following people for sharing their knowledge of the role of tourism in conservation in South Pacific countries and for details of the successful case study projects: Joseph Brider (Cook Islands), Isaac Rounds (Fiji), Julien Grignon (French Polynesia) and Patrick Pikacha (Solomon Islands).

8 Australia

Kimberley, Australia

Introduction

The interactions between tourism and conservation in Australia have been principally political, and at times highly controversial. Despite Australia's highly distinctive wildlife, there have as yet been very few attempts to emulate the African model of private conservation reserves funded through wildlife tourism. Likely reasons for this are outlined later. There are a small number of private reserves, and there are various government programmes intended to provide incentives for private conservation, but neither of these is linked closely to tourism. There is a small farm tourism sector which provides income for the rural landholders concerned, but which is only weakly linked to conservation. There is a well-established but complex system of protected areas nationwide, and many of these areas are managed and used for recreation as well as conservation, and serve as major attractions for both domestic and international tourists.

A wide variety of small-scale commercial tourism businesses operate tours inside these public parks which are broadly in line with the activities permitted for private visitors. The flow of visitors to public protected areas provides opportunities for commercial tourist accommodation, and there are many successful privately owned lodges on private land immediately adjacent to parks, or in some cases on enclaves within the parks themselves. Tourist accommodation in many small regional townships also relies heavily on self-drive tourists visiting nearby national parks. In a few national parks, there is fixed-site tourist accommodation on public land inside the parks themselves, but this is relatively rare. There is continuing pressure from the large-scale tourism property development sector to permit further such construction, but strong public opposition to this approach even where it has been embraced by the parks management agencies. Indeed, this public opposition extends to proposals by the parks agencies themselves.

Australia is a federated nation, and the majority of national parks are run by state government parks agencies. While there are informal coordinating mechanisms between these agencies, each is subject to the political directions and budget constraints of the particular state governments concerned. These governments compete against each other to attract tourism, and at times this competition can also involve national parks.

In a number of states there has also been an extended debate over the conservation values and management of publicly owned forest lands, with some areas being transferred to the parks agencies, albeit often after being logged first. The potential for regional tourism development has been a significant political argument for a number of these transfers. In the best-known example, the Wet Tropics of Queensland World Heritage Area, the successful conservation of an area formerly allocated to logging did indeed generate a regional tourism industry with annual income many times that of the former timber industry. In some parts of Australia, particularly the north, west and centre, there are also large areas allocated as Aboriginal reserves, where the interplay between tourism and conservation is heavily mediated by political issues associated with indigenous community development.

Public Park System

Australia has a three-tier system of government: federal, state and local. As a legacy of its colonial period, Australia has eight independently governed states and territories, namely Western Australia (WA), the Northern Territory (NT), South Australia (SA), Queensland (Qld), New South Wales (NSW), Victoria (Vic), Tasmania (Tas) and the Australian Capital Territory (ACT). The ACT was until recently governed directly by the federal government, but became an independent territory in the 1990s. There are also small areas within mainland Australia, and larger external territories such as the Australian Antarctic Territory, which are governed directly by the federal government. The rights and responsibilities of the state and federal governments respectively are defined in the Australian Constitution, which is similar in many ways to those of the USA and Canada, but different in some vital particulars.

Broadly, most powers relating to land tenure, land planning and land management fall within the role of the state and territory governments. This includes protected area management as well as primary industries such as agriculture, forestry, fisheries and mining. The federal government has strong constitutional powers in other areas, such as commerce and corporations. From a strictly legal perspective, it could use these powers in order to exercise indirect control over many activities currently regulated by the states. It does not do so in practice, however, because there is a strong political legacy which supports self-determination by the individual states and territories in these domains. Since the same individual citizens vote in both state and federal elections, a federal government which was perceived as overriding states' rights would be unlikely to survive subsequent elections unless it was seen as having a popular mandate for the particular reform concerned. The state and territory governments originally had the power to raise individual and corporate income taxes and excises, but they jointly ceded these powers to the federal government during the federation process, though they did retain control over certain other forms of taxation. In practice, therefore, the federal government exercises power either in areas where it has constitutionally allocated responsibilities, or in areas where large-scale federal funding is critical and can be provided with conditions attached.

From the particular perspective of tourism and conservation, the federal government is commonly involved in four main ways. It funds Tourism Australia, which is the principal international marketing body for the Australian tourism industry, and also compiles broad-scale statistical data on Australian tourism. At times, it prepares policy documents and funds small-scale grant programmes such as those associated with the former National Ecotourism Strategy (Fennell et al., 2001). It manages some areas of land directly, and others through joint management agreements with state governments or Aboriginal land councils. Perhaps most importantly, under the External Affairs power in the Australian Constitution, it is responsible for the effective implementation of international treaties and conventions, most notably the World Heritage Convention but also the UN Convention on Biological Diversity,

the Ramsar Convention and the Convention on International Trade in Endangered Species (CITES).

World Heritage

A High Court case in 1983, the Franklin Dam case, established that the External Affairs power enables the federal government to override state governments where the latter take actions which endanger World Heritage values. This power has been relied upon in a number of cases involving proposed large-scale developments in tourism, as well as other sectors, in or immediately adjacent to World Heritage Areas (Buckley, 2007b). The establishment and growth of the reef and rainforest tourism industry in northern Queensland has only been possible because the federal government used its powers related to World Heritage in order to halt rainforest logging in the Wet Tropics of Queensland World Heritage Area and restrict industrial fisheries within the Great Barrier Reef Marine Park. The federal government also exercised these powers to place conditions on development consent for a large-scale coastal resort–residential development at Hinchinbrook Harbour, in a narrow corridor between two World Heritage Areas (Buckley, 2009d).

More recently, the federal government's powers in relation to World Heritage have been called upon in relation to three tourism developments in the subtropical rainforest national parks of southern Queensland. These parks form part of the Gondwana Rainforests World Heritage Area, formerly known as the Central Eastern Rainforest Reserves Australia World Heritage Area. In one case, a local developer proposed the construction of a cableway through a section of Springbrook National Park, with unavoidable impacts on World Heritage Areas. Technically, this development did not proceed because it failed to gain consent from the Queensland State Government; but the political reality was that the State Government's decision was almost certainly influenced strongly by the knowledge that the federal government had both the ability and the intention to withhold consent, even if the state government were to grant it. This case is described in more detail by Buckley (2009d).

The second case involved a proposal by the Queensland Government to link and upgrade a number of actual and potential hiking routes within and near the same area, to create a so-called South-east Queensland Great Walk. The key political issue in that case was that parts of the proposed walk were in fact within the very northernmost part of the adjacent state of New South Wales, though accessed from the Queensland side. Concerns were expressed over the potential environmental impacts of the projected increase in visitor numbers in an area which was zoned as wilderness and intended to experience only very low visitation. In addition, the NSW Government was concerned over potential liability associated with proposed upgrades to tracks and lookouts in the NSW portion of the track. Following consultation, the Great Walk did proceed, but with no additional works in the NSW section. In practice it appears that the 'Great Walk' designation has brought very few additional visitors to these hiking trails, either new or pre-existing, so the issue has not proved critical. Use of sections of track for cross-country races, orienteering and multi-sport challenge events has far higher environmental impacts.

The third case involved an enclave of private land inside a National Park and World Heritage Area, part of the O'Reilly's Rainforest Resort (Buckley, 2003a, pp. 102–103) in the Green Mountains section of Lamington National Park. The O'Reilly family were pioneers in this area, and their farm pre-dated the National Park. Since the park was declared, they have run a highly successful tourist lodge, in addition to small-scale farming. The lodge had gone through a number of previous expansions, each successively more upmarket, but all within the same immediate physical area and all operated on a night-by-night hotel-style basis. This latest expansion, the 'Mountain Bowers' development, is a significant departure from that model (Buckley, 2009d). It is in a different and larger section of the privately owned enclave. It also has a much more complicated ownership structure, effectively a strata-titled (condominium-style) timeshare residential development, with the lodge as managing agent for individual owners who want to rent their properties out as short-term holiday accommodation. The individual houses were sold off the plan to raise the capital for construction, and the location inside a World Heritage Area featured very heavily in advertising materials. The new development is close to a creek which provides habitat for rare frog species, and concerns were expressed over the likelihood of increased roadkill from additional traffic along the access road, which runs through the World Heritage Area. The development was approved despite these concerns, perhaps in part because of the reputation already earned by the O'Reilly's Lodge and several generations of the O'Reilly family. Subsequently, O'Reilly's competitor at Binna Burra (Buckley, 2003a, p. 103) has also followed suit, with 'Sky Lodges', though at a much smaller scale.

Irrespective of the outcomes, the key feature of all these tourism developments within or immediately adjacent to World Heritage Areas is that they were subject to more detailed and comprehensive technical scrutiny than proposals within national parks controlled only by the state governments. Where there is no federal government involvement, political issues and power plays at state cabinet level can become significant. Although historically independent, most of the state government parks agencies are now subsidiary components of larger environmental agencies, subject to instructions from a director-general, a Minister for Environment and ultimately a state government cabinet. In Australia the technical standard of environmental impact assessment has historically been higher where federal government agencies have been involved (Buckley, 1989, 2009d). In addition, tourism industry associations and individual developers put continual and sometimes considerable pressure on state governments to permit developments which the relevant parks agency itself might not otherwise support.

Cross-state coordination

Each of the individual Australian states and territories has its own legislation for national parks and other protected areas, and its own approaches for the management of recreation and tourism. There is an Inter-Governmental

Agreement on the Environment (IGAE), be-tween the Australian federal government and each of the individual state and territory governments, and there are Ministerial Councils under the IGAE which are responsible for coordinating approaches to conservation and other aspects of environmental policy. There have at times been various task forces and other mechanisms to improve coordination between the states and territories in relation to management of tourism in protected areas.

Currently, there is an informal coordinating committee, the Tourism in Australia's Protected Areas Forum (TAPAF), established shortly after the 2001 Australian Academy of Science Fenner Conference on Nature Tourism and Environment (Buckley et al., 2003a). The Tourism in Australia's Protected Areas Forum has no executive powers, and each of its members operates through the organizations and legislation within their own government agencies. Since the TAPAF members include the most senior staff involved with management of tourism and recreation in each of the parks services, however, in practice it seems to have been highly effective in improving national coordination. Its main focus is on the smaller mobile commercial tourism enterprises which operate under renewable licences. For example, TAPAF has helped to harmonize aspects such as requirements for insurance and indemnifi-cation, and the types of technical operating conditions incorporated into commercial licences. Different agencies do, however, still introduce their own new programmes, such as the High Standard Tourism Programme established in 2004 by the Great Barrier Reef Marine Park Authority. In addition, TAPAF has not generally played a significant role as regards proposals for major fixed-site tourism develop-ments inside the protected area estate, and in practice these differ greatly between the various states and territories.

Western Australia

In Western Australia there was an extended period when the protected area agency was part of the same government department as the production forestry agency. This may well have created internal planning conflicts invisible to the public, but it did at least provide ample funding for tourism infrastructure. There are two particularly well-known examples of such infrastructure. The first is a canopy walkway in a section of tall forest known as the Valley of the Giants, an area of forest dominated by a tall eucalyptus species known as tingle (Ingram, 2007). The other is the Bibbulmun Track, a hiking track almost 1000 km in total length, which crosses between multiple different land tenures and was constructed as a tourist attraction through cooperative arrangements involving a number of different public and private stakeholders. This has been cited widely by industry commentators as an example of a parks–tourism partnership which has been successful from the tourism industry's com-mercial perspective. There does not seem to be any suggestion or indication, however, that this track has made any net positive contribution to conservation.

For some years the parks agency in Western Australia maintained a Web directory of tour operators licensed to visit national parks in that state, under the title of 'Nature Base'. That directory no longer seems to be operational, and tourism licensing systems have been standardized into departmental operations as in other states.

Northern Territory

Several of the national parks in the Northern Territory are very large in area and are owned and/or co-managed by Aboriginal peoples. As a result, there is more commercial tourism accommodation inside these parks than in other states. For example, there is the Gagadju Cooinda Lodge at Yellow Water in Kakadu National Park, the Seven Spirit Bay Wilderness Lodge in Gurig National Park on Cobourg Peninsula, and Minjungari tented camp run by Odyssey Safaris in Litchfield National Park. In a national review of the potential for privately funded infrastructure in public protected areas carried out some years ago (Buckley, 2004d), the Northern Territory Conservation Com-mission was the only one of the state parks agencies which expressed an interest in poten-tially permitting the development of private tourism accommodation inside a national park itself.

Its rationale was that in large national parks such as Kakadu, where tourist access is largely in self-drive 4WD vehicles, there may be advantages for the parks agency if tourists are concentrated at a single point rather than dispersed. The argument is that this can create a routine circuit drive where tracks can be maintained, reducing the number of inexperienced off-road drivers who need to be rescued. In addition, providing accommodation at a single point means that human waste can be managed in a sewage treatment plant, rather than dispersed in cat-holes (individually dug holes). The latter argument, however, is rather weak, first, since this outcome could equally be achieved through a parks service campsite, and second, since human waste is a miniscule input to Kakadu National Park ecosystems in comparison with that from feral buffalo. From a tourism perspective, the operators of the Gagadju Crocodile Hotel at Jabiru might also complain that new tourist accommodation in a less crowded part of the park could well cut heavily into their business.

Further south in the arid central Australian section of the Northern Territory, there is a long-standing history of private tourism accommodation within Uluru National Park, which is Aboriginal land co-managed by the parks agency. During the 1970s, when the entire Northern Territory was administered directly by the Australian federal government and the Pitjantjatjara people had no legal title to the park, there were three small motels close to the base of the Uluru monolith, as well as the parks service headquarters and ranger accommodation. In 1978 the Northern Territory established its own government, equivalent to those of the other states. In 1985 ownership of Uluru National Park was formally transferred to the Central Lands Council, representing the traditional Aboriginal owners of the area. Following the compilation of a new management plan, the old motels were demolished, the access road was moved further from the base of the monolith and reconstructed so as not to interrupt surface water flow, and new and much more upmarket resorts were constructed. In 2002, the upmarket nature tourism operator Voyages Inc. built a luxury

lodge, Longitude 131, as part of its national portfolio of similar properties. In 2003 this lodge burnt down, only 16 months after opening, but it was reconstructed. Voyages Inc. has recently sold off most of its portfolio, but retains Longitude 131. In addition to this private tourism accommodation within the park, the parks service also operates a campsite for self-drive visitors. As at Kakadu, there is no suggestion that private tourist accommodation at Uluru makes a net positive contribution to conservation, but, because of the historical development of the area, these hotels are now an entrenched component of the visitor experience and visitor management programmes.

While private tourist facilities as described above seem to be at best neutral for conservation in the Northern Territory national parks, tourism more generally may well have played a positive political role during an intense political conflict in the late 1990s between proposals to dedicate a further area for conservation, Kakadu Stage Three, and proposals to extend mineral exploration and perhaps production, principally of uranium, into that same area. This remained a contentious issue for over a decade, within national-level commissions of inquiry. Land was granted to an Aboriginal Land Trust and leased back to the parks service; mining commenced but the ore was not processed and the site was eventually rehabilitated. As is commonplace in such debates, many different types of evidence and many different political factors were involved in the final decision to go ahead with Stage Three of the National Park, and there is no published attempt to deconstruct exactly what role tourism may have played in the real decisions made. It was, however, certainly a significant factor presented and considered, particularly since Kakadu is a World Heritage Area.

South Australia

In South Australia, there was a major public controversy some decades ago when the parks service, under financial pressure from the state government, proposed to allow development of a private resort, including a golf course, inside one of the state's icon national parks at

Wilpena Pound. Public outcry at this proposal was so strong that it led to the amendment of relevant planning legislation, and tourist accommodation was subsequently built outside rather than inside the park. There are one or two small-scale commercial partnerships between private tourism enterprises and the parks service, notably at the Bent Wing Café in Naracoorte Nature Reserve (Buckley, 2004d, p. 22), but these were aimed purely at the provision of visitor facilities, with no direct relation to conservation. In the northern part of the state, there has for some decades been ongoing low-level friction between the different demands of oil exploration, cattle ranching and tourism, and the consequences of each for conservation. There is a considerable volume of self-drive tourism using 4WD vehicles, which make use of cattle station tracks, designated stock routes and oil exploration tracks as well as the relatively few public roads in the outback areas (Schmiechen, 2004). Surveillance and on-ground staffing levels in the conservation reserves are very low, even in comparison with private cattle properties (Schmiechen, 2004). In addition, minimal-impact practices for off-road driving and camping (Buckley, 2000) are often ignored. In these areas, tourism seems to have created significant direct ecological impacts without generating any countervailing political pressure for improved conservation.

At Arkaroola in the Flinders Ranges further south, however, a private property run principally for tourism over several decades does seem to have made a significant contribution to conservation, especially as regards eradication of feral animals such as goats, and management of access so as to minimize dispersed impacts from off-road driving (Arkaroola Pty Ltd, 2005).

Victoria

In Victoria, there have been two particularly controversial cases where large tourist infrastructure was built, or proposed, within national parks. At Wilsons Promontory National Park south-east of the state capital city of Melbourne, there is a large national parks campsite at Tidal River, the park entry point, which is accessible by road and very intensively used during holiday periods. The parks service itself proposed to build a large hotel at this campsite, effectively to replace the camping area. This proposal received very strong and vocal opposition from the Victorian public, with more public submissions than any other development proposal recorded in the state to that point, several thousand in total. Two principal concerns were expressed. The first was that a hotel would be much more expensive than a campsite, and this would make it financially impossible for many families to visit the park concerned. The second was that a campsite with communal facilities provides good opportunities for socializing between families, and that these opportunities would no longer exist if each were staying in a separate hotel room. Effectively, for many visitors the attraction was not the national park, which has a multi-day hiking circuit with small campsites which must be booked in advance. Rather, it was the Tidal River campsite itself, including an adjacent beach.

Another major controversy occurred at the Seal Rocks Sea Life Centre on Phillip Island (Buckley, 2004d, p. 13), where a private developer obtained a permit from the state government to build a resort inside the national park, with the very unusual special condition that the State Government could not impose restrictions which would prevent the resort from operating profitably. Once it had in fact started operations, the corporation concerned then claimed that it could not operate profitably because the development as approved was too small, and therefore that this special condition of development consent automatically gave the corporation the right to expand the scale of the resort. Following litigation and extensive public debate, the state government ultimately bought out the corporation's development rights, at a cost to the taxpayer of some Au$56 million (~US$50 million) (O'Connor, 2003).

In contrast to these two cases, there are also a number of examples from Victoria where, at least in the view of the parks service itself, successful partnerships have been formed with private enterprise. For example, the parks service formed a partnership with an Aboriginal corporation to build a visitor centre (Buckley, 2004d, pp. 20–21). The principal function of this arrangement was to improve visitor information about Aboriginal history and interests in the area concerned. There is also one case where a historic building in a peri-urban area, which happened to be owned by the parks service, was restored and run as a restaurant and convention centre by a private company, but with no particular relevance for conservation.

The parks service in Victoria has generally been very proactive in promoting parks for public outdoor recreation, under the slogan 'Healthy Parks, Healthy People'. Since Victoria is one of the smaller and more densely populated Australian states, it has also taken the lead in monitoring and managing individual visitors and commercial tour operators to minimize their impacts. For example, a review by Buckley et al. (2003b) found that Victoria had the most detailed, site-specific and activity-specific conditions in its licensing arrangements for commercial tourism enterprises operating inside the parks estate. Victoria also makes particular use of a variety of minimal-impact educational materials, such as the minimal-impact bushwalking guides for the Australian Alps, produced jointly with the NSW Parks Service; and externally produced minimal-impact codes for 4WD operations (Buckley, 2000). All these measures, however, were initiated by the parks service itself, not by the commercial tourism industry.

Tasmania

The tourism industry in Tasmania has a particular dependence on the natural environment, especially its national parks (Williams, 2004), and there seems to be a generally good working relationship between the state's parks agency and its tourism agency. Historically, however, there has been a large logging industry and a small but none the less significant mining industry, both with negative consequences for conservation. There are still significant areas of primary cool temperate rainforest in Tasmania which are of very high conservation value but are under very severe threat from the timber industry. The controversies have been particularly severe in areas such as the Styx and Tarkine Valleys. There are small tourism operations in each of these areas, but they do not seem to have very significant political power relative to the logging industry.

Forestry Tasmania, the state government agency responsible for public forests, suffered a significant negative impact on public relations in 1994 when the World Congress on Adventure Travel and Ecotourism was held in Hobart. Many of the delegates took advantage of buses provided by a local conservation NGO, and saw for themselves the degree of destruction being wrought in primary forests of high value for conservation and tourism. Following that debacle, the forestry agency decided to promote forest tourism, essentially in order to counteract negative public press and perception. The person they hired to head this effort, undeterred by the lack of funding provided by the forestry agency itself, applied successfully for a large federal government grant and built a treetop walk, the Tahune Airwalk, through an area of tall forest adjacent to a river. This rapidly proved exceedingly successful as a tourist attraction, greatly exceeding its revenue projections and leading Forestry Tasmania to develop a series of further tourist attractions. Their marketing skills, however, seem to have been rather rudimentary, as the second such development was initially advertised under its historical name of Dismal Swamp, and it was not for many years that it was renamed in a somewhat more positive tone. The new name, Tarkine Forest Adventures, is somewhat misleading and politically driven, but much more likely to attract visitors.

Since Tasmania is relatively small and has generally good roads and dispersed tourist accommodation, and since there is a car ferry from mainland Australia, there is a substantial self-drive domestic tourist industry where people travel from one attraction to another. The forest tourism attractions simply became additional destinations in these self-drive circuits, with a ready supply of visitors and customers. The same individual tourists might visit a national park one day and a state forest the next. Despite the success of these forest tourism ventures in economic terms, however, there seems little suggestion that they have made any significant contribution to conservation, e.g. by reducing logging, or leading Forestry Tasmania to seek a major revenue stream based on tourism, or even to recognize the potential significance of forest tourism for regional economies. It does not seem to have learnt, for example, from the experience of the US Forest Service in this regard.

Conservation in Tasmania has also suffered very severe impacts in the past from hydro-electric power development. In the early stages of controversy over the construction of the proposed Gordon-below-Franklin Dam, many people visited the area and rafted down the Franklin River in support of conservation efforts. Many people also visited the world-famous scalloped freshwater sandy beach of Lake Pedder, which was permanently destroyed by the Gordon River Dam. The commercial tourism industry, however, was not involved to any significant degree: these were individual wilderness travellers. Paradoxically, there is now a commercial boat-based tourism industry on the dam reservoir, known as Lake Gordon. When proposals have been put forward to demolish the dam and rehabilitate the river, motorized boat operators and private boat owners have actively opposed the draining of the lake. Currently, a small number of rafting tour operators run multi-day trips down the Franklin River, and there is a low-level contro-versy between different operators regarding a 4WD track which provides access part-way down the river. At least one operator uses this track for access, so as to offer a shorter trip; and at least one argues that it should be permanently closed so as to reduce environ-mental impact in what is otherwise a wilderness area (Buckley, 2003a, p. 113, 2006, pp. 81–82). As of early 2010 this track, the McCall Road, is apparently still operational, subject to permit from the parks agency.

A relatively large proportion of Tasmania lies within national parks, and in some areas there is privately operated infrastructure as well as that built and serviced by the parks agency itself. Cradle Mountain Lodge, for example, lies just outside the entrance to Cradle Mountain National Park, and Freycinet Lodge is at the entrance to Freycinet National Park on the east coast. At Mt Field National Park there is a small seasonally operated ski area, with club lodges but no commercial tourism accom-modation. Commercial tour operators can book space in park huts which are also available to the general public, for example along the Cradle Mountain track.

Overall, therefore, the contribution of com-mercial tourism to conservation in Tasmania is somewhat mixed. The public national parks are certainly a major attraction for visitors to Tasmania, and considerable resources are devoted to visitor management. Tourism may have played some minor rhetorical role in debate over the proposed damming of the Franklin River, but ultimately it was a High Court case on the constitutional powers of the Australian federal government in regard to World Heritage Areas that determined the outcome. Tourism infrastructure within state forests has demonstrated a demand for forest tourism, but there is no evidence that this has led Forestry Tasmania to improve conservation management of the public forest estate. Indeed, the forestry agency continues to log areas of highest value for both conservation and tour-ism, despite strong public political opposition.

New South Wales

The relationship between national parks and commercial tourism is particularly problematic at present in the state of New South Wales (NSW), especially as regards large-scale private developments inside the parks estate itself. New South Wales is generally proud that it has one of the world's first national parks at Royal National Park, which was declared shortly after Yellowstone in the USA. Over recent decades, the total area of land managed by the NSW Parks Service has continued to increase (Gilligan and Allen, 2004), though some of these additions are former forestry areas which may take hundreds or thousands of years to recover to their full conservation value. In recent decades, NSW has had a more decentralized park management system than Australia's other states and territories, with individual regions enjoying a high degree of autonomy.

The NSW Parks Service has generally been proactive in making its park management and monitoring plans available to the public through its website (Buckley et al., 2008c). It is responsible for management or co-management of three World Heritage Areas, namely

Gondwana Rainforest WHA (formerly Central Eastern Rainforest Reserves Australia WHA), Blue Mountains WHA and Lord Howe Island WHA. It is also responsible for managing Kosciusko National Park, the NSW portion of the Australian Alps National Parks.

There is large-scale historical tourism infrastructure development within Kosciusko National Park, associated with the ski industry. The same applies for the Victorian component of the Australian Alps. All the major NSW ski resorts, including a significant proportion of the accommodation, lie within Kosciusko National Park itself (Buckley et al., 2000; Pickering and Buckley, 2010). There is also a major road through the park connecting NSW and Victoria, and a number of minor roads providing access to some of the resorts and also for self-drive summer tourism. Some of these roads are associated with the dams and pipes of the Snowy Mountains Scheme, a large-scale water collection and diversion programme which provides hydroelectric power and water supplies for irrigated agriculture in inland areas. These are not generally associated with tourism except as regards road access.

The conditions under which the various ski resorts operate differ between the individual resorts. Some include accommodation and others do not; some are only permitted to operate in winter, others year-round; some are accessible by road even during winter, whereas others are reached by an over-snow shuttle service or a light rail link through a dedicated tunnel. Most of the NSW resorts are owned by a single operator, which is always seeking opportunities to expand the scale and scope of activities. The Australian ski industry has significant environmental impacts, however, including impacts on a number of endangered mammal species such as the mountain pygmy possum, Burramys parvus (Buckley et al., 2000; Pickering et al., 2003). Key impacts include the disturbance of critical habitat, e.g. for the mountain pygmy possum; complete removal of vegetation and soil in so-called supergrooming; crushing of under-snow burrows during snow grooming, exposing small mammals to increased predation (Sanecki et al., 2006); increased numbers of feral cats, dogs and foxes associated with the ski resorts; and the introduction of invasive plant species

on ski runs and access tracks, with indirect effects on native plant species through competition for pollinators (Pickering and Hill, 2007; Pickering et al., 2007). The ski resorts also use water from the local river systems for snow making, and propose to increase their consumption markedly in order to increase snow making as a counter to climate change (Pickering and Buckley, 2010). It is also likely that the resort operating companies may seek to gain development consent for additional summer activities in order to extend their revenue base (Pickering and Buckley, 2010). Overall, therefore, it appears that the ski tourism development within Kosciusko National Park has generated significant negative impacts on conservation, with no positive contributions.

Inside the boundaries of some NSW national parks, there are old buildings which the parks service is required to manage as items of European cultural heritage. From the parks service perspective, this obligation creates a relatively costly liability, since the buildings must be maintained to a safe standard. One approach adopted for a number of these buildings, though not without controversy, has been to lease them to private companies to run as commercial tourism facilities. For example, there are lighthouse keepers' quarters from the days before automation. One particularly controversial example was an old quarantine station on an island in Sydney Harbour; but the controversy was principally about private recreational access to the island. There does not seem to have been any suggestion that the island was of significant value for conservation of biodiversity; and the public does not seem to have been concerned about the potential cultural heritage value of the quarantine station buildings. The commercial redevelopment did go ahead after an extended period of negotiations between the parks service and the developer. Elsewhere on the NSW coast there are a number of other buildings owned by the parks service and operated as tourist accommodation or attractions, though with no particular significance for conservation. These include old lighthouses, and some cottages in Byron Bay. There are also buildings in some NSW National Parks that are owned and used by the parks service itself, but which are also available for rent to private individuals or educational groups.

By far the majority of visitor accommodation in NSW National Parks, however, is in campsites operated directly by the parks service itself. In heavily visited parks with road access, some of these campsites are quite heavily developed, with individually fenced car camping sites and large-scale cooking and ablutions facilities. Gibraltar Range National Park in the northern tablelands region of NSW provides an example. For a few national parks, camping opportunities are provided in privately run campsites, generally adjacent to the park concerned. The commercial viability of such operations relies heavily on what are essentially monopoly rights: in this area, there is effectively nowhere else available for park visitors to camp. Such operators are thus very sensitive to any proposals to establish alternative accommodation options within the parks concerned.

During 2009, one large-scale private tourist resort did indeed open within a national park in NSW, amid considerable controversy. It was, however, built on an area of former farmland recently incorporated into the park, and was apparently supported by local conservation NGOs. In addition, the NSW State Government has recently amended its parks legislation so as to provide greatly increased opportunities for further such developments in future. This was opposed strenuously by conservation groups (National Parks Association of NSW, 2010). This amendment appears to be a consequence of the particular political balance of power between the incumbent NSW Government, the principal parliamentary opposition in the State and a small number of independent senators in the NSW Government Upper House who have made particular demands in return for supporting other legislation. This is politics still in progress, and not fully deconstructible. It appears, however, that while there were also a small number of senators belonging to a Green party, these senators made demands which were essentially impossible for the incumbent government to accede to. As a result, in order to defeat formal opposition by a centre-right opposition, a centre-left incumbent government was forced to accept unpalatable demands with localized consequences from the political far right, rather than unpalatable demands with unworkably broad consequences from the political far left. That is, the Green representatives indirectly, but knowingly, forced an outcome with severe negative consequences for conservation.

The resort development which has already gone ahead, in the Blue Mountains National Park and World Heritage Area, reflects the same political landscape as that underlying the newly amended legislation, though not formally connected. The resort, known as Wolgan Valley Resort and Spa (2010), is owned, built and operated by Emirates Airlines and appears to be part of a general strategy by Emirates to build luxury nature resorts in a number of its key destination countries, in parallel to its Al Maha Resort in the desert landscapes inland from the city of Dubai. Al Maha includes a private reserve stocked with Arabian oryx and scimitar-horned oryx, both endangered species, and is surrounded by a co-managed public reserve. It does indeed seem to have made a contribution to the conservation of these particular species at least. The Wolgan Resort is built on a former pastoral landholding within the park and has involved relatively complex land swap arrangements. The resort itself and also the NSW parks agency apparently feel that these land swap arrangements have been beneficial for conservation, but some conservation groups argue otherwise.

Queensland

While commercial tour operators who take their clients into national parks in Queensland pay very similar per capita fees as commercial tour operators in other states (Buckley et al., 2003b), individual private visitors to national parks in Queensland are not required to pay entry fees, and tourism industry representatives have complained about this differential on a number of occasions. In particular, while Ecotourism Australia is a national organization, for historical reasons it has always had particularly close links with the Queensland State Government tourism agency. For a number of years it has been heavily involved in lobbying the Queensland Government parks agency to allow increased access for commercial tourism operations, and preferential conditions for members of Ecotourism Australia. This lobbying is currently carried out under the heading of 'TIPA', the Tourism in Protected Areas Initiative.

Individual visitors do have to book and pay for overnight camping in Queensland National Parks, using a rather poorly thought-out online system which makes it difficult or impossible for self-drive travellers to obtain a legal camping permit once they have actually arrived at a particular park. Historically, the number of camping permits issued has been recorded, but the number of day visitors to Queensland National Parks has not, except for those parks which are also World Heritage. In recent years, the more heavily frequented hiking tracks in some national parks have been equipped with track counters, but there are still no comprehensive visitor statistics for national parks in Queensland.

There are a number of privately owned tourist accommodation facilities on private land immediately adjacent to key national parks in Queensland, or in some cases on enclaves within these parks. Most of the parks involved are also World Heritage Areas: notably, the Gondwana Rainforest WHA, Wet Tropics of Queensland WHA and Great Barrier Reef WHA. There are a small number of private commercial tourism developments operating inside national parks in Queensland, each with its own particular history. At the Undara Lava Tubes in northern Queensland, for example, the area was formerly private land, and the owners gave the land to the parks service on condition that they be permitted to continue commercial tourism operations. The Skyrail® cableway near Cairns runs through sections of the Wet Tropics of Queensland WHA, but the area concerned was formerly managed by the Queensland state forestry agency, and the cableway was approved as part of a political package intended to generate new employment when World Heritage designation led to the cessation of logging. There are private tourist lodges on some of the islands managed by the Queensland parks agency within the Great Barrier Reef Marine Park, for example at Green Island near Cairns. There are also privately owned tourist facilities constructed directly on the outer ribbon reefs in one section

of the Great Barrier Reef Marine Park. Day visitors are ferried to the outer reefs in a high-speed wave-piercing catamaran, which then docks for the day alongside a permanent platform which provides a stable space to serve them lunch and fit them out with snorkelling or diving gear (Buckley, 2003a, pp. 121–122; 2006, pp. 168–172; Quicksilver Cruises, 2010).

Throughout Queensland, there are private tourist lodges immediately adjacent to national parks, or in some cases on enclaves of private land within the parks, which rely on the parks to attract their clientele. Examples include Crocodylus Village, Daintree Ecolodge and Silky Oaks Lodge in north Queensland, Kingfisher Bay on Fraser Island, Oasis Lodge at Carnarvon Gorge, Hinchinbrook Island Wilderness Lodge on Hinchinbrook Island, and Binna Burra and O'Reilly's Lodges in Lamington National Park (Buckley, 2003a). Most of these market themselves as ecotourism enterprises, and do indeed take steps to minimize on-site environmental impacts and to provide environmental education programmes for their clients. There is no indication, however, that any of them make a direct positive contribution to conservation. At some of these lodges, there has been a degree of friction between the lodge and the parks service over particular local issues. For example, Kingfisher Bay takes its clients through Fraser Island National Park, which is traversed by a number of sandy tracks, using large 4WD buses, which apparently create greater impacts than the smaller 4WD vehicles used by individual self-drive tourists.

At O'Reilly's in Lamington National Park, there has been a long-standing, though not serious, disagreement over the feeding of birds, notably parrots and bowerbirds, as a tourist attraction. This is prohibited in the park itself, but practised and indeed encouraged within the O'Reilly's enclave. For a visitor, the park and the lodge grounds are simply two adjacent sections of the same destination, with the same access road and carpark, and most visitors will cross repeatedly from one to the other and back during a single short visit, so this situation can be somewhat confusing. O'Reilly's argues that they have fed the birds for many decades with no adverse consequences evident, and that this provides the visitors with harmless enjoyment and opportunities to see species such as the Regents Bowerbird, which otherwise they might not. The parks service is concerned over: the indirect impacts of large local population increases for particular parrot species; the potential for these dense local populations to act as a reservoir of pathogens which could spread into broader populations throughout the park; and, perhaps most significantly, at the way in which bird feeding at the lodge contradicts or negates the educational message that visitors to parks should not interfere with interspecies interactions through feeding of wildlife. In late 2009, the bird feeding area was fenced off and licensed by the parks service.

Large-scale private conservation areas funded by tourism seem to be rather uncommon in Queensland. The best-known example is the 20 km^2 Mareeba Wetlands, west of Cairns in north Queensland, operated by the Mareeba Wetlands Foundation and funded at least partly through tourism (Nevard, 2004). There is an extensive and apparently successful programme of small-scale private conservation agreements throughout Queensland, as in several other states, but these do not seem to be linked to tourism. Likewise, there are a number of private properties operated as farm tourism businesses, especially near major tourist gateway towns (Ollenburg and Buckley, 2007), but without any particular focus on conservation.

Overall, therefore, it appears that in Queensland as elsewhere in Australia, the commercial tourism sector relies heavily on publicly funded protected area systems to provide many of its principal attractions; and, though many operators do take steps to minimize negative impacts, there are rather few examples of direct positive contributions to conservation.

Private Conservation

Private conservation reserves of any size are relatively uncommon in Australia, and those which do exist are not necessarily involved in tourism. In some regions of Europe, there are large private estates which contain woodlands, grasslands or wetlands of significant conservation value. In North America, the taxation system encourages the establishment of private conservation trusts and the sale of conservation easements. In parts of sub-Saharan Africa, there are large charismatic wildlife which attract enough high-paying tourists to support private game reserves as commercial tourist ventures. In Australia, there are analogues to each of these, but none of these mechanisms are so prevalent as elsewhere. In some parts of Australia there are indeed large private landholdings which have been in the same family for a number of generations, and a number of these are indeed significant for conservation; but there has not been such a historical tradition of managing with conservation in mind. There are a range of incentive programmes at all levels of government for conservation on private land in Australia, but these are neither consistent nor coordinated (Buckley, 2009e).

There are private corporations such as Earth Sanctuaries and the Australian Wildlife Conservancy which have bought and managed land specifically for conservation, with tourism as one income stream in some cases. There are private associations such as Birds Australia (2010) and private foundations such as the Mareeba Wetlands Foundation (2010) and the NSW Foundation for National Parks and Wildlife (2010) which have followed a similar approach. Australia does also have a wildlife tourism sector analogous to that of Africa, but far less well developed – perhaps because there are far fewer large diurnal animal species. There are a few public protected areas, such as Tidbinbilla Nature Reserve near Canberra, which are effectively run as outdoor zoos, and which rely on tourists for a major contribution to their total revenue. Because native wildlife in Australia legally belongs to the Crown rather than the landholder, there is far less opportunity for landowners to profit from conservation management of individual species. This contrasts with South Africa, for example, where there is an active market in many species of native wildlife, contributing both to wildlife tourism and to conservation breeding programmes.

Earth Sanctuaries Limited (ESL) was established in 1969 by Dr John Walmsley at

Warrawong, a 14 ha agricultural property in the Adelaide hills. Walmsley built a vermin-proof fence, eradicated feral animals, restored vegetation and reintroduced native wildlife (Earth Sanctuaries Ltd, 2002; Buckley, 2003a). Operating costs were funded through a range of small-scale tourist activities on site.

In 2000–2001, ESL was listed as a public company and embarked on a major acquisition programme, with six reserves totalling 880 km² in late 2001. This venture proved too ambitious financially, and in 2002 ESL had to sell most of the new acquisitions. They were not lost to conservation, however, since most were bought by the Australian Wildlife Conservancy (2010), which manages them successfully as private conservation reserves. In 2005 ESL was delisted, and Warrawong now operates as an independent private reserve (Warrawong Wildlife Sanctuary, 2010), with tourist accommodation on site. In 2007 the remaining assets of the delisted company were apparently bought by a property development company called Prudential Investments P/L. A newspaper article in July 2009 (Millar and Feneley, 2009) reported that Prudential Investments was still the owner of Waratah Park Earth Sanctuary near Sydney, having taken it over in 2006, but that NSW government authorities said that the company did not have a licence to care for >100 native animals in the park. In March 2010, local residents submitted a petition to the company and the state government to prevent housing development on this site (Savewaratah, 2010). Despite this rather inglorious conclusion for the ESL public listing experiment, Walmsley and Earth Sanctuaries Ltd did indeed make a significant contribution to conservation of native Australian wildlife, both by protecting habitat and individual animals and by increasing public interest in wildlife conservation (Buckley, 2003a). In addition, most of the reserves owned by ESL in its heyday were taken over successfully by the AWC, as below.

Founded in 2001, the Australian Wildlife Conservancy (AWC) is currently Australia's largest NGO landholder, with 20 properties totalling 25,000 km² in area. AWC employs about 80 staff, mostly in the field, and its annual operating costs are around Au$9 million (~US$8 million). Its principal income is from charitable donations, and it received $15 million in 2009, with the surplus allocated to ongoing land purchases. The reserves provide habitat for around 170 threatened animal species (Australian Wildlife Conservancy, 2010).

Tourist accommodation is available on three of the reserves. There is a small lodge at Yookamurra and permanent tented camps at Mornington in the Kimberley area of Western Australia and at Pungalina near Tennant Creek in the Northern Territory. Current rates are $250 per person per night twin-share full board at Mornington, and $475 per person all found at Pungalina. The latter includes tours and guides. Pungalina has only recently been purchased by AWC. Tourism is likely to become a more significant component of AWC's income stream in future decades.

At least two other Australian NGOs offer tourism opportunities on land bought for conservation. In the mallee eucalyptus woodlands of South Australia, Birds Australia owns the 544 km² Gluepot Reserve, which provides habitat for over 190 bird species. Visitors pay entry fees of $5 per vehicle per day, or $10 per vehicle for overnight stays. Tour operators using buses pay per person, but at lower rates. Birds Australia also owns the 2620 km² Newhaven Station in the Northern Territory, now managed jointly with AWC (Birds Australia, 2010). There does not seem to be any tourism operation at Newhaven.

On Springbrook Plateau, next to the Springbrook National Park section of the Gondwana Rainforests World Heritage Area, the Rainforest Conservation Society (2010) recently purchased a former private landholding to contribute to conservation, and in the process took over ownership of the Springbrook Lyrebird Retreat (2010), a small lodge which offers cabins and cottages at Au$250–$290 (~US$225–260) per couple per night, with a two-night minimum stay. The area of the property is apparently not stated on either website.

In addition to the NGOs mentioned above, there are a number of other conservation organizations in Australia involved in purchasing land for private conservation, but these are not generally involved in tourism operations. There are also a number of small private tourism lodges, listed by Buckley (2009d), whose landholdings effectively act as private reserves, but at far smaller scale than those outlined above.

Conclusions

The main interactions between tourism and conservation in Australia are those involving public protected areas, both in regard to operational management and in regard to changing land tenure, especially from logging to conservation. There is one large NGO, Australian Wildlife Conservancy, and a number of smaller NGOs and private ecolodge operators, which contribute to conservation through private landholdings and also operate tourism enterprises of various types. These operations are currently far less common in Australia than in sub-Saharan Africa and in South and Central America, but this may change in the future.

9 Arctic and Antarctic

King Penguins, Antarctica

Introduction

Commercial tourism may well play a significant political role in conserving the polar ecosystems of the Arctic and Antarctic (Snyder and Stonehouse, 2007), but both the conservation threats and the conservation mechanisms are complex. At the broad geographical scale, the principal threats to polar ecosystems are currently from climate change and from large-scale oil, gas and mineral explorations and exploitation. If the ice caps, glaciers and ice sheets suffer major break-up and melting, and the ocean suffers significant warming and acidification, this will cause major disruption to habitat, food chains, migrations and breeding behaviour for marine and terrestrial birds, mammals and other animal species which rely on the polar ecosystems for at least part of their life cycles. Large-scale oil exploration and production in the Arctic have already caused both very considerable impacts on the migration of terrestrial animals, and perhaps even more severe effects through noise impacts on marine species, including endangered cetaceans such as narwhal and bowhead whale. To date, the Antarctic Treaty has successfully protected the Antarctic against mining, but this is a fragile instrument at best. The International Whaling Convention provides a degree of protection for whale species in polar ecosystems as elsewhere, but does not protect them from whaling by countries such as Japan, Norway or Russia. As this book went to press, these whaling nations had apparently announced their intention to resume commercial whaling.

The potential role of polar tourism in conservation derives almost entirely from the possible creation of a political constituency which may be concerned over the fate of the polar regions and prepared to lobby for their protection. It is by no means clear if any such effect actually does occur. A study of Antarctic expedition cruise tourists by Bauer (2001) indicated that they were unlikely to act as conservation advocates as a result of their holiday experiences. It seems likely that film and television documentaries, which reach far wider audiences and also those who are already concerned about conservation, may have much more significant political effects. In addition, as noted in a more general context by Buckley (2009a, b), this mechanism can only make a net positive contribution to conservation if three conditions are all met simultaneously. These are: first, that lobbying by former tourists does actually yield conservation gains; second, that their decision to lobby was due to the tourism experience; and, third, that the conservation gains outweigh the aggregate conservation impacts of tourism in the area concerned. In polar regions, while physical impacts are much smaller than those of mining or climate change, biological impacts may be quite severe because tourism is concentrated in the areas of highest biodiversity.

Antarctic

In the Antarctic, while there is a small subsector of the tourism industry that relies on air access, by far the majority relies on access by boat. There are two main subsectors, the mainstream cruise ships and much smaller expedition cruise vessels. The former are not ice strengthened, and generally cannot put all their passengers ashore simultaneously except at ports with docks and gangways. They do, however, halt at the undeveloped sites visited by the expedition cruise vessels, and put some of their passengers ashore each time. Expedition cruise vessels, in contrast, are specifically equipped with sufficient inflatable boats and rapid-launch davits for them to be able to put their entire, much smaller, passenger complement ashore very rapidly, and may thus make several beach landings at different sites on a single day.

Passengers on expedition vessels receive lectures and detailed briefings about the species and ecosystems they can expect to see, and how they should behave in order to minimize impacts and disturbance. In addition, they are accompanied by experienced guides who monitor the passengers' behaviour and if necessary enforce minimal-impact codes, such as minimum approach distances to nesting seabirds. Many of the individual passengers on these expedition cruises already have high levels of environmental understanding and concern, and this creates a peer-group ethic which helps the guides to ensure that all passengers follow minimal-impact codes.

None of these factors necessarily apply on mainstream cruise ships. Even though those ships may only put a small proportion of their passengers ashore at any one time, the absolute number of passengers involved in any one landing may still be greater than for the much smaller expedition cruise vessels. The passengers do not necessarily have the same level of knowledge and concern about minimizing environmental impacts, and they are not necessarily accompanied by skilled and experienced natural history guides. In addition, all of the tour companies which operate the smaller expedition cruise vessels in Antarctic waters are members of IAATO, the International Association of Antarctic Tour Operators, and subscribe at least nominally to its code of conduct for both marine operations and landings. At least some of the larger cruise ship lines, in contrast, are not members of IAATO.

Both the expedition cruise vessels and the mainstream cruise ships concentrate their visits and landings in very specific parts of the Antarctic, with a strong focus on subantarctic islands and the Antarctic Peninsula. There are two main reasons for this. The first reason is logistic. These are the only areas with open-water access, though they require particularly skilled and cautious navigation, both because of floating icebergs and because of potential groundings. The other reason is that these areas have by far the majority of wildlife in the Antarctic region, and wildlife provide the principal tourist attractions. Elephant seals and other marine mammals, and penguin and sea-bird colonies, are in particular demand. A wide range of scientific research on these colonies (Buckley 2004e, 2009b, p. 162) confirms that disturbance by tourists can indeed have significant impact on breeding seabird colonies, through a number of mechanisms. The aggregate impact of tourism on the total population of any particular Antarctic species has not been assessed, but it certainly appears that tourism is currently the single largest source of impacts on many species. These direct negative impacts on conservation must be offset against any potential conservation gains through indirect political mechanisms.

In addition to the boat-based tourism in the Antarctic and subantarctic, there is a small fly-in fly-out ice-climbing operation at Patriot Hills, and air access to some of the national scientific bases operated by Antarctic Treaty nations and other countries in various parts of the Antarctic continent. There has also been considerable debate over the possibility of establishing fixed-site tourist accommodation and facilities on the Antarctic mainland. There are no such facilities at present.

High Arctic

The High Arctic includes the polar ice cap, Arctic islands and adjacent seas, and the most northerly parts of the continental margins. The oceans of the High Arctic are frozen over for much of the year, breaking up only briefly during summer. Even though the High Arctic is a polar region like Antarctica, patterns of tourism use in the High Arctic are rather different from those in the Antarctic. The Arctic ice cap is thin and floating, and can be crossed or cut by icebreaking vessels. Tourists can reach the pole in summer in an icebreaking vessel refitted as an expedition cruise ship. This contrasts with the Antarctic, where vessels can only penetrate the seasonally frozen fringes, not the far thicker floating ice shelves, and where the main ice cap is a thick perennial body of ice overlying a rock base. In addition, at least the fringes of the Arctic are inhabited, while the Antarctic is not, except for scientific bases. Tourism activities in the Arctic are thus somewhat more varied than those in the Antarctic.

The most extreme and correspondingly expensive options include the opportunity to descend to the ocean sea floor at the North Pole in a deep-sea submersible, or skydive on to the North Pole. A Russian operation establishes a base camp on the Arctic ice, approximately one degree latitude away from the North Pole, from late March to late April each year. Known as Barneo, this camp provides a base both for scientists conducting research and for tourist operations where their clients are taken to ski the last degree to the North Pole itself, dragging camping equipment in pulks, specialized ice sledges. Tourists can also reach the North Pole by flying to Barneo and travelling the last degree by helicopter.

The principal tourist gateways to the High Arctic are in Canada, at Resolute on Cornwallis

Island and Pond Inlet at the northern tip of Baffin Island; in Norway, at Longyearbyen on Svalbard, also known as Spitsbergen; and in Greenland, at Nunuk and Kangerlussaq. There are also seasonal fly-in tourism operations further north, e.g. on Canada's Ellesmere Island and elsewhere. Expedition cruise vessels can and do travel more widely. Tourists do also drive to Deadhorse on the northern continental coast of Alaska, although the access road, built to support oil and gas production, is not technically open to the public. Similarly, there are land-based tourism operations in the far northern areas of Norway and Sweden, centred around the reindeer-herding Sami people, and purpose-built tourist attractions such as the famed Ice Hotel. These areas are significantly further south. There is not, as yet, a significant international tourism industry in the Russian section of the High Arctic, except for the Barneo ice base, but this is likely to change.

High Arctic tourism is rather small in scale, and its impacts are unlikely to be significant in comparison with those of climate change and undersea oil exploration and production. The impacts of climate change on the Arctic ice cap, and the consequences for polar bear populations in particular, have been heavily publicized. The noise impacts of undersea oil exploration and production on marine mammals may also be severe but are much less well publicized. There is a significant tourism industry based on watching polar bears, and this industry may even have received a boost in client numbers because of the perception that polar bears are now endangered, in the same way that the East African wildlife safari industry received a boost in the 1970s because of the severe conservation threats to many of the icon species at that time. There does not seem to be any evidence, however, as to whether or not the bear-watching or marine and ice-based adventure tourism sectors in the Arctic have themselves played any significant role in the conservation of either marine or terrestrial species and ecosystems.

Conservation issues in much of the Arctic are strongly linked to the dynamics of indigenous communities, known in Canada and the USA as First Nations. In Pond Inlet at the northern tip of Canada's Baffin Island, for example, there is a relatively small tourism industry and it does not seem to have any significant effect either on local Inuit lifestyles or on the mineral exploration industry which uses Pond Inlet as a staging point. Indeed, the growth of mainstream cruise ship tourism in this region has apparently provided a new market for the illegal trade in protected wildlife such as narwhal tusks (Buckley, 2005). In addition, Inuit-owned tourism businesses operating out of Pond Inlet advertise that tourists should expect to see Inuit hunting, including hunting for marine mammals, as part of their experience.

Low Arctic

By far the majority of Arctic tourism takes place in the Low Arctic, which includes continental areas in Alaska, Canada, Scandinavia and Russia. From a tourism perspective, the principal attractions of the Low Arctic are scenery, landscapes and wildlife. There are extensive residential populations, and tourist access is relatively straightforward, with self-drive and independent backcountry travel opportunities readily available, in addition to organized commercial tours and expeditions. The south-western coastline of Alaska, including Admiralty Sound and Glacier Bay, are well-known tourist destinations in the North American Low Arctic; and so are Denali National Park in Alaska and northern Nunavut in eastern Canada. Iceland, parts of northern Norway and Sweden and much of northern Siberia in Russia also qualify as Low Arctic. Both large mainstream cruise ships and a variety of smaller vessels ply these coastlines routinely. There are tourist cruises on Glacier Bay in Alaska, for example; along both east and west coasts of Greenland; up the western coast of Norway; and along the coastline of the Kamchatka Peninsula in eastern Russia. Sea kayaks are available for rent in Juneau in Alaska, and there are extensive independent sea-kayaking opportunities in Admiralty Sound and Glacier Bay, as well as further north in Prince William Sound, accessed via Whittier (Buckley, 2006, pp. 123–128). Similarly, companies such as Southern Sea Ventures (2010) run unsupported sea kayak tours along the coastline of Kamchatka, and boat-supported sea kayak tours, in conjunction with Aurora Expeditions (2010), into Scoresby Sund on the east coast of Greenland.

There is a wide variety of well-known terrestrial wildlife-watching opportunities in the Low Arctic, with a particular focus on bears and reindeer. There are a number of Alaskan wildlife lodges which are famous for the opportunity to watch grizzly bears catching salmon. Bears are one of the major wildlife attractions for tourists in Denali National Park, and bear safety is one of the key issues in visitor management, especially for backcountry camping. Caribou are one of the key species in the Brookes Range in central northern Alaska, north of Denali; and reindeer in northern Scandinavia, Svalbard and Siberia. Grizzly bear are a major attraction in Kamchatka (Buckley, 2006, pp. 375–379).

The degree to which tourism may contribute to conservation in the Low Arctic is far from clear. In Russia, the reserves known as *zapovedniks* were established purely for conservation and science and were not originally open for tourism or recreation; but with the break-up of the former USSR, ecotourism became a significant factor in maintaining their operational funding (Chizhova, 2004). The major national parks of Alaska and northern Canada are part of the relevant national protected area systems, managed for conservation and also for individual private recreation. Parks such as Denali and Glacier Bay are heavily visited, and managing visitor infrastructure, safety and impacts is a major part of the day-to-day operations of the park. In less well-protected areas such as the Arctic National Wildlife Refuge in Alaska, however, where conservation use is continually under threat from proposed oil exploration, tourism and recreation may have a political role in maintaining them for conservation. Equally, however, it may well be that political conflicts between oil and conservation interests respectively are played out at national level without any significant reference to tourism.

Tourism has become an important component of the economy for some of the coastal towns in south-western Alaska, but it is not clear whether this has created any significant new conservation lobby. At Khutzeymateen, immediately south of the Alaskan border in northern Canada, two small-scale boat-based grizzly bear watching tour operators apparently did make a significant contribution to conservation of the bear population concerned, by providing logistic assistance for conservation groups who wanted to bring politicians to see the area for themselves (Buckley, 2010, pp. 153–154). This successfully protected one catchment area, its forests and its bears from logging and associated impacts.

Polar Expedition Cruises

Operational details and aspects of environmental management for cruise ship companies operating in polar regions have been described by Kriwoken and Rootes (2000) for Quark Expeditions, Buckley (2006, pp. 155–159) for Abercrombie and Kent (2010) and Buckley (2006, pp. 159–162) for Aurora Expeditions (2010). In the Antarctic, Quark Expeditions is a long-term member of IAATO and, according to Kriwoken and Rootes (2000), adheres to the IAATO Codes of Environmental Practice. In the Arctic, however, it apparently uses ice-breaking ships to cut through the polar ice cap to the North Pole itself. Abercrombie and Kent (2010) have run expedition cruises in the Antarctic using the *Explorer II*, renamed the *Minerva* in 2008. In 2010 it is using the newly built vessel *El Boreal*.

Aurora Expeditions (2010) operate in the Arctic, the Antarctic and also in Kamchatka, Papua New Guinea and along the Kimberley coastline of north-western Australia. During 2009 the company purchased a Russian-built polar vessel, the *Marina Svaeteva*, which it had previously used on a charter basis. In the Arctic, it operates a programme of cruises from Scotland to Iceland, across to Svalbard, around the main Svalbard island of Spitsbergen and back to Scotland. One of the key features is a partnership with the sea-kayaking company Southern Sea Ventures, which allows passengers to kayak in Arctic waters from the comfort of an expedition cruise vessel. A number of other expedition cruise companies offer similar itineraries, though most use chartered Russian vessels.

As noted by Buckley (2003a, 2006), Splettstoesser *et al.* (2004) and Snyder and

Stonehouse (2007), the principal destination for Antarctic expedition cruises is the Antarctic Peninsula: first since it is the closest to Ushuaia and the least ice-bound; and second since it provides easy opportunities for tourists to see penguin colonies. Many of these cruises, and also the large-scale non-expedition cruise ships, also visit a variety of subantarctic islands which are used extensively as breeding rookeries by seabirds and seals. Most Antarctic cruise ship operators are members of the industry association IAATO, the International Association of Antarctic Tour Operators, which promulgates minimal-impact guidelines; and the naturalist guides on expedition cruise vessels do indeed remind tour clients constantly of these concerns. Despite these measures, however, tourism does none the less create significant impacts on these colonies.

The impacts of disturbance by numerous landing parties of tourists who visit these colonies during the height of the breeding season may be considerable. The key issue is that seabird colonies are constantly under attack by other predatory birds such as skuas, which take advantage of even a moment's disturbance or distraction on the part of the parents, to snatch eggs or chicks. In very dense colonies such as those of many penguin species, disturbance can also lead chicks to stray into the nest territories of other adult birds, which then attack them. In addition, even if parent birds do not abandon their nests, they suffer significant physiological stress from closely approaching tourists (Giese et al., 1999), affecting the chance that they can successfully raise their offspring. All these types of impact are now well documented and have been reviewed by Buckley (2004e, 2009b, pp. 148–174).

Both Aurora Expeditions and Abercrombie and Kent do have a strong focus on natural history and conservation issues in polar regions. As noted previously, however (Buckley, 2009a; see Chapter 1), this does not necessarily, in itself, yield any improvement to conservation. It may simply serve to attract clients who have strong natural history or conservation interests already. Even if the tour experiences do indeed help to generate or maintain a political interest in conservation on the part of the participants, this will only make a net positive contribution

to conservation in practice if it leads those participants to take political action which makes a sufficiently large net contribution to conservation to outweigh the total aggregate negative impacts on conservation of the entire tour in which they took part. It is, of course, beyond the capabilities or responsibilities of the individual tour operators to track this entire chain of events. The most that they can reasonably be expected to do is to minimize the impacts of the tour itself as far as possible; to provide its clients with accurate and appropriate information about the areas visited and their conservation value and significance; to indicate ways in which clients could potentially become involved in conservation lobbying efforts if they so choose; and to become involved in such efforts themselves where appropriate opportunities arise.

Conclusions

In both the Arctic and the Antarctic, therefore, the relationship between tourism and conservation is somewhat ambiguous. On the positive side, tourism may help to contribute to public awareness of environmental impacts and threats to conservation from other industry sectors, but this contribution is probably quite small relative to the efforts of environmental NGOs, television documentaries and other mass-media information sources. On the negative side, tourism in polar regions certainly does produce environmental impacts, especially on wildlife which forms a key tourist attraction. In some areas, especially on the subantarctic islands, the impacts of tourism may well be more severe than any other impacts which these species currently face. In other areas, especially in the Arctic where both marine and terrestrial mammals are hunted and where there are other high-impact industries, the impacts of tourism are probably small, at least in relative terms.

It is possible that tourism may create a political lobbying force, e.g. to persuade national governments to endorse and maintain the conservation status of the Antarctic, but there is no evidence to date whether or not this actually occurs (Bauer, 1999). It remains unknown. It is also possible that the continual presence of tourists may provide some protection against deliberate vandalism or unintentional but severe impacts by vessels engaged in industrial fishing and whaling. This is completely unstudied to date. There are numerous reports, however, that tuna fishermen off the coast of South Australia have shot seals and that yachtsmen landing on islands in the Great Barrier Reef have disturbed large colonies of breeding terns. Similar impacts could easily occur on subantarctic islands.

The significance of Arctic expedition cruises for conservation are difficult to determine. They visit walrus colonies and seabird rookeries, but their environmental impacts seem low, since the birds nest on rocky cliffs which are much less accessible than their Antarctic counterparts. Unlike the Antarctic, in the High Arctic there are human residents, both indigenous and Western, who fish, hunt and trap wildlife; and tourism has relatively low impact in comparison. There is also a large-scale Arctic oil and gas exploration and production

industry, with major environmental impacts on both marine and terrestrial wildlife. There is as yet no evidence that tourism reduces any of these impacts, even where the same individual local residents may be involved in both tourism and hunting (Buckley, 2005).

In the Low Arctic, in contrast, tourism does seem to have generated some positive outcomes for conservation. At Churchill in Canada's Hudson Bay, as described in Chapter 4, tourism seems to have reduced the impacts of local residents on polar bears. At Khutzeymateen on the north-western coast of British Columbia, Canada, the assistance of two small-scale tour operators was critical in protecting one of the last unlogged areas of coastal temperate forest and its resident grizzly bear population.

Overall, it seems that tourism is now a significant part of the political dynamics of both the Arctic and the Antarctic, but it is difficult to determine whether the net outcome for conservation is positive or negative.

10 France and Francophone Nations

Julianna Priskin and Bruno Sarrasin

Mercantour NP, France

Introduction: Francophone Nations

The positive relationship between ecotourism and biodiversity conservation in countries where the cultural background is primarily associated with the French language has not been evaluated previously. Francophone cultures outside Europe are a legacy of the former colonial empires of France and also of Belgium (Congo, Burundi, Rwanda). France still has numerous dependent territories such as French Guiana, Guadeloupe, Martinique and La Réunion (Table 10.1). Today, the francophone world includes over 50 countries, of which 28 use French as an official language. With the exception of France, Belgium, Switzerland, Tunisia and Canada, tourism is not an important sector in most francophone countries, with international tourism arrivals well below one million per year (Table 10.1). Francophone countries which do promote and use tourism as a development tool include Senegal, Tunisia and numerous island states, such as the Seychelles and those in the Pacific Ocean. Many of these destinations continue to develop ecotourism as a niche product. Most West African francophone countries, in contrast, are poverty-stricken and rely largely on subsistence agriculture and international humanitarian aid. Most of these countries are also politically unstable, and this is reflected in the low numbers of international tourism arrivals and very limited ecotourism activities. The setting for ecotourism in publicly managed protected areas across francophone countries is highly variable, and only a few have more than the global average of 12% of territory in some kind of protection status (Table 10.1). Although they exist, the total number and the distribution of private conservation areas in these countries does not appear to be documented systematically.

The existence of ecotourism in francophone countries remains mostly marginal and a niche activity. In most areas, ecotourism is considered to have more potential than what is currently developed. For example, there are tour operators focusing on wildlife tourism in Gabon, Benin, Chad, Central African Republic, Mauritania, Mali, Côte d'Ivoire and Senegal with some eco-lodges, as well as private reserves that work in cooperation with conservation-oriented NGOs such as the World Wide Fund for Nature, Wildlife Conservation Society, Conservation International and so on. In most of these countries the management of nationally designated conservation estates is only ensured via international assistance. Madagascar remains one of the only francophone destinations that specifically promotes ecotourism as a vector for development and biodiversity conservation, where publicly and privately managed nature reserves offer a variety of settings for ecotourism (see also Chapter 4). Private conservation reserves that offer tourism opportunities represent a form of non-destructive land-use alternative, as compared with resource extraction industries linked to forestry and mining (Sarrasin, 2007).

With some exceptions, ecotourism in the francophone world has received very limited attention in the literature; yet each country would merit a close examination individually. As the core of francophone countries, France itself is an interesting case, since according to the UNWTO it attracts nearly 80 million visitors a year, ranking it the most visited nation in the world (United Nations World Tourism Organization, 2009). Moreover, in a European context France also has a large territory that offers a variety of settings for nature-based and ecotourism. Currently, this sector is estimated to be 30% of the entire tourism industry (Lamic, 2008; World Wildlife Fund France, 2008). However, the size of the French ecotourism market is difficult to estimate since it is not monitored specifically, and ecotourism specifically remains a small segment, although it has been reported to be increasingly diversified (Blangy, 1995; World Tourism Organization, 2002).

Today, the nature-based and ecotourism sector in France is also increasingly structured, and in 2009 the French national ecotourism association had approximately 300 members (P. Laguillon, personal communication, 2009). Most business members of this association were lodging establishments, and few corresponded to strict international ecotourism criteria as specified by the United Nations Environment Programme and World Tourism Organization (2002). Many French tour operators associated with nature-based ecotourism

Table 10.1. Francophone countries – tourism and protected area statistics.

Region and country or territory	Nationally designated terrestrial protected areas[a]		International tourism arrivals[b]	
	Number	% area	Millions	Year
EUROPE				
Belgium	502	3.20	7.1	2008
France	1541	15.37	79.3	2008
Luxembourg	58	16.64	0.91	2008
Monaco	1	0.25	0.29	2008
Switzerland	2146	28.58	8.6	2008
AFRICA AND INDIAN OCEAN				
Benin	49	23.16	0.17	2004
Burkina Faso	72	14.35	0.22	2004
Burundi	15	5.56	0.15	2005
Cameroon	39	10.11	0.19	2004
Cape Verde	1	0.01	0.29	2008
Central African Republic	32	18.19	0.008	2004
DR of Congo	n/a	n/a	0.061	2005
Chad	9	8.95	0.02	2000
Comoros	0	0.00	0.02	2004
Congo	14	10.29	0.02	2000
Côte d'Ivoire	240	21.14	0.18	2003
Djibouti	1	0.00	0.03	2005
Gabon	22	16.54	0.22	2003
Madagascar	53	3.09	0.23	2004
Mali	10	2.10	0.19	2008
Mauritania	3	0.87	0.03	2000
Mauritius	23	5.54	0.93	2008
Mayotte[c]	n/a	n/a	0.04	2007
Niger	6	6.64	0.06	2003
Réunion[d]	n/a	n/a	0.41	2005
Rwanda	5	7.62	0.1	2000
Senegal	109	25.01	0.88	2008
Seychelles	18	55.60	0.16	2008
Togo	90	11.10	0.07	2008
Tunisia	36	1.51	7	2008
PACIFIC OCEAN				
Vanuatu	32	4.46	0.09	2008
French Polynesia[c]	7	1.07	0.19	2008
Wallis and Futuna[c]	n/a	n/a	n/a	
New Caledonia[e]	n/a	n/a	0.1	2008
CENTRAL AND SOUTH AMERICA				
French Guiana[d]	33	5.81	0.07	2002
Guadeloupe[d]	n/a	n/a	0.46	2008
Martinique[d]	n/a	n/a	0.48	2008
Saint Barthélemy[c]	n/a	n/a	0.32	2007
Saint Martin[c]	n/a	n/a	0.46	2008

Table 10.1. Continued.

Region and country or territory	Nationally designated terrestrial protected areas[a]		International tourism arrivals[b]	
	Number	% area	Millions	Year
NORTH AMERICA				
Canada	5122	8.23	17.1	2008
Saint Pierre and Miquelon	n/a	n/a	0.02	2006

[a] Source: The World Database on Protected Areas for 2009.
[b] Source: United Nations World Tourism Organization international visitor arrival statistics.
[c] Overseas French Territory (TOM).
[d] Overseas French Department (DOM).
[e] Independent since 1998.

are involved in solidarity and fair-trade aspects of tourism, particularly in less developed African countries. In this sense, French tourism operators and many NGOs use the terms such as responsible, fair, equity, social, solidarity and sustainable tourism more often than, and interchangeably with, ecotourism, in their work towards equilibrium between economic, social and environmental components of the sector. The most active organizations in this sense include l'Union nationale des associations de tourisme (UNAT) and Tourisme et développement solidaire (TDS).

There are few examples as yet of positive contributions to biodiversity conservation by private industry, where industry has taken leadership without outside influences provided by organizations concerned with environmental protection and nature conservation and/or involvement and pressure from the government. The current trends, however, appear positive, and industry is showing signs of cooperating and working in partnership arrangements, especially with public sector organizations at the local and regional level throughout France. This chapter provides a brief insight into this process, mainly from secondary sources and some personal communications to validate a number of points. The chapter begins by tracing a historical evolution that established a context for a conservation network in France. The second part describes some of the tools and mechanisms currently in place to show how a positive relationship is fostered between tourism and conservation in publicly managed protected areas.

Pre-1960s: Historical Context for Establishment of Conservation Areas in France

The practical idea to set land aside for conservation arrived slowly and late in France compared with the rest of Europe (Cans, 2006). Many factors explain this tardy development, including the historical evolution of social attitudes to nature enshrined in Catholic ideals (Bozonnet and Fischesser, 1985; Viard, 1985). In consequence, nature was perceived as either something to fear, or something to control via engineering and cultivation (Rodary and Castellanet, 2003). Nature protection in France dates to the period of Louis XIV, although very much underpinned by 'resourcism', a utilitarian approach to protecting forests for wood production and protecting animals for hunting by rich nobility (Fromageau, 1985; Walter, 1990). As in the rest of Europe, the romantic art and poetic movement led to the heritage movement (Kalaora and Savoye, 1985) and, in this context, the upper classes, urbanite intellectuals and artists contributed foremost to the evolution of an ecological conscience in French society (Larrère, 1997). These groups advocated conservation to preserve picturesque landscapes and monuments in reaction to the adverse impacts that resulted from industrialization and agricultural expansion. In consequence, the first nature reserve in France was created in 1861 at Fontainebleau Forest just outside Paris. This reserve began to draw visitors almost immediately after its establishment. The first zoological society in the world was founded in France in 1854, by and large in response to wildlife massacres by hunters (Simonnet, 1991).

Prior to the early 20th century, tourism development in France was concentrated in purpose-built exclusive resorts, often considered well integrated into the landscape in the mountains and along the coast (Lozato-Giotart, 2006). Nature-based tourism expanded gradually from general countryside recreation, led by the curiosity of urban intellectuals and naturalists who wanted to see landmarks such as caves and waterfalls. These groups were the early founders of the Alpine Club (established in 1874) and the Touring Club (established in 1890), both of which played a pivotal role in the French conservation movement (Kalaora and Savoye, 1985; Clary, 1993). Their lobbying efforts resulted in the foundation of the Landscape Protection Association in 1901, which marked the arrival of the idea of conserving nature for its intrinsic value in France. At the turn of the 20th century, some tourism associations were also actively involved in the activities of the Touring Club to protect some of the natural monuments considered important for tourism (Rodary and Castellanet, 2003; Lepart and Marty, 2006). In 1913, legislation was passed to protect monuments and significant sites. For many decades subsequently, the role of naturalists, scientists and nature protection societies continued to be significantly more important than tourism in France's conservation movement (Raffin and Ricou, 1985). For example, in 1910, the Dauphinois Alpinist Society actively demanded the creation of the first national park in the Grand Chartreuse region in the south-east of France. This followed general conservation trends elsewhere, particularly the establishment of the first European National Park in 1909 in Sweden (Cans, 2006). Unfortunately, none of the early conservation-oriented organizations had any significant financial capacity to buy land for conservation, although several small private reserves were established as early as 1912. One example is Sept-Îles, which now extends over 170 ha and is managed by the Ligue de protection des oiseaux (LPO), the French representative of BirdLife International.

All conservation efforts were seriously hindered by the aftermaths of the two world wars and economic decline in rural areas (Préau, 1972). From a tourism perspective, the period between the 1940s and the end of the 1960s marked an era of unprecedented mass tourism development led by the state, as well as a period of ambivalence towards ecosystem protection (Michaud, 1983). The French government considered tourism as an inexhaustible motor of regional development in both mountain and coastal regions (Béteille, 1996). Starting with *Le Plan Neige* in 1946, the state embarked on a huge capital investment programme to build resorts, thereby purposefully positioning France on the global tourism scene (Préau, 1972). Much of this intervention was justified on the basis of potential demand, stipulated in consequence of increased tourism that resulted from paid vacations, growth in personal mobility and rising popularity of outdoor activities during the post Second World War period. This technocratic development resulted in serious negative biophysical impacts, such as converting almost the whole coast into concrete. In the Languedoc-Roussillon Region, however, a network of wetland protection sites was established (Clary, 1993). The fact that the French state played a central role in developing mass tourism, as well as leading most of the efforts in implementing natural resource protection measures, created a particularly paradoxical situation.

Phase I: Towards a Positive Relationship Between Tourism and Conservation 1960–1980s

Legislation to establish nature reserves was passed in 1957, and national parks in 1960 (Veyret and Ciattoni, 2004). The following decades set the scene for expanding a protected area network in France, beginning with the establishment of La Vanoise National Park in 1963 (Table 10.2). The national park creation process was modelled on the American system, but executed almost entirely in a top-down manner by the French government. The tourism industry played almost no role at all (Richez, 1992, p. 22). This process was also a reaction to decades of pressure from conservation-oriented organizations, including the Touring Club. Park creation was used as an instrument of regional development to avoid further anarchic and irreversible damage caused by agriculture and mass tourism in both coastal and mountain areas (Richez, 1992, p. 77).

The process took literally decades in France, because of complications related to land acquisition. Instead of expropriation, the government negotiated with landowners and 'communes' (equivalent to municipalities) to obtain land rights. The aim was to achieve local acceptance of state regulation over land as set out in the legislation for the establishment of national parks by the central government. However, compensation was not granted in return, and this created strong opposition by the large rural-dwelling population who owned many small parcels of land. Hence, the national park concept remained unacceptable in France for many years. Because of these land acquisition difficulties, the initial parks were established in mountainous regions, as mountain lands were still available in relatively large parcels and perceived as useless to agriculture (Barrué-Pastor, 1989). For the same reasons, it still remains difficult to implement management actions around parks, because of persisting resistance to conservation principles by rural landholders (Jardel, 1997; Lahaye, 2006).

Today approximately 95% of rural France remains in private ownership (World Wildlife Fund France, 2008).

Following the establishment of a national park network in the mid-1960s (Table 10.2), tourism did not grow exponentially as predicted in and around parks, and many people remained unemployed in rural areas. Initially, parks were not only perceived as unsuccessful by rural France, but they were also of little interest to tourism and the general population. The numbers of visitors to parks were negligible, even at the beginning of the 1980s (Richez, 1992). As French national parks were created according to IUCN criteria, the central core of parks resulted in the exclusion of human occupation (except in Cévennes) and this has been a continued source of land use conflicts (Bouvier et al., 1995; Veyret and Ciattoni, 2004). The periphery or the buffer zone of French national parks allows a variety of land uses, while tourism and recreation are permitted in both zones. For example, La Vanoise National Park (Table 10.2) still contains 60% of ski resorts in France in its periphery, but ski lifts stop literally at the border of the park's core, while tracks continue into it. In compensation for excluding many traditional land uses in the core areas of national parks during the 1960s–1970s, the French government provided massive subsidies to develop tourism

Table 10.2. Characteristics of national parks in France.

National park	Year of creation	Park land area, km² Centre	Periphery	Total	Central zone visitors 2007–2008
La Vanoise	1963	530	1450	1980	800,000
Port-Cros[a]	1963	17	0	30	1,500,000
Pyrénées	1967	457	2063	2521	1,500,000
Cévennes	1970	912	2297	3210	800,000
Écrins	1973	918	1780	2698	750,000
Mercantour	1979	685	1465	2150	600,000
Guadeloupe	1989	174	162	336	1,000,000
Amazonien de Guyane	2007	19,659	n/a	n/a	n/a
La Réunion	2007	1,054	n/a	n/a	430,000
Calanques[a]	2010 (planned)	125	340	465	1,300,000 (projected)

[a] Port-Cros also has a 13 km² maritime zone and Calanques a 2760 km² maritime zone, with an 820 km² core area and 1940 km² periphery.
Source: Website of each park. NB: Of the nine national parks in France, three are situated on territories outside Europe.

in their periphery areas (Clary, 1993, p. 177). Despite the adoption of new legislation for national parks in 2006, today the management of park periphery areas continues to be a source of problems throughout France (Lahaye, 2006), since about 32% of these lands are still used for forestry and 13% for agriculture (Veyret and Ciattoni, 2004). Hunting remains a particular problem (Larrère, 2003).

Phase II: Integration of Tourism and Conservation

It was really after the mid-1970s that attitudes changed, and tourism became part of the solution in integrating rural development and economic revival and started delivering any service to conservation in France (Cans, 1994). Nature-based and ecotourism started to develop incrementally and slowly, facilitated largely by the public sector (Blangy et al., 2002). The 1970s also marked the establishment of a complex hierarchy of public-sector institutions in France that affected both tourism and conservation (Michaud, 1983). Some of this facilitated a partnership between tourism and conservation, but mainly it led to the expansion and diversification of the French protected area network (Table 10.3; Nevers, 2005). Additionally, in 1976, legislation was passed for general nature protection to enable land to be set aside incrementally for conservation under a range of categories besides national parks. The establishment of a legal framework for regional park creation was particularly important. The

Table 10.3. Typology of the main protected areas in France where ecotourism and nature-based recreation occur.

Typology	French status of protection	IUCN categories	Number	Area, km^2	% of territory	Conservation	Tourism
National Park	Total National Parks (NP), central and buffer zones included	II (central zone); V (buffer zone)	9	12,924	2.36	Minor to major	Major
Regional Natural Park	Total Regional Natural Parks (RNP)	V	45	71,298	13.03	Minor	Major
	Sites included in a NP			154	0.03		
Nature Reserves	Total Nature Reserves (NR)	III or IV	323	28,480	5.21	Major	Minor
Biological Reserves	Total Biological Reserves		199	1,812	0.33		
	Managed Biological Reserves	IV	161	305	0.06	Minor	Minor
	Integrated Estate Biological Reserves	I	38	1,506	0.28	Major	Absent
Biosphere Reserves	Total MAB Zones	N/A	10	8921	1.63	Minor	Major
Natura2000 sites	Total Natura2000 sites	I to V	1,704	97,853	17.89		
	Sites included in a NP			6,578	1.20	Minor to major	Major
	Sites included in a NR			1,462	0.27		
	Sites included in a RNP			12,828	2.35		

(Source: Adapted from Giran (2003, pp.57–69) and Martinez (2007, pp.14 and 91–92).)

1980s and 1990s represented a period of decentralization of public-sector activities across France, as well as a period of elaboration and reinforcement of laws for environmental protection, to avoid past mistakes incurred by tourism. In 1985, 1986 and 1993, new legislation was passed to protect mountain ecosystems, coastal ecosystems and general landscapes respectively. These laws continue to affect tourism, notably by limiting its expansion and requiring landscape protection measures to control erosion and associated degradation.

One of the areas that benefited from these changes was the French coast, which had become almost completely urbanized and converted to concrete as a consequence of all the tourism developments. Established in 1975, the Coastal Conservancy (Giacobbi, 1997) began to acquire land to rehabilitate many areas, and in some cases to halt tourism development and exclude all recreation. The Coastal Conservancy manages over 700 km of coast today, and it continues to play an important coordinating role between local and regional public-sector authorities, and also occasionally tourism businesses (Giacobbi, 1997). Its weakness remains its limited financial capacity to manage land. It has no control over development proposals outside its properties, as this remains in the power of municipalities and regional public authorities (Lopez, 1999, p. 109). Today, the Conservancy accommodates some tourism and recreation in its reserves, and some of this is financed via partnerships with private-sector organizations, including tourism enterprises which donate funds towards rehabilitation works and coastal clean-ups (Legrain and Letourneux, 1994). Coastal areas are important to the French tourism sector and in 2004 they represented over 30% of overnight stays, as compared with less than 10% in mountains (Deboudt, 2004).

Today, about 15% of France is in some kind of reservation, of which 3% is under strict control by legislation and almost completely under public-sector management (Table 10.3). The protected area network in France remains fragmented and complicated, and its efficacy is often questioned (Giran, 2003). Most areas labelled as some kind of a 'reserve' exist primarily for biodiversity protection, but not necessarily with the complete exclusion of tourism and recreation. There are about 25 different types of conservation area in France, and many may overlap with one another (Atelier technique des espaces naturels, 2009). Most eco- and nature-based tourism occurs on lands reserved as national parks, regional natural parks, Natura2000 reserves, UNESCO Man and Biosphere Reserves and coastal reserves (Table 10.3). The management of human activities in these areas often creates complex issues, because it may involve organizations at the level of municipalities, counties, regions and nationally, as well as a range of non-government organizations (Breton, 2004; Veyret and Ciattoni, 2004).

Whatever the classification, in France most conservation estates are managed directly by government agencies, and, where tourism and recreation are permitted, there are regional public-sector associations that collectively contribute to managing them. Hence, funds for managing conservation areas used by tourism are derived largely from the national government, or from local and regional-scale funds collected via special local taxes, such as those added on to a stay at a lodging facility. In France, there are traditional beliefs that nature is a free commodity accessible to all, and that nature manages itself and therefore needs little funding for maintenance (Vourc'h, 1999). Many natural sites are accorded very basic management actions such as litter collections and clean-ups, and otherwise no specific efforts are made for ensuring the ecological integrity of the area. There appears also to be a culture in France to invest more in protecting cultural heritage places and humanized landscapes that represent past ways of life than in natural areas for preserving biodiversity values.

Linked to the idea that nature should be a free commodity, most places with any type of public conservation status are free to visit, including national parks. There is thus little or no direct funding contribution from tourism. Cross-country skiers are generally the only recreation group required to pay a fee for practising their activity: all other outdoor activities in natural areas are free throughout France. There are a few conservation areas where tourists are required to pay fees directly. This is the case, for instance, in the coastal reserve of Marquanterre, owned by the Coastal

Conservancy, where entry fees generate almost all the funds required for site management (Vourc'h and Natali, 2000). Elsewhere, funds collected from tourists via the sale of meals and various souvenir items in nearby shops may contribute indirectly to the management of conservation areas. At most conservation reserves where the local municipality or agency manages an area, it may collect parking fees and part of this sum may be used for management. This arrangement appears to be one of the most acceptable to the French public, because of the perception that the payment is for a specific service (Vourc'h, 1999).

As an example, at l'Ardèche Gorge Reserve, 12 municipalities are involved with the local tourism sector, and special lodging taxes form the basis for managing the Gorge Reserve via a mixed public–private-sector organization. It is estimated that businesses in the Gorge area allocate about 3% of their revenues to environmental management linked to natural spaces (Vourc'h and Natali, 2000, p. 32). At Sept Îles Nature Reserve, about 60% of site management is sourced from items sold in the boutique and guided tourism activities. Since 1993, there has also been a financial partnership with an organization of boat tour operators, who give a percentage of ticket sales to conservation works, and this represents around 5% of the reserve's revenues. Two-thirds of the reserve's revenue comes from interpretation activities and products sold to visitors, while a third is from public funds.

In general, publicly managed French conservation areas frequented by tourists are not adequately financed, and there are still opportunities to gain revenues from tourism (Vourc'h, 2007). How effectively tourism is contributing directly to the maintenance of some conservation areas is not clear, but this seems to be rare except on a few private conservation estates. There are a number of private nature reserves across France, and some of them have developed a combination of agro-ecotourism. For example, the company Aoubre in the south of France has developed a 30 ha private nature park, le Parc des Cèdres, in an effort to preserve a Mediterranean forest ecosystem. This is also a sustainable forest as certified by the European Forest Certification Council, and it offers a variety of low-impact nature-based

activities to visitors. There are other similar examples, but there does not appear to be any overall database providing coherent information about such places.

In most conservation areas where tourists are allowed to visit, ecotourism is promoted, because it is linked to visitor education and interpretation of heritage values. In turn, this provides a legitimate context for setting and maintaining publicly funded conservation areas in France, and this remains very important. Since the mid-1990s, many conservation areas throughout France have been managed using volunteer work. Some tourism and travel organizations actively promote volunteer work with conservation-oriented NGOs such as Ecovolontariat, Cybelle Planet, A Pas de Loup, Planète Urgence and LPO. The tourism sector more broadly does not have a culture of involvement with conservation works, but there are some exceptions. For example, the tour operator company Saïga offers trips to private and public conservation areas around the world where the experience directly exposes clients to conservation works in action, such as monitoring wildlife. Many of this company's visitor experiences also focus on supporting small local initiatives to resolve conservation issues, where an entry fee from a visit makes a financial contribution to a specific initiative. Examples include the reintroduction of salmon in the Loire River, or a stay with alpine mountain shepherds to expose clients to wolf conservation issues. The latter visitor experience is organized in direct association with a conservation-oriented organization A Pas de Loup, whose mission is to save wolves from further decline in alpine areas of France. Saïga was also responsible for the foundation of the latter organization (P. Marais, personal communication, 2009).

There are many more tour companies with similar profiles. One example is Escursia, which offers nature-based and ecotourism products to small groups in France and overseas which involve visiting protected areas, a strong education component and direct involvement with scientific monitoring in protected areas, e.g. whale monitoring in the Gulf Saint-Lawrence in Canada. Some accommodation establishments are also involved with conservation-related works. The Etap Hotel chain, for example, has establishments across France engaged in land restoration works, with the specific objective of creating habitats for birds. Their work is in cooperation and in partnership with the bird protection organization LPO. There are similar examples, at various scales, across the whole of France. Often they involve volunteer work by individual tour company staff. In Port-Cros National Park, for example, which includes marine and coastal sections, dive tour operators contribute actively to invasive weed control efforts (G. Landrieu, personal communication, 2009).

International organizations such as IUCN and WWF, as well as various European regional policies, continue to be a major influence in facilitating positive relationships between conservation and tourism in France (Nevers, 2005). For example, the European Charter for Sustainable Tourism in Protected Areas remains an important voluntary tool in many French parks, because it requires the tourism sector to work in partnership with park management authorities, and this is subject to verification by Europarc (Europarc, 2008). The Charter focuses on helping tourism operators and park managers achieve cooperation, using a checklist of 12 principles applied in a 5-year plan for each park (Lair, 2006). To date, the Charter's success is ascribed largely to the provision of networking and knowledge-sharing opportunities at a regional scale. This is important because it provides a setting for the tourism network in which conservation objectives at various scales become an element of their operations, even if only at the level of awareness of ecosystem management issues.

The World Wide Fund for Nature (WWF) also continues to facilitate positive relationships between tourism and conservation, even though none of the French parks are members of the WWF Pan Parks programme. WWF's Gîtes Panda initiative, however, is widely recognized in France as providing good practice in environmental management for rural accommodation in and around conservation areas. Gîtes Panda is an eco-label system (Font and Buckley, 2001) which specifies minimum thresholds for energy, water and waste management, and for the environmental education of guests. The initiative started in 1992, and in 2009 there were 230 Gîtes in

national parks and regional natural parks across France (C. Magdelenat, personal communication, 2009). Many Gîtes Panda guest houses are actively involved in restoring heritage buildings, and many offer only local products for consumption. Regional councils provide a small subsidy for establishments to earn the Gîtes Panda label, and park management agencies monitor each guest house to check compliance (Commission Internationale pour la Protection des Alpes, 2008). Most Gîtes Panda operators contribute to managing nearby natural areas, but these individual efforts and their cumulative effects remain undocumented to date (C. Magdelenat, personal communication, 2009).

Case Study: Cévennes National Park

Especially since the 1980s, tourism has increasingly been perceived as the most legitimate land use in and around conservation estates such as national and regional natural parks, because of its role in public education on conservation and environmental protection, and because it leads to economic development in nearby rural areas. Government conservation agencies provide support for the tourism industry to provide interpretation and guided activities to promote low-impact recreation, and in some cases to become involved in management works (Ministère de l'Économie, des Finances et de l'Emploi, 2009). One park where such a positive relationship exists between the private sector and the park management is Cévennes National Park (CNP), located in the southern highlands of France. This park has been a UNESCO World Biosphere Reserve since 1985, and a signatory to the European Charter for Sustainable Development since 1992.

CNP is an unusual case in the French context, for two reasons. First, about 600 people live in the core area of the park. Second, ecotourism in the park is managed through a local association, Écotourisme Cévennes, which works closely with park management (Daversin, 2009). The fact that the park is a signatory to the European Charter is very significant for Cévennes, because the park has a particularly complex political and institutional setting. This is due to the multitude of stakeholders involved at all levels of government, and especially to the high number of local government municipalities (M. Pin, personal communication, 2008). The core of CNP encompasses 910 km² across 52 municipalities, and 41,000 people live in a peripheral buffer zone which extends over 2370 km² and 117 municipalities. Adherence to the Charter also resulted in specific 5-year land management plans involving tourism. This affects how tourism-based enterprises operate in the park, monitored by a technical committee that assesses individual business activities. In practical terms, this means that each tourism business is required to have a 3-year action plan to ensure responsible operations in the park. While there are currently around 1000 tourism operations functioning within the park, however, only 75 of these are members of Écotourisme Cévennes, and only 43 have signed the European Charter. The association, which has been in existence since 2001, encourages other tour operators to join.

Écotourisme Cévennes remains a unique arrangement in a French national park context, especially since the establishment of the organization was initiated by a number of tourism professionals who wanted to work closely with park management and truly implement ecotourism principles. Écotourisme Cévennes plays an important role in promoting conservation through direct involvement in environmental education of park visitors, but it does not contribute directly to the environmental management of areas. In conjunction with park management, the association has been instrumental in creating additional interpretation facilities to improve public education about environmental issues. This includes the creation of an 'ecomuseum', and the organization of a variety of nature festivals (about 600 a year). While individual businesses may be involved directly in planning and carrying out these projects, however, most of the projects are financed by the state. The member businesses of Écotourisme Cévennes are distributed across the entire area covered by the park, and their combined net sales are estimated at over five million euros annually. In aggregate, they employ 140 people on a full-time equivalent basis, and offer 842 beds and 296 campsites

(Jaffuel and Pin, 2006, p. 222). There are also 20 Gîtes Panda in the park, and several other projects aimed at conserving the park's heritage value. For example, an old ski area at Mas de la Barque was converted to a nature resort by replacing ski infrastructure with hiking tracks and environmentally conscious lodging establishments (Jaffuel and Pin, 2006).

Cévennes NP offers around 1067 km of hiking trails in its core area and 2210 km in the buffer zone, along 257 separate trails. The park also maintains 510 km of horse riding trails. Visitor numbers to the park are estimated at over 800,000 annually. Around 330,000 visitors to the core of the park take part in organized educational activities (Ministère de l'Écologie, de l'Énergie, du Développement durable et de l'Aménagement du territoire, 2007). Ecotourism is particularly important at CNP, because it raises awareness about the importance of conservation, a notion that remains unpopular with certain stakeholders such as hunters in the park (Guerrini, 1995). Agro-ecotourism is increasingly important and encouraged, and in recent years the expansion of chestnut groves has provided an important setting for local organic food production (Crosnier, 2006). There are also increased efforts by tourism businesses to improve their energy, water and waste management, and overall these actions all contribute positive outcomes for the park area (Daversin, 2009).

Since around 95% of the total park is in private ownership, the management role of the park authority that administers state legislation is rather complex. This is on the one hand because management tries to keep a North American concept of national park, and on the other to accommodate traditional land uses such as forestry, grazing and hunting that are not consistent with conservation principles. Hunting, both professional and recreational, is permitted to avoid overpopulation of successfully reintroduced species such as deer and wild boar. Cévennes National Park, however, remains a setting for a wide variety of stakeholders with often divergent interests (Crosnier, 2006). Commonly, conservation objectives are accepted only so long as they do not affect certain traditions that are perceived as an important part of the local identity. Land use problems relate principally to hunting and to agriculture, even though the park provides financial assistance to farmers to avoid degradation (Guerrini, 1990). Activities such as four-wheel driving are also still permitted, with 80 km of tracks. This is paradoxical, since non-motorized outdoor activities receive higher support from tourism businesses and municipalities, because of their favourable economic impacts.

Regional Natural Parks: a Bottom-up Approach for Land Conservation

The regional natural park (RNP) concept is perhaps one of the most interesting approaches in achieving positive relationships between tourism development and land conservation in France. These parks are considered as 'conservation areas' in the broad sense, because their entire area is under a common management framework and they are classed as IUCN category V protected areas (Martinez, 2007). The origin of RNPs is related to the difficulties encountered with traditional national parks in France (Lepart and Marty, 2006). RNPs are very different from publicly managed national parks, because their creation represents a voluntary, bottom-up approach to setting land aside for conservation. Stakeholders from a given region establish each existing RNP following an application process to the Ministry of the Environment, in order to give formal recognition of the local heritage values to an area. Once an application is approved, the park's territory must be managed as an integrated entity, guided by a charter for the park and specific management plans. A park's charter engages all stakeholders to respect this engagement, and the territory is recognized for 12 years. The Ministry of the Environment administers and oversees the overall management of the park's territory. All stakeholders within a park territory are expected to adopt a 'wise use' approach to land and resource management. In tourism this generally translates to improved energy, water and waste management.

In 2009 there were 47 RNPs across France (Table 10.4). Each park contains a variety of land uses within a settled area, with a balance between natural and cultural land uses, such as agriculture and tourism. A range of mechanisms are used for management, including a private association (Lorraine), a foundation (Parc de Camargue) or a mixed syndicate including municipal, county or regional body (Vosges du Nord). This variation occurs since RNPs must be self-financed, and their investment funds may be derived from regional council, county council, national or European Union sources. RNPs may contain a variety of nature reserves within their territories, and only some of these allow visitors, with the majority set aside for conservation (Maupéoux et al., 2005). Setting land aside within RNPs for conservation purposes only is encouraged, and sometimes supported by tax incentives. Most RNPs address biodiversity conservation rather weakly, however, because their establishment does not include specific legislation for this. Legislation does require that environmental management efforts must uphold a certain minimum quality in land management, or a park may lose its status. Since the creation of the first RNP at the end of the 1960s, however, only one park has lost its status owing to inadequate environmental management (O. Sanch, personal communication, 2009).

In 2009 RNPs covered approximately 13% of France's land mass, or 7 million hectares including 3 million inhabitants. A growing number of regions throughout France are converting their territories to RNPs as an instrument for tourism development. Most such tourism is broadly based on nature and cultural heritage. As a result, RNPs across France are estimated to attract more than 30% of tourists throughout the year (André and Talbot, 2007). RNPs have been considered as a success from their inception, especially due to their bottom-up approach to implementing national policy (Préau, 1972; Laurens and Cousseau, 2000). Considerable know-how has been developed in the creation and management of RNPs, especially in organizing stakeholder groups, and this know-how has been exported to China, Brazil, Benin and elsewhere (Fédération des Parcs naturels régionaux de France, 2008).

Since implementation of RNP management plans or park charters is coordinated by government, the involvement of tourism in land management is not straightforward. In some

Table 10.4. Characteristics of regional natural parks in France. (Source: Fédération des Parcs naturels régionaux de France, 28 August 2007, except for PNR Pyrénées ariégeoises.)

Regional Natural Park	Region	Number of Rural Communes included	Park area, km²	Population 1999	Year of creation
Scarpe-Escaut	Nord-Pas de Calais	48	450	162,000	1968
Armorique (+ 600 km² marine)	Bretagne	39	1,120	55,670	1969
Brière	Pays de la Loire	18	490	75,000	1970
Camargue	Provence-Alpes-Côte d'Azur	2	865	8,000	1970
Forêt d'Orient	Champagne Ardenne	50	715	20,000	1970
Landes de Gascogne	Aquitaine	41	3,030	55,000	1970
Morvan	Bourgogne	94	2,260	33,000	1970
Vercors	Rhône-Alpes	68	1,780	30,500	1970
Corse	Corse	143	3,750	26,000	1972
Haut-Languedoc	Languedoc Roussillon Midi-Pyrénées	93	2,605	82,000	1973
Boucles de la Seine	Haute-Normandie	72	810	58,000	1974
Lorraine	Normande (ex Brotonne)	188	2,195	72,090	1974
Pilat	Rhône-Alpes	47	700	48,000	1974
Normandie-Maine	Basse-Normandie Pays de la Loire	150	2,340	85,500	1975
Montagne de Reims	Champagne Ardenne	69	500	35,000	1976
Vosges du Nord	Alsace Lorraine	111	1,300	83,000	1976
Martinique	Martinique	32	630	100,000	1976
Luberon	Provence-Alpes-Côte d'Azur	71	1,650	148,000	1977
Volcans d'Auvergne	Auvergne	153	3,950	88,000	1977
Haute-Vallée de Chevreuse	Île de France	21	245	46,500	1985
Caps et Marais d'Opale	Nord-Pas de Calais	152	1,320	186,500	1986
Haut-Jura	France Comté Rhône-Alpes	105	1,640	70,000	1986
Livradois-Forez	Auvergne	170	3,100	98,000	1986
Brenne	Centre	46	1,660	30,000	1989
Ballons des Vosges	Alsace Franche-Comté Lorraine	203	2,915	253,500	1989
Marais du Cotentin et du Bessin	Basse-Normandie	144	1,450	64,500	1991
Chartreuse	Rhône-Alpes	52	690	35,000	1995
Grands Causses	Midi-Pyrénées	94	3,160	63,500	1995
Massif des Bauges	Rhône-Alpes	58	810	52,500	1995
Vexin français	Île-de-France	94	655	79,000	1995
Loire-Anjou-Touraine	Centre Pays de la Loire	136	2,530	177,000	1996
Queyras	Provence-Alpes-Côte d'Azur	11	600	3,000	1997
Verdon	Provence-Alpes-Côte d'Azur	45	1,800	22,000	1997

Table 10.4. Continued.

Regional Natural Park	Region	Number of Rural Communes included	Park area, km²	Population 1999	Year of creation
Avesnois	Nord/Pas de Calais	129	1,250	131,000	1998
Perche	Basse-Normandie Centre	118	1,820	74,000	1998
Périgord-Limousin	Aquitaine Limousin	78	1,800	50,000	1998
Causses du Quercy	Midi-Pyrénées	97	1,750	25,000	1999
Gâtinais français	Île de France	57	635	70,000	1999
Monts d'Ardèche	Rhône-Alpes	132	1,800	56,000	2001
Guyane	Guyane	3	2,247	8,106	2001
Narbonnaise en Méditerranée	Languedoc Roussillon	20	800	28,000	2003
Millevaches en Limousin	Limousin	113	3,000	38,000	2004
Oise – Pays de France	Picardie Île de France	59	600	110,000	2004
Pyrénées catalanes	Languedoc Roussillon	64	1,371	21,000	2004
Alpilles	PACA	16	510	42,000	2007
Pyrénées ariégeoises	Midi-Pyrénées	142	2,500	42,000	2009
TOTAL		3,848	73,798	3,140,866	

parks, however, mechanisms have been developed to achieve cooperation between land conservation and tourism development. One of the better examples of cooperation is the RNP of Vosges du Nord, which has been a UNESCO MAB Reserve since 1989, and is now also a signatory to the European Charter of Sustainable Tourism Development. In 2009, this park also won an EDEN Award, a European initiative to recognize destination sustainability. Vosges du Nord Park extends over 1300 km², including 111 communes and 83,000 inhabitants. A positive relationship between park management and tourism has been achieved through the establishment of a conservation foundation in 2006 to support park management actions by tour operators. This subsequently became a factor in mobilizing further action to conserve heritage areas within the park. Its main objective is to raise funds through voluntary donations so as to help tourism enterprises to be more responsible in their management, while retaining tourism activity within the park area (Lair, 2006, p. 99). The foundation also aims to inform and educate tourism businesses about natural heritage protection.

As in many areas within park territory in France, nature and ecotourism in Vosges du Nord are associated with continuing agricultural activities (Barrué-Pastor 1989). Business in Vosges du Nord NRP contributes to the conservation foundation by selling foods certified by the label 'Le paysage a du Goût', which are produced from Highland cattle found within this particular park. Sales of bottled water from springs found in the park (l'eau Celtic) also contribute to the foundation. Additionally, some restaurants contribute 1 euro to the conservation foundation for every meal sold containing Highland cattle products. Since 1993, there has been a close relationship between tourism and the park, with industry contributing to resource management on a voluntary basis (Laurens and Cousseau, 2000, p. 243). All parks across France are currently encouraging agribusinesses to develop local value-added products that reflect the heritage value of the park. Products approved by the park federation are labelled as produits du terroir, and carry brand labels linked to the specific RNP (Féderation des Parcs naturels régionaux de France, 2009).

Tourism businesses are also encouraged to promote a park's brands via the network of lodging facilities *Hôtels au Naturel*. Essentially, any establishment may apply for this label if they are located inside a park, but they must demonstrate to park management that they manage resources to reduce environmental impacts, that they educate guests in low-impact recreation and that they offer educational activities, including guided nature interpretation. These hotels currently exist in seven parks, and in 2009 there were 21 individual establishments (M. Lasguines, personal communication, 2009). Park managers help such lodging operations implement management practices so they meet criteria and reduce their environmental impacts. The hotels, however, do not participate in land management efforts with parks staff, nor do they provide financial contributions towards land management. As with the rest of the tourism sector in RNPs, these hotels are considered valuable largely because of the role they play in educating guests about conservation issues. In Vosges Natural Park, for example, one local villa is actively involved in organizing tours and activities focused on botany, including weed control practices.

Conclusions

France represents an unusual case when considering positive relationships between tourism and land conservation. Traditionally and historically, France seems to have resisted conservation efforts because of a range of socio-economic and political reasons that might be explained by its large rural population and the fact that about 95% of land is privately owned. As the landscape is intensely humanized, it is extremely difficult to implement conservation measures, even on land already in conservation status. There appears to be some convergence between tourism and conservation, but this is rather ad hoc, since the French nature-ecotourism sector rarely contributes directly to biodiversity conservation efforts. It

seems that the main benefit that conservation areas receive from tourism is in visitor education and promotion of low-impact recreation activities. Clearly, much is still to be done, but at least mechanisms are now in place to coordinate the efforts of public-sector organizations and NGOs that involve the tourism sector.

The regional natural park concept seems to hold particular potential to achieve some kind of a balance between tourism and conservation. The example of Cévennes also highlights that the French protection system 'tolerates' a lot of activities in conservation areas, such as hunting, that do not really correspond to the definition of ecotourism or the mission of national parks. It appears that the French system is based on a rather pragmatic vision of integration between humans and nature, where traditional land-use activities seem to have priority. This is accompanied by a certain possibility of 'operational compromise' as far as those are concerned who are more respectful of the rules because it serves their interests. This also explains some of the issues linked to implementing practical management actions linked to conservation. The situation in France is certainly complex. The detailed roles of different stakeholders in conservation processes were beyond the scope of this chapter, but this also deserves attention in future, since one of the distinguishing characteristics of tourism and conservation in France resides in its political structure and the complex hierarchy of public institutions.

Acknowledgements

The authors wish to thank Annie Demers-Caron for her work with the compilation of secondary sources, and all individuals who gave time for interviews concerning conservation and tourism in France. A special thank you is extended to Sylvie Blangy and Ghislain Dubois for their comments on draft versions of this chapter.

11 South and Central America

Canopy tower, La Selva

Introduction

The links between tourism and conservation in South and Central America – as in other continents – may be considered in four main groups: public, community, private land and tour operations. Some public protected areas, but not many, rely on fees from visitors and tour operators for a significant component of their budgets, though there are commonly difficulties with revenue retention and distribution and issues relating to visitor impacts. Some local communities, including some indigenous communities, have established tourism operations as part of efforts to retain control and management of their traditional lands and gain a low-impact cash income. Many of these ventures have been assisted by local or international NGOs and/or grants, loans or donations from development assistance agencies or private donors. There are privately owned landholdings, many of them small but ecologically significant none the less, which are managed for a combination of conservation and tourism, with the balance differing between properties. Some of these are owned and run by expatriates, which creates local political tensions in some cases. Finally, there are tour operators, with various private ownership structures, which can in some cases contribute to conservation through a variety of mechanisms ranging from marketing and bookings to cash donations and political lobbying (Buckley, 2009a, b).

Since there is as yet no fully comprehensive collection of audited case studies from every continent, it is not yet possible to determine whether the relative frequencies of these four groups differ between continents to create regional signatures in conservation tourism. Such signatures were suggested by Buckley (2003a) for ecotourism but were not identified by Buckley (2006) for adventure tourism. Within the Amazon basin, for example, there are a number of well-known community tourism ventures supported by NGOs, notably Conservation International, but there are also private reserves and various partnerships between private tour operators and community landowners.

This chapter considers only a selection of countries in South and Central America, namely those where the most detailed or reliable data are available. Most of the countries covered, though only a few of the individual sites, have been visited by the principal author or the authors of individual case studies. Some of the case studies, notably in Mexico, Panama and Bolivia, have been described quite extensively in previous reports. A few, such as Chalalan in Bolivia and Posada Amazonas in Peru, have been subject to detailed independent academic research.

A number of the case studies mentioned either by Buckley (2003a), Zeppel (2006) or Stronza and Durham (2008) are not referred to here: either because little has changed from previous reports; or because conservation was not one of their goals; or because tourism is not their main mechanism; or because there is no reliable information on their outcomes. For example, Zeppel (2006) considers cases in Venezuela, Guyana and Suriname. Those nations are not included in this volume but deserve attention in future research. The same applies for the Chilean case study, Expediciones Chile on the Rio Futaleufu, described by Buckley (2003a, 2006). It is still there, still operating and still lobbying for conservation, but there are no significant updates to report.

The majority of cases reported in this chapter are in rainforest ecosystems, and most of them involve Indigenous peoples concerned to protect their territories against various incursions and to provide themselves with improved livelihoods. Many also involve external assistance from either NGOs or aid agencies. The social and political contexts of the interactions between these players are both fascinating and illuminating, but they are not the primary focus for this volume, which is concerned to assess conservation outcomes in so far as may be possible.

Mexico

Two case studies from Mexico, namely Ixcan Biological Station, in the Montes Azules Biosphere Reserve, and the Monarch Butterfly Biosphere Reserve (Buckley, 2003a), both seem to have suffered some deterioration over the past decade, and tourism apparently does not contribute to conservation in either area.

Ixcan Biological Station was an investment by Conservation International, intended to help protect Mexico's most biodiverse ecosystem (ENDESU, 2010; UNESCO, 2010c). It is located on the Lacantún River with access to the 6500 km^2 Lacandona Forest and a variety of Mayan ruins. According to Nations (2006), one Mexican government agency created the Biosphere Reserve, but another created a farming cooperative, Ejido Ixcan, on the same land; and in addition, squatters who are not members of the cooperative also moved into the Reserve and cleared forest. Conservation International's aim was to convince members of Ejido Ixcan that they could earn more through conserving the forest than through clearing it. The 18-room, three-storey Biological Station was built in 1996 at a cost of five million Mexican pesos (~US$400,000), and was planned to provide local employment and a community fund. According to Quintero (undated), the economic activity at Ixcan did not match local expectations, and the locals feel defrauded. According to local newspapers, the building was very poorly constructed and collapsed; with either fraud, flood or both being blamed (Gutierrez, 2008). It appears that there are several other small tourist lodges, but it is not clear that these have yielded any conservation outcomes.

The Monarch Butterfly Biosphere Reserve was declared by the Mexican government in 1986 (Barkin, 2000). Various local and international NGOs commenced training programmes for local residents (Oberhauser and Solensky, 2004). Well-known international nature tour operators such as Natural Habitat Adventures still lead tours there, but the majority of visitors are domestic tourists. The butterflies overwinter for 4 months, and Barkin (2000) proposed that the area could be marketed as a more general domestic nature and adventure tourism destination during the rest of the year. It appears that there are significant and growing conservation problems, but whether these are associated with, alleviated by or entirely independent from tourism is not clear from the published literature.

Zeppel (2006) also referred to an area known as Singayta where local people variously known as Huichol or Wixaritari were establishing an area to protect mangroves. An NGO known as the Global Greengrants Fund provided US$10,000 (El Manglar EPG, 2004). The detailed accounts for the grant, however, show that about $2000 were used to buy land and the remainder on telephone, transport, communications and 'professional honoraria'. The project has a website (Singayta, 2010) and there are village tours on offer. A recent report in a local newspaper, however (Eagle, 2009) says that the Huichol have built an ecotourism centre but that it has not had any visitors. Conservation outcomes are thus unclear.

Belize

The best-known case of conservation tourism in Belize is the Community Baboon Sanctuary, which has been operating for 25 years. The key species is the black howler monkey, referred to locally as baboons. Reports by Edington and Edington (1997) described the Sanctuary as an elongated area of 40 km^2 along the Belize River (Buckley, 2003a), where villagers conserve tree corridors and fruit trees and don't hunt monkeys. The Sanctuary went through some difficult periods in the early 1990s (Bruner, 1993), but now appears to have stabilized. It was managed for many years by the Belize Audubon Society, but management has now been taken over by a local Women's Conservation Group, and involves at least 120 landowners in seven villages (Jones and Young, 2004). The area has also been expanded to over 50 km^2. A 2008 tourist blog on Trip Advisor® refers to new lodges built in 2007 and good local guides. A 2009 blog on *Lonely Planet*'s ThornTree® site expresses some concerns over pricing but not service. A 2007 interview with a university ecologist in Belize (Young, 2007) stated that the Sanctuary receives about 15,000 visitors annually, three times more than a decade ago, and that the Women's Conservation Group has won over $120,000 in grants. The same interview notes threats to Belize's forests from logging, agricultural clearance and oil exploration and production. According to the organization Community Conservation (2010), formed by the expatriate originators of the Sanctuary concept, the Sanctuary has protected howler monkeys locally, donated monkeys to two other areas, supported ecological research and served as a model for community conservation funded by tourism within Belize.

The Cockscomb Basin Wildlife Sanctuary was first established in 1984, expanded to 415 km^2 in 1990 and declared officially in 1997 (Leikam et al., 2004). It also supports ocelot, tapir and other key wildlife species. In 1992–1994, black howler monkeys were translocated to Cockscomb Basin Wildlife Sanctuary from the Community Baboon Sanctuary (Horwich et al., 2002). A discussion by Clark (undated) about a decade ago states that it was managed by the Belize Audubon Society, BAS; that disagreements arose between BAS and members of the local Maya community; but that these were not so serious as to dissolve the Sanctuary. An economic analysis by Lindberg et al. (1996) indicated that, at that time, the Sanctuary's main source of income was from international donors, with tourism turnover <\$50,000 p.a. and profitability uncertain.

Two additional case studies in Belize were mentioned by Buckley (2003a) and Zeppel (2006): Chaa Creek Lodge and the Toledo Ecotourism Association. The 135 ha private reserve and resort operated by Chaa Creek Ltd is apparently doing well commercially. It received positive reports on basic environmental management issues such as septic tanks from Barnett (2001), but less favourable reports from Fritsch and Johannsen (2004, p. 123). Neither commented on conservation. The Toledo Ecotourism Association (2010) is also apparently still operational, but it is not clear whether or not it contributes to conservation. According to marketing information, it consists of ten villages in southern Belize, each with an eight-person dormitory-style guest house. Early reports (Buckley, 2003a) state that a total of 13 guest houses had been built, with assistance from WWF, TNC and USAID. An NGO called Plenty International (2010) promotes TEA as one of its achievements, but the relevant materials on its website date from 1999.

Guatemala

The Ecomaya initiative in Guatemala was established in 1998 with support from Con-

servation International, to promote ecotourism in the 16,000 km^2 Mayan Biosphere Reserve. The ecotourism marketing initiative was complicated through conjunction with: a local NGO, Pro-Peten; a language school, Ecoescuela; and a tourism eco-certification scheme, Alianza Verde. Evaluations carried out by Conservation International in 2001, as reported in Buckley (2003a), found that the Ecoescuela component had reduced the area of land under cultivation for 100 families. More recently, however, CI withdrew, business difficulties arose and Ecomaya collapsed. A salvage attempt by the Alianza Verde syndicate proved unsuccessful. The community tourism products established by Ecomaya were then rescued by a private tour operator, Tikal Connection (2010), which continues to offer them (M. Villamar, 22 April 2010, personal communication). Pro-Peten now seems to run the language school. It is not clear whether there have been any significant long-term conservation benefits.

Several other cases in Guatemala were mentioned by Zeppel (2006), with suggestions that tourism had reduced local wildlife hunting in various forests, but there are no recent independent evaluations. A number of tour companies and NGOs now operate in Tikal National Park. An NGO known as RARE (2010), which specifies its aims as 'social marketing', says that, in 2005, tourism operations distributed US\$600 to a community benefit fund for 19 families and that this was used for school education. Recent reports on the San Pedro Volcano, included as a case study by both Buckley (2003a) and Zeppel (2006), indicate that it has experienced a tourism boom, but with negative consequences for conservation and local communities, as outsiders moved in to take advantage of commercial opportunities. This is exactly what the local residents had been trying to avoid, so it appears they were not successful.

Costa Rica

Costa Rica is well known worldwide as a natural history tourism destination, and the Monteverde Cloud Forest (2010) is perhaps its oldest and best-known example of private conservation funded by tourism. The Reserve was established in 1972 on a 14 km^2 farm, and has grown to ~105 km^2 in 2009 through a series of externally funded land purchases. It covers operational costs by charging entrance fees to visitors, with a turnover of over \$1 million per year. It was described in some detail by Honey (2008). The Reserve provides protection for the cloud forest watershed, vegetation and birds, including the rare resplendent quetzal. There has apparently been accelerated degradation immediately outside the Reserve, however, with strip development along access roads as locals took advantage of opportunities generated by the flow of tourists (Aylward *et al.*, 1996; Weaver, 1999). The Monteverde Cloud Forest Reserve has apparently catalysed the establishment of other reserves in the area, but also the growth of unplanned tourism.

Another long-established and well-known private lodge and reserve in Costa Rica is Rara Avis (2010) at 700 m elevation in the Sarapiqui area, not far from San José. It was established in 1983 by founder Amos Bien. It is close to Braulio-Carrillo National Park, and the company also lobbied successfully for an extension of the National Park to make its boundaries contiguous with the private reserve. The original reserve is 4 km^2 in area, and a second adjacent section of 5.6 km^2 is held by independent owners (Rara Avis, 2010). There are two lodges, one also serving as a biological research station. Several hundred bird species are recorded from the surrounding area, including great green macaw, umbrella birds and sunbittern (Rara Avis, 2010).

Costa Rica is also known for a number of long-standing and successful nature, eco- and adventure tour operators which bring international visitors to smaller lodges throughout the country. Perhaps best known of these are Costa Rica Expeditions (2010) and Horizontes Tours (2010). Costa Rica Expeditions (2010) was started as a rafting company in 1978. In 1986 it opened Tortuga Lodge at Tortuguero, an important nesting ground for the endangered Atlantic green sea turtle. Tourism, along with international conservation efforts, has been credited with reducing turtle hunting and egg collecting and reversing a former decline in the local turtle population. Tortuga Lodge is not the only hotel there, but Michael Kaye, founder of Costa Rica Expeditions, is credited as a pioneer of environmental concern in the Costa Rica tourism industry. Horizontes Tours (2010) started as a ticketing agency in 1984, and was run for many years by co-founders Tamara Budowski and Margarita Forero. In 2008 it was bought out by four members of its operational management team. Over the years it has made a series of small but significant donations to the Costa Rica national parks system and local NGOs, reported by Buckley (2003a) as averaging US\$2500 per year.

Panama

In 1995, Conservation International provided US\$20,000 to subsidize the establishment of a rainforest lodge adjacent to La Amistad National Park in the Bocas del Toro region of Panama. The site is important for migratory birds and also for quetzal and harpy eagle. Known as Wekso Ecolodge, the lodge was converted from a former jungle training camp and is operated as a community enterprise by Naso indigenous people along the Teribe River, through a local NGO known as Odesen (2010). The lodge is rather small, and, despite promotion in *Time* magazine (Walsh, 2009) and in research texts such as Buckley (2003a), Zeppel (2006) and Paiement (2007), it does not seem to have been a commercial success. Recent travel blogs are complimentary about the guides' knowledge but scathing about logistics and service. It is not clear how much it may contribute to conservation. Paiement (2007) reports that Naso villagers still hunt forest wildlife and, while they mostly hunt at least 2 hours' walk from the lodge and villages, this is only because there are no longer any animals closer to home. It is possible, however, that, even if the lodge is not a successful venture commercially and has not reduced hunting by the local Naso people, that it may have had political significance in maintaining a forested buffer zone to La Amistad National Park, if only by focusing international attention on the area.

Zeppel (2006) also mentioned projects known as Embera, at Chagres National Park, and Nusagandi, in the San Blas Mountains. Various tour companies operate in the former, taking tourists to a 'demonstration village' built by local residents, but there is no indication whether this contributes to conservation. The Nusagandi project has been described in detail in a report for the Worldwide Fund for Nature (Chapin, 2000). According to that report, the project was initiated in 1983 by the Kuna indigenous people in the San Blas area. Since 1938 the Kuna had occupied and controlled the 3260 km² Indigenous Reserve of Comarca Kuna Yala. The Kuna people in this Comarca live principally on coastal lowlands and near-shore islands, with higher-elevation areas inland still bearing intact rainforest (Chapin, 2000, p. 7). These areas were being colonized by non-Kuna agricultural squatters, and the Government of Panama was planning a new road funded by USAID. Nusagandi is the point at which the proposed road corridor enters Comarca Kuna Yala.

The Kuna people were concerned over territorial encroachment. Conservation groups such as WWF were concerned over impacts on an area of relatively undisturbed rainforest. PEMASKY was the acronym of a project set up to establish a rainforest reserve along the border. With funds from US donors, its staff surveyed the inland border of Comarca Kuma Yala, along the continental divide, and established park guards. According to Chapin (2000), PEMASKY's technical operations were managed by specialists from a tropical agri-culture centre in Costa Rica. Between 1983 and 1991, PEMASKY received over US$1.2 million from the Inter-American Foundation, MacArthur Foundation and WWF. In the mid-1980s it employed over 20 staff and was spending over US$300,000 p.a. By 1987 it ran out of money and in 1988 it effectively collapsed, though maintaining a bold front externally for several years subsequently (Chapin, 2000). According to Chapin (2000), PEMASKY did achieve what the Kuna people wanted, namely border protection. It did not achieve what conservation NGOs wanted, namely a model for indigenous-led conservation throughout the Central American tropics. It may well have achieved some net conservation gains on the ground, however, first if it halted agricultural clearance, and second if it halted the USAID-funded road. The report by Chapin (2000) does not clarify either of these issues.

Ecuador

Introduction

Tourism is second only to oil production in the Ecuador economy, and the two are sometimes in conflict. There are four main geographical regions within Ecuador, and each has its own characteristic forms of tourism. Best-known internationally are the offshore islands of the Galapagos, famous worldwide for their conser-vation significance, but threatened by fisheries and by continuing immigration from mainland Ecuador. Along the mainland coastline there are beach resorts interspersed between fishing ports. The highlands of the Andes are famous for trekking, mountaineering and scenic drives, and also for markets, crafts and rural tourist accommodation in either farms, lodges or the smaller towns. On the upper slopes of the Andes there are areas of cloud forest, of high conservation value. East of the Andes, Ecuador extends into the upper portions of the Amazon basin, and in this region there are complex interactions and sometimes conflicts between the oil industry and various indigenous peoples, in which tourism plays a significant role.

Galapagos

Most of the islands in the Galapagos are national parks, where tourism is regulated closely by the Ecuador Ministry of the Environ-ment. Attempts by the Ministry to maintain protection for the Galapagos, however, have met with opposition from two quarters. The first is the fishing industry, which objected strongly to the declaration of a marine park, and protested by killing seals and other wildlife on the outer islands. This led to international outrage, but the fisheries industry had strong representation within the government of Ecuador and lobbied strongly for concessions. The economic significance of the international tourism industry based on the wildlife of the Galapagos Islands was almost certainly a significant factor in these political negotiations. As with most political negotiations, however, details are not publicly available.

The other major problem for conservation on the Galapagos Islands is caused by the success of the tourism industry itself. Despite various master plans purportedly limiting the total number of tourists permitted to visit the Galapagos, in fact the number has simply continued to increase indefinitely. This has brought three major impacts. The first is simply increasing pressure of visitor numbers throughout the islands. The second is that boats from the mainland have inadvertently introduced new species to the Galapagos, which is of particular concern for conservation. Most of these are insect species. The third is that the economic opportunities associated with growth in the tourism industry have attracted internal migrants and settlers from mainland Ecuador to move to the Galapagos, where they settle in the township areas outside the national park itself. Since the number of migrants far exceeds the capacity of the tourism industry to provide new employment, particularly for unskilled staff, these settlers have taken up subsistence agriculture, clearing native vegetation and creating significant conservation impacts. Since the township areas are outside the jurisdiction of the parks service, it was unable to prevent this continuing migration; and, once people had actually taken up residence in the Galapagos, they formed a political constituency which created continuing difficulties for conservation. Overall, the relationships between tourism, residents, fisheries and conservation in the Galapagos have been mixed. The politics are still contentious, as indicated by a recent government press release (Ecuador, Ministerio del Ambiente, 2010).

Amazon Basin

In the Amazon basin, the role of tourism in conservation seems to have been more positive (Rodriguez, 2008). The principal threat to the natural environment appears to be from the mineral and petroleum industries, and from associated secondary development which follows the creation of new access roads. The principal defenders of the rainforest ecosystems have been its Indigenous inhabitants, who have fought for land rights so as to maintain their traditional lifestyles and territories, but in the process have also indirectly provided some protection for the rainforest species and eco-

systems. Tourism has been a significant component of these efforts (Borman, 2008). A number of Indigenous communities throughout the Oriente region have opened jungle lodges and ecotourism ventures, both as a source of funding for legal actions and to provide a direct political constituency for their interests. Some of these groups have received support from international non-government organizations and development assistance agencies. Some are run directly by local communities, others by enthusiastic expatriates. Many of these lodges are far from cheap. Access, especially by air, may only be available on certain days each week, so many of the lodges market multi-night packages which include meals and local activities as well as accommodation. Typical activities include: forest hikes, by day and sometimes also by night; local journeys in canoes or dugouts; swimming in rainforest creeks; and visits to local communities to take part in various subsistence tasks or observe commodified religious ceremonies.

Currently, the range of indigenous rainforest peoples involved in tourism includes the Cofan, Siona, Huaorani, Achuar and Quichua or Kichwa groups such as the Sani and Napo Runa. The Quichua peoples migrated downslope from the Andes to the Amazon after Spanish colonization of the uplands. The other peoples referred to are indigenous to the Amazon basin. Different lodges are based in different Indigenous territories. The politics of oil exploration, Indigenous land rights, tourism and conservation have been described in particular detail for the Cofan people of the Cuyabeno area in the northern Oriente region, most recently by Borman (2008).

A review of ecotourism case studies by Buckley (2003a) included four examples from the Ecuadorean Oriente. Since then, the number of rainforest lodges has burgeoned, with most of them marketed by numerous different tour operators. There are now also cruising riverboats, which effectively act as mobile lodges. Of the four examples listed in 2003, it appears that all are still operational but with different degrees of success and different levels of contribution to communities and conservation respectively. The Quichua Capirona community near the town of Tena, reported as thriving by Brandon (1996), cited in Buckley (2003a), now offers a volunteer programme but does not feature prominently in tour operator itineraries and is not mentioned in the *Lonely Planet* guide to Ecuador. The organization RICANCIE, described by Drumm (1998) and cited by Buckley (2003a), also still exists but, as of late 2009, Ecuadorean tour operators reported that it does not function effectively and refused to book tours to these villages even if they had advertised them previously. The tour company Tropic Ecotours (2010), described by Drumm (1998) as closely linked to the Huaorani peoples of the Quehueri'ono villages, apparently now operates a lodge known as the Huao Lodge (Rodriquez, 2008) or the Huaorani Ecolodge (2010). Tropic Ecotours also sells a wide variety of other Ecuadorean lodges and tours, apparently in order to cross-subsidize the Huaorani. The Cofan people still operate occasional tours to their community at Zabalo, east of Cuyabeno Wildlife Reserve, but according to Borman (2008) there was a major downturn in visitor numbers because of border incursions from Colombia, so it is not clear whether tourism is still a major contributor.

There are currently two areas with numerous lodges, namely the Cuyabeno and Napo River areas in northern Oriente. On the Cuyabeno River the best known lodge is Cuyabeno Lodge itself, in Siona territory in the Cuyabeno Wildlife Reserve, but there are many others nearby. On the Napo River there are numerous lodges. Oldest and best-known of these is La Selva Jungle Lodge (2010), described in a separate case study below. Other lodges in this area include Sacha Lodge and the Napo Wildlife Centre in the Sani Quichua area. It appears that moves by the Ecuador government in 2009 to enforce a minimum threshold of sanitation, hygiene and service quality led to abandonment of some lodges in both the Napo and Cuyabeno areas, but there are many still operational in both.

There is also a third and less accessible area in southern Oriente, apparently with only a single lodge, the Kapawi Ecolodge in the Achuar territory. This was established as a joint venture between an Achuar community association and a commercial tour operator, Canodros SA (2010), which also sells a range of other tours and packages. Despite winning various awards historically and taking part in the Amazon Exchange described by Stronza and Gordillo (2008), the Kapawi lodge seems to have experienced some difficulties. According to Rodriguez (2008, p. 159), the partnership 'ended prematurely in 2008'; and certainly, during much of 2009, the Kapawi website was blank except for the opening page. As of early 2010, however, it appears on the Canodros website, so perhaps the partnership has been re-established.

Cuyabeno Lodge

Cuyabeno Lodge (2010) lies on Laguna Grande, the Great Cuyabeno Lake, in the 6000 km^2 Reserva de Produccion Faunistica Cuyabeno (2010) or Cuyabeno Wildlife Reserve, in the province of Sucumbios. The lodge has been open since 1989 and is operated by Neotropic Turis (2010). It is reached by a 2.5 hour motorized canoe ride downstream from the reserve entrance at El Puente. There is a reserve entry fee of US$20 for foreigners. The lodge uses local Siona people to operate all its boats, and also takes guests to a Siona village, where traditional food preparation techniques are demonstrated and various artefacts are for sale. The area around the lodge supports a diverse assemblage of wildlife, including two-toed sloth, woolly anteater or tamandua, ten different primate species including the night monkey, freshwater dolphin and a wide variety of birds and invertebrates. Bulk bottled drinking water is provided for guests, and washing water is drawn from the lagoon. Guests are also taken to swim in the lagoon, as well as spotlighting for caiman and fishing for piranha in the rivers. Electric power is provided by solar panels and a generator. Propane is used for cooking and heating water. Organic waste is composted, and sewage and sullage are treated in a three-chamber septic system. The history of the lodge and the reserve are summarized on the lodge's website. There are a number of other lodges nearby. The lodges do not contribute to conservation, land tenure or land management, but they contribute indirectly by providing income for the Siona people without clearing the forest, and providing a political counterbalance to continued oil exploration and production.

Napo Wildlife Center

Despite its name, the Napo Wildlife Center (2010) is in fact a 12-cabin tourist lodge, or, according to its own promotional materials, an 'ultimate alternative luxury eco-hotel'. It is on the banks of the black-water Anangucocha Lake within the 214 km^2 territory of the Anangu Quichua people, which lies inside the 9800 km^2 Yasuni National Park and UNESCO Biosphere Reserve. According to the NWC website, the local community built four shelters and a kitchen for tourism in the 1990s, but this venture was unsuccessful. The current lodge was built in 2003, and the NWC website says it was financed by an Ecuadorean NGO called EcoEcuador. Note, however, that a US-based organization called Tropical Nature (2010), associated with a US travel company named Tropical Nature Travel, also claims to have established NWC. The NWC website says that 'ownership was transferred to the Anangu community in 2007'. Rodriguez (2008, p. 159) says that 'the partnership for the Napo Wildlife Center ... ended in 2007', which suggests a somewhat different interpretation of events. The lodge apparently has low-impact energy and waste treatment technologies. It has a canopy tower, making it especially popular for birdwatchers, with a total of 568 bird species recorded. Napo Wildlife Center seems to be well regarded by Ecuadorean naturalist guides. Whether it has contributed to conservation depends, perhaps, on how it may have altered the lifestyles and behaviour of the Anangu people, since they are resident inside Yasuni National Park. If income from NWC has reduced subsistence agriculture and hunting and/or led the Anangu people to protect Yasuni against external encroachment, then the net outcome would be positive.

La Selva

The direct translation of the Spanish 'La Selva' is 'forest' or 'jungle', and there are hence a number of properties by that name throughout the rainforests of South and Central America. In particular, there is a well-known biological research station at La Selva in Costa Rica, but the lodge described here is on the Napo River in Ecuador. Established over two decades ago, it is reputedly the first tourist lodge built in the western Amazon, not only in Ecuador, but in the entire region. When it was built, many of its guests were apparently concerned that wildlife could get into the rooms at night. In consequence, the older rooms were built in a style which now seems rather small, dark and enclosed. Newer rooms are more contemporary in design.

The lodge is built on an area leased from a neighbouring Quichua community. The community has title to a 90 km^2 area, and La Selva pays a fixed monthly rent for a small section of this land, on which it has built the lodge and associated facilities, a large butterfly breeding house, a 45 m canopy tower and a number of narrow and unsurfaced hiking trails. Nearby residents grow cash and subsistence crops and a variety of medicinal, poisonous or otherwise useful plants. The reason that this area can support a continuing high diversity of forest birds and mammals is because the forest cover is still largely continuous over an extended area, not only in the section leased by the lodge. By providing employment and lease fees for the local community, the lodge may well contribute to conservation outside as well as inside its lease areas.

The lodge itself is built on a low hill at the edge of Garzacocha Lagoon, a black-water lake which drains into the Napo River. Access is by boat down the Napo from the river town of Coca, on foot along a 500 m boardwalk between the river and the lagoon and then by dugout canoe across the lagoon. Because of these lease and access arrangements, the lodge and its hiking area are undisturbed by boat traffic on the Napo River or by any other lodges or settlements. With the combination of the canopy tower, the forest hikes, dugout trips on Garzacocha Lagoon and visits to a riverbank parrot clay-lick on the other side of the Napo, guests have excellent opportunities to see a wide variety of birds and monkeys. A group visiting for a few days in December 2009, for example, saw five species of monkey including the rare pygmy marmoset; and over 50 bird species including tanagers and troupials, hawks and herons, parrots and macaws, toucans and aracaris, kingbirds and kingfishers, caciques and oropendulas, and many more; and an unconfirmed sighting of the highly endangered greater curassow.

El Monte

El Monte Sustainable Lodge is a small but very well-appointed lodge on a private reserve near the town of Mindo, at about 1500 m elevation in montane cloud forest on the western slopes of the Andes. Mindo is famous for its birdwatching, most notably the reliable opportunity to see the lek displays of the Andean cock of the rock. This is a bright red bird with a large circular crest, and the males carry out a competitive communal display of singing and dancing in particular trees at dawn every day. There are many other icon bird species in these cloud forests, some of them extremely rare and highly prized by birdwatching tourists. These include, for example, the club-winged manakin and a large number of different hummingbird species. As a result, Mindo has several lodges catering to international birdwatching tourists, as well as a number of lodges and guest houses catering principally to domestic tourists on short-break holidays from Quito, a few hours' drive away. Indeed, it appears that around 80% of Mindo's 2000 residents are supported by tourism. Mindo has also become something of a destination for local amenity migration, with wealthier residents of Quito building second homes or weekend cottages. Most of this development, however, has little or no connection to conservation. In addition to its birdwatching opportunities, El Monte Lodge is known for its quiet, out-of-town streamside location, its comfortable cabins, its spacious central area, its outstanding vegetarian cuisine and its friendly owners, Tom Quesenbery and Mariella Tenorio. All of these aspects are accurately described in the *Lonely Planet* guide to Ecuador (St Louis *et al.*, 2009).

There is a public protected area close to Mindo, the 190 km^2 Nambilla National Park, and a number of private landholdings, which are still largely forested and currently also contribute to conservation, but which do not necessarily have any connection with tourism. El Monte, however, though relatively small, is designed and operated as a conservation tourism enterprise, with international tourism funding the lodge which in turn supports the reserve. In addition, birdwatching tourists staying at El Monte help to support local birdwatching guides, some of whom are now sufficiently famous to be mentioned individually in the *Lonely Planet* guide to Ecuador. Since the prime viewing sites for the cock of the rock can change from year to year and are not currently on the El Monte reserve, these guides also take guests from the El Monte Lodge to other properties, with payments to both local guides and local landowners. These payments provide incentives for these landowners to maintain the forested areas on their properties, so as to keep a healthy population of the birds, which in turn attract paying tourists. Indeed, El Monte has recently changed its preferred cock of the rock viewing site from one property to another, specifically because the landowner of the former site had cleared much of his forested land, leaving only the trees used for the leks.

Mindo lies on a major road from Quito to the coast of Ecuador. Some years ago there was a proposal to build a major pipeline from the oilfields of the Ecuadorean Amazon across the Andes to a coastal port, running directly through the cloud forests near Mindo. Driven by the combined concerns of tourism and conservation, the residents of Mindo and conservationists worldwide mounted strong opposition to this proposal. The owners of El Monte played a significant role in this campaign, and this in itself represents a significant contribution to conservation, in addition to the lodge's own private reserve.

Bolivia

There are two particularly well-known conservation tourism initiatives in Bolivia, at Mapajo and Chalalan respectively. Both have significant external support from NGOs and international donors. The Mapajo Project (2010) is a small tourist lodge operated by five T'simane and Moseten indigenous communities inside the Pilon Lajas UNESCO Biosphere Reserve. An area of 4000 km^2 was declared as a reserve by UNESCO in 1977 and the Bolivian government in 1992, and as an Indigenous territory in 1997. It is apparently under threat from small-scale agricultural colonization, illegal logging, poaching and population growth. The Mapajo Project was presumably conceived as a source of income and hence support for conservation by the Indigenous communities along the Quiquibey River. The Reserve is managed by the Bolivian National Parks agency SERNAB, and community development aspects by the agency PRAIA, Programa Regional de Apoyoa los Pueblos Indigenas de la Cuenca del Amazonas. The Mapajo Lodge consists of six cabins and can accommodate up to 16 guests, who generally stay for either two or five nights. It has 20 km of trails.

The Mapajo Project received international donor funding totalling around US$200,000 (Parks Watch, 2010) from France, the UK, Belgium, Canada, the UNDP, Conservation International and PRAIA. This was around $5500 for each of the 36 reported families of the communities concerned. Other sources refer to around 50 families in six villages (Mapajo Ecoturismo Indigena, 2010). The project was handed over to the community in 2006 but experienced financial difficulties (Conservation Strategy Fund, 2008). A cost–benefit analysis by the Conservation Strategy Fund (2008) found a major drop in visitor numbers from 2005 to 2006, especially through travel-agency sales. Direct sales fell from US$21,000 in 2005 to US$17,000 in 2006 and increased to US$32,000 in 2007. The operation has only been profitable about half the time. The analysis by CSF (2008) concluded that without further investment it will suffer financial collapse, but that it could become profitable if marketing, service quality and infrastructure were all improved. More broadly, this analysis concluded that community-based tourism is a major component in Bolivia's national tourism strategy, but that <10% of enterprises have become self-sustaining.

The cost–benefit analysis by CSF (2008) indicates that, at the time of that analysis, direct costs per guest-night totalled US$29 and that this represented 50% of the total price charged, leaving insufficient funds for marketing and maintenance. It also noted that staff are provided by the community on a rotational basis, so that 80% of community members earn wages, but none stay long enough to learn relevant skills. In addition, the lodge is very severely overstaffed, with a staff:client ratio of 8:1. Operations are thus highly inefficient. According to Parks Watch (2010) the project, recently renamed Mapajo Ecoturismo Indigena SRL, receives only 200–300 visitors annually of the 13,000 tourists who visit the gateway town of Rurrenabaque. Access is difficult and there is little wildlife, owing to continued hunting. Commercial tour operators still offer tours to Mapajo. Its conservation outcomes apparently have not been subject to independent investigation.

The Chalalan Ecolodge (2010) in Madidi National Park, in contrast, has been studied quite extensively. Declared in 1995, Madidi National Park is 19,000 km^2 in area, is highly biodiverse and extends from the Andes to the Amazon. The lodge is operated by the local community of San Jose de Uchupiamonas, who are descended from local Tacana people and the Quichua people who migrated downslope from the Andes. The area had a history of rubber logging in the late 1880s and early 1900s, and a period of intensive hunting for animal skins around 1970 (MacQuarrie cited in Stronza, 2004). There were two early experiments with forest tourism in this area. The first took place in the 1970s, when a tour company called TAWA built a small hunting and fishing lodge near San Jose (Stronza, 2004). The second was a bunkhouse camp in San Jose built by Colibri Tours in 1992, in partnership with three residents of San Jose. This was unsuccessful but laid the groundwork for Chalalan (Stronza, 2004).

Conservation International became involved because they were already conducting research on biodiversity in Madidi. It was CI which lobbied successfully for the establishment of the Madidi National Park and Area for Integrated Management, and which bid successfully for IADB funding in 1998, as below. The San Jose residents supported it because they were concerned over likely encroachment on their lands by logging companies.

Initial construction in 1995 was supported by Conservation International (2010), and the lodge was handed over to the community in 2001. It is relatively small, a set of cabins with maximum capacity of 24 visitors, shared bathrooms and a central kitchen and dining area. It received external funding of US$200,000 from Conservation International directly and US$1.25 million from the Inter-American Development Bank (IADB) via Conservation International, of which about $900,000 was available in Bolivia itself (Stronza, 2004). It appears that the lodge first generated a profit either in 2000 (Stronza, 2004, p. 47; Peaty and Portillo, 2009) or in 2001 (Stronza, 2004, p. 33) with figures of $22,000, $20,000 and $15,000 being quoted respectively. According to Peaty and Portillo (2009), Chalalan received 1136 visitors in 2006. According to Conservation International (2002), the lodge has provided economic benefits for 60 families as an alternative to logging and as an incentive not to hunt wildlife. The report by Stronza (2004) says that 74 families received shareholder dividends and the whole community gained from a community fund. A survey of 64 respondents in San Jose de Uchupiamonas indicated that Chalalan provided the main source of income for 56% of that sample, and that their average cash expenditure in 2003 was US$70 per month. This income, however, was used largely to buy shotguns, chainsaws, wristwatches and radios. In addition to descriptions by Conservation International (2002) and the accounts of the IADB, Chalalan Ecolodge has been referred to repeatedly in travel magazines (Cahill, 2004), government reports (Garcia and Ricalde, 2001), conference proceedings and case study compilations (Buckley, 2003a; Zeppel, 2006). Visitor blogs refer to a high concentration of wildlife around Chalalan.

The only detailed independent study, however, seems to be that reported by Stronza (2004), Gordillo et al. (2008), Stronza and de Vasconcellos Pêgas (2008), Stronza and Gordillo (2008) and Jamal and Stronza (2009), from an ethnographic investigation and community exchange project known as Trueque Amazonicas, the Amazon Exchange. This took place during 2003–2004 at a cost of over $140,000.

The evaluation of Chalalan by Stronza (2004) catalogues the numerous social challenges it faced and the ways in which they were addressed. In summary, it takes around a decade for a lodge of this type to become established. Her report also outlines conservation threats and benefits. Madidi National Park was, and indeed still is, under threat from mining, possible oil exploration and even a proposed hydroelectric dam which would flood over 2500 km^2 of the park, including Chalalan. From the perspective of San Jose residents, Chalalan provides additional material well-being and a tool in maintaining their territory. From the perspective of Conservation International, Chalalan gives the San Jose residents both means and incentive to defend Madidi National Park, especially against oil exploration. The lodge has not stopped local people hunting, but it may have reduced hunting in the vicinity of the lodge itself, with anecdotal evidence of improved wildlife sightings (Stronza, 2004, p. 62). The report by Peaty and Portillo (2009) refers to two large-scale conservation achievements or actions, in addition to local-scale reductions in hunting and clearance. Apparently, Chalalan was instrumental in the cancellation of a logging concession in 2000; and it is campaigning currently against a proposed dam on the Beni River.

Peru

Huascaran

Huascaran National Park in Peru's Cordillera Blanca is a major tourist destination, immediately after Machu Picchu in popularity (Torres, 1996). Established in 1975, it later received international funding from the USA and the Netherlands to produce a strategy to use tourism to fund conservation (Torres, 1996). In practice, however, it appears that, while tourism does indeed generate revenue, little of that revenue is returned to the park, and impacts from tourism have increased, along with threats to conservation from mining, grazing and industrial water use (Shoobridge, 2005; UNEP, 2007; Byers, 2009).

Huascaran National Park is 3400 km^2 in area, accessible from Lima and popular for mountaineering, hiking, biking and skiing. It is a significant reservoir of Andean biological diversity (UNEP, 2007), with seven different ecological zones, and also includes 33 pre-Inca archaeological sites (Torres, 1996). According to a management review by UNEP (2007), tourism is creating serious environmental and social impacts. The park collects entrance fees but is only allowed to keep 10% of these, with the remainder used elsewhere by INRENA, Peru's National Institute of Natural Resources. There are 78 mining concessions and nine operating mines in the park, with significant impacts especially on water quality. A hydroelectric power company extracts water and plans to build dams inside the park, and the Ministry of Transport takes rock and gravel for road building. A census conducted by INRENA in 2004 found around 10,000 cattle, 12,000 sheep and 300 horses in the park. According to UNEP (2007) there are 850 people living inside the park, ~5000 in a buffer zone and a quarter of a million in neighbouring townships (Shoobridge, 2005). There are two main entrances where visitors must pay fees, but also a number of unsupervised smaller entrances where they do not. In 2000, the park received close to 100,000 Peruvian visitors and close to 15,000 foreigners. There are 24 trekking circuits and around 50 tourist agencies, 300 guides and 175 lodges in the local region (Shoobridge, 2005; UNEP, 2007). There are also significant impacts from burros used as pack-stock for tourists and from garbage and human waste (Byers, 2009).

Overall, it appears that, while tourism is only one of a number of high-impact uses, the potential for tourism to fund conservation management is not being realized. Tourism is indeed generating revenue, but it is not being retained to manage impacts within the park.

Posada Amazonas

Posada Amazonas is a lodge on the Tambopata River, in a 20 km^2 community reserve which forms part of the 100 km^2 communal territory of La Comunidad Nativa de Infierno, CNI. It lies in the buffer zone of the 10,000 km^2 Bahuaja-Sonene National Park, itself part of a 17,000 km^2 reserve complex in the Amazon region of south-eastern Peru. The Infierno community consists of about 600 individuals in about 150 families, some of them from the indigenous Ese'eja people and some of them *riberenhos*, mestizo immigrants to the riverbank areas. La Comunidad Nativa de Infierno has formed a commercial association,

the Kee'way Association, for its commercial dealings with tourists. Infierno is about 17 km by road or 2 hours by boat from Puerto Maldonado, gateway town and capital of the Madre de Dios region of Peru. Puerto Maldonado is an hour's flight from Cuzco.

Posado Amazonas is a 20-year commercial partnership between CNI and a private tour operator, Rainforest Expeditions (RFE), which owns the 13-room Tambopata Research Centre and lodge in the 2750 km^2 Tambopata National Reserve, 4 to 6 hours by boat upstream of Posada Amazonas. Rainforest Expeditions was founded by Eduardo Nycander and Kurt Holle. It was described by Nycander (2002) in a UNWTO compendium of sustainable tourism case studies. The commercial agreement between RFE and CNI commenced in 1996 and terminated in 2006. It divided decision-making powers 50:50 between CNI and RFE, and profits 60:40 with the larger share going to the community. Funding for construction totalling US$350,000 was provided by a Canadian aid-agency grant of $240,000 and loan of $110,000. Funds for staff and community training were provided by two grants of US$50,000 each, from the World Bank and the MacArthur Foundation.

Posada Amazonas has been subject to quite extensive independent study. The most detailed report is that of Stronza (undated) from the US$140,000 Amazon Exchange programme (Trueque Amazonas) between this lodge and two others. There are subsequent analyses by Stronza (2007), Gordillo *et al.* (2008), Stronza and de Vasconcellos Pêgas (2008), Stronza and Gordillo (2008) and Jamal and Stronza (2009); and additional reports by Pauca (2001) and Gordillo (2005). The outline below is drawn largely from Stronza (undated).

The lodge is variously reported as having either 24 or 48 rooms and able to accommodate up to 60 guests. As of 2006 it was receiving over 6000 visitors annually. It has a canopy tower, variously reported as 30 m or 47 m high. It started operations in 1998, and was profitable from the outset, but the first 2 years' profits went to paying off the $110,000 loan. It was a key condition of the agreement that CNI should not build any other lodge on their land during the term of the agreement or allow any other operator to build one. The agreement thus gave Rainforest Expeditions exclusive rights to tourism operations on the CNI land until 2016. This was required in order to give RFE the opportunity to recoup its investment, given the expected slow growth in profitability. In fact, however, it appears that this has now been renegotiated and CNI is building an independent lodge. This is possible since Posada Amazonas is overbooked. There are a number of other river lodges downstream of Infierno and Puerto Maldonado, and 70 in the entire Madre de Dios region, but RFE is the largest tour operator in the region and hosts 25% of the total visitor-nights (Anon., 2008).

By 2006 the lodge was earning an annual profit of around US$500,000, of which 60% went to CNI, in addition to wage earnings of around $150,000 p.a. Revenue to CNI is divided between a community fund and individual families. In 2006, average household incomes increased by $600 from this tourism dividend, representing a 25% increase. According to Stronza (undated), profits are divided 50:50 between the Ese'eja and *riberenho* groups, but the number of households in each group is not reported. The community fund has apparently been used for community projects in education, health, communication and access. The individual components have been used in various ways, but some families at least have used them to buy chainsaws, shotguns, boats and alcohol, increasing impacts on rainforest flora and fauna. Some individuals earning wages from the lodge have also hired other community members to clear more forest for crops, using a swidden–fallow agricultural system known locally as *chacra*.

The area supports a range of flora and fauna of high value for both tourism and conservation. Plants include Brazil nut, ceiba tree, orchids and medicinals. Mammals include jaguar, tapir, giant otter, capybara and peccary, and birds include macaws, toucans and harpy eagle. There are community prohibitions against hunting in communal reserve areas or fishing in an oxbow lake where the giant otters live. These prohibitions are flouted by some members, but the community has applied sanctions on at least some occasions. Members of an Ecuadorean Amazon lodge, Kapawi, who visited during the Amazon Exchange programme, commented that there is far more wildlife at Posada Amazonas than at Kapawi, where the local Achuar people still hunt routinely around the lodge area.

According to CNI members reported by Stronza (undated), local threats to conservation include clearing for farms, selective logging of two palm species and the shihuahuaco tree and continuing hunting and fishing. The shihuahuaco is a key species for parrots and eagles, but is used locally to make charcoal. Local measures to combat these threats include an 'adopt a shihuahuaco' programme, nest boxes, prohibitions on palm cutting and a biological monitoring programme. It appears that these are broadly but not entirely successful.

More significantly, the entire area is now threatened both by the potential granting of oil exploration licences and by the InterOceanic Highway, which cuts through the rainforest <15 km from Infierno. Rainforest Expeditions and CNI have lobbied against oil exploration. Rainforest Expeditions has lobbied the highway construction consortium to establish a no-development buffer zone, in order to prevent uncontrolled ribbon degradation, as has occurred along other roads. CNI used $12,000 from its community fund in 2006 to apply for legal title to a 17 km^2 concession area as a buffer between its community lands and the highway.

In community lands such as those at Posada Amazonas, community dynamics and social aspects play a major role in conservation outcomes. Social concerns, processes, solutions and outcomes have been studied in some detail at this site. There have clearly been a number of stumbling blocks, some severe, but they seem to have been overcome. Most importantly for conservation, the Posada Amazonas partnership does seem to have created sufficient income and employment for local community members, as well as a local sense of ownership through joint management, for them to appreciate the significance of the rainforest and its wildlife for their own immediate well-being, and they are hence prepared to take communal action to protect it insofar as they are able. A single local community has little political power against the oil industry or a billion-dollar highway, but Posada Amazonas has received international recognition and can bring an international spotlight to bear on these issues and government actions.

Heath River Wildlife Centre

Zeppel (2006) included several additional case studies in Peru besides those mentioned here. Some of these are apparently still operational, but with no information on conservation outcomes. The Heath River Wildlife Centre, however, is of particular interest because of a link to the Napo Wildlife Centre in Ecuador. A conservation NGO known as Tropical Nature (2010) apparently operates a tourism subsidiary, Tropical Nature Travel, to support its overall goal of a 'Tropical Nature Conservation System'. According to its website, it set up both the Napo and Heath River centres. The latter is 4 hours by boat from Puerto Maldonado, the same gateway town as for Tambopata and Posada Amazonas. Heath River is a tributary. There is apparently also an upmarket 35-room lodge on a 100 km² private reserve near Tambopata (Inkaterra, 2010) but no independent reports are available.

Brazil

Brazil is an enormous country with globally significant biodiversity but a rapidly growing population and economy, which creates severe conservation conflicts. In addition to national parks and state parks, it has a system of private reserves, Reservas Particulares do Patrimonio Natural or RPPNs. These involve legal covenants on the land title so as to require continuing conservation management even if the property is sold. There are similar systems in many other countries. As in other countries, some but not all RPPNs are adjacent to public protected areas; some but not all RPPNs operate tourism enterprises either to generate funds or as a tool for conservation education; and some but not all conservation tourism enterprises involve RPPNs.

This section describes four conservation tourism ventures: Fazenda Rio Negro and Pousada Caiman, in the great grassy wetlands of the Pantanal; Cristalino Jungle Lodge in the Mato Grosso, the Amazon rainforest; and Una Ecopark in the Mata Atlantica, the heavily threatened Atlantic coastal rainforest. There are other examples in each of these areas, but those selected here are particular well-established.

Fazenda Rio Negro is a former cattle ranch, 77 km² in area, bought by Conservation International in 1999 and established as a private reserve in 2001. Part of the property is a listed RAMSAR site. It operates several small tourist lodges and a small research station. It appears that as of 2000/2001 it was receiving only around 350 commercial tourists per annum, of whom about two-thirds were from Brazil and the remainder mainly from Europe and North America. It also received another 300 or so visitors each year on a variety of educational and research programmes. It offers fishing, four-wheel-drive tours, horse riding, canoeing and hikes to watch birds and other wildlife. The most recent and detailed description is given in a 116-page Conservation International report (Correa da Silva and Amaral, 2008). While an area barely 8 km × 10 km is a drop in the proverbial ocean compared with the overall expanse of the 100,000 km² Pantanal wetlands, Fazenda Rio Negro does seem to have made conservation contributions well beyond its immediate boundaries: both as a base for scientific research used for conservation lobbying and as a demonstration project for other private landholders in the Pantanal.

Also in the Pantanal region is Pousada Caiman, a lodge on the Caiman Ecological Refuge, established by owner Roberto Klabin in 1985 on a cattle ranch, Estancia Caiman. The property as a whole is 530 km² in area, of which two-thirds are used to run cattle, one-third is reportedly reserved for conservation and 56 km² is within the RPPN Dona Aracy Klabin. There are four lodges on the property. Beginning in 2009, the Refuge has charged 30 Brazilian reais per visitor, about US$17, to support the RPPN. It also supports conservation projects on jaguar, Amazon parrot and hyacinth macaw. The last of these helped to increase the macaw population from 1500 in 1987 to 5000 in 2005, by providing artificial nests, reducing poaching and encouraging other property owners not to fell macaw nest trees. Hyacinth macaws are apparently worth $25,000 each on the international black market (Hinchberger, 2004). It appears that the continual presence of macaw researchers is in itself a significant deterrent to poachers.

Cristalino Jungle Lodge (2010) lies in an RPPN variously listed as 77 km^2, 100 km^2 or 176 km^2 in area, adjoining Cristalino State Park which is variously listed as 680 km^2 or 1849 km^2 in area. A much larger area nearby, 21,588 km^2 in total, is controlled by the Brazilian Air Force but is reported as in good condition for conservation. A number of blogs about Cristalino Jungle Lodge (e.g. Underwood, 2009), and marketing materials from travel agents, feature interviews with owner Vitoria da Riva Carvalho. In these interviews, she mentions first that her family has owned land here for generations, and secondly that, in their view, Cristalino Sate Park was declared, or at least enlarged, specifically as a result of lobbying by the Cristalino Jungle Lodge. Areas to the south, not within reserves, are apparently subject to wholesale logging and agricultural clearance.

Cristalino lies within the Alta Floresta region of Brazil's Mato Grosso province. The area as a whole supports numerous bird species of high conservation significance, including red-throated piping-guan, bare-throated fruit-crow, white-bellied parrot and ladder-tailed nightjar (Cristalino Jungle Lodge, 2010). The lodge appeals particularly to birdwatchers and has a 45 m canopy tower. The family da Riva Carvalho also operates the Cristalino Ecological Foundation (2010), distinct from the commercial operations of the lodge. The Foundation apparently receives assistance from an international NGO, Fauna and Flora International (2010).

Una Ecopark (2010) in Brazil's Atlantic coastal forest is rather different from the other three examples. First, it apparently does not offer tourist accommodation on site, but earns tourist revenue only by charging entrance fees. Second, most of its visitors are local school groups, and it sees its role as local education as well as on-site conservation. The Una Ecopark is a private reserve 3.8 km^2 in area, immediately adjacent to the publicly owned Una Biological Reserve. It has a 2 km hiking trail and a canopy walkway. According to KfW Entwicklungsbank (2005), the German international aid agency had invested some 57 million euros in projects aimed at protecting Brazil's Atlantic coastal forest. According to Eagles and Hillel (2009),

for example, there is another public reserve nearby, Conduru State Park, financed by the Inter-American Development Bank from 1994 to 2006.

Una Ecopark was established in 1998 as a joint initiative of Conservation International (2010), the Institute for Socio-environmental Studies of Southern Bolivia, and a private donor (Conservation International, 2002, cited in Buckley, 2003a). More recently it seems to have received most of its external support from the Wildlife Conservation Trust (Mallinson, 2001). It covers 60% of its operational costs from gate takings, with around 30,000 visitors each year, of whom about one-third are students. The Una Ecopark is mentioned in a variety of tourism destination handbooks including the Brazil editions of the *Footprint®* and *Lonely Planet®* travel guides (St Louis *et al.*, 2009). Interactions between the park and residents in the nearby village of Jacqueiral were analysed by Nobrega (2005), based on interviews. He found that these interactions were generally positive, with improved education and also higher agricultural production in nearby areas.

Argentina

Agustina Barros, ICER.

Private conservation

Argentina is the second largest country in South America and the eighth largest in the world. It contains 18 different ecoregions: humid environments such as the subtropical rainforest and the Patagonian cool temperate forest; semi-arid regions such as the Espinal, Pampas and the Monte; and arid areas such as the High Andes, Puna and Patagonian Steppe (Burkart *et al.*, 1999; Fundación Vida Silvestre Argentina, 2010a). More than 20,000 plant species, 380 species of mammals and over 1000 species of birds are found in these regions (Narosky and Yzurieta, 1987; Barquez *et al.*, 2006; Zuloaga *et al.*, 2008).

Biodiversity conservation efforts on public lands started in 1922 with the creation of Nahuel Huapi National Park in Patagonia

(Argentina, Administracion de Parques Nacionales, 2007). Currently, Argentina has about 435 protected areas, but only 35 of these are national parks. The remainder are managed under a variety of provincial administrative arrangements (Argentina, Administracion de Parques Nacionales, 2007). In total, protected areas cover 7% of the country. To comply with the Convention on Biological Diversity, to which Argentina is a signatory, this proportion would have to increase to 15% (Moreno et al., 2008).

Since over 80% of Argentina is privately owned (Morales, 2009), it is increasingly critical to involve private landowners in order to expand the area dedicated to conservation. Fundación Vida Silvestre Argentina (FVSA), a national NGO dedicated to biodiversity conservation, has been a pioneer in the creation of privately protected areas. In 1979, FVSA created Argentina's first wildlife refuge, the 32 km^2 'Campos del Tuyu' in the Pampas Region of Buenos Aires, to help protect endangered populations of pampas deer. This reserve was subsequently donated to the public national park system (Argentina, Administracion de Parques Nacionales, 2009).

Since 1987, FVSA has run a national programme of wildlife refuges which operate through agreements with landowners (FVSA, 2008). FVSA carries out ecological assessments, constructs management plans and conducts annual monitoring. The landowner is responsible for the financial costs (FVSA, 2008). In exchange, FVSA also provides technical advice on the management of income-generating activities such as ecotourism, organic farming and cattle grazing. In provinces where legislation recognizes private protected areas, FVSA assists in bringing these refuges into the provincial protected areas network (Moreno et al., 2008). To date, FVSA has assisted in the establishment of 14 wildlife refuges with a total area of 1800 km^2, some of them now operational for over a decade.

The initiatives commenced by FVSA have also been taken up by other national and local organizations, including Fundación ProYungas, Aves Argentinas, Fundación Hábitat y Desarrollo and Fundación de Historia Natural Félix de Azara. More recently, this approach has also been taken up within Argentina by international NGOs such as the Conservation Land Trust (CLT) and The Nature Conservancy (TNC). There are now 123 individual initiatives with a total area of 7290 km^2, 0.26% of the country (Morales, 2009). Agreements between landowners, NGOs and provincial governments differ from case to case. Most of them are for 10–20 years' duration (Moreno et al., 2008). Agreements for FVSA Wildlife Refuges are for only 5 years, but can be renewed automatically (FVSA, 2008).

Unlike public protected areas, private reserves can continue to operate agricultural and grazing activities as well as conservation and tourism. The landowners receive tax incentives, generally a partial exemption from property taxes. These exemptions range from 40% for multiple-use areas, up to 100% for areas dedicated entirely to conservation (Moreno et al., 2008). These economic incentives have proved effective for properties >1 km^2 in area, but not for smaller areas (Morales, 2009). In the view of conservation NGOs, government support for private conservation remains inadequate. In their view, specific legislation and policies with effective economic incentives would be needed for private conservation to become widespread (FARN and FVSA, 2007a, b, c).

Tourism and other economic activities

Most conservation initiatives by NGOs and private landowners in Argentina are financed by farming and/or tourism. Some of these initiatives use community-based tourism activities to connect protected areas. Other projects, carried out by international NGOs, use external funding to encourage private landowners to shift from traditional economic activities to more sustainable land-use practices. The Nature Conservancy (2010), for example, is working with farmers and landowners in the Patagonian grasslands to improve the management of sheep grazing regimes. TNC aims to help preserve over 160,000 km^2 of temperate grasslands by 2015 (The Nature Conservancy, 2010).

According to a survey carried out by FVSA across 48 private conservation initiatives, the main activities were grazing (52%) and ecotourism (42%), with forestry, fishing and agriculture at lower percentages (Morales, 2009). There are good prospects for increased ecotourism in these areas, since currently half of all international tourists to Argentina visit protected areas. Nine of FVSA's 14 current wildlife refuges have established ecotourism and tourism activities (FVSA, 2009; 2010a). Most of these refuges have their own promotional websites. FVSA provides additional support by publishing online brochures. Some examples are outlined below.

At Peninsula de Valdez in Patagonia, an icon site for watching the southern right whale, and at Puerto Iguazu near Iguazu Falls, FVSA is attempting to build local community capacity in ecotourism, promote responsible tourism practices and improve tourist infrastructure (FVSA, 2010b). FVSA wildlife refuges at Cerro Blanco in the Sierras Grandes in Cordoba, Aurora del Palmar in Entre Rios, San Antonio, in Corrientes and Yaguarundi in Misiones offer tourist activities such as horse riding, climbing and abseiling, wildlife safaris and canoeing.

Yacutinga and Yaguarundi wildlife refuges, in the buffer zone of Iguazu Falls National Park and the 'Transboundary Green Corridor of the Atlantic Forest', have apparently adopted ecotourism and halted extraction of the palm tree *Euterpe edulis* (FVSA, 2010a), which is endemic and endangered (Chediak, 2008). Tourism activities at Yaguaroundi (2010) include accommodation, guided ecotours, birdwatching and handicraft sales from the local indigenous community Guavirá Poty.

Yacutinga Wildlife Refuge (2010) conserves 5.7 km^2 of the Interior Atlantic Forest, and receives around 800 tourists each year, largely from overseas (Groves, 2003). The refuge operates a low-impact lodge with a four-person staff, and offers local tours featuring birdwatching, medicinal plants and nocturnal wildlife. It also operates a small research station which supports projects on impact monitoring, captive breeding of capybara, environmental education, forest restoration and ethnobotany. The station runs a volunteer programme for visitors and students.

The Wildlife Refuge Aurora del Palmar, in the province of Entre Rios, lies adjacent to the Uruguay River international tourism corridor and the National Park El Palmar. The Refuge is 13 km^2 in area, including seasonal wetlands and grasslands and 2 km^2 of old-growth Yatay palm trees (*Butia yatay*). Aurora del Palmar joined the FVSA Wildlife Refuge network in 1998, and is now also part of the Entre Rios provincial protected areas network. It is a family concern, which includes farming, forestry and organic food production as well as ecotourism. Ecotourism activities include hiking, horse riding, canoeing, birdwatching and photography. Aurora del Palmar also runs a school environmental education programme, with assistance from the ornithological foundation Aves Argentinas. The Refuge is economically self-sustaining, with ecotourism now the main source of revenue (Morales, 2009). Revenue is sufficient to fund conservation projects on regeneration of the Yatay palm, reintroduction of rhea, environmental education programmes and tour guide training. In conjunction with El Palmar National Park, Aurora del Palmar is lobbying for creation of the first Ramsar site in Entre Rios (Aurora del Palmar, 2010).

In the provinces of Jujuy and Salta in northwestern Argentina, the local NGO Fundación ProYungas (2010) has established a conservation programme in the subtropical cloud forest ecosystem known as Yungas. The programme operates within the 21,000 km^2 Alto Bermejo Basin. Three-quarters of this region lies within the Yungas Biosphere Reserve, created in 2002, and Fundación ProYungas operates largely with private landowners and local communities in the remaining area. The Foundation has established a community-based tourism project, involving 65 grass roots organizations which offer tourist products along the Ruta Alto Bermejo. This is a tourist route linking the Biosphere Reserve and a cultural World Heritage Site at Quebrada de Humahuaca. Local indigenous communities have developed their own websites to promote local trekking routes. These are traditional trails used historically by local communities to trade food and livestock between the arid land of the Puna and the cloud forest of the Yungas. The Ruta Alto Bermejo Project is carried out in conjunction with an organiszation known as Programa Andes Tropicales (PAT) (2010), which also supports community-based tourism in Bolivia and Venezuela. PAT is co-financed by regional and international organizations including the Andean Corporation, the CODESPA Foundation in Spain and the International Finance Corporation.

The Conservation Land Trust (2010), CLT, is an international NGO dedicated to the establishment and expansion of protected areas in Argentina and Chile. In Argentina, CLT has helped to establish El Piñalito provincial park in the subtropical rainforest of Misiones. In Patagonia, CLT and the local NGO Conservación Patagonica (2010) have bought land for conservation at El Rincon, bordering Perito Moreno National Park. CLT, FVSA and Conservación Patagonia also contributed to the establishment of Argentina's first national coastal protected area, the 600 km^2 Monte Leon National Park (2010). Declared in 2004, this park protects a significant section of coastline, important in the conservation of orca, southern right whale and Magellanic penguin colonies. Monte Leon National Park and Peninsula de Valdez Provincial Reserve have become prime tourism destinations for coastal wildlife watching.

The principal ecotourism and private conservation project operated by the Conservation Land Trust (2010) is situated in the marshes of Esteros, in the province of Corrientes. The private reserve has a total area of 690 km^2 and incorporates the estancias of El Socorro and San Alonso, previously run for cattle grazing. The reserve's principal income is from ecotourism, including accommodation and guided birdwatching, horse riding, fly fishing and canoeing. Estancia el Socorro (2010) also offers a tour of savannah and wetlands rehabilitation. The CLT initiative also provides training for surrounding communities in land restoration and sustainable farming practices as well as ecotourism.

Current challenges

Private conservation efforts in Argentina are increasing: NGOs are playing a key role in these initiatives; and ecotourism is an increasingly important economic activity in both public and privately owned protected areas. At a national scale, tourism has increased from 500,000 visitors in 1990 to 2,700,000 visitors in 2006 (APN, 2007).

Private reserves near national parks and other major tourism destinations, such as El Palmar, Estancia el Socorro and Yacutinga, can fund their operations successfully through a combination of ecotourism and farming. Elsewhere, however, support from both national and local governments needs to be improved if these efforts are to succeed (FARN and FVSA, 2007a, b). In other Latin American nations such as Chile and Brazil, for example, there are landholder incentives for private conservation including tax exemptions, financial compensation for land-use restrictions and funding for ecotourism demonstration projects (Grieg-Gran, 2000; Morales, 2009). Argentina could benefit from similar programmes.

Conclusions

Every country in South and Central America is different, and these differences are reflected in conservation tourism projects, but there seem to be some distinctive characteristics for this continent none the less. First, the majority of these projects are in highly biodiverse forested areas. There are one or two in the grassland–wetland complexes of the Brazilian Pantanal, but none are reported from the pampas of Argentina, the deserts of southern Peru and northern Chile or the paramo and other montane ecosystems above the treeline in the Andes. Second, a relatively high proportion of these forest examples seem to involve Indigenous peoples. Some of these peoples are quite small in number, with only a few thousand or even a few hundred individuals in total. Their current lifestyles, history of interaction with colonial civilizations and other Indigenous peoples and current involvement in commercial tourism differ, but there seem to be some features in common. The third characteristic of these South American examples is that a relatively high proportion involve international NGOs, donors or expatriate entrepreneurs, at least in some countries. The US-based NGO Conservation International, for example, has been involved in a number of these cases; and US expatriates established lodges such as

El Monte and La Selva in Ecuador, and tour operations such as Costa Rica Expeditions and Expediciones Chile (Buckley, 2006). Cases such as Pousada Caiman and Cristalino Jungle Lodge in Brazil, in contrast, were established by well-off local landowners.

It appears that, in Brazil at least, preferential tax treatment has probably provided the principal incentive for the establishment of registered private reserves, RPPNs. In addition, it seems that, in some provinces at least, there are legal planning requirements to set aside 20% of pastoral properties for conservation. There is thus both a tax carrot and a planning stick for landowners who have areas of significant conservation value to establish RPPNs. It therefore needs only a very small additional incentive, on either the stick or carrot side, for property owners to establish tourism businesses as an adjunct to cattle ranching. Pousada Caiman, for example, had a heritage homestead which was converted to tourist accommodation. In the case of Cristalino Jungle Lodge, the private property concerned, as well as the surrounding area, was apparently under threat from oil exploration, and registering it as part of the national patrimony may provide some legal and political protection which would not be available to a property run solely for cattle. In each of these cases, however, these additional incentives remain speculative, and the landowners concerned may well also have had personal interests in conservation.

12 Southern and East Africa

J. Guy Castley

!Xaus Lodge, !Ae! Hai Kalahari Heritage Park, South Africa

Introduction

Africa, a continent synonymous with wildlife and promoted as the global destination to view the Big Five, has emerged in recent years as a leading region in advancing conservation strategies and promoting sustainable tourism. The legacy of the Big Five lives on and these flagship species (Walpole and Leader-Williams, 2002; Lindsey *et al.*, 2007) continue to attract visitors to Africa. However, the diversity of approaches to achieve sustainable tourism and conservation outcomes has increased (Eagles, 2009). It is a measure of the success of African countries that they have identified key develop-ment opportunities, enabling them to adapt to changing circumstances (Barnes *et al.*, 2002; Langholz and Kerley, 2006; Child, 2009). A common theme binds these approaches to-gether, namely tourism and its many manifest-ations (ecotourism, adventure tourism, nature tourism, green tourism, pro-poor tourism), which are shown to be successful conservation tools (Gössling, 1999; Krüger, 2005; Buckley 2008b).

Tourism continues to be one of the leading sectors of the global economy and many African countries have identified this as an avenue for sustainable development (Wilkie and Carpenter, 1999; Libanda and Blignaut, 2008). Tourism provides jobs, economic bene-fits and opportunities for capacity building within these nations (Saarinen *et al.*, 2009b). While the need to improve the livelihoods of so many of Africa's population is of paramount importance, this does not come without the recognition of the natural resource base which underpins these tourism opportunities. Con-sequently, conservation lies at the heart of ensuring a sustainable future (Brandon and Margoluis, 1996). However, the route followed to achieve this sustainable livelihood objective through tourism, and particularly ecotourism, is varied. Many African countries, conservation agencies, NGOs, tourism operators and private individuals have undertaken their own 'safari', in the process making Africa a global leader in this particular field. The need to address the requirements of the African environment (eco-logical, social, cultural, economic and political) has necessitated a response that is African in origin. The notion that Africa provides its own

solutions to its own problems is one that is relevant to our current overview of conservation tourism models and strategies.

This chapter first reviews the range of models used that contribute to the conservation and development objectives of various stakeholders, principally through the collaborative efforts between private landowners, communities, non-government organizations and public protected area agencies. It then uses a case study approach to look specifically at the manner in which these initiatives deliver sustainable conservation and tourism outcomes, and the key mechanisms used to achieve this. In doing so it identifies and summarizes the lessons learned through these processes. Second, the chapter identifies some challenges that lie ahead to ensure that Africa continues to be a leader in promoting responsible tourism activities, ensuring the continued con-servation of our natural environment.

As a starting point, this chapter looks largely beyond the boundaries of formal protected areas. Formal protected areas in Africa cannot protect all elements of biodiversity despite some countries having more than 40% of their habitats listed as protected (IUCN and UNEP, 2009). It is therefore the efforts and interventions that are undertaken on private land (including communal areas) that need to be harnessed to achieve conservation objectives. As such, this chapter reviews the importance of private conservation efforts in southern Africa and how these have been supported by ecotourism.

The review of the spectrum of approaches in this chapter, as applied in various African countries, is based on a combination of personal knowledge of these operations, reviews of academic articles and online media and publi-cations. The examples chosen to represent this classification of African approaches are not expected to cover all operational scenarios, and this analysis is restricted to an overview of the capacity of such models to address conser-vation and sustainable development objectives. Furthermore, the chapter does not present a comprehensive assessment of two of the larger ecotourism operations (&Beyond and Wilder-ness Safaris) as these are discussed at length in other chapters.

As stated previously, conservation efforts cannot be confined to public estates to achieve desired biodiversity conservation objectives.

Many studies have demonstrated the value that private lands bring both to conservation and to social development objectives (Thackway and Olsen, 1999; Jones *et al.*, 2005; Sims-Castley *et al.*, 2005; Langholz and Kerley, 2006), and how ecotourism in particular facilitates the crystallization of these benefits (Buckley, 2003a, 2009b). Growth within private wildlife reserve networks and the associated ecotourism industry has increased considerably in southern and East Africa in the past 20 years, driven by demand for wildlife and nature tourism products (Jones *et al.*, 2005), and there are now a number of different ownership and management scenarios (Langholz and Lassoie, 2001; Carter *et al.*, 2008).

The conservation of natural resources remains a fundamental requirement in supplying viable ecotourism products (Brandon and Margoluis, 1996). While the private sector may be able to meet conservation objectives while providing profitable ecotourism destinations, the strategies used have various advantages and disadvantages (Langholz and Lassoie, 2001). Some of the concerns raised by Langholz and Lassoie (2001) are still relevant today. First, many profitable concerns still cater to an affluent minority and as a result may alienate local communities, leading to future conservation and social development problems. Second, ownership and management of these reserves and the inclusion of local communities in decision making processes where necessary may be critical to the long-term viability of these areas and their ability to meet conservation objectives. Lastly, growth within this sector continues, and, while private reserves are one of the tools to achieve conservation benefits, there are still many questions that require attention. This chapter intends to review various approaches to conservation on private lands and how benefits arising from these initiatives achieve multiple objectives.

Within Africa, the success of many private ventures has been achieved through the establishment of freehold conservancies (e.g. many Kenyan wildlife areas), privately owned reserves, conservancies and community conservation areas (Krug, 2001; Carter *et al.*, 2008). However, while well-managed and financially secure private reserves may be able to contribute significantly to the conservation of species and habitats, concerns have been raised about the ability of private reserves and community-based programmes to conserve ecological processes (Kiss, 2004; Jones *et al.*, 2005). In southern Africa in particular, where many reserves are relatively small, this presents future conservation problems. For example, the conservation or stocking of certain species (e.g. elephant, large predators) can compromise the conservation of biodiversity on these reserves as a result of the scale of localized impacts (e.g. damage to vegetation, excessive predation pressure). Further research is required to address the consequences of such conservation approaches directed towards creating an ecotourism product as there are limitations to these approaches that impact negatively on conservation efforts (Cousins *et al.*, 2008). The precise contribution that private reserves, including areas owned by private individuals, trusts, NGOs, communities, corporations, etc., make to conservation is dependent on the nature of the role within the conservation and ecotourism industry. It is therefore necessary to review the diversity of models through which the private sector operates.

Diversity of Models

Overview

Conservation and ecotourism models in Africa can essentially be categorized either as initiatives that operate as stand-alone entities (e.g. private individuals with sole ownership of land, etc.); or those that capitalize on the benefits of conservation through some form of joint venture. While the isolated operations may be successful, as will be demonstrated later, it is the joint venture models that have proved to be the focus of African conservation and sustainable development success stories. Generally, these two broad models rely on two essential components. The first is that there is sufficient tourism demand to see large African mammals; and the second is that the conversion from an agricultural or pastoral form of land use to one of wildlife conservation (i.e. the development of a tourism product) is a feasible alternative to generate adequate economic returns. Increasing trends in tourist numbers to African states (Balmford *et al.*, 2009; Rogerson, 2009;

Saarinen *et al.*, 2009) indicate that there is sufficient demand to view Africa's wildlife, as well as scenic landscapes. However, this may lead to conservation efforts driven by tourism demand (Cousins *et al.*, 2008), which ultimately undermine the fundamental requirements of biodiversity conservation. Wildlife ranching and tourism present a better land-use alternative to traditional farming practices (Kerley *et al.*, 1995, 1999; Davies *et al.*, 1997; Sims-Castley *et al.*, 2005; Relly, 2008). However, shifting land-use practices does not come without significant investment in capital (economic and social) and human resources. The removal of livestock from the land and subsequent restoration and rehabilitation, particularly if the landscape has undergone significant transform-ation (e.g. overgrazing, habitat removal, fragmentation, etc.), present ongoing chal-lenges. Other factors affecting these tourism models include the proximity to other reserves or public protected areas, the ease of access, level of service provision and social respon-sibilities. Weaver and Lawton (2007) apportioned these into supply, demand, impacts, institutions and external environment categories. While mindful of all these factors, it is anticipated that the supply and demand aspects will dominate the factors within wildlife-based ecotourism operations.

This section reviews the various models under the two broader categories (stand-alone and joint venture models) and provides examples of how these work within the African ecotourism and conservation context, using a selected review of case studies (Table 12.1). These approaches may not be universal in their applicability to African situations, as this will be determined by the socio-political climate, legislative procedures, economic and political stability and the actions and interventions of key players or champions in the tourism and conservation development process. However, they provide an overview of the suite of approaches that can be used to achieve con-servation and social development objectives.

Stand-alone operations

Under this model, private landowners make a conscious decision to develop an ecotourism

product that can be provided on the open market. This particular model is relatively commonplace in southern Africa, particularly in South Africa and Namibia where a considerable proportion of the land area is under private ownership. Advances and interest in wildlife-based tourism operations in South Africa are relatively recent. Prior to 1994, under the previous apartheid regime, tourism to the country was insignificant, but under the post-apartheid government there was a concerted effort to investigate the economic potential of tourism (Binns and Nel, 2002; Visser and Rogerson, 2004).

These opportunities manifest themselves in two scenarios. First, for many existing private landowners the economic returns from wildlife-based ecotourism were greater than those obtained through conventional farming methods (Kerley *et al.*, 1995; Sims-Castley *et al.*, 2005; Cousins *et al.*, 2008) and there has been a rapid conversion of land-use practices. However, owners also state that their motivation for entering into such land-use practices is driven by a desire to conserve the environment or for aesthetic reasons (Langholz, 1996; van der Waal and Dekker, 2000).

Second, there has been another suite of landowners (both local and international entrepreneurs) who have specifically entered the market with a view to establishing an ecotourism product through the creation of luxury private game reserves. The former scenario has seen the establishment of many private game reserves and wildlife ranches in the savannah regions of South Africa. Many of these were established as hunting reserves or they contributed to live game trading enterprises (van der Waal and Dekker, 2000; Reilly *et al.*, 2003; Bothma *et al.*, 2009). Despite the focus towards trophy hunting and wildlife ranching these properties were still seen to have conser-vation value as well as ecotourism potential. However, only 35.5% of these properties gained revenue through tourism activities (largely dominated by game viewing) and even fewer (7.9%) targeted the foreign tourist market (van der Waal and Dekker, 2000).

The development of luxury private game reserves has undoubtedly strengthened southern Africa's conservation and sustainable tourism profile. Individuals, principally conservationists,

Table 12.1. Selected case studies of African conservation and tourism models.

Property	Ownership	Model	Size (km²)	Benefits[a] to Conservation	Benefits[a] to Community
Erindi Private Game Reserve, Namibia	Private	Stand-alone	710	Yes	Yes
Kagga Kamma Nature Reserve, Western Cape, South Africa[b]	Private	Stand-alone	150	Yes	No
Kichaka Game Reserve, Eastern Cape, South Africa	Private	Stand-alone	80	No	No
Lalibela Game Reserve, Eastern Cape, South Africa	Private	Stand-alone	75	?	No
Thanda Private Game Reserve, Kwazulu-Natal, South Africa	Private	Stand-alone	140	Yes	Yes
Tswalu Desert Reserve, Northern Cape, South Africa[b]	Private	Stand-alone	1000	Yes	Yes
!Ae!Hai Kalahari Heritage Park, Kgalagadi Transfrontier Park, Northern Cape, South Africa[b]	Community	Contractual (community/ public sector)	500	?	Yes
Kuzuko Private Game Reserve, Eastern Cape, South Africa[b]	Private	Contractual (public/private sector)	160	Yes	Yes
Gorah Elephant Camp – Addo Elephant National Park, Eastern Cape, South Africa[b]	Private	Concession (public/private sector)	N/A[c]	?	Yes
African Parks Network/Peace Parks Foundation[b]	Private	Partnership (public/private sector)	Variable	Yes	Yes
Manda Wilderness Game Reserve/Nkwichi Lodge, Mozambique	Community/ Private	Partnership (community/ private)	1200	Yes	Yes
Madikwe Game Reserve, North West Province, South Africa[b]	Public/ Private	Partnership (public/private/ community)	750	Yes	Yes
Ol Pejeta Conservancy, Laikipia, Kenya	Private	Partnership (NGO/private/ community)	360	Yes	Yes
Welgevonden Private Game Reserve, Limpopo Province, South Africa[b]	Private	Partnership (private/corporate sector)	450	Yes	No
Tau Game Lodge – Madikwe Private Game Reserve, North West Province, South Africa	Private	Partnership (public/private sector)	N/A[d]	?	Yes
Kwandwe Game Reserve, Eastern Cape, South Africa[b]	Private	Corporate – &Beyond	220	Yes	Yes
Rooipoort Nature Reserve – Venetia Limpopo Game Reserve, South Africa[b]	Corporate	Corporate – De Beers Consolidated Mines	400/350	Yes	No
Sanbona Wildlife Reserve, Western Cape, South Africa	Private	Corporate – The Mantis Group	540	Yes	Yes

Table 12.1. Continued.

Property	Ownership	Model	Size (km²)	Benefits[a] to Conservation	Benefits[a] to Community
Shamwari Game Reserve, Eastern Cape, South Africa[b]	Private	Corporate – The Mantis Group	250	Yes	Yes
Khama Rhino Sanctuary, Serowe, Botswana	Community	Community-based	93	Yes	Yes
Mokolodi Nature Reserve, Gaborone, Botswana	Community	Community-based	30	Yes	Yes

[a] Benefits are those stated or demonstrated from websites (via images, statistics presented, etc.).
[b] Reserves where the author has personal knowledge of operations.
[c] The Gorah Elephant Camp is a 50 km² concession within the Addo Elephant National Park main camp.
[d] Tau Game Lodge is a single leasehold concession within the 750 km² Madikwe Game Reserve.

philanthropists and business entrepreneurs, have made significant business investments into establishing high-quality ecotourism experiences in line with both conservation and socio-economic objectives. The capital investment required for these ventures is significant and includes a range of costs additional to the land purchase costs. These include removal of non-essential and derelict infrastructure, erection of wildlife fences, restoration of habitats and alien vegetation removal, reintroduction of wildlife and the design, environmental assessment and construction of tourism-related infrastructure (e.g. lodges, roads, airstrips). There are a significant number of such operations that have become established within the last 20 years, primarily in South Africa and Namibia, and many have received global acclaim for their efforts. Furthermore, the emerging focus towards responsible and sustainable tourism in southern Africa (Spenceley et al., 2002; Spenceley, 2008a) has seen many of these private reserves actively engaging with local communities to ensure that the benefits from ecotourism accrue to both conservation and community development and empowerment. There are a number of examples that will be discussed in further detail in the case studies section of this chapter.

One of the concerns surrounding many stand-alone conservation tourism reserves is that the areas being managed are generally relatively small. These areal restrictions create numerous problems, particularly when introducing large charismatic species such as elephant and rhino and top predators such as

lion and African wild dog (Druce et al., 2004; Mackey et al., 2006; Hayward et al., 2007; Slotow and Hunter, 2009). Many of the issues linked to the size of the conservation area can be reduced, or at the very least diverted, for some time by increasing the available land area for species through further land purchase or certain joint venture arrangements. Consequently ecotourism can make a significant contribution to the conservation of threatened species such as the African wild dog (Lindsey et al., 2005; Gusset et al., 2008) on many reserves.

Joint Venture Models

A multitude of joint venture models have brought about conservation, ecotourism and community benefits (Langholz and Lassoie, 2001; Carter et al., 2008; Eagles, 2009). These models range from those between private and public partners to those between community groups and NGOs. Each of these models has varied success in relation to both conservation and socio-economic development objectives and all have associated strengths and weaknesses. This chapter outlines five African models classified under joint venture operations including: (i) contractual arrangements; (ii) concession or commercialization arrangements; (iii) private partnerships; (iv) corporate initiatives; and (v) community-based/NGO arrangements (Table 12.2).

The first two models commonly see agreements being made between public conservation

Table 12.2. Typology of joint venture operations in African conservation tourism.

Model	Description	Stakeholders	Commitment	Tenure	Conservation benefit	Community benefit	Successful examples
Contractual agreements	Negotiated public/ private; public/ community agreements	Public conservation agencies, private sector, local communities	Management and institutional support from the public sector, commitment to conservation and landholdings from private/community partner	Generally medium- to long-term agreements in the order of 20–100 years	Increased land area for conservation, increased wildlife population viability, potential to protect species with large range sizes	Opportunities for ecotourism development using existing public resource base, employment and SMME/BEE opportunities.	Kuzuko Game Reserve, Eastern Cape (SA), Makuleke Region of the Kruger National Park (SA), !Ae!Hai Kalahari Heritage Park (SA)
Concessions and commercialization	Transfer of goods and service provision to a third-party operator (e.g. lodge, restaurant)	Public conservation agencies, private sector, local communities – concession partners selected via open tender	Public protected areas provide the resource base upon which the private-sector business models are based. Private sector provides capital investment and percentage of turn-over to public agency	Generally short- to medium-term operations of 5–20 years (e.g. lodge concessions operate on longer leases and restaurants/shops on shorter leases)	Potentially no direct conservation benefit as developed within existing protected area estate. Additional benefits accrue through diversifying revenue streams to direct towards conservation actions	Equal opportunity employment and, with South Africa, the need to demonstrate black economic empowerment in operations. Support of regional SMME and BEE outside protected areas	Gorah Elephant Camp, Addo Elephant National Park, Jock Safari Camp, Kruger National Park
Partnerships	Joint ventures where partners have a common interest in one or more objectives	Private sector (landowners, investment groups), NGOs, community groups and trusts	Shared commitment to transparent decision making to achieve multiple objectives, particularly when including local communities. Unambiguous identification of stakeholders' roles and responsibilities required	Variable duration depending on the nature of the partnership. For example, some donor agencies may initiate community projects and then withdraw after an implementation phase	Expansion of protected area estate on private lands through establishment of conservancies. Creation of a viable conservation resources base underpinning development potential. Increased awareness of the benefits of conservation	Complete community engagement is critical to success of social development projects. These range from direct employment to capacity building and development of SMMEs	Thanda Private Game Reserve/Mduna Royal Reserve, Kwazulu-Natal (SA), Welgevonden Private Game Reserve, Limpopo (SA). Ol Pejeta Conservancy, Kenya. African Parks network

Continued

Table 12.2. Continued.

Model	Description	Stakeholders	Commitment	Tenure	Conservation benefit	Community benefit	Successful examples
Corporations	Ecotourism product administered and marketed by large corporations, some in partnerships with other agencies to deliver certain products	Private ecotourism and hospitality companies with interests in multiple lodge, adventure tourism facilities in African and beyond	Significant capital investment from private sector. Includes land acquisition, infrastructure development, product development (wildlife introduction), hospitality training and corporate social responsibility	Long-term ventures due to the level of commitment from the private sector. Many operations include land acquisition and areas set aside for conservation in perpetuity	Expansion of protected area estate on private lands. Conservation of wildlife including in many cases charismatic and threatened species. Habitat restoration and recovery following changes in historical land use	Community uplifting through corporate social responsibility and responsible tourism initiatives. Include contributions to education, health care, employment, empowerment and stimulation of SMME opportunities	Various groups run successful operations in Africa. These include &Beyond, Wilderness Safaris, Mantis Group, Hunter Hotels Group and the Singita Group
Community-based natural resource management	Initiatives driven primarily by local communities. Some may be in isolation (entirely through communities) while others are supported by NGOs assist as project and the private sector	Local communities, often structured into a community trust or management group. NGOs and the private sector and development partners and share a common vision with the community	Communities must have the desire to consider alternative forms of land use that can deliver on sustainable development priorities such as poverty reduction, education and health care. A level of community cohesion is required to engage project partners and also to plan strategically for community development projects	As communities commonly hold the native title to the land upon which these ventures operate, tenure should be secure in the medium to long term as long as the conversion to conservation land uses provides anticipated benefits. Tenure may be affected by ecotourism marketplace, as well as geographical isolation	Shifts in land-use patterns leading to downstream conservation benefits. Expansion of protected areas estates and reintroduction of wildlife. Conservation of natural and cultural heritage	Such models can address socio-economic development needs. Ecotourism revenue can be directed towards poverty alleviation schemes, business development and improvement in basic services (health, education)	Manda Wilderness Project (collaboration between the Manda Wilderness Community Trust and Nkwichi Lodge) in Mozambique, Khama Rhino Sanctuary and Mokolodi Nature Reserve in Botswana

agencies and private concerns, whether these are individuals, communities or corporate companies. The remaining three models include multiple stakeholders involved with the establishment, marketing, implementation and operation of various conservation, ecotourism and sustainable resource utilization initiatives.

Contractual arrangements

Contractual agreements are infrequently used to achieve conservation and ecotourism benefits on private land. However, these have been applied by public conservation authorities to establish agreements with community groups to implement joint management arrangements within public national parks and reserves (Grossman and Holden, 2009). Examples of such arrangements within South Africa include the jointly managed areas of the Richtersveld National Park, and lands restored to the Makuleke (north-eastern South Africa) and ‡Khomani San/Mier (north-western South Africa) communities within the Kruger National Park and Kgalagadi Transfrontier Park respectively. In these cases the South African National Parks (SANParks) has negotiated long-term conservation and management agreements with the communities. More recently SANParks has also negotiated the inclusion of a number of private reserves into the public protected area network. It could be argued that the conservation gains of such initiatives are negligible, given that: (i) the areas were already set aside for conservation and therefore make no further contribution to the areal extent of the conservation estate; or (ii) the change in tenure (in the case of land reverting back to traditional owners) may lead to an increase in extractive resource use, which may bring about changes to these areas. However, if the areas are indeed new additions, as is the case with many private reserve negotiations, then there are likely to be ongoing benefits from the conversion to more sustainable land-use practices and an overall increase in the consolidated area of any particular protected area. Larger areas provide protected habitats with buffers from external influences while also allowing for wider dispersion of fauna and flora within these areas (Hansen and DeFries, 2007). Under these circumstances the benefits that accrue to the enhanced functioning of ecological processes (e.g. predator–prey interactions, wildlife migrations) can be significantly greater.

Contractual areas may also make financial contributions to public conservation agencies through the development of associated ecotourism activities in these sites, but there is invariably a quid pro quo relationship as agencies tend to assist with the reintroduction of wildlife, as well as conducting ongoing conservation management and monitoring. However, it is important to realize that the intended cooperative arrangements do not always materialize and there are also examples where contractual agreements have ongoing management concerns. The contractual agreements between public agencies and local communities are examples from South Africa, providing a basis for discussion when reviewing these case studies later in this chapter.

Concessions and commercialization

Concession agreements and commercialization have been widely adopted by SANParks as a model that allows private enterprise to provide a range of services while contributing (through delivering agreed percentages of turnover) to the ongoing conservation costs of SANParks (Castley et al., 2009a; Mabunda and Wilson, 2009). These services include the development, management and marketing of luxury lodge facilities, but also the management of smaller business units such as shops, restaurants, laundry and general cleaning services, fuel suppliers and gardening. The strategy has met with mixed reactions, with some arguing that such intervention is effective in increasing the conservation performance of SANParks while others, including members of the public, remain unconvinced (Mabunda and Wilson, 2009).

Despite the realized economic benefits there are a number of important lessons to be learned related to such processes. These centre on: (i) the selection process and identification of vendors; (ii) a review of services and ecotourism activities that have the potential to be outsourced; (iii) the loss of control over activities and subsequent decline in service levels (e.g.

restaurants); (iv) the impact of overly optimistic market predictions and subsequent sustainability issues; and (v) the need for greater adoption of broad-based black economic empowerment initiatives in commercial partnerships (Varghese, 2008). Notwithstanding these important lessons, SANParks has been able to increase its net economic return from these ventures, contribute to equitable socio-economic development promoting the contributions of historically disadvantaged groups and increase its contributions to park expansion and biodiversity conservation initiatives (Varghese, 2008; Castley *et al.*, 2009b).

While the long-term success of this particular model has yet to be evaluated, it is evident that it is able to provide tangible benefits, largely through the additional revenue stream available to public conservation agencies (Saporiti, 2006). However, how these funds are disbursed is important and where these are not directed towards conservation-related objectives (e.g. land purchase for expansion of protected area estate, threatened species research, etc.) the extent of conservation benefits is questionable. It is therefore necessary to develop a deeper understanding of the complexity of these agreements, drawing from the lessons learned to ensure that any future negotiations are based on sound empirical data relevant to particular situations (i.e. nature of the industry, type of private partner involved, market surveys, trends in the industry, etc.) (Varghese, 2008; Mabunda and Wilson, 2009).

Partnerships

Partnership arrangements commonly arise between stakeholders with vested interests in conservation, responsible tourism and social development. These interests are not mutually exclusive and require an integrated management approach. Partnerships can be negotiated between private individuals, corporations, service providers, business and industry, investment partners, conservation and development NGOs, educational institutions, public conservation agencies, not-for-profit organizations and communities, ultimately providing a particular level of governance for protected areas (Eagles, 2009). This is especially relevant when con-

sidering partnerships with communities which are frequently approached from a Western perspective, where the views, attitudes and priorities may not align with those of local community groups (Cater, 2006). Engaging these communities from the bottom up is important as they may be able to provide valuable perspectives on priority issues at the outset of any negotiations (Mavhunga, 2007), where all stakeholders are able to share their insight and wisdom when considering alternative approaches to achieving shared goals (Walpole, 2006).

Partnerships will also invariably identify implementing authorities responsible for ensuring that agreed project outcomes are delivered. It is also conceivable that there will be multiple implementing authorities. For example, a private reserve may be instrumental in the development of a lodge and ecotourism venture while a partner community may be required to establish a community trust to ensure that revenue arising from tourism activities can be disbursed into appropriate social development projects. As a result of these diverse requirements it will be necessary to clearly articulate the responsibilities of each partner, particularly in agreements with multiple partners (Buckley, 2009b). Partnerships can achieve diverse tangible outcomes at local, regional, national and international scales (Buckley, 2002) and this chapter elaborates on some examples of these in a review of selected case studies.

Corporate flagships

One of the features of the African safari experience is the delivery of a reputable product where the supplier is well recognized as a leader in the industry. Here the renown of corporate ecotourism and hospitality providers is central to the success of these operations. These international profiles have been developed over many years of promotion and marketing to ensure a sustained demand for these destinations. Throughout Africa a selection of wildlife tourism operators have gained global esteem, including groups such as &Beyond (formerly Conservation Corporation Africa), Wilderness Safaris, Singita Lodges and the Mantis Group. We present a brief synopsis of this particular model for conservation tourism here, as individual chapters elsewhere in this volume are devoted to some of these groups. One of the central features binding these corporate groups is that they operate multiple luxury lodge facilities within public protected areas (see concession agreements), community lands or private game reserves. The tenure of these private reserves also differs considerably. Some may be single ownership properties (e.g. Shamwari Game Reserve, Eastern Cape) while others are conglomerates of privately owned properties that form part of a larger conservancy (e.g. Sabi Sands or Timbavati regions to the west of the Kruger National Park, South Africa), while others still are part of community/ government co-management areas (e.g. Ngorongoro Crater Conservation Area, Tanzania). We present a case study that exemplifies the corporate model of conservation tourism later in this chapter highlighting some of the conservation benefits.

Aside from the direct conservation benefits there is an opportunity to spread the benefits, beyond the boundaries of the reserves themselves (Bushell and Eagles, 2007). These operations work together with communities through a range of corporate social responsibility programmes to achieve social development objectives. Direct employment within reserves is one of the key benefits for members of local communities. However, corporate entities often partner with other agencies to deliver on economic empowerment objectives (i.e. establishment of business opportunities run by communities), and a range of community projects, such as improved education, promotion of equity in job creation and provision of health care. While many corporate joint ventures report on their community involvement activities on public websites, there is little detailed analysis of how these operations deliver on specified targets to quantify such success. This may be through the employment of members from the local community as part of tourism operations, through to the support of community development programmes that deliver on goals such as education, health care, sanitation and empowerment. Furthermore, the reported benefits may also not adequately capture the views from within the local communities that would give an objective assessment of the equitable distribution of benefits.

None the less, these corporate models do provide the foundations for local communities to enter into ecotourism ventures themselves. Importantly this may be either in isolation or through partnerships with public, private or NGO partners. A critical contribution by the private sector to stimulate such community empowerment is the mentoring and development of the business skills required to operate such enterprises to ensure that these are sustainable in the long term. For example, within South Africa there is a drive to encourage the development of small, medium and micro-enterprises (SMMEs) that facilitate black economic empowerment to address the needs of those communities previously disadvantaged by the former apartheid regime. To highlight the importance of the local communities, we expand briefly on the contributions of community-based tourism and conservation models in the next section and focus here on the conservation elements, as discussions around the socio-economic and development aspects have been discussed in detail elsewhere (Nelson, 2008; Spenceley, 2008c).

Community participation models

Conservation and ecotourism have evolved from simply being contributory mechanisms to regional economic development to ones that make concerted efforts to achieve economic goals through a combination of community-based and pro-poor tourism initiatives (Spenceley and Seif, 2003; Goodwin, 2009). This changing paradigm of tourism is acutely evident in developing countries and Africa has seen a diversity of models to address these social challenges. While there is no dissent about the need to improve local livelihoods and that tourism can provide a means to achieve this (Barnes et al., 2002; Jones et al., 2005; Libanda and Blignaut, 2008), just how communities engage with the tourism and ultimately the conservation process is varied.

Community-based natural resource management (CBNRM) is a land management term which has become widespread in several continents over recent decades, particularly in southern Africa, Asia and Latin America (Salafsky et al., 2001). Fundamentally, it refers simply to the devolution of land management decisions and practices to local communities resident on the land concerned. In practice, however, it comes with several additional connotations. The first is that it commonly involves some form of community title to the land involved, whether through freehold under modern land law, a long-term community lease from the national government concerned or some form of traditional or customary land ownership system. The precise bundles of rights and responsibilities conferred by such titles and the precise definitions of who can share in those rights and responsibilities are critical aspects of any CBNRM system. The second is that, while CBNRM does not necessarily involve either tourism or conservation, in practice these have been important components of CBNRM approaches in several countries (Libanda and Blignaut, 2008; Sebele, 2010); and, equally, CBNRM has been a key component or context of attempts to link tourism and conservation. In sub-Saharan Africa, links between tourism, conservation and CBNRM are particularly strong in Namibia (Barnes et al., 2002) and Botswana.

In Namibia, early examples at Nyae-Nyae and #Khoadi //Hoas were reported by WTO (2002) and summarized in Buckley (2003a). Since that time the number of cases has grown very rapidly, and there are currently over 50 CBNRM areas in Namibia, many incorporating tourism operations (Spenceley, 2008c; NACSO 2009). Wildlife tourism does not necessarily spell an end to higher-impact uses such as livestock grazing or commercial or subsistence hunting in these areas. However, it does provide economic benefits linked directly to wildlife viewing prompting the modification of land and wildlife management practices in favour of conservation, at least in some instances. Community-based natural resource management is also very extensive in Botswana, and wildlife tourism operations are widespread. The greatest densities are in the north-east corner of the country, accessible from Victoria Falls, and in the Okavango area, accessible by air from Maun. Several large wildlife tourism operators maintain multiple lodges in Okavango CBNRM areas, which are known legally as

wildlife management areas, and these are considered in detail elsewhere in this volume.

Two different approaches are in common use in communal areas. In some cases the actual tourism operations are run by local communities directly, often with assistance from international donors and aid agencies at the establishment stage. In others, the community leases tourism operating rights to a private tourism enterprise. The details of such arrangements can vary considerably. These may include, for example: financial arrangements, exclusivity of access to particular areas, responsibility for wildlife and infrastructure management, and obligations to provide preferential employment or entrepreneurial opportunities for members of particular local communities. Not all of these arrangements will be successful for a variety of reasons, but there are a number of cases where arrangements with private operators have indeed provided benefits both for local communities and for conservation. Several particularly well-regarded examples operated by Wilderness Safaris are discussed in an earlier chapter while we present some additional case studies later in this chapter.

In summary, CBNRM arrangements have indeed helped to conserve significant areas and wildlife populations, including endangered species; and associated tourism enterprises do indeed provide significant local employment – as also occurs with public protected areas in this region. However, increased employment also generates secondary growth in local resident populations, only some of whom are employed; and this creates indirect negative impacts on conservation, as well as increasing demands on local social services and infrastructure. This issue is less significant where community landholders of a CBNRM area are defined at the time the area is established and have the right to exclude others from moving into their area. It is of greater concern where there are local municipalities with open access. Despite these second-order issues, it does appear that CBNRM systems in southern Africa provide a platform allowing ecotourism to provide incentives for the conservation of biological diversity. None the less, Kiss (2004) urges caution when looking at the perceived benefits of community-based ecotourism as, despite appearances, these initiatives may not be contributing to real conservation targets such as protecting large areas, viable populations and heterogeneous ecosystems. Hence she suggests that alternative approaches such as direct payment to communities for the supply of ecosystem services may be just as successful in achieving social development goals, allowing scarce financial resources to be directed to more pressing conservation requirements.

Conservation Tourism Case Studies

Overview

The six models presented in the preceding section demonstrate that it is possible to achieve conservation benefits while meeting socio-economic objectives. It is also clear that each of these models has its associated strengths and weaknesses and that there are opportunities to learn from each. This section presents an overview of selected case studies for each of these models in turn, to demonstrate how benefits have been achieved. This review of selected case studies draws from the personal experiences of the author. For the majority of examples, the author has either visited or is familiar with the conservation and tourism activities within these areas. For the others, information for this review was drawn primarily from the published literature and online sources (e.g. a reserve's official website), supplemented by personal experience within the southern African protected area management sector.

Tswalu Desert Reserve

Tswalu Desert Reserve is the single largest private wildlife reserve in South Africa and covers more than 1000 km² of arid savannah landscapes in the southern Kalahari. This stand-alone reserve was initially set aside for hunting purposes by the late Stephen Boler, but has been expanded and converted to a purely conservation and ecotourism land use after being purchased by Nicky Oppenheimer (of De Beers Consolidated Diamond Mining) in 1998. Unlike many other smaller reserves

throughout southern Africa, the extensive landscapes conserved have facilitated the reintroduction of viable populations of many wildlife species, including threatened species such as the arid-adapted ecotype of the critically endangered black rhinoceros (*Diceros bicornis bicornis*). As a member of the Relais & Châteaux group, the reserve has blended the conservation objectives with that of an exclusive ecotourism experience, and as such only 30 guests are allowed in the reserve at any one time. The relative isolation of Tswalu adds to the wilderness qualities and issues associated with access are circumvented by guests being flown in on private charter flights from either Johannesburg or Cape Town. The emphasis at Tswalu is about restoring the natural habitats from their previously highly degraded states to that which is more representative of the Kalahari today. In achieving this Tswalu has tried to move beyond the ubiquitous Big Five attractions, despite having these for visitors to look at, to allow guests to determine how they interact with the landscape and environment through personally tailored ecotourism activities.

Conservation efforts at Tswalu are coordinated by a resident ecologist and include the monitoring and management of predator populations and threatened species. The desire to ensure that reserve management is informed by scientific research resulted in the establishment of the Tswalu Foundation in 2008. Since its inception the foundation has supported 26 research studies, undertaken by a range of tertiary institutions and students, ranging from those investigating arachnid communities to those tracking the movement and behaviour of top-order carnivores. Ultimately this research will provide the basis for informed conservation decision making at Tswalu.

Experiencing Tswalu's wilderness is likely to be limited only to the wealthy but the benefits from these visitors can support local communities and initiatives through the increased regional revenues generated by the reserve. The reserve employs 142 staff (a staff:guest ratio of 3:1 if fully booked), with the majority sourced from the neighbouring communities. The direct benefits to staff have been significant, with the provision of energy-efficient housing (solar water heaters, etc.), education and sporting facilities. This attention to social development has already seen a dramatic increase in adult literacy levels. The wider community has benefited by the construction of a health care clinic. This provides free health services, in partnership with the state government and an international team of medical professionals, to any residents in the neighbouring regions. Tswalu has also made smaller contributions to community empowerment by donating a vehicle and ostriches to communally run tourism and ranching operations respectively.

The success of Tswalu is driven by a number of factors. First, the size of the reserve is significant and captures a mosaic of habitats that is able to support a rich diversity of fauna and flora. Second, while those experiencing the conservation and hospitality qualities of Tswalu may be limited, the ongoing support and engagement with neighbouring communities strengthen relationships and build confidence in community support for conservation projects. Third, the development and implementation of a conservation ecotourism project of this magnitude requires significant financial investment. The majority of private landowners in southern Africa are unlikely to be able to provide the capital investment required (land purchase, rehabilitation, appropriate boundary fencing, supporting infrastructure such as roads and airstrips, tourism facilities, staff development and support, etc.) to establish such expansive reserves. Lastly, the vision of the landowner is critical to the success. Had the reserve not been purchased by one with a conservation philosophy, then the outcome could have been significantly different. Furthermore, having a team of dedicated staff who share this vision and are committed to achieving conservation and social development goals is fundamental to the ongoing success of the reserve.

Thanda Private Game Reserve

Thanda Private Game Reserve lies at the other end of the stand-alone private reserve spectrum, and at 72 km² is one of the smaller areas reviewed for this chapter. Thanda is located in the Kwazulu-Natal Province of South Africa in an area known for its wildlife diversity. Thanda is owned by Swedish entrepreneur Dan Olofsson and was opened to the public in 2004. While the reserve offers guests a chance to view South Africa's wildlife up close and personal, it prides itself on the indulgent opulence of its exclusive accommodation as a member of the Leading Hotels of the World. Despite its small size Thanda supports populations of the Big Five and has partnered with Ezemvelo KZN Wildlife to reintroduce a small population of eastern black rhinoceros, *Diceros bicornis minor*, as part of WWF's Black Rhino Range Expansion Project. A breeding pack of African wild dog has also been reintroduced but the small size of the reserve is a cause for concern, given the prey and habitat requirements of the species. Thanda has a resident ecologist and contributes to broader regional programmes that seek to expand the range of elephant populations by reducing the extent of fenced environments across the landscape. These initiatives, coordinated through the Space for Elephants and Thanda Foundations, serve as mechanisms to address landscape function by stimulating the movement and migration of wildlife across conservation areas and relatively unpopulated areas.

Thanda has also made significant contributions in addressing corporate social responsibility aspects through partnership agreements. The Thanda Foundation was established to direct attention to the socio-economic and development needs of the three neighbouring communities. This foundation provides a mechanism to raise funds for both community and conservation projects and initiatives. An example of a successful partnership at a local level is the agreement set up between the Thanda Private Game Reserve and two neighbouring local communities, the Mdletshe Tribal Authority and the Mandlakhazi Tribal Authority in Kwazulu-Natal, South Africa. Operating through the Mdletshe Mandlakhazi Community Trust, Thanda PGR has negotiated the expansion of conservation lands to include additional portions of His Majesty King Zwelithini Goodwill kaBhekuzulu's land to establish the Mduna Royal Reserve, effectively doubling the size of the conservation area to just over 147 km². Already the expansion of the conservation estate has seen the introduction of additional black rhino as part of the range expansion programme mentioned earlier. This partnership also seeks to empower the local communities to develop their own ecotourism product. To facilitate this process, Thanda has compiled a business plan and completed economic and financial modelling to ensure that the community partnership venture is sustainable. As part of the agreement to extend the size of the reserve, Thanda leases the land back from the community. This provides the community with an income stream of the order of US$234,000 each year. Thanda also highlights its efforts to provide bridging finance to enable additional wildlife to be reintroduced into the community area. In return, Thanda receives exclusive traversing rights over the community lands to extend its own ecotourism activities.

In addition to these empowerment benefits Thanda has also improved the livelihoods of 143 staff employed directly on the reserve or at the lodge, as well as contracting the services of local dance troupes for tourist entertainment. Additional contract staff are employed via subcontractors to work on alien vegetation removal and other labour-intensive projects. The Mdletshe Mandlakhazi Community Trust has also identified and implemented important social development programmes with the assistance of the Thanda Foundation, Thanda PGR's corporate and social responsibility arm. These programmes include those that provide education, equitable employment opportunities, skills development, AIDS education and medical treatment as well as black economic empowerment opportunities to enable communities to enter the conservation and ecotourism marketplace. As a measure of the success of these programmes, the AIDS awareness campaign with the slogan 'AIDS-Free, That's Me' has been rolled out to 40 schools in the region, reaching over 40,000 children, with its message of AIDS awareness and prevention to enable children to make informed sexual choices.

Thanda provides an example of how it is possible to achieve both conservation, ecotourism and social development objectives through the promotion of conservation land use and luxury ecotourism. It appears that the management of Thanda have embraced the need to narrow the gap between the opulence of an exclusive wildlife reserve and the needs of local communities and this is demonstrated by their many partnerships and efforts to achieve benefits beyond their boundaries. While Thanda may be considerably smaller than Tswalu, the key criteria for success of these stand-alone initiatives are largely similar.

Kuzuko Game Reserve

The Addo Elephant National Park (AENP) in the Eastern Cape, South Africa, is an example of a public protected area that is undergoing significant expansion, using a number of strategies and models to incorporate land for conservation (Castley et al., 2009b). To this end, South African National Parks (SANParks) have entered into a number of contractual agreements with private landowners neighbouring the park, and the largest is the Kuzuko Private Game Reserve. The Kuzuko contractual area has seen the inclusion of an additional 160 km² (±10% of the total national park area) into the AENP. As part of the agreement, SANParks have reintroduced key wildlife species such as African elephant, the desert ecotype of the black rhino, Cape mountain zebra and large predators such as lion and cheetah. In preparing the property for ecotourism, Kuzuko management also cleared more than 230 km of internal livestock fencing, removed derelict and redundant structures (e.g. farm buildings, dams, reservoirs, windmills), in the process removing 20 tons of metal from the property. They also actively removed alien vegetation from over 2.5 km² of habitat, improving the quality of these areas. Ongoing revegetation projects using native species such as spekboom, *Portulacaria afra*, reduce the effects of decades of overgrazing by livestock. These rehabilitation works contribute to conservation by restoring natural habitats, but also through the provision of ecosystem services, particularly carbon sequestration (Mills and Cowling, 2006, 2010).

Kuzuko have constructed a luxury ecotourism lodge atop a hill within the contractual area overlooking the rugged semi-arid landscape and the dense thicket vegetation in the valleys below. The lodge has 24 individual units which can accommodate 48 guests (excluding accompanying children). Guests are able to take part in a number of activities including standard game drives but also walking safaris which allow guests accompanied by suitably qualified rangers to encounter the wildlife of the area at close range. Many of these walking safaris utilize the tracking collars deployed on wildlife species to enable rangers to locate and direct guests to find these individuals from the ground. This serves a dual purpose in that it provides the guests an opportunity to see the wildlife at close hand but also enables the rangers to record movement patterns and behavioural observations that can be used for assisting in the management of the species.

Makuleke/‡Khomani San and Mier communities

While a number of contractual arrangements have been made with private ecotourism reserves such as Kuzuko, SANParks have also entered into negotiations with local communities. In some cases these agreements are long-standing, such as with the joint management of the Richtersveld National Park in the far north-west of South Africa on the border with Namibia. In others the contracts are more recent and have come about as a result of successful land claims by a number of communities neighbouring public protected areas. The land restitution process in post-apartheid South Africa has seen the transfer of historical land title back to local communities within the last 10 years. Some of these successful community land claims have been within public protected areas, notably the Kruger National Park and Kgalagadi Transfrontier Park, which has seen some 250 km² of land reverting back to each of the Makuleke, ‡Khomani San and Mier communities respectively.

While these landholdings were deproclaimed as part of the national park estate, the communities agreed to continue with the existing conservation land-use practices and entered into contractual park arrangements with SANParks (Grossman and Holden, 2009). These contractual agreements were intended to result in co-management partnership

arrangements where these areas would be managed through the establishment of joint management boards where communities and park officials would agree on management strategies. While the framework for collaboration may be present, actual constructive collaboration may not yet have been achieved in reality (Grossman and Holden, 2009). Nonetheless, the foundations for future collaborations that are able to deliver on both conservation and social development objectives are present.

An example of how it is possible to merge conservation and community development is demonstrated by the development of the luxury !Xaus (meaning 'heart') lodge facility in the ‡Khomani San/Mier !Ae!Hai Kalahari Heritage Park within the south-western boundary of the Kgalagadi Transfrontier Park. The communities, SANParks and the South African government reached an agreement in May 2002 related to land restitution and future land use. This resulted in the ownership of the land being handed back to the communities, who then leased the land back to SANParks to continue with the conservation efforts in this area. This 500 km² area of communal land lies to the south-west of the ephemeral Auob River and allows visitors to experience the wildlife as well as historical cultures of the region. The Bushmen were nomadic hunter-gatherers that roamed much of the arid regions of the central Kalahari but today few of the elders are alive to share their experience with the younger generations and park visitors.

The !Xaus Lodge is owned entirely by the community but has benefited through the assistance of management partners who provide hospitality services and marketing support. Visitors to the lodge enter the park through the SANParks main entrance at Twee Rivieren in the south and then follow the characteristically dry Auob riverbed before crossing the many red sand dunes to reach the lodge. The development itself has a central lodge and 12 individual chalets, each situated on top of a dune ridge with a veranda overlooking a large salt pan that serves to attract wildlife to the area. The communities received a tourism development grant to assist in the construction of the lodge, which is managed by a black empowerment company, Transfrontier Park Destinations. The local communities have benefited in a number of ways from this land restitution process, which has simultaneously maintained the historical conservation values of the area: first, the communities have rightfully received title to the land; second, they receive ongoing revenue by leasing the land back to SANParks to manage this area as part of the larger transfrontier national park; third, they receive tourism revenue generated through the development of a luxury ecotourism lodge facility; fourth, members from the local communities have gained employment at the lodge; and, lastly, there is the potential for further social development and upliftment as the communities are given a 10% equity share of the lodge management company.

Unlike the predominantly self-drive wildlife viewing undertaken in the larger part of the transfrontier park, visitors to this area are able to experience the hidden signs of the animals. Bushmen trackers, whose skills are passed down from generation to generation, have learned to read the tracks (spoor) in the sand dunes and routinely escort visitors out into the dunes to share their local knowledge of the area, the animals and their behaviour. Visitors are also able to visit local cultural villages where various locally crafted souvenirs are for sale.

SANParks staff work closely with the communities to ensure that conservation and social objectives can be achieved. These efforts are largely driven by the 'People and Conservation' arm of SANParks and include initiatives such as environmental education workshops, field-guide and biodiversity training. The contrasts between these two contractual model scenarios (e.g. Kuzuko vs. !Xaus) as described above highlight the fact that the model is not a 'one size fits all' approach. Each contract should be seen as a dynamic co-management framework that is intended to bring about sustained conservation, ecotourism and socio-economic benefits to all stakeholders through continuous and constructive dialogue (Castley et al., 2009b).

Gorah Elephant Camp

The Gorah Elephant Camp within the Addo Elephant National Park is an example of where a private concession within a public protected area has been successful. Here a private tourism and hospitality provider (Hunter Hotels Group, a member of Relais & Châteaux) was granted a concession lease over 50 km² within the main elephant camp (135 km²) of the AENP. The Gorah Elephant Camp, operating under the larger corporate Hunter Hotels banner, restored a historical farmhouse, protected by the National Heritage Resources Act (Republic of South Africa, 1999) in South Africa, and converted this into a luxury lodge and built an additional 11 tented units. The chosen style of this accommodation was designed such that it is of a relatively lower environmental impact and can be removed (if necessary) with little additional impact. Gorah Elephant Camp offers visitors a combination of ecotourism activities, including game drives and guided bush walks in Big Five territory, while providing five-star hospitality service.

Gorah Elephant Camp, and other concessions like it, may not contribute directly to conservation activities, e.g. setting aside conservation land and protecting species, as these ecological services are provided by the park the concession is established in. However, they certainly contribute to raising the awareness of guests to the needs for conservation and that such practices are conducted in a responsible and sustainable manner. As a result, many concession partners are engaged with corporate and social responsibility initiatives in addition to providing guests with a rewarding wildlife viewing experience. Of course, not all concessions may be as successful as the example used here from the AENP. For example, many of the concession contracts granted in the Kruger National Parks have had to be renegotiated following a joint submission by the individual concessionaires, who approached SANParks after it became clear that these lodges were unable to meet their financial contractual obligations (Varghese, 2008).

Madikwe Game Reserve

Examples of regional partnerships that have been effective at achieving conservation, ecotourism and community development outcomes include the Madikwe Game Reserve in South

Africa, and the Ol Pejeta Conservancy in Kenya. The 750 km² Madikwe Game Reserve, established in 1991, lies on the border with Botswana, in the North West Province, South Africa. The reserve was established under a tripartite 'partnership for conservation' agreement between government (then Bophutha-tswana Parks Board, now the North West Parks and Tourism Board), private sector and local communities. While identified as a partnership for conservation, the intent was driven by the identified economic potential of wildlife conservation and ecotourism that could be used to stimulate ecologically sustainable development within the region where the needs of the people are placed before that of conservation (Davies *et al.*, 1997). At the time this was a significant departure from the standard ecotourism models, which were built squarely on the foundations of biodiversity preservation (Relly, 2008). None the less, while the socio-economic objectives may be paramount at Madikwe, these cannot be achieved without the conservation of the natural resource base.

The state provided the land through the purchase of degraded cattle farms and reintroduced numerous wildlife species, in one of the largest translocation exercises in the country, to create an ecotourism product. As a result, Madikwe protects populations of the Big Five as well as a number of threatened species, including the black (*Diceros bicornis minor*) and white rhinoceros, African wild dog, roan (*Hippotragus equinus*) and sable antelope (*Hippotragus niger*) and tsessebe (*Damaliscus lunatus*). However, the contributions by the private sector, who invested in the reserve through the construction and management of private wildlife lodges, were pivotal to the success of the joint venture. There are 21 commercially run lodges within Madikwe and it has been these lodges that have generated the revenues to ensure that the Madikwe Game Reserve acts as an economic engine in the region, as portions of the concession fees paid to the state are directed towards the local communities to stimulate and finance community development projects.

Individual lodges provide employment for neighbouring communities and many assist in community development projects. For example, the Tau Game Lodge has established the Tau

Foundation, which contributes to the improvement of infrastructure and education facilities in the nearby town of Supingstad. The lodge has established vegetable gardens and improved rainwater capture facilities at these schools, which aim to improve the education environment for children. In addition, Tau offers guests to the lodge the opportunity to contribute to rehabilitation efforts within Madikwe through the Tau Tree Fund as part of a collaborative effort with the South African Department of Water Affairs and Forestry. Here guests can buy and plant a selection of threatened tree species, such as the marula (*Sclerocarya birrea cafra*), from the region within the Tau Lodge lease area.

Ol Pejeta Conservancy

The Ol Pejeta Conservancy in the Laikipia District in Kenya is a 360 km² conservation area co-owned by Fauna and Flora International (FFI), the Arcus Foundation and Lewa Conservancy and is jointly managed by FFI and a number of other development partners in the various specialized areas (e.g. ecological monitoring, conservation management, community development, livestock management, ecotourism development). The conservancy acts as a model for conservation efforts in East Africa as it combines wildlife conservation philosophies with traditional pastoral lifestyles, where wildlife and livestock are supported on Ol Pejeta in a mixed system. As part of its mission statement, Ol Pejeta aims to use wildlife tourism and complementary enterprises to provide returns for conservation and community development. Although management and development of the conservancy were only recently taken over by FFI, already they have been in the spotlight for their conservation efforts. The most recent of these initiatives has seen the reintroduction of four of the last known northern white rhinoceros (*Ceratotherium simum cottoni*) from a Prague zoo as part of a breeding programme. In addition to these species rescue programmes, the conservancy also protects populations of a number of other threatened species, including a significant population of eastern black rhino (*Diceros bicornis michaeli*), Grevy's zebra

(*Equus grevyi*) and Jackson's hartebeest (*Alcelaphus buselaphus lelwel*).

The conservancy has established multiple partnerships in various operational units, with agreements with six different operators to run and manage ecotourism within the conservancy. Ecotourism partners providing accommodation within the conservancy include Serena Hotels, Gamewatchers Safaris (Porini Camps), Kicheche Camps and Insiders Africa. Ecotourism revenue is generated by visitors paying a daily conservation fee that is channelled back into research and monitoring efforts as well as security management (i.e. anti-poaching units, fence patrols and maintenance, etc.). Ecotourism is also used as a conduit to channel valuable resources into the local communities, and Ol Pejeta supports a number of community outreach and development projects. These include initiatives that address education, health, agricultural extension and community ecotourism ventures. The commitment to conservation and community development is demonstrated through the constitution of the conservancy, which requires all profits to be reinvested to further wildlife conservation and community outreach. While Ol Pejeta is a not-for-profit agency, it does not preclude the ongoing contributions through donor agencies, and these avenues are actively pursued to provide additional financial support to supplement income through ecotourism. As a result Ol Pejeta has raised and disbursed more than US$1 million within the local communities over the past 3 years. Donor support is also likely to be critical to the success of the conservancy, as visitor numbers can fluctuate considerably as a result of political instability affecting the reserve's ability to be completely self-sufficient.

African Parks Foundation

While Ol Pejeta and Madikwe provide examples of where partnerships can achieve conservation benefits at a local level, there are those that have successfully tackled conservation, tourism and sustainable development issues at an international level. These include the projects currently being implemented by the African Parks and Peace Parks Foundations. This discussion considers only the former. The African Parks Foundation was established in 2000 by a group of conservationists and businessmen whose vision it was to address the immediate conservation challenges across the African continent. The African Parks Foundation, as a private park management agency, has pioneered the effective long-term management of protected areas in Africa in partnership with relevant governments by combining conservation best practice with business expertise. African Parks Foundation emphasizes the financial sustainability of its projects and parks through stimulating tourism, private investment and payments for ecosystem services. It is through these mechanisms that they aim to address the African priorities of poverty alleviation and economic development (Fearnhead, 2009). African Parks have identified four critical partnerships necessary to establish park management projects. These include agreements with: (i) government; (ii) communities, (iii) financial partners; and (iv) commercial investors (Fig. 12.1).

While governments retain the ownership of the parks and wildlife, they must share the same philosophical approach to park management and be prepared to delegate responsibilities to African Parks to implement the project itself. Agreements with governments create a legal mechanism for African Parks to operate within an individual country but there is still a need to involve local communities, particularly those adjacent to these parks. The voice of the community needs to be considered at the outset to ensure that these considerations are incorporated into project objectives. The avenues for community involvement range from formal to informal mechanisms. Park management is costly and African Parks negotiates with financial partners to cover portions of both capital and operational costs prior to committing to conservation projects. Commercial investors are brought into the park management framework once the initial establishment and development phase is completed. These investors contribute to the park through the development of ecotourism lodges and other enterprises, which then form the pathway for income streams arising from entrance fees, concession fees, etc. Ultimately, once fully established, African Parks projects can then look towards becoming

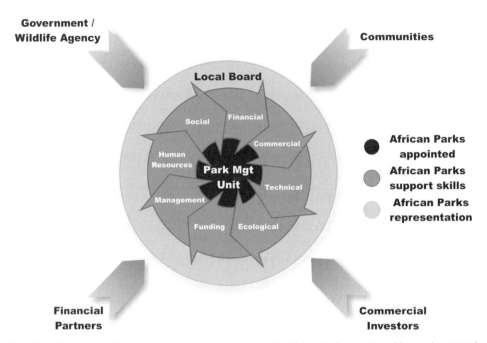

Fig. 12.1. The African Parks Foundation business model, identifying the key partnership requirements for effective park management (Mgt), conservation and social development (reproduced with permission: African Parks Foundation – www.african-parks.org).

self-sustaining to reduce their dependence on donor funding.

Since the establishment of African Parks, there have been a number of park management contracts negotiated, and African Parks currently manages five national parks in four African states (Zambia, Malawi, Rwanda, Democratic Republic of Congo). The transfer of management to African Parks has resulted in the reintroduction of wildlife in many cases, as well as the improvement of infrastructure and facilities. This includes provision of resources and staffing to facilitate wildlife monitoring and increased anti-poaching patrols but also to develop ecotourism facilities to encourage visitation to these parks.

While African Parks has been successful in many circumstances and has brought about positive changes for conservation there are cases where negotiations and agreements have not had positive outcomes. For example, African Parks has previously entered into management agreements with the Ethiopian government to manage the Nech Sar and Omo

National Parks in southern Ethiopia. However, African Parks withdrew from these agreements as a result of international pressure from human rights groups concerned about the rights and welfare of communities that had historical access to land within and adjacent to these national parks. It is therefore clear that, while this business approach works well under certain situations, it is not amenable to every situation and requires a concerted effort to ensure that local communities are fully engaged in these processes. This suggests that formal mechanisms for including communities in park management negotiations are preferred over informal strategies.

The Mantis Group

The growth in the wildlife ecotourism sector within southern Africa has seen a number of private operators enter the market. While many of these operate as stand-alone ventures, as described earlier, there are those that have consolidated their business activities into formal corporate structures with global reputations. Shamwari Game Reserve in the Eastern Cape, South Africa, is the flagship of the Mantis Group, and forms the basis for this case study review. At 250 km² the reserve makes a significant contribution to the protection of the region's biodiversity assets. The reserve is situated in the Maputaland–Pondoland–Albany hotspot (Steenkamp et al., 2004), an area recognized for its diversity and endemic floral communities as a result of the transitional boundaries between five of South Africa's seven terrestrial biomes (Lubke et al., 1986; Victor and Dold, 2003). Established and developed as a premier wildlife destination over the past 18 years, Shamwari acts as an example of boutique-style ecotourism. The approach adopted in the development and marketing of Shamwari has been the brainchild of local entrepreneur Adrian Gardiner, and the success achieved at Shamwari has seen the expansion of additional reserves and lodges owned and managed by the Mantis Group throughout South Africa (e.g. Sanbona Wildlife Reserve in the Western Cape, Nkomazi Game Reserve in Mpumalanga, Jock Safari Lodge, a Kruger National Park concession) and more recently continental Africa (e.g. Nyungwe Forest Lodge, Gorilla Nest Lodge in Rwanda). The Mantis Group have also partnered with international ecotourism operators to offer luxury ecotourism packages abroad (e.g. partnering with 'explora' packages to the Atacama, Patagonia in Chile and Rapa Nui on Easter Island as well as the White Desert expeditions to the Antarctic).

The Mantis Group has a stated philosophy of responsible and ecologically sensitive development which supports environmental conservation through community development projects and conservation of resources. It is therefore necessary to review these principles against tangible outcomes, and we present a review of some key areas here, again using Shamwari as an example. One of the first conservation benefits to be considered is that of the conversion of land from an agricultural or pastoral land use to one supporting wildlife and biodiversity conservation. This has previously been identified as one of the most efficient forms of land use, particularly in the

Eastern Cape region of South Africa (Kerley et al., 1995, 1999). The removal of livestock from private land and further consolidation to expand these units into viable reserves has allowed the recovery of natural vegetation communities. The second land-use improvement with a conservation benefit relies on the creation of an ecotourism product which requires the reintroduction of wildlife to increase the wildlife viewing potential for tourism. While this practice is commonplace in South Africa and Namibia, there are risks associated with such reintroduction strategies, as a number of authors have highlighted (Castley et al., 2001; Spear and Chown, 2009).

Undoubtedly, the reintroduction of extralimital species provides an opportunity to create a more diverse wildlife experience, but the potential costs to biodiversity conservation may be more subtle. Many of the private landowners in South Africa, including the icons such as Shamwari, have reintroduced such extralimital species into their reserves. Species that are commonly reintroduced beyond their natural range include the southern white rhinoceros (Ceratotherium simum simum), giraffe (Giraffa camelopardalis), black (Connochaetes gnou) and blue wildebeest (Connochaetes taurinus), red lechwe (Kobus leche), nyala (Tragelaphus angasii), impala (Aepyceros melamphus) and waterbuck (Kobus ellipsyprymnus). Apart from the South African endemic black wildebeest, which is a highveld grassland species, the remaining species are associated with African savannah ecosystems, which did not occur naturally in the subtropical thicket ecosystems of the Eastern Cape. Notwithstanding these potential conservation challenges, Shamwari and many other private reserves throughout southern African have facilitated the recovery of wildlife species that were previously hunted almost to extinction (Bothma et al., 2009). However, it is necessary to be mindful of the lure to continue conservation efforts centred on the few charismatic species, such as elephant, at the expense of the broader biodiversity requirements. Elephants, for example, can have significant impacts on the environment (Lombard et al., 2001; Kerley and Landman, 2006), although the mechanisms driving these impacts remain poorly understood (Landman et al., 2008).

Khama Rhino Sanctuary/Mokolodi Nature Reserve

A model that is frequently advocated to achieve conservation and social objectives is community-based natural resource management (CBNRM). The principal model for tourism and conservation in CBNRM areas in northern Botswana involves private tourism corporations rather than community-run tourism enterprises. Different views have been expressed by different authors as to the implications of this model for the community landholders. Mbaiwa (2008) argues that the tourism operations are enclave developments which exploit local communities, with the result that tourism has not fundamentally addressed sustainable development needs (Mbaiwa and Darkoh, 2009). Massyn (2008), however, argues that local communities have in fact driven hard and astute business bargains with the commercial tour operators, under which they gain substantial net benefits for the use of their resources; and that if anyone is being exploited, it is the goodwill of the tour operators towards the local communities. While the disparity of views related to community participation and benefit cannot be resolved here, it is worth mentioning that there are also conservation tourism areas in south-eastern Botswana that are run entirely by local communities. This review considers two examples of such community-run operations in Botswana, the Khama Rhino Sanctuary near Serowe and the Mokolodi Nature Reserve on the outskirts of Gaborone. These areas may not be large, or able to provide luxury-style tourism accommodation, but they do demonstrate that local communities are able to achieve social development objectives by offering a range of ecotourism products supported by conservation efforts.

The Khama Rhino Sanctuary is a 93 km² area managed through a community trust established in 1993. The initiative arose from community interest in 1983 to restore the land to a previous state, effectively changing the land use from livestock farming to conservation. In developing the sanctuary, the community has been supported both by corporations such as De Beers and Debswana, which sponsored boundary fencing, and by the Botswanan government, especially the defence force,

which provides 24-hour protection, and various wildlife management agencies, which provided either donated or exchanged rhino for the sanctuary. The ongoing operation of the sanctuary is also made possible through the partnerships and agreements with a multitude of other external donor agencies. Khama Rhino Sanctuary currently supports a small but significant population of white rhinoceros as well as two black rhino. While the rhino populations are the focus of the community reserve, the broader objectives are to promote the conservation of the area's biodiversity to provide a means to generate income through ecotourism for the neighbouring communities. Ecotourism facilities are available at a rate that is considerably more affordable than many of the luxury lodges reviewed here. In addition to an environmental education centre that caters specifically for school groups brought to the reserve, there are eight chalets and 13 campsites accommodating visitors to the area.

The 30 km² Mokolodi Nature Reserve acts as one of Botswana's community-run reserves that contributes to conservation initiatives. Established in 1994, the reserve's objectives are to promote wildlife conservation and environmental education for the children of Botswana. This aim is achieved by adopting a sustainable use philosophy centred on ecotourism. While the reserve was initially supported through donor funding and support, it is now able to sustain its operations independently while providing an avenue for social development. Before the reserve was established the cattle ranching land use employed nine people, while the reserve now employs 70 staff from the local communities. The reserve works closely with the neighbouring village community to maintain strong linkages that contribute to both conservation and social upliftment. Aside from protecting a variety of wildlife species on the reserve, Mokolodi has also made an important conservation contribution in national relocation exercises to reintroduce populations of white rhinoceros to other parts of Botswana. Animals from Mokolodi have been reintroduced to Mombo Camp in the Moremi Game Reserve in the Okavango region, as well as the Tuli Block in the south-east. The reserve also houses one of two wildlife rehabilitation centres within Botswana.

Even within these community-managed areas there is inequitable distribution of benefits, which negatively impacts on the livelihoods and conservation attitudes of local communities (Sebele, 2010). Therefore, as Mbaiwa (2008) has argued, there is room for improvement to extend the reach of CBNRM activities to further reduce conflicts between conservation and communities.

Manda Wilderness Trust

Another avenue through which communities can access the benefits of conservation is through agreements with private-sector partners. Partnering with private tourism operators enables communities to capitalize on a wide range of added benefits, such as marketing, product development, business planning and hospitality services. This is likely to reduce the existing gap between private luxury lodges and community lodges (Dixey, 2008). An example demonstrating the achievement of dual conservation and community objectives is the Manda Wilderness Project in Mozambique. This project is a partnership between the Manda Wilderness Community Trust (representing 15 local communities), the Manda Agricultural Project and Nkwichi Lodge. The project has seen the community assign more than 1000 km² of communal lands to a conservation land use, where the cessation of hunting (dogs and snares) and slash-and-burn agriculture has already seen the environment responding positively, with increases in bird and small mammal communities. Furthermore, and in conjunction with the luxury Nkwichi lodge, the Trust has delivered on a number of community development programmes. These include the construction of six schools, provision of health care, training in sustainable agricultural practices, employment and downstream economic flows to each community, equity in community representation and the empowerment and assignment of management rights to the natural resources on communal lands and lake areas. This case study demonstrates the positive outcomes that well-planned synergies between communities and private partners can bring.

Mountain Gorilla Tourism

The conservation of the endangered mountain gorilla (*Gorilla beringei beringei*) in the Virunga Mountains is an example of how ecotourism can benefit the conservation of iconic species. The conservation of such iconic species can result in increased tourism and visitation, with resultant economic benefits for local communities, but also international recognition for government conservation actions. The Virunga Mountains span the border between Uganda, Rwanda and the Democratic Republic of the Congo, and provide the only remaining habitat for this species. It is confined to Afro-montane areas above 1500 m, persisting in two small isolated subpopulations in relatively small national parks such as Bwindi and Mgahinga. If gorillas leave the forest in order to raid crops grown nearby, they are likely to be killed by the villagers who depend on those crops. During times of political instability in particular, they are subject to significant poaching. Adults are killed in order to sell body parts, and juveniles are captured for the illegal international wildlife trade. Finally, the mountain gorillas are at risk from disease potentially transmitted by humans, as occurred on at least one occasion for the lowland gorillas (Butynski and Kalina, 1998).

Given that tourism has been identified as a key conservation strategy for the gorilla, the links between gorilla tourism and gorilla conservation, including the role of local communities and of international donors and conservation agencies, have been examined and reviewed on a number of occasions (McNeilage, 1996; Archabald and Naughton-Treves, 2001; Adams and Infield, 2003; Buckley 2003a, 2006). Very broadly, the gorillas live in extended family groups known as troops, which occupy broad territorial areas and can travel significant distances from day to day. Some of these groups have been habituated to human visitors. At Mgahinga National Park, for example, trackers lead small groups of tourists to the point where the gorillas were last seen, and follow their trail through the forest. Once the gorillas are encountered, the tourists are allowed to watch them for a maximum of 1 hour, and then return to the park's headquarters. Only adult tourists in good health are allowed to take part; the maximum number of tourists each day is strictly enforced through a quota system; and tourist behaviour once gorillas are encountered is subject to a well-defined code of behaviour to avoid disturbance to the gorillas. Gorilla-watching permits are sold via a system which is intended to prevent profiteering and to provide equity between commercial tour clients and independent travellers. However, gorilla sightings are not guaranteed since the habituated troops may cross international borders into neighbouring countries, where guides and clients are not allowed to follow.

The distribution of funds received from the gorilla-watching permits has also been examined on several occasions (Archabald and Naughton-Treves, 2001; Adams and Infield, 2003). As in many such instances, there is uncertainty and dispute over the allocation of permit fees both within the park services and also to local communities and individuals. Within the park services, the key issue is whether these fees, which are paid in US dollars, should be retained locally for gorilla conservation efforts in the parks concerned or made available to the park services or indeed the country's national treasury as a whole. Similar issues apply for park visitor fees worldwide.

Local residents may receive part of the funds associated with gorilla tourism through three principal mechanisms. Individual villagers living near the forest parks may receive compensation if their crops are damaged by gorillas. Locals may be employed as part of the gorilla tourism operations, or they may be able to sell produce or other goods to those operations. And third, a proportion of the revenue generated by gorilla tourism is allocated, in theory at least, to the provision of benefits for local communities. It is by no means clear, however, that these various benefits actually materialize fully in practice. According to Archabald and Naughton-Treves (2001), 22 parishes (approximately ten villages in each parish) around Bwindi and Mgahinga National Parks received a total of $80,000 in benefits between 1995 and 1997, but the allocation of these funds at an appropriate scale was contested by community respondents. While all respondents felt that communities neighbour-

ing these parks should benefit from revenue-sharing schemes, 35% felt that this should be at the parish level, 15% felt that funds should be allocated to villages, 24% felt that those directly affected by the park should be compensated and the remaining 26% were ambivalent. While gorilla ecotourism can indeed generate valuable external sources of income for local communities and promote conservation efforts, Archabald and Naughton-Treves (2001) identified four key areas critical to successful revenue-sharing schemes. They highlighted: the importance of long-term institutional support (emphasized by the changes in policy within Uganda relating to revenue sharing); the appropriate identification of target communities and project types; transparency and accountability; and lastly adequate funding.

While it seems likely that tourism does indeed contribute to gorilla conservation in the Virunga Mountains, it seems to do so by multiple indirect social and political mechanisms. Financial contributions, from both the park fees and the commercial tourism industry, form only a rather small and indirect part of the overall picture. The majority of funds available for conservation management of the parks and gorilla populations, including monitoring and anti-poaching patrols, are provided by international conservation donors. The gorilla-watching fees collected by the parks agencies themselves are not earmarked for local use.

Published information on the economics of the commercial gorilla-watching tourism industry is sparse. The sector contains two distinct tiers, which interact only during the actual gorilla-tracking activity. There is an upmarket component, where relatively wealthy international clients book gorilla-watching tours through international agents and operators, who then use domestic tour operators in the capital cities or gateway airports of the countries concerned in order to arrange in-country transport, accommodation and gorilla-tracking permits. These clients do not interact at all with local residents unless the latter are employed at lodges or guest houses. The establishment of the Gorilla Nest Lodge in Rwanda by the Mantis Group serves as an indication of the potential success of merging upmarket eco-tourism and conservation. The second component is essentially part of the global backpacker market, travelling either independently on local transport, or more commonly in groups in so-called overlander bus tours. These visitors generally stay and eat in local facilities operated by the park services itself. These park facilities and private tourist accommodation nearby provide similar employment and entrepreneurial opportunities for local residents.

Money from park fees and tourism enterprises may not go directly to gorilla conservation or local community benefits. However, the gorilla-watching tourism industry is a flagship component of national tourism strategies for the countries concerned, and brings in significant revenues to the larger domestically based tour operators, who may have some political influence. In addition, the existence of the gorilla-watching tourism industry may possibly help to promote international public concern and hence financial support for gorilla conservation. This mechanism, however, remains speculative: it is at least equally possible that such concern is generated principally by wildlife documentaries, and that commercial tourism plays no significant role.

Achieving Conservation Benefits

Overview

The preceding sections of this chapter have alluded to the positive contributions various conservation and ecotourism models make to achieving biodiversity conservation objectives. This section expands on three key conservation targets identified through this process, namely: (i) increasing the conservation estate; (ii) protecting populations of species; and (iii) conserving functional landscapes and ecosystems. Following this review, this section highlights some possible limitations to achieving conservation goals.

Expanding the conservation estate

In terms of the contribution by private and community landowners (hereafter landowners)

to the expansion of conservation lands in Africa, there has been phenomenal growth, with ongoing interest in the industry. In southern Africa in particular, the contributions that landowners have made to setting aside land far exceed that formally conserved within the public protected area networks. In South Africa the figure is approximately three times as much as the public estate of just over 6% (Cousins et al., 2008; Bothma et al., 2009), while in Namibia, where 43% of the land is under private ownership, wildlife conservancies encompass more than 40,000 km² (approximately 5% of the total land surface area) (Barnes and Jones, 2009). While these trends are encouraging and likely to continue, given the higher economic returns from tourism (Barnes and Jones, 2009), it is necessary to recognize the potential impacts associated with such private initiatives. Many of these decisions are taken by the individual owners and as such may not address conservation priorities as identified in national planning initiatives (e.g. the National Biodiversity Strategy and Action Plan – NBSAP, in South Africa). Consequently the potential exists for many biomes and ecosystems to be over-represented while others remain neglected. However, a recent study by Gallo et al. (2009) has demonstrated that private reserves can make significant contributions to achieving biodiversity conservation targets at regional scales. This highlights the need to include private conservation areas into future conservation planning initiatives in order to ensure that the best targets can be achieved.

Protecting populations

Conservation efforts on private reserves have seen a significant increase in the populations of many species, including those on the IUCN Red Lists (Barnes and Jones, 2009; Bothma et al., 2009). However, the translocation and movement of wildlife are poorly regulated within South Africa, despite efforts to establish a national wildlife translocation policy. Consequently there are few restrictions other than the requirement to ensure adequate enclosure (a measure of wildlife ownership), which limits the movement of species among private reserves. Despite these concerns, there has undoubtedly been a general recovery of wildlife species populations, including many charismatic and threatened species. These include the conservation of black (*Diceros bicornis bicornis* and *D. b. minor*) and white rhinoceros (*Certotherium simum simum*) and African wild dog in southern Africa and mountain gorilla in central Africa.

In the past decade, the number of rhino protected within South Africa has increased, bolstered by the legal trade in the species, which has enabled both species to be held by landowners (Castley and Hall-Martin, 2003; Hall-Martin and Castley, 2003). For many landowners, the motivation for reintroducing white rhinoceros stems from the desire to establish a Big Five reserve that caters for the tourist perception of the quintessential African safari focused on charismatic megafauna (Kerley *et al.*, 2003; Boshoff *et al.*, 2007). White rhino are more readily available on the open market in South Africa (Castley and Hall-Martin, 2003) and are consequently easier to introduce to areas than the black rhino, which would have been the historically appropriate species within certain areas. While some reserves support populations of both black and white rhino it is invariably the white rhino that is reintroduced first. There are also fewer black rhino available on the free market, as a result of their critically endangered status, but recent initiatives have seen the private sector making significant contributions to the conservation of this species, particularly the *D. b. minor* ecotype.

The WWF/Ezemvelo Kwazulu-Natal Wildlife Black Rhino Range Expansion Project has seen founder populations of black rhino being reintroduced into private game reserves as part of a programme to re-establish the species in the wild throughout its historical range and increase the performance of the species as a whole. The first founder population of 15 animals was reintroduced into the 200 km² Mun-ya-Wana Private Game Reserve in 2004 and there have been more recent introductions on to community-run private reserves. The partnerships forged between the conservation NGO (WWF), a public conservation agency (Ezemvelo KZN Wildlife) and private landowners (Mun-ya-Wana,

Zululand Rhino Reserve, Pongola Game Reserve, Somkhanda Game Reserve, Thanda Private Game Reserve, Mduna Royal Reserve) have been instrumental in achieving better conservation outcomes for the species (Sherriffs, 2007). The access to suitable habitat has increased by 25% (in Kwazulu-Natal, South Africa) and the population size has increased, precluding the need to offer surplus black rhino as hunting trophies once public reserves could no longer support growing populations. Similar conservation programmes are in place for the arid-adapted black rhino ecotype (*D. b. bicornis*). The numbers of this subspecies are significantly lower than those of the south-central ecotype and the bulk of the subspecies is conserved on public protected areas in Namibia and South Africa (Emslie, 2008). However, recent multilateral partnership agreements between the Ministry of Environment and Tourism, SANParks and private landowners have seen individuals of this subspecies introduced to private reserves (e.g. Tswalu Desert Reserve, Kuzuko Reserve, Ongava Reserve in Namibia) to secure the long-term viability and genetic diversity of the larger metapopulation.

The continued growth in southern white rhino populations is a further conservation success story supported by the growth within the private sector. The numbers of this species have increased substantially on private reserves, and there is an active wildlife market for the translocation of this species among private game reserves in southern Africa (Castley and Hall-Martin, 2003). The prices paid for white rhino continue to increase, and public conservation agencies make use of rhino sales as a means of revenue generation to increase conservation funds. For example, SANParks routinely offers white rhino on game auctions to private buyers, and then commits these funds to other conservation programmes such as park expansion and development initiatives. The one significant disadvantage of this system is that since white rhino may still be hunted legally, and black rhino under certain conditions, in South Africa, this provides an avenue for unscrupulous individuals to further the illegal trade in rhino horn. None the less, despite the actions of this minority, the conservation benefits have been significant.

Conserving functional landscapes

The conservation of functional ecosystems has previously been identified as an important strategy to ensure the conservation of all levels of biodiversity. However, these functional units exist at multiple scales, which increases the complexity associated with their management (Poiani et al., 2000). However, Poiani et al. (2000) argue that for future conservation efforts to be successful these need to be implemented at the coarsest level possible to capture the regional- and landscape-level patterns and processes in a dynamic nested framework. We argue therefore that private reserves and conservancies make less significant contributions to conserving ecological processes across landscapes as these areas are commonly small in size and frequently located across the landscape based on opportunity rather than the need to address conservation priorities at a regional scale.

Therefore there is a need to identify how private reserves, communal lands and public–private partnerships are able to achieve regional conservation objectives for conserving functional landscapes. It is possible to consider how this can be achieved under current land-use scenarios. First, many individual property owners are involved in broader regional initiatives that seek to connect landscapes and create biodiversity corridors. This may be through the establishment of private-sector conservancy agreements that effectively increase the overall size of conservation areas but can also be driven by regional planning programmes that seek to use a combination of strategies to establish linkages and biodiversity corridors across landscapes (Rouget et al., 2006, see Chapters 2 and 3). Another example is provided by the Heritage Park, a partnership concept with a combined vision to link the Madikwe Game Reserve with the Pilansberg National Park through the inclusion of a further 1670 km² of land in a phased roll-out. However, despite these plans there seems to have been little progress on this initiative to date. In another initiative, the Landmark Foundation, a South African conservation NGO established in 2004, is championing regional change in land use to conservation as a means to build a conservation economy. One of their projects aims to connect the Addo Elephant National Park with other conservation areas such as the Baviaanskloof Wilderness Area by establishing a network of conservancies within a regional conservation corridor. Through these initiatives the potential exists to achieve ecosystem function objectives. Achieving these regional conservation measures to conserve functional ecosystems not only requires detailed systematic conservation planning assessments to identify priority areas for consolidation, but also inclusive public participation to ensure that the views of all stakeholders are considered. A final requirement is the need for an implementation plan that clearly identifies the roles and responsibilities of those responsible for implementing any regional conservation plans (Knight et al., 2006).

Potential limitations

While the increasing trend in the number of private reserves and wildlife populations is encouraging, it is necessary to acknowledge the potential limitations associated with these private initiatives. These can be categorized into three key areas: (i) landowner motivation; (ii) land-use practices; and (iii) an understanding of conservation principles. We discuss the implications of each of these briefly to emphasize their relevance to ensuring ongoing conservation benefits from tourism.

The sharp increase in private wildlife reserves has been driven by landowners recognizing the potential of alternative sources of income. Within South Africa, many of the reserves are established in the Limpopo and North-West Provinces (van der Waal and Dekker, 2000; Reilly et al., 2003; Bothma et al., 2009) and originated as owners shifted from agricultural and pastoral production systems to wildlife ranching, ecotourism, mixed farming and hunting blocks. The incentive to make this change in land use is driven by a desire either to tap into an alternative income stream, to make a positive contribution to conservation activities at a local, regional and national level, or to engage with local communities in sustainable development opportunities, or a combination of the former. For private landowners in the business of providing a luxury wildlife experience, coupled to programmes that provide an enriching cultural experience that demonstrate corporate and social responsibility, the capital outlay in establishing these reserves and their associated tourism ventures is significant. However, many state that their aim is to improve the conservation of habitats and species while providing a responsible tourism product (Sims-Castley et al., 2005). None the less, Cousins et al. (2008) point out that private land is not protected by legislation as are public parks and reserves, and it is therefore possible that landowners can opt to revert back to some former land use that is no longer compatible with conservation. While this may be less likely where owners have invested considerable capital into the development of luxury lodges and reserves, it still presents a potential risk.

In an effort to make conservation more accessible to local communities, the need to address issues associated with poverty, health and education within local communities is increasing among private operators. However, there are still many reserves that have not embedded the essential elements of corporate social responsibility into their operations, emphasizing a requirement for such practices within private reserves (Langholz and Kerley, 2006). Those properties that contribute to community development programmes through the provision of financial resources, construction programmes, educational facilities and capacity building and empowerment demonstrate that it is possible to address social requirements while ensuring the conservation of biodiversity (Spenceley, 2008c).

While landowner motivation and land-use practices may drive the decision to enter into wildlife or conservation tourism ventures, this says little of the resultant management approach. The manner in which landowners approach the preservation of the constituent biodiversity within a specific reserve, irrespective of size, is determined by their philosophical approach to conservation and their under-standing of conservation principles. While tourism can, under some circumstances, act as a tool to improve conservation outcomes (Buckley, 2008b, 2009b), it is still important to choose the right tool for the job. This point is illustrated by discussing the need of landowners

to create a tourism product that will attract top-end clients and then continue to attract these clients. Within southern Africa, and South Africa in particular, where the buying and selling of wildlife at game auctions is commonplace, many landowners have easy access to a diversity of wildlife. When faced with a reserve where the fauna native to the area are cryptic and solitary, the introduction of gregarious herding species as well as iconic drawcard species is commonplace. Many private reserves in South Africa stock species that are extralimital (native species, but outside their natural range) in order to create a tourism viewing product or to offer these species as part of hunting packages (Castley et al., 2001). While tourists may find these species enticing, the potential impacts on biodiversity and ecosystem functioning are likely to present the greatest threat through performing novel functions, but further quantitative research is required (Spear and Chown, 2009). The intention of some landowners may be to remove these species in the long term, once natural wildlife populations have recovered but this task is not easily done, particularly for those that breed profusely (e.g. impala).

Conservation and Tourism Challenges

While conservation tourism provides valuable benefits for biodiversity and sustainable development, it is important to reflect on these from a long-term perspective. There are a number of areas that are likely to affect both conservation and tourism in Africa over the next 50 years and we outline what we feel to be some of the key issues here. These can be categorized as: (i) external forces that cannot be controlled by conservation agencies or ecotourism operators; and (ii) in situ factors that can be manipulated to achieve either conservation or tourism objectives or both.

Climate change and political instability have been highlighted as key areas of concern (Hall, 2009; Saarinen et al., 2009). Climate change research continues to predict dramatic con-sequences for the earth's natural systems under current warming scenarios (IPCC, 2007). While much research has concentrated efforts on identifying species and ecosystem responses to global warming scenarios, there has been a recent drive to consider how such species and systems, including humans, will adapt to climate change. Climate change adaptation is not merely about the resilience and resistance of natural ecosystems, but about the measures society introduces to minimize the predicted negative consequences. Thuiller *et al.* (2006) predict dramatic shifts in mammal species, where 25–40% of African mammals could be critically endangered by 2080 as a result of climate change. Given that these mammals are central to the establishment of viable wildlife-viewing destinations, the impacts on tourism could be severe. Achieving conservation objectives in the future will therefore be dependent on interventions taken within both the public and the private sector. Climate change may also affect existing public and private ecotourism products, but the ability of the private sector to deal with such change is likely to be determined by the size and location of properties within the landscape. The ability to capture latitudinal as well as aridity gradients within these zones that enable wildlife to migrate between core habitats will be important. However, while the potential exists for climate change to affect tourism dramatically (Turpie *et al.*, 2002), these impacts have been poorly quantified, with few empirical data to support the existing climate modelling scenarios (Boko *et al.*, 2007). It is therefore necessary to determine how ecotourism operators have accounted for potential climate change impacts, as this is likely to influence the long-term sustainability of these operations, affecting both conservation and social development outcomes.

Political instability and civil war in many African countries have led to the reduction in visitor arrivals to many countries in recent years (e.g. Côte d'Ivoire, Zimbabwe). While this directly affects the numbers of tourists visiting areas, it also has the potential to impact directly on conservation efforts as a result of escalation in poaching, subsistence extraction (e.g. bushmeat harvesting) and active targeting of tourism venues and visitors. There are a number of examples where tourists have become victims of such violent conflicts (e.g. tourists killed by DRC rebels while visiting

mountain gorilla sites), but these internal conflicts also affect the management of parks. For example, the headquarters of the African Parks-managed Garamba National Park were targeted early in 2009, resulting in loss of life and damage to infrastructure. Despite these incidents, African Parks, who were already managing the park, have continued with their activities in this park to achieve conservation outcomes. In other areas the cessation of civil conflicts and subsequent development have led to an increase in investment, including within the tourism sector (e.g. Mozambique).

While many of the models outlined previously have demonstrated benefits for conservation, communities and the tourism industry as a whole, it is important to point out that these may not be generally applicable in all situations. Issues that may impede the implementation of some models (e.g. luxury fly-in/fly-out lodges on privately owned land) include the ability of investors to own property in some areas. Land tenure rights vary from one African country to the next, but this will be a key issue in promoting the development of sustainable ecotourism facilities that also deliver conservation benefits. Furthermore, the ownership of wildlife, particularly in ecotourism models, may be a critical factor to ensure the viability of tourism products. This is particularly relevant in many East African countries, where wildlife is still controlled by the state, whereas southern African countries, notably South Africa, Namibia and Zimbabwe, permit private ownership (Muir-Leresche and Nelson, 2000). In other countries, while the state may hold the rights to wildlife, these are nominally for the benefit of the people of these countries, and in some situations may include the rights to resource utilization (Cirelli, 2002). The devolution of authority to local communities in other African states will be critical to promote empowerment, but these communities also need support in the development of ecotourism ventures to ensure that these are viable and self-sustaining while continuing to protect the environment.

As a means to address some of these community aspects, the tourism portfolio of the South African national government deliberately adopted responsible tourism as a strategy within South Africa (Spenceley *et al.*,

2002). One of the key features of the responsible tourism model is the three-way link between tourism, conservation and local communities. Specifically, the responsible tourism model involves the use of wildlife-viewing tourism to provide economic benefits for local communities, and hence an incentive for them to conserve animals and habitat. These incentives can take many forms but must provide communities with benefits that exceed livelihood costs at all levels (Kiss, 2004). This broad model applies across a range of governments, jurisdictions and land tenures in sub-Saharan Africa. This includes countries with unstable as well as stable governments, and areas under private, public or community tenure. Examples are provided in several recent volumes, notably Spenceley (2008a), Saarinen *et al.* (2009a) and Suich *et al.* (2009), where the achievements of this strategy are highlighted (Spenceley, 2008b).

The successful implementation of responsible tourism practices is linked to destinations. Tourists, whether local or international, seek out destinations based on a range of selection criteria. There is therefore a need to ensure that tourism planning takes potential markets into consideration in the promotion and presentation of destination drawcards. As part of this marketing strategy, tourism operators, particularly those entering the market, need to be cognizant of the potential environmental limitations that could impact upon the success of both tourism and conservation objectives. Accessibility and the provision of basic services remain key issues although the appeal and lure of the destination are emerging as important factors in driving demand (Saarinen *et al.*, 2009b). The attractiveness of destinations, particularly in southern Africa, is actively promoted via websites, blogs, visitor comments and visual galleries, such that potential visitors are able to determine well in advance what it is that makes any particular destination appealing. Promotion of the African safari has diverged from the classical wildlife viewing experience to one that offers access to awe-inspiring landscapes, unique species or communities, valued-added services such as spas and wellness centres, as well as the personalized attention given by staff, rangers and field guides. This is exemplified by the growth in the high-end

luxury destination, where visitors expect to receive exemplary service in relation to both the accommodation, food and service but also the wildlife-viewing experience.

One of the factors that can be managed is the need to instil an appreciation for the natural biodiversity value of a region and the development of a better understanding of the ecological structure and function of the representative ecosystems at tourism destinations. The icon wildlife species known as the Big Five (lion, elephant, rhinoceros, buffalo and leopard), and in some cases the Big Seven (the inclusion of African wild dog and cheetah in terrestrial habitats, but whales and great white sharks in marine parks), continue to attract visitors to African destinations (Kerley *et al.*, 2003), performing an important socio-economic role (Walpole and Leader-Williams, 2002). While this bestows a modicum of conservation benefit for individual animals, many of these areas are unable to maintain populations of these species as they are too small or isolated or do not have the appropriate habitats to support viable populations. Nevertheless, many operators with a poor understanding of the ecological ramifications in certain situations continue to introduce these species (Mackey *et al.*, 2006; Hayward *et al.*, 2007; Landman *et al.*, 2008), while the broader consequences of these actions are poorly understood (Castley *et al.*, 2001; Spear and Chown, 2009). Reintroductions of charismatic predators are often based on local objectives and can devalue larger conservation priorities for such species (Slotow and Hunter, 2009).

Intensive and well-directed management efforts to control growing populations in confined areas (e.g. hunting, contraception, translocation) can result in positive local conservation outcomes with little impact on the behavioural and social structure of target species (Gusset *et al.*, 2008; Kettles and Slotow, 2009). Proponents advocating the value of these reintroduction practices argue along the lines of maintaining genetic diversity, by collaboration in captive breeding programmes, or through repatriation programmes aimed at the conservation of the species. However, the real conservation benefits of rehabilitation centres, captive-bred populations and the repatriation of individuals to the wild touted by many private operators as important conservation activities remain to be quantified. There is therefore a need to identify alternative tourism drawcards that will continue to entice visitors to these destinations while minimizing the potential impacts on ecosystem function. Tourists need to be conditioned through appropriate marketing strategies to there being larger conservation issues at play than the perpetuation of a single-species approach to conservation.

Conclusions

Tourism and conservation seem to have had relatively close links throughout the post-colonial history of sub-Saharan Africa. There are four key issues of particular relevance in any intra-continental comparisons. The first is that parks and wildlife, tourism and the links between them only thrive in countries which are safe and stable and have well-maintained infrastructure. War, terrorism, large-scale corruption or other breakdowns of law and order produce an almost immediate collapse in tourism and a longer-term deterioration in protected area systems and wildlife populations.

The second is that the role of parks and tourism in generating foreign exchange depends on the broader economic context at national and local scales, but these links can be complex. Botswana, for example, has a thriving wildlife tourism industry even though its economy relies principally on diamond mining. Angola, in contrast, also relies principally on mining, but has had little or no wildlife tourism. At a more local scale, the degree to which communities may be prepared to conserve wildlife and habitat as a basis for tourism and the degree to which they are prepared to work in the tourism industry may depend strongly on other economic opportunities available. For projects which receive initial funding from international aid agencies, for example, local residents may well be glad to accept such funding as long as it is available, but then abandon the project as soon as external funding ends.

The third key issue is that the links between tourism and conservation in sub-Saharan Africa include public, community and private land. As demonstrated in this chapter, there are somewhat different models for different land tenures, and there are also links across and between these different tenures. In particular, larger public protected areas provide the principal reservoir for native wildlife conservation, but private reserves can extend this area significantly. Leasing private tourism rights inside public protected areas can generate significant returns to support conservation efforts, but this also requires long-term institutional policy to ensure that these funds are not redirected elsewhere. In addition, private tourism enterprises are a key factor in conservation efforts on community lands, since they enable the community landowners to generate more revenue from conservation than they could achieve on their own. However, fully inclusive community engagement is still in its infancy in many countries, and will require concerted efforts across the spectrum of models presented in this chapter to achieve positive change for merging conservation and social objectives.

Finally, it is worth noting that at least a few of the commercial conservation tourism enterprises which commenced operations in sub-Saharan Africa have been particularly successful in expanding their activities into new countries and even continents, in a way which does not seem to have happened in other regions.

Acknowledgements

Some sections of this chapter, notably that on mountain gorillas in Uganda, were first drafted by Ralf Buckley on the basis of relevant field experience.

13 Conclusions

Elephant at close range

As outlined in Chapter 1, there are a number of different mechanisms by which tourism can, potentially at least, make positive net contributions to conservation. Subsequent chapters reconsider these mechanisms from a variety of different perspectives, at scales from individual companies, communities and conservation organizations to entire countries. The aim of this concluding chapter, therefore, is to evaluate the evidence relevant to each of the mechanisms outlined in Chapter 1, using the cases and country studies presented in the later chapters.

In this volume, we have presented a selection of case studies worldwide either where commercial tourism has, in so far as we can judge, made some contribution to conservation by one of a variety of mechanisms; or, in a few cases, where it was designed to do so but apparently did not succeed. Before attempting to draw any general conclusions, we must first note that these case studies were deliberately selected as some of the best-documented examples of conservation tourism worldwide. They are not in any way representative of the global tourism industry as a whole. They show what is possible, not what is routine. In so far as we can judge, most of the case studies presented in this volume are world leaders in conservation tourism. With these caveats in mind, and drawing also on other literature in this field as reviewed in Chapter 1, the following conclusions can be reached:

1. Conservation tourism does exist. There are examples, around the world, where commercial tourism operations are making a net positive contribution to conservation of biological diversity and ecosystem services.

2. Conservation tourism is small. The examples presented in this volume, and others which resemble them but for which no reliable data yet exist, currently constitute only a tiny fraction of the total tourism industry worldwide. In some cases their achievements have been leveraged well beyond their immediate local impacts. The bulk of the mainstream tourism industry, however, remains very different from the small subsector presented here.

3. Conservation tourism is important none the less. While tourism and conservation are largely independent throughout most of the world, in those instances where they overlap, the interaction is important to both (Buckley, 2008b). In many cases that interaction is very one-sided, with the tourism sector gaining at the expense of conservation. The case studies in this volume represent the much smaller proportion where there is indeed a gain for conservation, and generally also for local communities, in addition to the commercial tourism operators.

4. Conservation tourism adds to parks. There are many countries, developed as well as developing, where public-sector protected area agencies face shortfalls in finance and resources, lack of political power relative to other sectors, or lack of access to land of high conservation value. In these circumstances, commercial tourism can, under appropriate conditions, play a significant role in supporting conservation on either private, community or public lands. As efforts to improve landscape-scale conservation connectivity gain momentum as one mechanism to adapt to climate change, conservation tourism will become increasingly significant.

5. Conservation tourism is not accurately accounted for. The net economic, social or environmental contributions of conservation tourism enterprises, either individually or in aggregate, are largely unknown: first, because of incomplete information on the set of enterprises to be included; second, since there is not yet any well-established accounting protocol to measure, compare and aggregate the social and environmental contributions; and, third since the raw data for such accounting exercises are rarely available. There are only a small number of individual private reserves whose achievements have been analysed in detail (Buckley, 2003a; Sims-Castley et al., 2005; Langholz and Kerley, 2006).

6. Conservation tourism mechanisms differ in significance. While there are many different potential mechanisms for commercial tourism to contribute to conservation, in practice some are far more significant ecologically than others. Different mechanisms may be more or less significant at different spatial scales. Broadly, mechanisms which involve minor modifications to commercial tourism operations in order to reduce local environmental impacts, or small cash or in-kind contributions to conservation groups, local communities or parks agencies, are unlikely to make any major contribution to conservation, even though they are promoted heavily by tourism industry organizations. Similarly, despite the industry emphasis on eco-certification and awards, there is little or no evidence that these actually yield any net marginal contribution to conservation, especially since they focus principally on environmental management technologies.

7. Political mechanisms are most far-reaching. The mechanisms which are most significant in a global conservation context are those which involve large-scale political lobbying, land-use or land tenure changes; where commercial tourism forms one of a suite of tools which, taken together, can effectively increase the overall area of the global conservation estate. Positive political effects can occur when tourism provides an incentive for governments to provide protection for ecologically valuable areas which are under threat from other sectors. Negative political effects can also occur, however, notably when property developers use ecotourism as an excuse to build high-impact infrastructure and private resorts inside protected areas. The scale of such effects depends particularly on the longevity and permanence of the structures concerned.

8. Effective conservation tourism tools show regional signatures. The mechanisms which are the most widespread and effective differ between countries and regions, depending on both political and economic factors. That is, there are regional signatures in the conservation tourism sector, as identified for ecotourism (Buckley, 2003a, 2009b) but not adventure tourism (Buckley, 2006, 2010). Experiments by companies such as &Beyond (2010) to transfer African models to other continents are thus of particular interest for future research in this field.

9. Private reserves are key in rich stable countries, where both wealth and stability are relative measures which must be considered in a regional context. In countries with strong economies, stable land tenure systems and a high proportion of land in private ownership, the most effective mechanism is the establishment of private reserves funded by upmarket lodges. This model is used in

countries which fulfil those three conditions, especially in southern Africa and Latin America.

10. Community partnerships are key for communal land tenure. Many countries have large areas of relatively undeveloped land held under various forms of communal tenure. These may represent an unbroken descent of traditional tenure systems, as in several South Pacific nations; or modern government recognition of minority Indigenous rights, as in parts of Australia and the Americas; or modern codification of majority land-use systems, as in parts of sub-Saharan Africa. In each of these cases, conservation tourism can only operate effectively through partnerships with existing community control systems, even if those partnerships also involve private tour operators, NGOs or national and international government agencies.

11. In less wealthy nations, tourism can support public protected areas. Many developing countries have parks which exist on paper but are very poorly resourced for on-ground management, because national governments are indebted, impoverished, ineffective, or have other priorities. Such parks are commonly subject to encroachment and illegal use. Tourism is often the only or least destructive local land use which can provide both local economic incentives and the on-ground human presence to protect parks and endangered species against such impacts.

12. In developed nations, commercial tourism forms a small proportion of recreational visitation to existing public protected areas, and small-scale commercial tour operators are managed largely in line with independent visitors. Parks agencies believe that recreational use provides them with an ongoing political constituency, but there is no actual evidence for this, and in fact it seems more likely that the conservation constituency is far more widespread and diffuse than local recreational users. Pressures for access to public parks by large-scale tourism developers create continuing political difficulties for conservation. Private reserves do contribute to conservation in some developed nations. In many nations, only a small proportion of these are currently funded by tourism, but the role of tourism may well become more widespread in future.

13. Conservation tourism will be affected by climate change. Efforts to mitigate climate change will increase the costs of international travel, and may also change its social perception in northern nations which generate outbound tourism. The relative attractiveness of different tourist destinations may also change (Buckley, 2008c). Conservation efforts which rely on income from international nature and wildlife tourists may falter if these flows are cut or reduced. This has already happened in areas where tourism has been reduced through political instabilities or disease.

14. Conservation tourism will be increasingly important under climate change. The world's protected area systems are necessary but not sufficient to protect global biodiversity and ecosystem services. Their effectiveness may be reduced further by climate change, especially in areas experiencing more intense and frequent droughts or changed temperature regimes. Many hundreds of species-scale ecological effects of climate change have already been identified, and many more involving decoupling of interspecies interactions. One of the few possible adaptive responses by human social systems is to improve landscape-scale connectivity, and off-reserve conservation tourism is one key component of these efforts (Buckley, 2008a; Gallo *et al.*, 2009). Another key response, however, is to improve the resilience of ecosystems in existing protected areas, and one key step is to reduce the impacts of tourism.

15. From a policy perspective, it appears that conservation tourism is indeed growing at present and will indeed become a more significant component of both the tourism and conservation sectors in future. From a research perspective, this volume barely begins to catalogue the many newly formed conservation tourism enterprises. We need to compile a much more comprehensive set, with more complete social, economic and environmental information, and attempt a global-scale comparative analysis of net outcomes and the factors that influence them. A number of cooperative research efforts are already under way, in various countries, with this aim in mind; and we invite all of our colleagues worldwide who share these interests to contact us with their own insights and examples.

References

Abercrombie and Kent (2010) Abercrombie & Kent. Available at: http://abercrombiekent.com (accessed 8 April 2010).

Adams, W.M. and Infield, M. (2003) Who is on the gorilla's payroll? Claims on tourist revenue from Ugandan National Park. *World Development* 31, 177–190.

Airey, D. and Chong, K. (2010) National policy-makers for tourism in China. *Annals of Tourism Research* 37, 295–314.

Allendorf, T. (2007) Residents' attitudes toward three protected areas in southwestern Nepal. *Biodiversity and Conservation* 16, 2087–2102.

&Beyond (2010) &Beyond. Available at: http://www.andbeyond.com/ (accessed 16 February 2010).

Anderson, A., Roberts, R., Dickinson, W.R., Clark, G., Burley, D., de Biran, A., Hope, G. and Nunn, P.D. (2006) Times of sand: sedimentary history and archaeology at the Sigatoka Dunes, Fiji. *Geoarchaeology* 21, 131–154.

André, O. and Talbot, E. (2007) *40 ans. Parcs naturels régionaux de France*. Fédération des parcs naturels régionaux de France, Paris.

Anon. (2008) The Americas: rumble in the jungle. *The Economist* 387(8575), 58.

Anon. (2010a) Jiuzhaigou Nature Reserve. Available at: http://www.lonelyplanet.com/china.sichuan/jiuzhaigou-nature-reserve (accessed 13 February 2010).

Anon. (2010b) Jiuzhaigou Nature Reserve. Available at: http://wikitravel.org/en/jiuzhaigou-nature-reserve (accessed 13 February 2010).

Archabald, K. and Naughton-Treves, L. (2001) Tourism revenue-sharing around national parks in Western Uganda: early efforts to identify and reward local communities. *Environmental Conservation* 28, 135–149.

Argentina, Administración de Parques Nacionales (APN) (2007) *Las Áreas Protegidas de la Argentina: Herramienta Superior para la Conservación de nuestro patrimonio natural y cultural*, (ed.) Aires, C.A. Administración de Parques Nacionales, Buenos Aires, Argentina.

Argentina, Administración de Parques Nacionales (APN) (2009) *ECOS DEL PARQUE Periódico del Parque Nacional Nahuel Huapi*. Issue 9. Administración de Parques Nacionales, Buenos Aires.

Arkaroola Pty Ltd (2005) Arkaroola's history. Available at: www.arkaroola.com.au/history (accessed 14 April 2010).

Arunachal Tourism (2010) Government approved local tour operations. Available at: http://www.arunachaltourism.com/tour.htm (accessed 4 March 2010).

Atelier technique des espaces naturels (ATEN) (2009) Tableau comparatif des espaces naturels de France. Available at: http://www.espaces-naturels.fr (accessed 18 June 2009).

Aurora del Palmar (2010) La Aurora del Palmar: Refugio de Vida Silvestre. Available at: http://www.auroradelpalmar.com.ar/ (accessed 1 April 2010).

Aurora Expeditions (2010) Cruising to the heart of nature. Available at: http://www.auroraexpeditions.com.au/site/home.aspx (accessed 8 April 2010).

Australian Wildlife Conservancy (2010) Australian Wildlife Conservancy. Available at: http://www.awc.org.au/ (accessed 16 February 2010).

Aylward, B., Allen, K., Echeverria, J. and Tosi, J. (1996) Sustainable ecotourism in Costa Rica: the Monteverde Cloud Forest Reserve. *Biodiversity and Conservation* 5, 315–343.

Baines, G., Hunnman, P., Rivers, M.-J. and Watson, B. (2002) *South Pacific Biodiversity Conservation Program: Terminal Evaluation Mission Final Report*. UNDP, New York.

Bakkes, C. (2010) *In Bushveld and Desert: A Game Ranger's Life*. Human & Rousseau, Cape Town, South Africa.

Balme, G.A., Slotow, R. and Hunter, L.T.B. (2009) Impact of conservation interventions on the dynamics and persistence of a persecuted leopard (*Panthera pardus*) population. *Biological Conservation* 142, 2681–2690.

Balmford, A., Beresford, J., Green, J., Naidoo, R., Walpole, M. and Manica, A. (2009) A global perspective on trends in nature-based tourism. *PLoS Biology* 7, 1–6.

Barkin, D. (2000) The economic impacts of ecotourism: conflicts and solutions in the highland Mexico. In: Godde, P.M., Price, M.F. and Zimmermann, F.M. (eds) *Tourism Development in Mountain Regions*. CAB International, Wallingford, United Kingdom, pp. 157–171.

Barnes, J. (2008) Community-based tourism and natural resource management in Namibia: local and national economic impacts. In: Spenceley, A. (ed.) *Responsible Tourism*. Earthscan, London, United Kingdom, pp. 343–360.

Barnes, J. and Jones, B. (2009) Game ranching in Namibia. In: Suich, H. and Child, B. with Spenceley, A. (eds) *Evolution and Innovation in Wildlife Conservation: Parks and Game Ranches to Tranfrontier Conservation Areas*. SASUSG, IUCN, Earthscan, London, United Kingdom, pp. 113-126.

Barnes, J.I., MacGregor, J. and Weaver, L.C. (2002) Economic efficiency and incentives for change within Namibia's community wildlife use initiatives. *World Development* 30, 667–681.

Barnes, K.N. (ed.) (2000) *The Eskom Red Data Book of Birds of South Africa, Lesotho and Swaziland*. BirdLife South Africa, Johannesburg, South Africa.

Barnett, P. (2001) Fair trade in tourism: 'Belize: the Lodge at Chaa Creek'. *UNEP Industry and Environment* 24(3-4), 1–49.

Barquez, R.M., Diaz, M.M. and Ojeda, R.A. (eds) (2006) *Mamiferos de Argentina: Sistematica y Distribución*. Sociedad Argentina para el Estudio de los Mamiferos (SAREM), Buenos Aires, Argentina.

Barron, E.J. (2009) Beyond climate science. *Science* 326, 643.

Barrué-Pastor, M. (1989) Cent ans de législation montagnarde: des images contradictoires de la nature. In: Mathieu, N. and Jollivet, M. and Association des ruralistes français (eds) *Du Rural à l'environnement: la Question de la Nature Aujourd'hui*. L'Harmattan, Paris, France, pp. 225–233.

Basiuk, R. (2000) Borneo: reaping the fruits of ecotourism. Available at: http://www.unesco.org/courier/2000_05/uk/doss25.htm (accessed 5 March 2010).

Batjargal, B. (2004) Mongolia: grassland of wisdom and natural beauty. *China's Foreign Trade* 24, 32–35.

Bauer, T. (1999) Towards a sustainable tourism future: lessons from Antarctic. In: Weir, B., McArthur, S. and Crabtree, A. (eds) *Developing Ecotourism into the Millenium. Proceedings of the Ecotourism Association of Australia*. Ecotourism Association of Australia, Brisbane, Australia, pp. 275–278.

Bauer, T.G. (2001) *Tourism in the Antarctic: Opportunities, Constraints, and Future Prospects*. The Haworth Hospitality Press, New York, USA.

Beaumont, N. (1998) The conservation benefits of ecotourism: does it produce pro-environmental attitudes or are ecotourists already converted to the cause? In: *Progress in Tourism and Hospitality Research: Proceedings of the Eighth Australian Tourism and Hospitality Research Conference*. Bureau of Tourism Research, Canberra, pp. 273–275.

Beqa Adventure Divers (BAD) (2010) Take a bite. a week of the best shark dive in the world. Every year guaranteed. Available at: http://www.beqadiving.com/ (accessed 4 March 2010).

Béteille, R. (1996) *Le Tourisme vert*. Presses universitaires de France, Paris, France.

Bhagwat, S. (2009) Conservation: the world's religions can help. *Nature* 461, 37.

Bierbaum, R. and Zoellick, R. (2009) Development and climate change. *Science* 326, 771.

Binns, T. and Nel, E. (2002) Tourism as a local development strategy in South Africa. *Geographical Journal* 168, 235–247.

Birds Australia (2010) Conservation through knowledge. Available at: http://www.birdsaustralia.com.au/ (accessed 16 April 2010).

Blangy, S. (1995) Écotourisme, tourisme durable et tourisme rural. *Cahier Espaces* 42, 60–68.

Blangy, S., Dubois, G. and Kouchner, F. (2002) L'écotourisme, un concept fructueux pour le tourisme français. *Espaces Tourisme et Loisirs* 195, 48–55.

Boko, M., Niang, I., Nyong, A., Vogel, C., Githeko, A., Medany, M., Osman-Elasha, B., Tabo, R. and Yanda, P. (2007) Africa. In: Parry, V., Canziani, O.F., Palutikof, V., van der Linden, P.J. and Hanson, V. (eds) *Climate Change 2007: Impacts, Adaptation and Vulnerability. Contribution of Working Group II to the Fourth Assessment Report of the Intergovernmental Panel on Climate Change.* Cambridge University Press, Cambridge, United Kingdom, pp. 433–467.

Borman, R. (2008) Ecotourism and conservation: the Cofan experience. In: Stronza, A. and Durham, W.H. (eds) *Ecotourism and Conservation in the Americas.* CAB International, Wallingford, United Kingdom, pp. 21–29.

Borneo Adventure (2010) The Borneo specialist. Available at: http://www.borneoadventure.com/public/home/default.asp (accessed 1 March 2010).

Borneo Rainforest Lodge (2010) Danum Valley and the Borneo Rainforest Lodge. Available at: http://www.borneorainforestlodge.com/ (accessed 1 March 2010).

Boshoff, A.F., Landman, M., Kerley, G.I.H. and Bradfield, M. (2007) Profiles, views and observations of visitors to the Addo Elephant National Park, Eastern Cape, South Africa. *South African Journal of Wildlife Research* 37, 189–196.

Bothma, J. du P., Suich, H. and Spenceley, A. (2009) Extensive wildlife production on private land in South Africa. In: Suich, H. and Child, B. with Spenceley, A. (eds) *Evolution and Innovation in Wildlife Conservation: Parks and Game Ranches to Transfrontier Conservation Areas.* SASUSG, IUCN, Earthscan, London, United Kingdom, pp. 147–162.

Bouvier, M., Hervieu, M. and Balfet, M. (1995) Valorisation de l'environnement et tourisme. Le cas du Parc National des Pyrénées. *Téoros* 14, 60–66.

Bowerman, K. (2008) Part 2. In: Pellegrini, T. (ed.) *Fast Track, Week 44.* BBC News, London (video).

Bozonnet, J.-P. and Fischesser, B. (1985) La dimension imaginaire dans l'idéologie de la protection de la nature. In: Cadoret, A. (ed.) *Protection de la nature, histoire et idéologie. De la Nature à l'environnement.* L'Harmattan, Paris, France, pp. 193–207.

Brandon, K. (1996) *Ecotourism and Conservation: Key Issues.* World Bank Environment Paper 033, World Bank, Washington, DC.

Brandon, K. and Margoluis, R. (1996) The bottom line: getting biodiversity conservation back into ecotourism. In: Miller, J.A. and Malek-Zadeh, E. (eds) *The Ecotourism Equation: Measuring the Impacts.* Yale Bulletin Series, No. 99, Yale University, New Haven, Connecticut, USA, pp. 28–38.

Breton, J.-M. (2004) *Tourisme, environnement et aires protégées.* Karthala-CREJETA, Paris, France.

Bricker, K. (2001) Ecotourism development in the rural highlands of Fiji. In: Harrison, D. (ed.) *Tourism and the Less Developed World: Issues and Case Studies.* CAB International, Wallingford, United Kingdom, pp. 235–250.

Bricker, K. (2003) Ecotourism development in Fiji. In: Dowling, R.K. and Fennell, D.A. (eds) *Ecotourism Policy and Planning.* CAB International, Wallingford, United Kingdom, pp. 187–204.

Brooks, T.M., Mittermeier, R.A., da Fonseca, G.A.B., Gerlach, J., Hoffman, M., Lamoreux, J.F., Mittermeier, C.G., Pilgrim, J.D. and Rodrigues, A.S.L. (2006) Global biodiversity conservation priorities. *Science* 313, 58–61.

Bruner, F.Y. (1993) Evaluation of model of private-ownership conservation: ecotourism in the community baboon sanctuary in Belize. Thesis, School of Public Policy, Georgia Institute of Technology.

Brunnschweiler, J.M. (2010) The Shark Reef Marine Reserve: a marine tourism project in Fiji involving local communities. *Journal of Sustainable Tourism* 18, 29–42.

Brunnschweiler, J.M. and Earle, J.L. (2006) A contribution to marine life conservation efforts in the South Pacific: the Shark Reef Marine Reserve, Fiji. *Cybium* 30, 133–139.

Buckley, R.C. (1989) *Precision in Environmental Impact Prediction: First National Environmental Audit, Australia.* ANU Press, Canberra. ISBN 0 86740 364 0.

Buckley R.C. (1994) A framework for ecotourism. *Annals of Tourism Research* 21, 661–669.

Buckley, R.C. (2000) *Green Guide for 4WD Tours: Best-practice   Environmental Management for 4WD and Off-road Tours.* CRC Tourism, Gold Coast, Australia.

Buckley, R.C. (2002) Public and private partnerships between tourism and protected areas. *Journal of Tourism Studies* 13, 26–38.

Buckley, R.C. (2003a) *Case Studies in Ecotourism.* CAB International, Wallingford, United Kingdom.

Buckley, R.C. (2003b) Environmental inputs and outputs in ecotourism geotourism with a positive triple bottom line? *Journal of Ecotourism* 2, 76–82.

Buckley, R.C. (ed.) (2004a) *Environmental Impacts of Ecotourism.* CAB International, Wallingford, United Kingdom.

Buckley, R.C. (ed.) (2004b) *Tourism in Parks: Australian Initiatives*. Griffith University, Gold Coast, Australia.

Buckley, R.C. (2004c) Environmental impacts of motorized off-highway vehicles. In: Buckley, R.C. (ed.) *Environmental Impacts of Ecotourism*. CAB International, Wallingford, United Kingdom, pp. 83–97.

Buckley, R.C. (2004d) *A Natural Partnership*, vol. 2. *Innovative Funding Mechanisms for Visitor Infrastructure in Protected Areas*. TTF Australia, Sydney, Australia.

Buckley, R.C. (2004e) Impacts of ecotourism on birds. In: Buckley, R. (ed.) *Environmental Impacts of Ecotourism*. CAB International, Wallingford, United Kingdom, pp. 187–209.

Buckley, R.C. (2005) In search of the narwhal: ethical dilemmas in ecotourism. *Journal of Ecotourism* 4, 129–134.

Buckley, R.C. (2006) *Adventure Tourism*. CAB International, Wallingford, United Kingdom.

Buckley, R.C. (2007a) Adventure tourism products: price, duration, size, skill, remoteness. *Tourism Management* 28, 1428–1433.

Buckley, R.C. (2007b) Thresholds and standards for tourism environmental impact assessment. In: Schmidt, M., Glasson, J., Emmelin, L. and Helbron, H. (eds) *Standards and Thresholds for Impact Assessment*. Springer, Heidelberg, Germany, pp. 205–215.

Buckley R.C. (2008a) World Wild Web: funding connectivity conservation under climate change. *Biodiversity* 9, 71–78.

Buckley, R.C. (2008b) Tourism as a conservation tool. In: Raschi, A. and Trampetti, S. (eds) *Management for Protection and Sustainable Development*. Consiglio Nationale della Ricerche, Montecatini, Italy, pp. 19–25.

Buckley, R.C. (2008c) Climate change: tourism destination dynamics. *Tourism Recreation Research* 33, 354–355.

Buckley, R.C. (2009a) Evaluating the net effects of ecotourism on the environment: a framework, first assessment and future research. *Journal of Sustainable Tourism* 17, 643–672.

Buckley, R.C. (2009b) *Ecotourism: Principles and Practices*. CAB International, Wallingford, United Kingdom.

Buckley, R.C. (2009c) Parks and tourism. *PLoS Biol* 7, e1000143.

Buckley, R.C. (2009d) Tourism enterprises and sustainable development in Australia. In: Leslie, D. (ed.) *Tourism Enterprises and Sustainable Development*. Routledge, New York, pp. 126–138.

Buckley, R.C. (2009e) Submission on NSW draft sea-level rise policy statement and accompanying draft technical note 2009. NSW Dept Environment and Climate Change.

Buckley, R.C. (2010) *Adventure Tourism Management*. Elsevier, Oxford, United Kingdom.

Buckley, R.C., Pickering C. and Warnken, J. (2000) Environmental management for alpine tourism and resorts in Australia. In: Goode, P.M., Price, M.F. and Zimmerman, F.M. (eds) *Tourism and Development in Mountain Regions*. CAB International, Wallingford, United Kingdom, pp. 27–45.

Buckley, R.C., Pickering, C.M. and Weaver, D. (eds) (2003a) *Nature-based Tourism, Environment and Land Management*. CAB International, Wallingford, United Kingdom.

Buckley, R.C., Witting, N. and Guest, M. (2003b) Visitor fees, tour permits and asset and risk management by parks agencies: Australian case study. In: Buckley, R.C., Pickering, C.M. and Weaver, D.B. (eds) *Nature-based Tourism, Environment and Land Management*. CAB International, Wallingford, United Kingdom, pp. 51–59.

Buckley, R.C., Zhong, L.-S., Cater, C. and Chen, T. (2008a) Shengtai luyou: cross-cultural comparison in ecotourism. *Annals of Tourism Research* 35, 945–968.

Buckley, R.C., Ollenburg, C. and Zhong, L.S. (2008b) Cultural landscape in Mongolian tourism. *Annals of Tourism Research* 35, 47–61.

Buckley, R.C., Robinson, J., Carmody, J. and King, N. (2008c) Monitoring for management of conservation and recreation in Australian protected areas. *Biodiversity and Conservation* 17, 3589–3606.

Burkart, R., Bárbaro, N.O., Sánchez, R.O. and Gomez, D.A. (1999) *Eco-regiones de la Argentina*. Administración de Parques Nacionales, Buenos Aires.

Burslem, D.F.R.P., Whitmore, T.C. and Denmark, N. (1998) A thirty-year record of forest dynamics from Kolombangara, Solomon Islands. In: Dallmeier, F. and Comiskey, J.A. (eds) *Forest Biodiversity Research, Monitoring and Modeling. Conceptual Background and Old World Case Studies*. UNESCO, Paris and Parthenon, Carnforth, Lancs, pp. 633–645.

Bushell, R. and Eagles, P.F.J. (2007) *Tourism in Protected Areas: Benefits Beyond Boundaries*. CAB International, Wallingford, United Kingdom.

Butynski, T.M. and Kalina, J. (1998) Gorilla tourism: a critical look. In: Milner-Gullard, E.J. (ed.) *Conservation of Biological Resources*. Blackwell, Oxford, United Kingdom, pp. 294–313.

Byers, A. (2009) A comparative study of tourism impacts on alpine ecosystems in the Sagarmatha (Mt. Everest) National Park, Nepal and the Huascaran National Park, Peru. In: Hill, J. and Gales, T. (eds) *Ecotourism and Environmental Sustainability: Principles and Practices*. Ashgate, Farnham, United Kingdom, pp. 51–71.

Cahill, T. (2004) Madidi National Park, Bolivia: call of the wild. *National Geographic Traveler* 21, 52–58.

Canodros SA (2010) Unforgettable experiences with responsability [*sic*]. Available at: http://www.canodros.com/htm/inicio-en.html (accessed 9 February 2010).

Cans, R. (1994) Les trois âges de la politique française de l'environnement. *Aménagement et Nature* 116, 23–27.

Cans, R. (2006) *Petite Histoire du mouvement écolo en France*. Delachaux et Niestle, Paris, France.

Carlisle, L. (2007) Conservation and community development: the Conservation Corporation Africa model. In: Bushell, R. and Eagles, P.J.F. (eds) *Tourism and Protected Areas: Benefits Beyond Boundaries*. CAB International, Wallingford, United Kingdom, pp. 244–265.

Carter, E., Adams, W.M. and Hutton, J. (2008) Private protected areas: management regimes, tenure arrangements and protected area categorization in East Africa. *Oryx* 42, 177–186.

Castley, J.G. and Hall-Martin, A.J. (2003) The status of the southern white rhino (*Ceratotherium simum simum*) on private land in South Africa in 2001. *Pachyderm* 34, 33–44.

Castley, J.G., Boshoff, A.F. and Kerley, G.I.H. (2001) Compromising South Africa's natural biodiversity – inappropriate herbivore introductions. *South African Journal of Science* 97, 344–348.

Castley, J.G., Patton, C. and Magome, H. (2009a) Parks for people: the performance of South African National Parks. In: Suich, H. and Child, B. with Spenceley, A. (eds) *Evolution and Innovation in Wildlife Conservation: Parks and Game Ranches to Transfrontier Conservation Areas*. SASUSG, IUCN, Earthscan, London, pp. 393–407.

Castley, J.G., Knight, M. and Gordon, J. (2009b) Making conservation work: innovative approaches to meeting conservation and socio-economic objectives (an example from the Addo Elephant National Park, South Africa). In: Suich, H. and Child, B. with Spenceley, A. (eds) *Evolution and Innovation in Wildlife Conservation: Parks and Game Ranches to Transfrontier Conservation Areas*. SASUSG, IUCN, Earthscan, London, pp. 307–324.

Cater, E. (2006) Ecotourism as a western construct. *Journal of Ecotourism* 5, 23–39.

Ceballos-Lascurain, H. (1996) *Tourism, Ecotourism and Protected Areas: the State of Nature-based Tourism Around the World and Guidelines for its Development*. IUCN, Gland, Switzerland.

Chalalan Ecolodge (2010) Leading the way in ecotourism in Bolivia. Available at: http://www.chalalan.com/ (accessed 17 February 2010).

Chape, S., Blyth, S., Fish, L., Fox, P. and Spalding, M. (eds) (2003) *2003 United Nations List of Protected Areas*. UNEP-WCMC and WCPA. IUCN, Gland, Switzerland and Cambridge, United Kingdom.

Chapin, M. (2000) *Defending Kuna Yala*. WWF, Washington DC, 34 pp. Available at: http://www.worldwildlife.org/bsp/publications/aam/panama/panama.html (accessed 23 February 2010).

Chatterjee, P. (1997) Dam busting. *New Scientist* 155, 34–37.

Chediak, S. (2008) Aprovechamiento Sustentable del Palmito Misionero. Temas de la Biodiversidad del Litoral Fluvial Argentino III. *Miscelánea INSUGEO* 17(2), 309–316.

Child, B. (2009) Innovations in state, private and communal conservation. In: Suich, H. and Child, B. with Spenceley, A. (eds) *Evolution and Innovation in Wildlife Conservation: Parks and Game Ranches to Transfrontier Conservation Areas*. SASUSG, IUCN, Earthscan, London, pp. 427–440.

China Gezhouba Group Corporation (2010) Xiangjiaba hydropower project. Available at: http://www.gzbgj.com/english/article.asp?id=569 (accessed 8 March 2010).

China, Ministry of Environmental Protection (2008) Communique of environmental statistics of China. Available at: http://zls.mep.gov.cn/hjtj/qghjtjgb/200809/t20080924_129355.htm (accessed 20 April 2010) (In Chinese).

China Rivers Project (2010) Protecting China's river heritage for people and wildlife, and fostering river based recreation in China. Available at: http://www.chinariversproject.org/ (accessed 22 February 2010).

Chizhova, V.P. (2004) Impacts and management of hikers in Kavkazsky State Biosphere Reserve, Russia. In: Buckley, R.C. (ed.) *Environmental Impacts of Ecotourism*. CAB International, Wallingford, United Kingdom, pp. 377–381.

Chu, S.-J. and Xu, G. (2004) Conflictive and coordination Chanism in land use and ecosystem conservation in a mountainous area of North Zhejiang: the case of Tianmushan Nature Reserve. *Resources and Environment in the Yangtze Basin* 13(1): 25–28 (in Chinese).

Cirelli, M.T. (2002) Legal trends in wildlife management. *FAO Legislative Study* 74: 73 pp. Food and Agriculture Organization of the United Nations, Rome. Available at: ftp://ftp.fao.org/docrep/fao/005/y3844E/y3844e01.pdf (accessed 23 April 2010).

Clark, C. (undated) Lessons from co-management regimes in Belize. Available at: http://sorrel.humboldt.edu/~storage/clark/co-managament.pdf [sic] (accessed 26 April 2010).

Clary, D. (1993) *Le Tourisme dans l'espace français*. Masson, Paris, France.

Commission Internationale pour la Protection des Alpes (2008) CIPRA. Available at: www.cipra.org/alpknowhow/bestpractice.2005–11-24.4717292482 (accessed 29 June 2008).

Community Conservation (2010) Catalyzing communities for conservation since 1989. Available at: http://www.communityconservation.org/ (accessed 17 February 2010).

Connor, R., Houlbrook, R. and Tarihao, F. (1996) Local conservation area ownership and traditional management. In: Wallace, H. (ed.) *Developing Alternatives: Community Development Strategies and Environmental Issues in the Pacific*. Victoria University of Technology, Melbourne, Australia, pp. 29–45.

Conservación Patagonica (2010) The future Patagonia National Park. Available at: http://www.conservacionpatagonica.org/monteleon.htm (accessed 1 April 2010).

Conservation Finance Alliance (2003) *The Conservation Finance Guide*. IUCN, Gland.

Conservation International (2002) *Una Ecopark, Brazilian Atlantic Forest*. Conservation International, Washington, DC.

Conservation International (2010) People need nature to survive. Available at: http://www.conservation.org (accessed 16 February 2010).

Conservation Land Trust (2010) The Conservation Land Trust. Available at: http://www.theconservationlandtrust.org/eng/mision_introduccion.htm (accessed 1 April 2010).

Conservation Strategy Fund (CSF) (2008) Help support conservation. Available at: http://conservation-strategy.org/ (accessed 9 February 2010).

Correa da Silva, M. and Amaral, V. (eds) (2008) *Fazenda Rio Negro, Tradicão e conservacão no Pantanal Mato Grossense*, Conservacão Internacional Brasil, Campo Grande (in Portuguese).

Costa Rica Expeditions (2010) Costa Rica Expeditions. Available at: http://www.costaricaexpeditions.com/wl3/index.php (accessed 8 February 2010).

Cousins, J.A., Sadler, J.P. and Evans, J. (2008) Exploring the role of private wildlife ranching as a conservation tool in South Africa: stakeholder perspectives. *Ecology and Society* 13: Article 43. Available at: http://www.ecologyandsociety.org/vol13/iss2/art43/ (accessed 23 April 2010).

Craul, M., Chikhi, L., Sousa, V., Olivieri, G.L., Rabesandratana, A., Zimmermann, E. and Radespiel, U. (2009) Influence of forest fragmentation on an endangered large-bodied lemur in northwestern Madagascar. *Biological Conservation* 142(12), 2862–2871.

Cristalino Ecological Foundation (2010) Fundacao Ecologica Cristalino. Available at: http://www.fundacaocristalino.org.br/br_index.php (accessed 22 February 2010).

Cristalino Jungle Lodge (2010) An Amazon sanctuary. Available at: http://www.cristalinolodge.com.br/ (accessed 9 February 2010).

Crooks, K.R. and Sanjayan, M. (eds) (2006) *Connectivity Conservation*. Cambridge University Press, Cambridge, United Kingdom.

Crosnier, C. (2006) Biodiversité et pertinence des pratiques locales dans la réserve de biosphère des Cévennes. *Revue Internationale des Sciences Sociales* 187(1), 159–168.

Cuyabeno Lodge (2010) The Cuyabeno Lodge. Available at: http://www.cuyabenolodge.com/ (accessed 27 April 2010).

Daversin, B. (2009) The Role of Tourism Businesses with Conservation Initiatives in Cévennes National Park. Chargé de mission tourisme durable, Parc national des Cévennes, Florac, France.

Davies, R., Trieloff, C. and Wells, M. (1997) *Financial and Economic Objectives and Management of the Madikwe Game Reserve*. Madikwe Development Series Number 5, North West Parks and Tourism Board, Rustenberg, South Africa..

Deboudt, P. (2004) Tourisme littoral, préservation des espaces naturels et gestion intégrée de la zone côtière en France: le cas de la côte d'Opale. *Hommes et Terres du Nord* 2, 37–48.

de Loma, T.L., Osenberg, C.W., Shima, J.S., Chancerelle, Y., Davies, N., Brooks, A.J. and Galzin, R.

(2008) A framework for assessing impacts of Marine Protected Areas in Moorea (French Polynesia). *Pacific Science* 62(3), 431–441.

de Oliveira, J.A.P. (2005) Tourism as a force for establishing protected areas: the case of Bahia, Brazil. *Journal of Sustainable Tourism* 13, 24–49.

Derocher, A.E. and Stirling, I. (1990a) Distribution of polar bears (*Ursus maritimus*) during the ice-free period in western Hudson Bay. *Canadian Journal of Zoology* 68, 1395–1403.

Derocher, A.E. and Stirling, I. (1990b) Observations of aggregating behaviour in adult male polar bears (*Ursus maritimus*). *Canadian Journal of Zoology* 68, 1390–1394.

Derocher, A.E. and Stirling, I. (1995) Temporal variation in reproduction and body mass of polar bears in western Hudson Bay. *Canadian Journal of Zoology* 73, 1657–1665.

Dixey, L.M. (2008) The unsustainability of community tourism donor projects: lessons from Zambia. In: Spenceley, A. (ed.) *Responsible Tourism: Critical Issues for Conservation and Development.* Earthscan, London, United Kingdom, pp. 323–342.

Donohoe, H.M. and Needham, R.D. (2006) Ecotourism: the evolving contemporary definition. *Journal of Ecotourism* 5, 192–210.

Doyle, M., Stanley, E., Harbor, J. and Grant, G. (2003) Dam removal in the United States: emerging needs for science and policy. *EOS* 84, 29–36.

Druce, D., Genis, H., Braak, J., Greatwood, S., Delsink, A., Kettles, R., Hunter, L. and Slotow, R. (2004) Population demography and spatial ecology of a reintroduced lion population in the Greater Makalali Conservancy, South Africa. *Koedoe* 47, 103–118.

Druce, H.C., Pretorius, K. and Slotow, R. (2006) The effect of mature elephant bull introductions on ranging patterns of resident bulls: Phinda Private Game Reserve, South Africa. *Koedoe* 49, 77–84.

Druce, H.C., Pretorius, K. and Slotow, R. (2008) The response of an elephant population to conservation area expansion: Phinda Private Game Reserve, South Africa. *Biological Conservation* 141, 3127–3138.

Drumm, A. (1998) New approaches to community-based ecotourism management. In: Lindberg, K., Epler-Wood, M. and Engeldrum, D. (eds) *Ecotourism: a Guide for Planners and Managers.* Ecotourism Society, North Bennington, Vermont, pp. 97–123.

Dyck, M.G. and Baydack, R.K. (2004) Vigilance behaviour of polar bears (*Ursus maritimus*) in the context of wildlife-viewing activities at Churchill, Manitoba, Canada. *Biological Conservation* 116, 343–350.

Eagle, A. (2009) Huichol ecotourism centre awaits visitors. *Guadalajara Reporter* 31 July.

Eagles, P.F.J. (2009) Governance of recreation and tourism partnerships in parks and protected areas. *Journal of Sustainable Tourism* 17, 231–248.

Eagles, P.F.J. and Hillel, O. (2009) Improving protected area finance through tourism. Task Force on Tourism and Protected Areas, World Commission on Protected Areas, Secretariat of the Convention on Biological Diversity, 14 pp. Available at: http://www.ahs.uwaterloo.ca/~eagles/documents/EaglesandHillelArticleonEconomicsandFinanceofTourisminProtectedAreas.pdf (accessed 9 September 2009).

Earth Sanctuaries Ltd (2002) Welcome to Earth Sanctuaries Online. Available at: www.esl.com.au (accessed 10 September 2002).

Earth Science Expeditions (ESE) (2010) Exploring the rivers of western China. Available at: http://www.shangri-la-river-expeditions.com/ (accessed 22 February 2010).

Ebedes, H., van Rooyen, J. and du Toit, J.G. (2002) Capturing wild animals. In: Bothma, du P.J. (ed.) *Game Ranch Management*, 4th edn. Van Schaik Publishers, Pretoria, South Africa, pp. 382–440.

Ecuador, Ministerio del Ambiente (2010) DPNG aclara publicacion de Diario el Universo. Boletin de Prensa PR.C.P003.R002 – 20/04/2010-No.039. Available at: http://www.ambiente.gov.ec/contenido.php?cd=2177 (accessed 22 April 2010).

Edington, J.M. and Edington, M.A. (1997) Tropical forest ecotourism: two promising projects in Belize. In: Stabler, M.J. (ed.) *Tourism and Sustainability: Principles to Practice.* CAB International, Wallingford, United Kingdom, pp. 163–167.

Ekstrom, J.M.M., Jones, J.P.G., Willis, J., Tobias, J., Dutson, G. and Barré, N. (2002) New information on the distribution, status and conservation of terrestrial bird species in Grande Terre, New Caledonia. *Emu* 102, 197–207.

El Manglar Environmental Protection Group (2004) *Final Report for Global Greengrants Fund* 50, 50–078. EMEPG, San Blas, Mexico.

Emslie, R. (2008) Rhino population sizes and trends. *Pachyderm* 44, 88–95.

ENDESU (2010) Espacios naturales y desarrollo sustenable. Available at: www.endesu.org.mx/ (accessed 27 April 2010).

Estancia el Socorro (2010) Estancia el Socorro, Estoncia San Alonso. Available at: http://www.rincondelsocorro.com/esteros-ibera/esteros-ibera.htm (accessed 6 April 2010).

Europarc (2008) Welcome to the Europarc Federation. Available at: www.europarc.org/international/europarc.html (accessed 29 June 2008)

Farrington, M. (2009) Saving paradise. Conservation of Tetepare. *Melanesian Geo* 7, 22–25.

Fauna and Flora International (2010) Conserving threatened species and ecosystems worldwide. Available at: http://www.fauna-flora.org/ (accessed 9 February 2010).

Fearnhead, P. (2009) Privately managed protected areas. In: Suich, H. and Child, B. with Spenceley, A. (eds) *Evolution and Innovation in Wildlife Conservation: Parks and Game Ranches to Transfrontier Conservation Areas.* SASUSG, IUCN, Earthscan, London, pp. 409–426.

Fédération des Parcs naturels régionaux de France (FPNRF) (2008) *Rapport d'activités.* Fédération des Parcs naturels régionaux de France, Paris.

Fédération des Parcs naturels régionaux de France (FPNRF) (2009). Una autre vie s'invente ici. Available at: http://www.parcs-naturels-regionaux.tm.fr/fr/accueil/ (accessed 2 June 2009).

Feng, X.-Q. (2005) Community co-management. Available at: http://www.cntms.org/ProductShow.asp?ClassID=&ID=496 (accessed 20 April 2010) (in Chinese).

Fennell, D.A., Buckley, R.C. and Weaver, D.B. (2001) Policy and planning. In: Weaver, D.B. (ed.) *Encyclopedia of Ecotourism.* CAB International, Wallingford, United Kingdom, pp. 463–478.

Filardi, C. and Pikacha, P. (2007) A role for conservation concessions in Melanesia: customary land tenure and community conservation agreements in the Solomon Islands. *Melanesian Geo* 5, 18–23.

Flannery, T.F. (1996) Mammalian zoogeography of New Guinea and the southwestern Pacific. In: Keast, A. and Miller, S.E. (eds) *The Origin and Evolution of Pacific Island Biotas, New Guinea to Eastern Polynesia: Patterns and Processes.* SPB Academic Publishing, Amsterdam, Netherlands, pp. 399–406.

Font, X. and Buckley, R.C. (eds) (2001) *Tourism Ecolabelling.* CAB International, Wallingford, United Kingdom.

Fritsch, A. and Johannsen, K. (2004) *Ecotourism in Appalachia: Marketing the Mountains.* The University Press of Kentucky, Lexington, Kentucky.

Fromageau, J. (1985) Réflexions relatives à l'histoire du droit et de la protection de la nature. In: Cadoret, A. (ed.) *Protection de la Nature: Histoire et idéologiee. De la Nature à l'environnement.* L'Harmattan, Paris, France, pp. 208–220.

Fundación Ambiente y Recursos Naturales (FARN) and Fundación Vida Silvestre Argentina (FVSA). (2007a) *Conclusiones del Taller Construyendo Modelos de Colaboración entre el Sector Público y Privado para Potenciar la Conservación en Tierras Privadas de la Argentina.* FARN and FVSA, Buenos Aires.

Fundación Ambiente y Recursos Naturales (FARN) and Fundación Vida Silvestre Argentina (FVSA) (2007b) *Conclusiones del Taller la Conservación Privada como Instrumento para la Ampliación del Sistema de Áreas Protegidas en la Argentina.* FARN and FVSA, Buenos Aires.

Fundación Ambiente y Recursos Naturales (FARN) and Fundación Vida Silvestre Argentina (FVSA) (2007c) *Síntesis de Resultados del Taller La Conservación Privada como Herramienta para el Logro de la Sustentabilidad Ambiental, Social y Económica. Experiencias y Propuestas.* FARN and FVSA, Buenos Aires.

Fundación ProYungas (2010) El Proyecto Rutas del Alto Bermejo. Available at: http://www.proyungas.org.ar/nuestrotrabajo/rab.htm (accessed 1 April 2010).

Fundación Vida Silvestre Argentina (FVSA) (2008) *Manual de Funcionamiento de la Red de Refugios de Vida Silvestres.* FVSA, Buenos Aires, Argentina.

Fundación Vida Silvestre Argentina (FVSA) (2009) *Red de Refugios de Vida Silvestre.* Available at: http://www.vidasilvestre.org.ar/programaDescripcion.php?idSeccion=94 (accessed 27 April 2010).

Fundación Vida Silvestre Argentina (FVSA) (2010a) Listado de Refugios de Vida Silvestre. Available at: http://www.vidasilvestre.org.ar/descargables/tierras_privadas.pdf (accessed 27 April 2010).

Fundación Vida Silvestre Argentina (FVSA) (2010b) Programa de Turismo Responsable. Available at: http://www.vidasilvestre.org.ar/descargables/turismo_responsable.pdf (accessed 27 April 2010).

Gallo, J.A., Pasquini, L., Reyers, B. and Cowling, R.M. (2009) The role of private conservation areas in biodiversity representation and target achievement within the Little Karoo region, South Africa. *Biological Conservation* 142(2), 446–454.

Garcia, J. and Ricalde, D. (2001) Training in the service industry makes the local community independent: the case of the Chalalan Ecolodge-Madidi National Park, Bolivia. *Industry and Environment* 24(3–4), 58–61.

Gardner, T.A., Caro, T.I.M., Fitzherbert, E.M., Banda, T. and Lalbhai, P. (2007) Conservation value of multiple-use areas in east Africa. *Conservation Biology* 21(6), 1516–1525.

Gaugris, J.Y. and van Rooyen, M.W. (2008) A spatial and temporal analysis of Sand Forest tree assemblages in Maputaland, South Africa. *South African Journal of Wildlife Research* 38, 171–184.

Giacobbi, L.-M. (1997) La protection des espaces littoraux dans les régions touristiques: le cas des acquisitions du Conservatoire du littoral dans le Var. In: Wolkowitsch, M. (ed.) *Tourisme et milieux.* Editions du CTHS, Paris, France, pp. 29–44.

Giese, M., Handsworth, R. and Stephenson, R. (1999) Measuring resting heart rates in penguins using an artificial egg. *Journal of Field Ornithology* 70, 49–53.

Gilligan, B. and Allen, C. (2004) Resource and visitor management in NSW National Parks. In: Buckley, R.C. (ed.) *Tourism in Parks: Australian Initiatives.* Griffith University, Gold Coast, Australia, pp. 132–149.

Giran, J.-P. (2003) *Les Parcs nationaux. Une Référence pour la France, une chance pour ses territoires.* Lavoisier, Paris, France.

Goodman, D.S.J. (2004) The campaign to 'open up the west': national, provincial-level and local perspectives. *The China Quarterly* 158, 317–334.

Goodwin, H. (2009) Reflections on 10 years of pro-poor tourism. *Journal of Policy Research in Tourism, Leisure and Events* 1, 90–94.

Gordillo, J. (2005) *Posada Amazonas Lodge. Case Study, Sharing Innovative Experiences.* Report to Third World Network of Scientific Organizations, Trieste, Italy.

Gordillo, J.F., Hunt, C. and Stronza, A. (2008) An ecotourism partnership in the Peruvian Amazon: the case of Posada Amazonas. In: Stronza, A. and Durham, W.H. (eds) *Ecotourism and Conservation in the Americas.* CAB International, Wallingford, United Kingdom, pp. 30–48.

Gössling, S. (1999) Ecotourism: a means to safeguard biodiversity and ecosystem functions? *Ecological Economics* 29, 303–320.

Gössling, S. and Hultman, J. (eds) (2006) *Ecotourism in Scandinavia: Lessons in Theory and Practice.* CAB International, Wallingford, United Kingdom.

Grieg-Gran, M. (2000) *Fiscal Incentives for Biodiversity Conservation: The ICMS Ecológico in Brazil.* Environmental Economics Programme. Discussion Paper. World Wide Fund for Nature and International Institute for Environment and Development, London.

Grossman, D. and Holden, P. (2009) Towards transformation: contractual national parks in South Africa. In: Suich, H. and Child, B. with Spenceley, A. (eds) *Evolution and Innovation in Wildlife Conservation: Parks and Game Ranches to Transfrontier Conservation Areas.* SASUSG, IUCN, Earthscan, London, pp. 357–372.

Groves, V. (2003) *Plan de Monitoreo de Condiciones Ambientales de las Areas de Uso Turistico Refugio de Vida Silvestre Primer Inventario de Condiciones. Programa Refugio de Vida Silvestre Argentina – Yacutinga Lodge.* FVSA, Buenos Aires, Argentina.

Grumbine, R.E. (2007) China's emergence and the prospects for global sustainability. *Bioscience* 57, 249–255.

Guerrini, M.-C. (1990) Systèmes de pouvoir et gestion du territoire dans le sud du Parc national des Cévennes. Conjuger stratégie(s) et territoire(s)? *Strates* 5, 1–8.

Guerrini, M.-C. (1995) Le Parc National des Cévennes. La question de l'environnement: recherches parallèles en Espagne et en France. Parcs espagnols, parcs français. *Strates* 8, 1–20.

Gurung, H. (2008) Fusioning: a grounded theory of participatory governance in the Annapurna Conservation Area, Nepal. PhD thesis, Griffith University, Gold Coast, Australia.

Gusset, M., Ryan, S.J., Hofmeyr, M., van Dyk, G., Davies-Mostert, H.T., Graf, J.A., Owen, C., Szykman, M., Macdonald, D.W., Monfort, S.L., Wildt, D.E., Maddock, A.H., Mills, M.G.L., Slotow, R. and Somers, M.J. (2008) Efforts going to the dogs? Evaluating attempts to re-introduce endangered wild dogs in South Africa. *Journal of Applied Ecology* 45, 100–108.

Gutierrez, T. (2008) Ixcan, centro ecoturistico en abandono. Available at: http://www.oem.com.mx/diariodexalapa/notas/n667153.htm (accessed 22 April 2010).

Hall, C.M. (2009) Tourism policy and politics in southern Africa. In: Saarinen, J., Becker, F., Manwa, H. and Wilson, D. (eds) *Sustainable Tourism in Southern Africa: Local Communities and Natural Resources in Transition.* Channel View Publications, Bristol, United Kingdom, pp. 42–60.

Hall-Martin, A.J. and Castley, J.G. (2003) The status of the black rhinoceros (*Diceros bicornis*) on private land in South Africa in 2001. *Pachyderm* 34, 24–32.

Hansen, A.J. and DeFries, R. (2007) Ecological mechanisms linking protected areas to surrounding lands. *Ecological Applications* 17, 974–988.

Hayward, M.H., Adendorff, J., O'Brien, J., Sholto-Douglas, A., Bissett, C., Moolman, L.C., Bean, P., Fogarty, A., Howarth, D., Slater, R. and Kerley, G.I.H. (2007) The reintroduction of large carnivores to the Eastern Cape, South Africa: an assessment. *Oryx* 41, 205–214.

Hillman, B. (2003) Paradise under construction: minorities, myths and modernity in northwest Yunnan. *Asian Ethnicity* 4, 175–188.

Hillman, B.M. and Barkmann, J. (2009) Conservation: a small price for long-term economic well-being. *Nature* 461, 37.

Hinchberger, B. (2004) Hyacinth Macaw Project: saving endangered birds in the Pantanal. brazilmax.com: *The Hip Guide to Brazil*, web post, 28 October, Marseilles, France. Available at: <http://www. brazilmax.com/news.cfm/tborigem/pl_pantanal/id/7> (accessed 15 September 2009).

Hitchins, P.M. (1992) *An Aerial Census of Black and Square-lipped Rhinoceros in Northern Botswana, 18 September to 2 October 1992*. Report to the Department of Wildlife and National Parks, Gaborone, Botswana.

Hoagland, E. (2009) Jiuzhaigou – China's mystic waters. *National Geographic*. Available at: http://ngm. nationalgeographic.com/2009/03/jiuzhaigou/hoagland-text (accessed 27 April 2010).

Holmern, T., Nyahongo, J. and Roskaft, E. (2007) Livestock loss caused by predators outside the Serengeti National Park, Tanzania. *Biological Conservation* 135, 534–542.

Honey, M. (2008) *Ecotourism and Sustainable Development*, 2nd edn. Island Press, Washington, DC.

Hong, Y. and Zhuo, M. (2001) Research on the exploitation of Shangri-la ecotourism and the Tibetan community culture in Northwest Yunnan. *Tourism Tribune* 16(2), 78–79 (in Chinese).

Horizontes Tours (2010) Nature tours. Available at: http://www.horizontes.com/eng/ (accessed 8 February 2010).

Horwich, R.H., Koontz, F., Saqui, E., Ostro, L., Silver, S. and Glander, K. (2002) Translocation of black howler monkeys in Belize. *Re-introduction News* 21, 10–12.

Huaorani Ecolodge (2010) Huaorani Ecolodge. Available at: http://www.huaorani.com/ (accessed 9 February 2010).

Hunnam, P. (2002) *Lessons in Conservation for People and Projects in the Pacific Islands Region*. UNDP, New York.

Imbu Rano Lodge (2010) Welkam to Imbu Rano Lodge – Solomons Rainforest at its best. Available at: http://www.imburano-lodge.com/ (accessed 4 March 2010).

IMF (2008) International Monetary Fund gross domestic product (GDP) data list 2008. Available at: www. imf.org/external/data.htm (accessed 4 March 2010).

Indonesian Environmental Conservation Information Center (2010) http://www.wiserearth.org/ organization/view/d94e06f0a2bf7afa081b85e038c2a859.

Ingram, C. (2007) Certification in protected areas: a Western Australian case study. In: Black, R. and Crabtree, A. (eds) *Quality Assurance and Certification in Ecotourism*. CAB International, Wallingford, United Kingdom, pp. 266–298.

Inkaterra (2010) Reserva Amazonica lodge. Available at: http://www.inkaterra.com/en/reserva-amazonica (accessed 23 April 2010).

International Rivers (2010) Jinsha River dams. Available at: http://www.internationalrivers.org (accessed 12 March 2010).

IPCC (2007) *Climate Change 2007: Synthesis Report. Contribution of Working Groups I, II and III to the Fourth Assessment Report of the Intergovernmental Panel on Climate Change*, ed. Pachauri, R.K. and Reisinger, A. IPCC, Geneva, Switzerland, 104 pp.

IUCN and UNEP (2009) *The World Database on Protected Areas (WDPA)*. UNEP–WCMC. Cambridge, United Kingdom.

Jaffuel, R. and Pin, M. (2006) La Charte européenne du tourisme durable dans le Parc national et réserve de biosphère des Cévennes (France). La rencontre entre un concept et un territoire. In: Gagnon, C. and Gagnon, S. (eds) *L'Ecotourisme entre l'arbre et l'écorce. De la Conservation au développement viable des territoires*. Presses de l'Université du Québec, Québec, pp. 211–228.

Jamal, T. and Stronza, A. (2009) Collaboration theory and tourism practice in protected areas: stakeholders, structuring and sustainability. *Journal of Sustainable Tourism* 17, 169–189.

Jardel, J.-P. (1997) Écotourisme et environnement: vers un tourisme soutenable. Le cas du sylvotourisme dans la région Alpes–Provence–Côte d'Azur. In: Wolkowitsch, M. (ed.) *Tourisme et milieux*. Editions du CTHS, Paris, France, pp. 85–98.

Jensen, O. (2009) The activation of local service suppliers by incoming tour operators in a 'developing' destination – the case of Madagascar. *Current Issues in Tourism* 12, 144–163.

Jones, B.T.B., Stolton, S. and Dudley, N. (2005) Private protected areas in east and southern Africa: contributing to biodiversity conservation and rural development. *Parks* 15, 67–77.

Jones, C.B. and Young, J. (2004) Hunting restraint by Creoles at the Community Baboon Sanctuary, Belize: a preliminary survey. *Journal of Applied Animal Welfare Science* 7(2), 127–141.

Jones, J.P.G., Andriamarovololona, M.M. and Hockley, N. (2008) The importance of taboos and social norms to conservation in Madagascar. *Conservation Biology* 22, 976–986.

Kalaora, B. and Savoye, A. (1985) La protection des régions de montagne au XIXe siècle: forestiers sociaux contre forestiers étatistes. In: Cadoret, A. (ed.) *Protection de la Nature: Histoire et Idéologie. De la Nature à l'environnement*. L'Harmattan, Paris, France, pp. 6–23.

Kareiva, P., Chang, A. and Marvier, M. (2008) Development and conservation goals in World Bank projects. *Science* 321, 1638–1639.

Keast, A. (1996) Pacific biogeography: patterns and processes. In: Keast, A. and Miller, S.E. (eds) *The Origin and Evolution of Pacific Island Biotas, New Guinea to Eastern Polynesia: Patterns and Processes*. SPB Academic Publishing, Amsterdam, Netherlands, pp. 477–512.

Keast, A. and Miller, S.E. (1996) *The Origin and Evolution of Pacific Island Biotas, New Guinea to Eastern Polynesia: Patterns and Processes*. SPB Academic Publishing, Amsterdam, Netherlands.

Kerley, G.I.H. and Landman, M. (2006) The impacts of elephants on biodiversity in the Eastern Cape subtropical thickets. *South African Journal of Science* 102, 395–402.

Kerley, G.I.H., Knight, M.H. and de Kock, M. (1995) Desertification of subtropical thicket in the Eastern Cape, South Africa: are there alternatives? *Environmental Monitoring and Assessment* 37, 211–230.

Kerley, G.I.H., Boshoff, A.F. and Knight, M.H. (1999) Ecosystem integrity and sustainable land-use in the thicket biome, South Africa. *Ecosystem Health* 5, 104–109.

Kerley, G.I.H., Geach, B.G.S. and Vial, C. (2003) Jumbos or bust: do tourists' perceptions lead to an under-appreciation of biodiversity? *South African Journal of Wildlife Research* 33, 13–21.

Kettles, R. and Slotow, R. (2009) Management of free-ranging lions on an enclosed game reserve. *South African Journal of Wildlife Research* 39, 23–33.

KfW Entwicklungsbank (2005) Welcome to KfW Entwicklungsbank. Available at: http://www.kfw-entwicklungsbank.de/EN_Home/index.jsp (accessed 7 April 2010).

Kirkpatrick, J.B. and Hassall, D.C. (1981) Vegetation of the Sigatoka sand dunes, Fiji. *New Zealand Journal of Botany* 19, 285–297.

Kiss, A. (2004) Is community-based ecotourism a good use of biodiversity conservation funds? *Trends in Ecology and Evolution* 19, 232–237.

Knight, A.T., Cowling, R.M. and Campbell, B.M. (2006) An operational model for implementing conservation action. *Conservation Biology* 20, 408–419.

Kolas, A. (2004) Tourism and the making of place in Shangri-La. *Tourism Geographies* 6, 262–278.

Kriwoken, L.K. and Rootes, D. (2000) Antarctic tourism: tourism on ice: environmental impact assessment of Antarctic tourism. *Impact Assessment and Project Appraisal* 18, 138–149.

Krug, W. (2001) *Private Supply of Protected Land in Southern Africa: a Review of Markets, Approaches, Barriers and Issues*. Report to Environment Directorate, Organization for Economic Cooperation and Development (OECD), Paris, France.

Krüger, O. (2005) The role of ecotourism in conservation: panacea or Pandora's box? *Biodiversity and Conservation* 14, 579–600.

Lahaye, N. (2006) Lorsque conservation et tourisme se confrontent: le cas du Parc national des Pyrénées et ses conflits d'usages. In: Gagnon, C. and Gagnon, S. (eds) *L'Ecotourisme, entre l'arbre et l'écorce: de la Conservation au développement viable des territoires*. Presses de l'Université du Québec, Québec, pp. 171–209.

Lair, F. (2006) *La Charte européenne du tourisme durable au sein des espaces protégés. Bilan et bonnes pratiques des cinq années d'application de la CETD*. Fédération des parcs naturels régionaux de France, Paris, France.

Lamic, J.-P. (2008) *Tourisme Durable: utopie ou réalité? Comment Identifier les voyageurs et voyagistes éco-responsables?* L'Harmattan, Paris.

Landman, M., Kerley, G.I.H. and Schoeman, D.S. (2008) Relevance of elephant herbivory as a threat to important plants in the Addo Elephant National Park, South Africa. *Journal of Zoology* 274, 51–58.

Langholz, J. (1996) Economics, objectives, and success of private nature reserves in sub-Saharan Africa and Latin America. *Conservation Biology* 10, 271–280.

Langholz, J.A. and Kerley, G.I.H. (2006) *Combining Conservation and Development on Private Lands: an Assessment of Ecotourism-based Private Game Reserves in the Eastern Cape.* Centre for African Conservation Ecology, Nelson Mandela Metropolitan University, Port Elizabeth, South Africa.

Langholz, J.A. and Lassoie, J.P. (2001) Perils and promise of privately owned protected areas. *Bioscience* 51, 1079–1085.

Larrère, C. (1997) *Du Bon Usage de la nature: pour une philosophie de l'environnement.* Aubier, Paris, France.

Larrère, R. (2003) Le conflit entre les chasseurs et les protecteurs de la nature. *La Ricerca Folklorica* 48(1), 45–51.

La Selva Jungle Lodge (2010) Adventure and service brought by our native staff. Available at: http://www.laselvajunglelodge.com/ (accessed 9 February 2010).

Last Descents River Expeditions (2010) Rafting in China. Your adventure of a lifetime may save a river. Available at: http://www.lastdescents.com/ (accessed 29 March 2010).

Laurens, L. and Cousseau, B. (2000) La valorisation du tourisme dans les espaces protégés européens: quelles orientations possibles? *Annales de Géographie* 109(613), 240–258.

Lavena Coastal Walk and Lodge (2010). Lavena coastal walk. Available at: http://bnhp.org/lavena_coastal_walk_home.htm (accessed 4 March 2010).

Lee, W.H. and Moscardo, G. (2005) Understanding the impact of ecotourism resort experiences on tourists' environmental attitudes and behavioural intentions. *Journal of Sustainable Tourism* 13, 546–565.

Lees, A.C. and Peres, C.A. (2008) Conservation value of remnant riparian forest corridors of varying quality for Amazonian birds and mammals. *Conservation Biology* 22, 439–449.

Leggett, K.E.A. (2006) Home range and seasonal movement of elephants in the Kunene region, northwestern Namibia. *African Zoology* 41, 17–26.

Legrain, D. and Letourneux, F. (1994) Les 7,000 jours du conservatoire du littoral. *Aménagement et Nature* 116, 67–75.

Leikam, G., Otis, S., Raymond, T., Sielken, N. and Sweeney, T. (2004) *Evaluation of the Belize Audubon Society Co-management Project at Crooked Tree Wildlife Sanctuary and Cockscomb Basin Wildlife Sanctuary, Belize, MS, Ann Arbor.* University of Michigan, Ann Arbor, Michigan.

Lepart, J. and Marty, P. (2006) Des réserves de nature aux territoires de la biodiversité: l'exemple de la France. *Annales de Géographie* 115(651), 485–507.

Letocart, Y. and Salas, M. (1997) Spatial organisation and breeding of Kagu *Rhynochetos jubatus* in Rivière Bleue Park, New Caledonia. *Emu* 97, 97–107.

Li, W., Ge, X. and Liu, C. (2005) Hiking trails and tourism impact assessment in protected areas: Jiuzhaigou Biosphere Reserve, China. *Environmental Monitoring and Assessment* 108, 279–293.

Libanda, B. and Blignaut, J.N. (2008) Tourism's local benefits for Namibia's community based natural resource management areas. *International Journal of Ecological Economics and Statistics* 10, 40–52.

Lindberg, K., Enriquez, J. and Sproule, K. (1996) Ecotourism questioned: case studies from Belize. *Annals of Tourism Research* 23, 543–562.

Lindsey, P.A., Alexander, R.R., du Toit, J.T. and Mills, M.G.L. (2005) The potential contribution of ecotourism to African wild dog *Lycaon pictus* conservation in South Africa. *Biological Conservation* 123, 339–348.

Lindsey, P.A., Alexander, R., Mills, M.G.L., Romanach, S. and Woodroffe, R. (2007) Wildlife viewing preferences of visitors to protected areas in South Africa: implications for the role of ecotourism in conservation. *Journal of Ecotourism* 6, 19–33.

Liu, J. (2010) China's road to sustainability. *Science* 328, 50.

Lockwood, M., Worboys, G. and Kothari, A. (2006) *Managing Protected Areas: A Global Guide.* Earthscan, London, United Kingdom.

Lombard, A.T., Johnson, C.F., Cowling, R.M. and Pressey, R.L. (2001) Protecting plants from elephants: botanical reserve scenarios within the Addo Elephant National Park, South Africa. *Biological Conservation* 102, 191–203.

Lopez, E. (1999) Protéger pour mieux développer: le rôle du conservatoire de l'espace littoral et des rivages lacustres. *Cahier Espaces* 62, 106–112.

Lozato-Giotart, J.-P. (2006) *Le Chemin vers l'écotourisme: Impacts et enjeux environnementaux du tourisme aujourd'hui*. Delachaux et Niestlé, Paris, France.

Lubke, R.A., Everard, D.A. and Jackson, S. (1986) The biomes of the eastern Cape with emphasis on their conservation. *Bothalia* 16, 251–261.

Lunn, N.J. and Stirling, I. (1985) The significance of supplement food to polar bears during the ice-free period of Hudson Bay. *Canadian Journal of Zoology* 63, 394–411.

Mabunda, D.M. and Wilson, D. (2009) Commercialization of national parks: South Africa's Kruger National Park as an example. In: Saarinen, J., Becker, F., Manwa, H. and Wilson, D. (eds) *Sustainable Tourism in Southern Africa: Local Communities and Natural Resources in Transition*. Channel View Publications, Bristol, United Kingdom, pp. 116–133.

Mackey, R.L., Page, B.R., Duffy, K.J. and Slotow, R. (2006) Modelling elephant population growth in small, fenced, South African reserves. *South African Journal of Wildlife Research* 36, 33–43.

Magee, D. (2006) Powershed politics: Yunnan hydropower under great western development. *The China Quarterly* 185, 23–41.

Mahal, A. (2004) Economic implications of inertia on HIV/AIDS and benefits of action. *Economic and Political Weekly* 39, 1049–1063.

Mallinson, J.J.C. (2001) Saving Brazil's Atlantic rainforests: using the golden-headed lion tamarin *Leontopithecus chrysomelas* as a flagship for a biodiversity hotspot. *Dodo, Journal of the Wildlife Preservation Trust* 37, 9–20.

Mapajo Ecoturismo Indigena (2010) Indigenous Ecotourism, Mapajo Ecotourism Indigena. Available at: www.madidi.com/mapajo.html (accessed 7 April 2010).

Mapajo Project (2010) Bird Bolivia. Available at: http://www.birdbolivia.com/Mapajo%20Lodge.htm (accessed 17 February 2010).

Mareeba Wetlands Foundation (2010) Savanna and wetland reserve. Available at: http://www.mareebawetlands.com/ (accessed 16 April 2010).

Marie, C., Sibelet, N., Dulcire, M., Rafalimaro, M., Danthu, P. and Carrière, S. (2009) Taking into account local practices and indigenous knowledge in an emergency conservation context in Madagascar. *Biodiversity and Conservation* 18(10), 2759–2777.

Martinez, C. (2007) *Analyse du dispositif français des aires protégées au regard du programme de travail 'aires protégées' de la Convention sur la Diversité Biologique. État des lieux et propositions d'actions*. Commission des aires protégées du Comité français de l'Union mondiale pour la nature (IUCN), Paris, France.

Marton-Lefevre, J. (2010) Biodiversity is our life. *Science* 327, 1179.

Massyn, P.J. (2008) Citizen participation in the lodge sector of the Okavango Delta. In: Spenceley, A. (ed.) *Responsible Tourism: Critical Issues for Conservation and Development*. Earthscan, London, United Kingdom, pp. 225–238.

Maupéoux, G. and Roux, A. (2005) *Mission d'évaluation et de réflexion sur la politique des parcs naturels régionaux. Rapport définitif*. Conseil général des ponts et chaussées, Inspection générale de l'environnement, Conseil général du génie rural, des eaux et des forêts, Paris.

Mavhunga, C. (2007) Even the rider and a horse are a partnership: a response to Vermeulen & Sheil. *Oryx* 41, 441–442.

Mbaiwa, J.E. (2004) Causes and possible solutions to water resource conflicts in the Okavango River Basin: the case of Angola, Namibia and Botswana. *Physics and Chemistry of the Earth* 29, 1319–1326.

Mbaiwa, J.E. (2008) The realities of ecotourism development in Botswana. In: Spenceley, A. (ed.) *Responsible Tourism: Critical Issues for Conservation and Development*. Earthscan, London, United Kingdom, pp. 205–223.

Mbaiwa, J.E. and Darkoh, M.B.K. (2009) The socio-economic impacts of tourism in the Okavango Delta, Botswana. In: Saarinen, J., Becker, F., Manwa, H. and Wilson, D. (eds) *Sustainable Tourism in Southern Africa: Local Communities and Natural Resources in Transition*. Channel View Publications, Bristol, United Kingdom, pp. 210–230.

McCauley, D.J. (2006) Selling out on nature. *Nature* 443, 2728.

McDonald, K. (2007) Damming China's Grand Canyon: pluralization without democratization in the Nu River Valley. PhD thesis, University of California Berkeley, San Francisco.

McNeilage, A. (1996) Ecotourism and mountain gorillas in the Virunga volcanoes. In: Taylor, V.J. and Dunstone, N. (eds) *The Exploitation of Mammal Populations*. Chapman and Hall, London, United Kingdom, pp. 334–344.

Mertha, A. (2008) *Water Warriors: Political Pluralization in China's Hydropower Policy*. Cornell University Press, New York.

Michaud, J.-L. (1983) *Le Tourisme face à l'environnement*. Presses universitaires de France, Paris, France.

Millar, R. and Feneley, R. (2009) One school friend free at home as the other sweats in a Dubai jail. *Sydney Morning Herald*. 27 July 2009. Available at: http://www.smh.com.au (accessed 18 April 2010).

Mills, A.J. and Cowling, R.M. (2006) Rate of carbon sequestration at two thicket restoration sites in the Eastern Cape, South Africa. *Restoration Ecology* 14, 38–49.

Mills, A.J. and Cowling, R.M. (2010) Below-ground carbon stocks in intact and transformed subtropical thicket landscapes in semi-arid South Africa. *Journal of Arid Environments* 74, 93–100.

Ministère de l'Écologie de l'Énergie, du Développement durable et de l'Aménagement du territoire. (MEEDDAT) (2007) *Établissement Public du Parc National des Cévennes. Contrat d'objectifs état – Parc National des Cévennes*. République français, Paris.

Ministère de l'Économie des Finances et de l'Emploi (MEIE) (2009) *Plan d'action tourisme*. République française, Paris.

Monte Leon National Park (2010) Parque Nacional Monte Leon. Available at: http://www.parquesnacionales. gov.ar/i/03_ap/26_mleon_PN/26_mleon_PN.htm (accessed 1 April 2010).

Monteverde Cloud Forest (2010) Monteverde Costa Rica. Available at: http://www.monteverdeinfo.com/ (accessed 17 February 2010).

Mooney, H. and Mace, G. (2009) Biodiversity policy challenges. *Science* 325, 1474.

Morales, F. (2009) Análisis comparativo de las estrategias y movimientos de Conservacion en Tierras Privadas en Argentina, Chile, Brasil y España. Master's thesis. Universidad Autonoma de Madrid, Madrid.

Moreno, D., Carminati, A., Machain, N. and Roldan, M. (2008) Reseña sobre las Reservas Privadas en Argentina. In: Chacon, C.M. (ed.) *Voluntad de Conservar*. The Nature Conservancy and Fundación Bioversidad, San José, pp. 7–33.

Morley, C.G. (2004) Has the invasive mongoose *Herpestes javanicus* yet reached the island of Taveuni, Fiji? *Oryx* 38, 457–460.

Morrison, C., Naikatini, A., Thomas, N., Rounds, I., Thaman, B. and Niukula, J. (2004) Importance of Waisali Reserve, Vanua Levu for herpetofauna conservation in Fiji. *South Pacific Journal of Natural Sciences* 22, 71–74.

Moss, R.H., Edmonds, J.A., Hibbard, K.A., Manning, M.R., Rose, S.K., van Vuuren, D.P., Carter, T.R., Emori, S., Kainuma, M., Kram, T., Meehl, G.A., Mitchell, J.F.B., Nakicenovic, N., Riahi, K., Smith, S.J., Stouffer, R.J., Thomson, A.M., Weyant, J.P. and Wilbanks, T.J. (2010) The next generation of scenarios for climate change research and assessment. *Nature* 463, 747.

Muir-Leresche, K. and Nelson, R.H. (2000) Private property rights to wildlife: the Southern African experiment. Unpublished report, University of Zimbabwe and University of Maryland.

Murphy, D.D. and Noon, B.R. (2007) The role of scientists in conservation planning on private lands. *Conservation Biology* 21, 25–28.

NACSO (2008) *Namibia's Communal Conservancies*. Namibian Association of CBNRM Support Organizations, Windhoek.

NACSO (2009) *Namibia's Communal Conservancies: a Review of Progress 2008*. Namibian Association of CBNRM Support Organizations (NACSO), Windhoek.

Napo Wildlife Center (2010) Ecuador Amazon Ecolodge. Available at: http://www.napowildlifecenter.com/ (accessed 26 February 2010).

Narosky, T. and Yzurieta, D. (1987) *Guía para la Identificación de las Aves de Argentina y Uruguay*. Vazquez Mazzini, Buenos Aires, Argentina.

National Parks Association of NSW (2010) Protecting nature through community action. Available at: http:// www.npansw.org.au/website/ (accessed 15 April 2010).

National Parks of Indonesia (2010) National Parks Indonesia. Available at: http://indonesianationalparks. com/ (accessed 5 March 2010).

National Parks of Malaysia (2010) Malaysia's National Parks and Preserves. Available at: http://www. geographia.com/malaysia/nationalparks.htm (accessed 5 March 2010).

National Trust Fiji (2010) Our heritage in trust. Available at: http://www.nationaltrust.org.fj/ (accessed 4 March 2010).

Nations, J. (2006) *The Maya Tropical Forest: People, Parks and Ancient Cities*. University of Texas Press, Austin, Texas.

Natural Habitat Adventures (NHA) (2010) The nature people. Available at: http://www.nathab.com/ (accessed 9 March 2010).

Nelson, F. (2008) Livelihoods, conservation and community-based tourism in Tanzania: potential and performance. In: Spenceley, A. (ed.) *Responsible Tourism: Critical Issues for Conservation and Development*. Earthscan, London, United Kingdom, pp. 305–322.

Neotropic Turis (2010) Cuyabeno Lodge. Available at: http://www.neotropicturis.com/index.html (accessed 27 April 2010).

Nevard, T. (2004) The Mareeba Wetlands: planning for wildlife management through tourism. In: Buckley, R.C. (ed.) *Tourism in Parks: Australian Initiatives*. Griffith University, Gold Coast, Australia, pp. 175–184.

Nevers, J.-Y. (2005) Les politiques publiques sont-elles efficaces? Hors-série: Les enjeux sociaux de l'environnement. *Sciences Humaines* 49, 70–74.

New Caledonia Southern Province Sud (2010) Nouvelle-Calédonie, Tourismse Province Sud Available at: http://www.province-sud.nc/ (accessed 4 March 2010).

New Caledonia Tourism (2010) Tourisme Point-Sud. Available at: www.nouvellecaledonietourisme-sud.com (accessed 4 March 2010).

Nobrega, W.R. de M. (2005) Tourism in natural areas and its relationship with the local community: a reflection on the ecopark of Una-Ba. *Caminhos de Geografia* 2(15), 13–19 (in Portuguese).

North-West Parks and Tourism Board (2010) This is Madikwe. Available at: http://www.madikwe-game-reserve.co.za/ (accessed 22 April 2010).

NSW Foundation for National Parks and Wildlife (2010) Foundation for National Parks and Wildlife. Available at: http://www.fnpw.com.au/ (accessed 16 April 2010).

Nycander, E. (2002) Posada Amazonas: un proyecto ecoturistito en el Parque Nacional Bahuaja-Sonene. In: WTO (comp.) *Sustainable Development of Ecotourism: a Compilation of Good Practices*. World Tourism Organization, Madrid, pp. 183–185.

Oberhauser, K. and Solensky, M. (2004) *The Monarch Butterfly: Biology and Conservation*. Cornell University Press, New York.

O'Connor, A. (2003) Workers' lament at Seal Rocks. *The Age* 21 November, Fairfax, Melbourne, Australia.

Odesen (2010) Projecto Odesen. Available at: http://www.bocas.com/odesen.htm (accessed 9 February 2010).

Ollenburg, C. and Buckley, R. (2007) Stated economic and social motivations of Australian farm tourism operators. *Journal of Travel Research* 45, 444–452.

Orangutan Conservancy (2010) Dedicated to the conservation of orangutans and their rainforest home. Available at: http://www.orangutan.com/ (accessed 1 March 2010).

O'Shea, M. (2006) *In the Naga's Wake: the First Man to Navigate the Mekong, from Tibet to the South China Sea*. Allen and Unwin, Crows Nest, Australia.

Paiement, J.J. (2007) The tiger and the turbine: indigenous rights and resource management in the Naso Territory of Panama. PhD thesis. McGill University, Montreal, Quebec.

Parks Watch (2010) Pilon Lajos Biosphere and communal lands. Available at: http://www.parkswatch.org (accessed 23 April 2010).

Parsons, E.C.M. and Rawles, C. (2003) The resumption of whaling by Iceland and the potential negative impacts in Icelandic whale-watching market. *Current Issues in Tourism* 6, 444–448.

Pauca, E. (2001) Rainforest expeditions and the native community of Infierno: a joint venture for profit, development and conservation. Available at: http://www.perunature.com/lodge/apa/conservationimpact#16apa (accessed 23 April 2010).

Peaty, D. and Portillo, A. (2009) Community-based tourism in Bolivia: projects and perspectives. *Ritsumeikan Journal of International Studies* 21(1), 111–120.

Petit, M. (ed.) (2008) *Les Raies pastenagues de Moorea. Eléments de biologie et d'écologie 2008*. Report produced by Te Mana o Te Moana. Available at: www.temanaotemoana.org/downloads/pink_whiprays_study_summary.pdf (accessed 4 March 2010).

Pickering, C.M. and Buckley, R.C. (2010) Climate response by the ski industry: the shortcomings of snowmaking for Australian resorts. *Ambio* (in press).

Pickering, C.M. and Hill, W. (2007) Impacts of recreation and tourism on plant biodiversity and vegetation in protected areas in Australia. *Journal of Environmental Management* 85, 791–800.

Pickering, C.M., Harrington, J. and Worboys, G.L. (2003) Environmental impacts of tourism on the

Australian Alps protected areas: judgment of protected area managers. *Mountain Research and Development* 23, 247–254.

Pickering, C.M., Hill, W. and Bear, R. (2007) Indirect impacts of nature based tourism and recreation: association between infrastructure and exotic plants in Kosciuszko National Park. *Journal of Ecotourism* 6, 146–157.

Pikacha, P. (2007) The wildlife of the Bauro Highlands, Makira Island, Solomon Islands. *Melanesian Geo* 5, 8–11.

Pikacha, P. (2009) *Wild West. Rainforests of Western Solomon Islands*. Melanesian Geo Publications, Honiara, Solomon Islands.

Pilkington, R. (2002) Articles and archives: spring. Available at http://www.ursusinternational.org/ (accessed 24 March 2010).

Pitlagano, M.L. (2007) Movement patterns, home ranges and mortality for reintroduced white rhinoceros in the Moremi Game Reserve, Botswana. MSc thesis, Norwegian University of Life Sciences, Norway.

Plenty International (2010) Belize – The Toledo Ecotourism Association. Available at: http://www.plenty.org/Belize-ecotourism.html (accessed 7 April 2010).

Poiani, K.A., Richter, B.D., Anderson, M.G. and Richter, H.E. (2000) Biodiversity conservation at multiple scales: functional sites, landscapes, and networks. *BioScience* 50, 133–146.

Ponseti, M. and Lopez-Pujol, J.L. (2006) The three gorges dam project in China: history and consequences. *Revista HMiC* 4, 1–37. ISSN 1696-4403. Available at: http://seneca.uab.es/hmic (accessed 20 April 2010).

Préau, P. (1972) De la protection de la nature à l'aménagement du territoire: l'expérience caractéristique du parc national de la Vanoise. *Aménagement du Territoire et Développement Régional: les Faits, les Idées, les Institutions* 5, 118–171.

Pressey, R.L., Cabeza, M., Watts, M.E., Cowling, R.M. and Wilson, K.A. (2007) Conservation planning in a changing world. *Trends in Ecology and Evaluation* 22, 583–592.

Programa Andes Tropicales (PAT) (2010) Turismo de Base Comunitario. Available at: http://www.andestropicales.org/Sitios_Trabajo.html (accessed 27 April 2010).

Quicksilver Cruises (2010) Quicksilver is the Great Barrier Reef. Available at: http://www.quicksilver-cruises.com/ (accessed 8 April 2010).

Quintero, S.M. (undated) El ecoturismo: ¿una alternativa para el desarrollo comunitario en la selva lacandona? Estudio de caso en el ejido ixcan. Unpublished Masters thesis. San Cristóbal de las Casas, Chiapas, Mexico.

Raffin, J.-P. and Ricou, G. (1985) Le lien entre les scientifiques et les associations de protection de la nature: approche historique. In: Cadoret, A. (ed.) *Protection de la Nature. Histoire et Idéologie. De la Nature à l'Environnement*. L'Harmattan, Paris, France, pp. 61–74.

Rainforest Conservation Society (2010) Australian Rainforest Conservation Society. Available at: http://www.rainforest.org.au/ (accessed 16 April 2010).

Rara Avis (2010) Rainforest Lodge and Reserve. Available at: http://www.rara-avis.com/ (accessed 8 February 2010).

RARE (2010) Inspiring conservation. Available at: http://rareconservation.org/news/articles.php?id=3 (accessed 23 February 2010).

Read, J.L. and Moseby, K. (2006) Vertebrates of Tetepare Island, Solomon Islands. *Pacific Science* 60, 69–79.

Read, T. (2002) *Navigating a New Course. Stories in Community Based Conservation in the Pacific*. UNDP, New York.

Reilly, B.K., Sutherland, E.A. and Harley, V. (2003) The nature and extent of wildlife ranching in Gauteng province, South Africa. *South African Journal of Wildlife Research* 33, 141–144.

Relly, P. (2008) Madikwe Game Reserve, South Africa – investment and employment. In: Spenceley, A. (ed.) *Responsible Tourism: Critical Issues for Conservation and Development*. Earthscan, London, United Kingdom, pp. 267–284.

Republic of South Africa (1999) Natural Heritage Resources Act. Act 25 of 1999. *Government Gazette* 406. (19974), Cape Town, South Africa.

Reserva de Produccion Faunistica Cuyabeno (2010) La magia de la amazonia ecuatoriana. Available at: http://www.reservacuyabeno.org/ (accessed 25 April 2010).

Reti, I. (2003) People in protected areas in the South Pacific. In: *Proceedings of the Fifth South Pacific*

Conference on Nature Conservation and Protected Areas, Vol. 2. Conference Papers, SPREP, Apia, Western Samoa pp. 12–14.

Richez, G. (1992) *Parcs Nationaux et tourisme en Europe.* L'Harmattan, Paris, France.

Ricketts, T.H., Soares-Filho, B., da Fonseca, G.A.B., Nepstad, D., Pfaff, A., Petsonk, A., Anderson, A., Boucher, D., Cattaneo, A., Conte, M., Creighton, K., Linden, L., Maretti, C., Moutinho, P., Ullman, R. and Victurine, R. (2010) Indigenous lands, protected areas, and slowing climate change. *PloS Biology* 8, 1–4.

Rivers Fiji (2010) Welcome to Rivers Fiji, home to pure Fiji Adventure. Available at: http://www.riversfiji. com/ (accessed 4 March 2010).

Rodary, E. and Castellanet, C. (2003) Les trois temps de la conservation. In: Rodary, E., Castellanet, C. and Rossi, G. (eds) *Conservation de la Nature et développement: l'intégration impossible?* Éditions Karthala, Paris, France, pp. 5–44.

Rodrigues, A.S.L. (2006) Are global conservation efforts successful? *Science* 313, 1051–1052.

Rodriguez, A. (2008) Tourism, indigenous peoples and conservation in the Ecuadorean Amazon. In: Stronza, A. and Durham, W.H. (eds) *Ecotourism and Conservation in the Americas.* CAB International, Wallingford, United Kingdom, pp. 155–162.

Rogerson, C.M. (2009) Tourism development in southern Africa: patterns, issues and constraints. In: Saarinen, J., Becker, F., Manwa, H. and Wilson, D. (eds) *Sustainable Tourism in Southern Africa: Local Communities and Natural Resources in Transition.* Channel View Publications, Bristol, United Kingdom, pp. 20–41.

Ross, K. (1987) *Okavango, Jewel of the Kalahari.* BBC Books, London, United Kingdom.

Rouget, M., Cowling, R.M., Lombard, A.T., Knight, A.T. and Kerley, G.I.H. (2006) Designing large-scale conservation corridors for pattern and process. *Conservation Biology* 20, 549–561.

Round River (2010) Round River conservation studies. Available at: http://www.roundriver.org/ (accessed 19 April 2010).

Russell, C. and Enns, M. (2002) *Grizzly Heart.* Random House, Toronto, Ontario, Canada.

Russell, D. and Stabile, J. (2003) Ecotourism in practice: trekking the highlands of Makira Island, Solomon Islands. In: Harrison, D. (ed.) *Pacific Island Tourism.* Cognizant Communications Corporation, New York, pp. 38–57.

Saarinen, J., Becker, F., Manwa, H. and Wilson, D. (eds) (2009a) *Sustainable Tourism in Southern Africa: Local Communities and Natural Resources in Transition.* Channel View Publications, Bristol, United Kingdom.

Saarinen, J., Becker, F., Manwa, H. and Wilson, D. (2009b) Introduction: call for sustainability. In: Saarinen, J., Becker, F., Manwa, H. and Wilson, D. (eds) *Sustainable Tourism in Southern Africa: Local Communities and Natural Resources in Transition.* Channel View Publications, Bristol, United Kingdom, pp. 3–19.

Sachs, J.D., Baillie, J.E.M., Sutherland, W.J., Armsworth, P.R., Ash, N., Beddington, J., Blackburn, T.M., Collen, B., Gardiner, B., Gaston, K.J., Godfray, H.C.J., Green, R.E., Harvey, P.H., House, B., Knapp, S., Kumpel, N.F., Macdonald, D.W., Mace, G.M., Mallet, J., Matthews, A., May, R.M., Petchey, O., Purvis, A., Roe, D., Safi, K., Turner, K., Walpole, M., Watson, R. and Jones, K.E. (2009) Biodiversity conservation and the millennium development goals. *Science* 325, 1502–1503.

St Louis, R., Burningham, L., Dowl, A. and Grosberg, M. (2009) *Lonely Planet Ecuador and the Galapagos Islands.* Lonely Planet, Footscray, Australia.

Salafsky, N., Cauley, H., Balachander, G., Cordes, B., Parks, J., Margoluis, C., Bhatt, S., Encarnacion, C., Russell, D. and Margoluis, R. (2001) A systematic test of an enterprise strategy for community-based biodiversity conservation. *Conservation Biology* 15(6), 1585–1595.

Samways, M.J., Hitchins, P.M., Bourquin, O. and Henwood, J. (2010) Restoration of a tropical island: Cousine Island, Seychelles. *Biodiversity Conservation* 19, 425–434.

Sanecki, G.M., Green, K., Wood, H. and Lindenmayer, D. (2006) The implications of snow-based recreation for small mammals in the subnivean space in south-east Australia. *Biological Conservation* 129, 511–518.

Saporiti, N. (2006) Managing national parks: how public–private partnerships can aid conservation. Public policy for the private sector, World Bank Group, Public Policy Journal, Note 309. Available at: http://www.ifc.org/ifcext/psa.nsf/AttachmentsByTitle/Viewpoint_SANP/$FILE/VP_National+Parks.pdf (accessed 23 April 2010).

Sarrasin, B. (2007) Géopolitique du tourisme à Madagascar: de la protection de l'environnement au développement de l'économie. *Hérodote* 127, 124–150.

Save the Rhino Trust (SRT) (2010) Save the Rhino Trust – Namibia. Available at: http://savetherhinotrust. org/ (accessed 19 April 2010).

Savewaratah (2010) Save Waratah Park Earth Sanctuary. Available on: http://www.gopetition.com.au/ petitions/save-waratah-park-earth-sanctuary.html (accessed 18 April 2010).

Schmiechen, J. (2004) Crossing borders: future directions for heritage tourism in the Lake Eyre Basin. In: Buckley, R.C. (ed.) *Tourism in Parks: Australian Initiatives*. Griffith University, Gold Coast, Australia, pp. 99–131.

Sebele, L.S. (2010) Community-based tourism ventures, benefits and challenges: Khama Rhino Sanctuary Trust, Central District, Botswana. *Tourism Management* 31, 136–146.

Shackley, M. (1995) Just started and now finished – tourism development in Arunachal Pradesh. *Tourism Management* 16, 623–625.

Shangri-La River Expeditions (SLRE) (2010) Exploring the rivers of western China. Available at: http:// www.shangri-la-river-expeditions.com/ (accessed 20 April 2010).

Shen, X.-J., Su, C.-J. and Li, W.-J. (2008) Jiuzhaigou ecotourism areal system: temporal evolution of entropic change. *Wuhan University Journal of Natural Science* 13, 303–308.

Sherley, G. (1999) Taking the first step to save our endangered Pacific Island birds. *Conservation Area Live Link* 1, 1–4.

Sherriffs, P. (2007) Update on the Black Rhino Range Expansion Project: local community receives black rhinos. *Pachyderm*, 43, 116–117.

Shoobridge, D. (2005) *Protected Area Profile – Peru. Huascaran National Park*. ParksWatch, Lima, Peru.

Shultis, J.D. and Way, P.A. (2006) Changing conceptions of protected areas and conservation: linking conservation, ecological integrity and tourism management. *Journal of Sustainable Tourism* 14, 223–237.

Simonnet, D. (1991) *L'Ecologisme*. Presses universitaires de France, Paris, France.

Sims-Castley, R., Kerley, G.I.H., Geach, B. and Langholz, J. (2005) Socio-economic significance of ecotourism-based private game reserves in South Africa's Eastern Cape province. *Parks* 15, 6–18.

Singayta (2010) Ecotourism in Singayta, Mexico. Available at: http://www.singayta.com (accessed 23 February 2010).

Skyer, P. (2004) *Namibia's Communal Conservancies*. Namibian Association of Community-based Natural Resource Management Organisation (NACSO), Windhoek, Namibia.

Slotow, R. and Hunter, L.B. (2009) Reintroduction decisions taken at the incorrect scale devalue their conservation contribution: the African lion in South Africa. In: Hayward, M.W. and Somers, M.J. (eds) *Reintroduction of Top-order Predators*. Wiley-Blackwell, Chichester, United Kingdom, pp. 43–71.

Snyder, J. and Stonehouse, B. (2007) *Prospects for Polar Tourism*. CAB International, Wallingford, United Kingdom.

Southern Sea Ventures (2010) Tropical and polar sea kayak tours. Available at: http://www. southernseaventures.com/ (accessed 8 April 2010).

Spangenberg, J.H., Martinez-Alier, J., Omann, I., Monterroso, I. and Binimelis, R. (2009) The DPSIR scheme for analysing biodiversity loss and developing preservation strategies. *Ecological Economics* 69, 9–11.

Spear, D. and Chown, S.L. (2009) Non-indigenous ungulates as a threat to biodiversity. *Journal of Zoology* 279, 1–17.

Spenceley, A. (ed.) (2008a) *Responsible Tourism: Critical Issues for Conservation and Development*. Earthscan, London, United Kingdom.

Spenceley, A. (2008b) Implications of responsible tourism for conservation and development in South Africa. In: Spenceley, A. (ed.) *Responsible Tourism: Critical Issues for Conservation and Development*. Earthscan, London, United Kingdom, pp. 361–374.

Spenceley, A. (2008c) Local impacts of community-based tourism in southern Africa. In: Spenceley, A. (ed.) *Responsible Tourism: Critical Issues for Conservation and Development*. Earthscan, London, pp. 285–304.

Spenceley, A. and Seif, J. (2003) Strategies, impacts and costs of pro-poor tourism approaches in South Africa. PPT Working Paper No. 11, Overseas Development Institute, London. 41 pp. Available at: http://www.research4development.info/PDF/Outputs/Mis_SPC/R8120-PPT11.pdf (accessed 23 April 2010).

Spenceley, A., Relly, P., Keyser, H., Warmeant, P., McKenzie, M., Mataboge, A., Norton, P., Mahlangu, S. and Seif, J. (2002) *Responsible Tourism Manual for South Africa*. Department for Environmental Affairs and Tourism, Pretoria, South Africa.

Spiteri, A. and Nepal, S.K. (2008) Evaluating local benefits from conservation in Nepal's Annapurna conservation area. *Environmental Management* 42, 391–401.

Splettstoesser, J., Landau, D. and Headland, R.K. (2004) Tourism in the forbidden landscapes. In: Singh, T.V. (ed.) *New Horizons in Tourism*. CAB International, Wallingford, United Kingdom, pp. 27–36.

SPREP (2003) *Sustainable Development: Successful Case Studies from the Pacific*. South Pacific Regional Environment Programme, Apia, Samoa.

Springbrook Lyrebird Retreat (2010) Springbrook is a nature lover's paradise. Available at: http://www.lyrebirdspringbrook.com/ (accessed 16 April 2010).

Steenkamp, Y., Van Wyk, B., Victor, J., Hoare, D., Smith, G., Dold, A. and Cowling, R. (2004) Maputaland–Pondoland–Albany. In: Mittermeier, R.A., Robles-Gil, P., Hoffmann, M., Pilgrim, J.D., Brooks, T., Mittermeier, C.G. and da Fonseca, G.A.B. (eds) *Hotspots Revisited: Earth's Biologically Richest and Most Endangered Ecoregions*. CEMEX, Mexico City, Mexico, pp. 218–229.

Stronza, A. (2004) Chalalan. Unpublished Case Study Report to Conservation International. Texas A&M University, Austin, Texas, 78 pp.

Stronza, A. (2007) The economic promise of ecotourism for conservation. *Journal of Ecotourism* 6, 210–230.

Stronza, A. (undated) Trueque Amazonico. Lessons in community-based ecotourism. Unpublished Report to Critical Ecosystems Partnership Fund, 122 pp.

Stronza, A. and de Vasconcellos Pêgas, F. (2008) Ecotourism equations: do economic benefits equal conservation? In: Stronza, A. and Durham, W.H. (eds) *Ecotourism and Conservation in the Americas*. CAB International, Wallingford, United Kingdom, pp. 163–176.

Stronza, A. and Durham, W.H. (eds) (2008) *Ecotourism and Conservation in the Americas*. CAB International, Wallingford, United Kingdom.

Stronza, A. and Gordillo, J. (2008) Community views of ecotourism. *Annals of Tourism Research* 35, 448–468.

Suich, H. (2008) Tourism in transfrontier conservation areas: the Kavango–Zambezi TFCA. In: Spenceley, A. (ed.) *Responsible Tourism*. Earthscan, London, United Kingdom, pp. 187–204.

Suich, H., Child, B. and Spenceley, A. (eds) (2009) *Evolution and Innovation in Wildlife Conservation: Parks and Game Ranches to Transfrontier Conservation Areas*. SASUSG, IUCN, Earthscan, London.

Sukau Rainforest Lodge (2010) Sukau Rainforest Lodge. Available at: http://www.sukau.com/ (accessed 5 March 2010).

Sukhdev, P. (2009) Costing the earth. *Nature* 462, 277.

Svoronou, E. and Holden, A. (2005) Ecotourism as a tool for nature conservation: the role of WWF Greece in the Dadia–Lefkimi–Soufli Reserve in Greece. *Journal of Sustainable Tourism* 13, 456–467.

Tabin Lodge (2010) Tabin Wildlife Resort. Available at: http://www.tabinwildlife.com.my/ (accessed 5 March 2010).

Tetepare (2010) The last wild island. Available at: http://www.tetepare.org/ (accessed 4 March 2010).

Tetepare Descendants Association (2010) The last wild island. Available at: http://www.tetepare.org/about-the-tda.html (accessed 4 March 2010).

Thackway, R. and Olsen, K. (1999) Public/private partnerships and protected areas: selected Australian case studies. *Landscape and Urban Planning* 44, 87–97.

The Nature Conservancy (2010) Protecting nature, preserving life. Available at: http://www.nature.org/ (accessed 22 February 2010).

Thorsen, M., Shorten, R., Lucking, R. and Lucking, V. (2000) Norway rats (*Rattus norvegicus*) on Fregate Island, Seychelles: the invasion; subsequent eradication attempts and implications for the island's fauna. *Biological Conservation* 96, 133–138.

Thuiller,W., Broennimann, O., Hughes, G., Alkemade, J.R.M., Midgley, G.F.and Corsi, F. (2006) Vulnerability of African mammals to anthropogenic climate change under conservative land transformation assumptions. *Global Change Biology* 12, 424–440.

Tikal Connection (2010) Tour operator. Available at: http://www.tikalcnx.com/ (accessed 8 February 2010).

Tisdell, C., Wilson, C. and Nantha, H.S. (2005) Policies for saving a rare Australian glider: economics and ecology. *Biological Conservation* 123, 237–248.

Toledo Ecotourism Association (2010) Services Toledo Ecotourism Association. Available at: http://www.southernbelize.com/tea.html (accessed 23 February 2010).

Torres, M. (1996) Participatory planning for ecotourism development in the Peruvian Highland. *Yale School of Forestry and Environmental Science Bulletin* 99, 284–294.

Tropical Nature (2010) Conservation through ecotourism. Available at: http://www.tropicalnature.org/ (accessed 27 April 2010).

Tropical Nature Travel (2010) Welcome to Tropical Nature Travel. Available at: http://www.tropicalnaturetravel.com/travel/index.html (accessed 27 April 2010).

Tropic Ecotours (2010) Journeys in nature. Available at: http://www.tropiceco.com/ (accessed 9 February 2010).

Tuiwawa, M. (ed.) (2004) *Baseline Floral and Faunal Survey of the Waisali Reserve, Cakaudrove, Vanua Levu, Fiji Islands, 2–6th March 2004.* Unpublished report prepared for the National Trust of Fiji, 24 pp, available from National Trust of Fiji.

Turpie, J., Winkler, H., Spalding-Flecher, R. and Midgley, G. (2002) *Economic Impacts of Climate Change in South Africa: a Preliminary Analysis of Unmitigated Damage Costs.* Southern Waters Ecological Research and Consulting and Energy Development Research Centre, University of Cape Town, South Africa.

Ultimate Descents (2010) Journeys of exploration and discovery throughout the Himalayas. Available at: http://www.ultimatedescents.com/ (accessed 5 March 2010).

Una Ecopark (2010) Una Ecopark/Biological Reserve. Available at: http://www.brazadv.com/brazil_tours/ecoparque_una.htm (accessed 22 February 2010).

Underwood, K. (2009) 'Cristalino Jungle Lodge: a resort actually saving the rainforest', viewed 18 September 2009. *Treehugger* web post, 12 April. Available at: <http://www.treehugger.com/files/2009/04/cristalino-jungle-lodge-a-resort-actually-saving-the-rainforest.php> (accessed 18 March 2010).

UNESCO (2010a) Jiuzhaigou Valley scenic and historic interest area. Available at: http://whc.unesco.org/en/list/637 (accessed 23 February 2010).

UNESCO (2010b) Biosphere reserve information – China – Tianmushan. Available at: http://www.unesco.org/mabdb/br/brdir/directory/biores.asp?mode=all&code=CPR+12 (accessed 23 February 2010).

UNESCO (2010c) Building peace in the minds of people. Available at: http://www.unesco.org/new/en/unesco/ (accessed 8 February 2010).

United Nations Environment Programme (UNEP) (2007) *User's Manual on the CBD Guidelines on Biodiversity and Tourism Development,* ed. Tapper, R. Secretariat of the Convention on Biological Diversity, Montreal, Canada.

United Nations Environment Programme and World Tourism Organization (UNEP) (2002) *Québec Declaration on Ecotourism.* UNEP and WTO, Québec.

United Nations World Tourism Organization (UNWTO) (2009) *World Tourism Barometer 7(2).* UNWTO, Madrid.

Van der Waal, C. and Dekker, B. (2000) Game ranching in the Northern Province of South Africa. *South African Journal of Wildlife Research* 30, 151–156.

Varghese, G. (2008) Public–private partnerships in South African National Parks: the rationale, benefits and lessons learned. In: Spenceley, A. (ed.) *Responsible Tourism: Critical Issues for Conservation and Development.* Earthscan, London, United Kingdom, pp. 69–84.

Venter, O., Laurance, W.F., Iwamura, T., Wilson, K.A., Fuller, R.A. and Possingham, H.P. (2009) Harnessing carbon payments to protect biodiversity. *Science* 326, 1368.

Veyret, Y. and Ciattoni, A. (2004) *Géo-environnement.* A. Colin, Paris, France.

Viard, J. (1985) Protestante, la nature? In: Cadoret, A. (ed.) *Protection de la nature: Histoire et idéologie. De la Nature à l'environnement.* L'Harmattan, Paris, France, pp. 161–164.

Victor, J.E. and Dold, A.P. (2003) Threatened plants of the Albany Centre of Floristic Endemism, South Africa. *South African Journal of Science* 99, 437–446.

Visser, G. and Rogerson, C.M. (2004) Researching the South African tourism and development nexus. *GeoJournal* 60, 201–215.

Vourc'h, A. (1999) Faire participer le tourisme à la gestion des sites naturels. *Cahier Espaces* 62, 90–96.

Vourc'h, A. (2007) *Comment les aires protégés peuvent-elles développer des stratégies de tourisme durable?* 6th European Tourism Forum, Sustainable Management of Tourism Destinations, Algarve, Portugal.

Vourc'h, A. and Natali, J.M. (2000) *Sites naturels: Contributions du tourisme à leur gestion et à leur entretien. Guide de savoir-faire.* Agence française de l'Ingénierie Touristique, Paris, France.

Wagner, L. (2003–2009) Seeing orang-utans in south-east Asia. Available at: http://www.lonelyplanet.com/ thorntree/thread.jspa?threadID=307278 (accessed 8 February 2010).

Walpole, M. (2006) Partnerships for conservation and poverty reduction. *Oryx* 40, 245–246.

Walpole, M.J. and Leader-Williams, N. (2002) Tourism and flagship species in conservation. *Biodiversity and Conservation* 11, 543–547.

Walsh, B. (2009) Ecotourism: Wekso Ecolodge Panama, viewed 17 August 2009. *Time in Partnership with CNN.* 7 May. Available at: http://www.time.com/time/specials/packages/ article/0,28804,1888728_1888734_1888929,00.html (accessed 18 March 2010).

Walter, F. (1990) *Les Suisses et l'environnement une histoire du rapport à la nature du XVIIIe siècle à nos jours.* Zoé, Geneva.

Wang, X.P., Yu, S.L. and Zhu, J.X. (2008) Achievement and perspectives of effective management for Tianmushan Reserve in Linan City, Zhejiang Province. *Resources and Environment in the Yangtze Basin* 17, 962–967.

Warrawong Wildlife Sanctuary (2010) Warrawong Wildlife Sanctuary. Available at: http://www.warrawong. com (accessed 19 April 2010).

Watling, D. (2001) *A Guide to the Birds of Fiji and Western Polynesia, Including American Samoa, Niue, Samoa, Tokelau, Tonga, Tuvalu and Wallis and Futuna.* Environmental Consultants (Fiji) Ltd, Suva, Fiji.

Watson, A. and Borrie, W. (2003) Applying public purpose marketing in the USA to protect relationships with public lands. In: Buckley, R.C., Pickering, C.M. and Weaver, D.B. (eds) *Nature-based Tourism, Environment and Land Management.* CAB International, Wallingford, United Kingdom, pp. 25–34.

Wearing, S. and Neil, J. (2009) *Ecotourism: Impacts, Potentials and Possibilities,* 2nd edn. Butterworth-Heinemann, Oxford, United Kingdom.

Weaver, D.B. (1999) Magnitude of ecotourism in Costa Rica and Kenya. *Annals of Tourism Research* 26, 792–816.

Weaver, D.B. (2001) *The Encyclopedia of Ecotourism.* CAB International, Wallingford, United Kingdom.

Weaver, D.B. and Lawton, L.J. (2007) Twenty years on: the state of contemporary ecotourism research. *Tourism Management* 28, 1168–1179.

Wei, Z., Yang, J. and Han, G. (1999) The management of rangeland for tourism. *Inner Mongolia Grassland Industry* 3, 34–37 (in Chinese).

White, R., Murray, S. and Rohweder, M. (2000) *Pilot Analysis of Global Ecosystems.* World Resources Institute, Washington, DC.

Wilderness Lodge (2010) The Wilderness Lodge, Solomon Islands. Available on http://www. thewildernesslodge.org/ (accessed 4 March 2010).

Wilderness Safaris (2010) Our journeys change people's lives. Available at: http://www.wilderness-safaris. com/ (accessed 19 April 2010).

Wilkie, D.S. and Carpenter, J.F. (1999) Can nature tourism help finance protected areas in the Congo basin? *Oryx* 33, 332–338.

Williams, P. (2004) Natural attractions: Tasmanian parks. In: Buckley, R.C. (ed.) *Tourism in Parks: Australian Initiatives.* Griffith University, Gold Coast, Australia, pp. 170–174.

Willis, K.J. and Bhagwat, S.A. (2009) Biodiversity and climate change. *Science* 326, 806–807.

Wolgan Valley Resort and Spa (2010) Wolgan Valley Resort and Spa, Australia. Available at: http://www. emirateshotelsresorts.com/wolgan-valley/en/ (accessed 8 April 2010).

World Expeditions (2010) Take the path less travelled. Available at: http://www.worldexpeditions.com/au/ index.php (accessed 1 March 2010).

World Tourism Organization (WTO) (2000) *Sustainable Development of Tourism: a Compilation of Good Practices.* WTO, Madrid.

World Tourism Organization (WTO) (2002) *The French Ecotourism Market. Special Report.* WTO, Madrid.

World Wide Fund for Nature (2010) For a living planet. Available at: http://www.panda.org (accessed 27 April 2010).

World Wildlife Fund France (2008) Pour une planète vivante. Available at: www.wwf.fr/ (accesed 29 June 2008).

WWF China (2008) *Qinling Giant Panda Landscape Conservation and Sustainable Development Project.* WWF China, Xian, 21 pp.

Yacutinga Wildlife Refuge (2010) Reserva Natural. Available at: http://www.yacutinga.com/fact-sheet-iguazu-lodge-es.html (accessed 1 March 2010).

Yaguaroundi (2010) Reserva Yaguaroundi. Available at: www.yaguaroundi.com.ar (accessed 27 April 2010).

Yang, D. and Naughton, B. (eds) (2004) *Holding China Together: Diversity and National Integration in the Post Deng Era.* Cambridge University Press, Cambridge, United Kingdom.

Yang, M. and Gan, Y. (2001) Discussion on approaches for the sustainable development of grassland. *Sichuan Grassland* 3, 8–11 (in Chinese).

Young, C. (2007) The state of forests and ecotourism in Belize: An interview with Colin Young, a Belizean ecologist. Interview 16 November. Available at: mongabay.com http://news.mongabay.com/2007/1116–interview_young_belize.html (accessed 18 March 2010).

Yu, L. and Goulden, M. (2006) A comparative analysis of international tourists' satisfaction in Mongolia. *Tourism Management* 26, 1331–1342.

Zeppel, H. (2006) *Indigenous Ecotourism: Sustainable Development and Management.* CAB International, Wallingford, United Kingdom.

Zhong, L.S., Niu, Y.F, Liu, J.M. and Chen, T. (2005) Development of grassland tourism resource in Inner Mongolia autonomous region. *Journal of Arid Land Resources and Environment* 19(2), 105–110 (in Chinese).

Zhong, Z. (2001) *Study on the Ecological Environment by Remote Sensing at the End of 20th Century.* Inner Mongolia Peoples Press, Huhehaote, pp. 165–169 (in Chinese).

Zuloaga, F.O., Morrone, O. and Belgrano, M.J. (eds) (2008) *Catalogo de las Plantas Vasculares del Cono Sur: Argentina, Sur de Brasil, Paraguay y Uruguay.* Missouri Botanical Garden Press, St Louis, Missouri.

Index

Note: Page numbers in *italic* refer to tables; those in **bold** refer to figures